D0442897

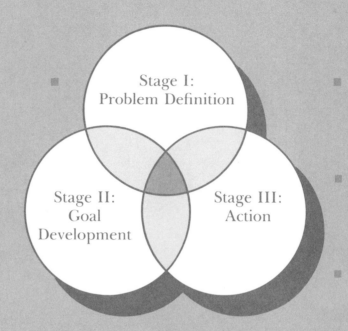

Third Edition

The Skilled Helper

A Systematic Approach to Effective Helping

Third Edition

The Skilled Helper

A Systematic Approach to Effective Helping

Gerard Egan
Loyola University of Chicago

Brooks/Cole Publishing Company
Pacific Grove, California

Brooks/Cole Publishing Company
A Division of Wadsworth, Inc.
© 1986 by Wadsworth, Inc., Belmont, California 94002. All rights reserved. No part of
this book may be reproduced, stored in a retrieval system, or transcribed, any any form
or by any means—electronic, mechanical, photocopying, recording, or otherwise—without the prior written permission of the publisher, Brooks/Cole Publishing Company,
Pacific Grove, California 93950, a division of Wadsworth, Inc.

Printed in the United States of America
10 9 8

Library of Congress Cataloging in Publication Data

Egan, Gerard.
   The skilled helper.

   Bibliography: p.
   Includes indexes.
   1. Counseling. 2. Helping behavior. I. Title.
BF637.C6E38   1985   158′.3   85-14956

ISBN 0-534-05904-X

Sponsoring Editor: *Claire Verduin*
Marketing Representative: *Thomas L. Braden*
Editorial Assistant: *Linda Wright*
Production Editor: *Ellen Brownstein*
Manuscript Editor: *Pamela Evans*
Permissions Editor: *Carline Haga*
Interior and Cover Design: *Katherine Minerva*
Art Coordinator: *Judith Macdonald*
Interior Illustration: *Art by AYXA*
Typesetting: *Omegatype Typography, Inc., Champaign, Illinois*
Cover Printing: *Phoenix Color Corp., Long Island City, New York*
Printing and Binding: *R. R. Donnelley & Sons Co., Crawfordsville, Indiana*

About the Author

Gerard (Gerry) Egan is Professor of Psychology at Loyola University of Chicago and currently coordinator for the program in Community and Organizational Development at the downtown campus. His doctorate is in clinical psychology. He does consulting work with a variety of organizations and conducts workshops in counseling, counselor education and training, and organization design, assessment, and consultation. He has taught in England and conducted workshops in Canada, Europe, Australia, and Africa. His other publications—all with Brooks/Cole Publishing Company—include the following:

- *Exercises in Helping Skills, Third Edition*
- *Change Agent Skills in Helping and Human Service Settings*
- *Face to Face: The Small Group Experience and Interpersonal Growth*
- *Interpersonal Living: A Skills/Contract Approach to Human Relations Training in Groups*
- *You & Me: The Skills of Communicating and Relating to Others*

Preface

There is a constant tension between psychology's "two cultures" (Kimble, 1984): one behavioral or scientific, the other humanistic. C. P. Snow (1964), who had friends in both camps, thought he saw possibilities for the merging of the two cultures.

> I have been thoroughly impressed by a body of intellectual opinion, forming itself, without organisation, without any kind of lead or conscious direction, under the surface of the debate. . . . This body of opinion seems to come from intellectual sources in a variety of fields—social history, sociology, demography, political science, economics, government (in the American academic sense), psychology, medicine, and social arts such as architecture. It seems a mixed bag, but there is an inner consistency. All of them are concerned with how human beings are living or have lived—and concerned, not in terms of legend, but of fact [pp. 69–70].

Both camps favorably reviewed *The Skilled Helper* when it was first published: the behaviorists as an effective humanistic text, the humanists as an effective behavioral text. Since I consider both "cultures" to be essential—and complementary—I have tried to further blend the two in this edition. The technology of helping, like the technology of medicine, is always in need of humanizing.

Since helping as a formal profession is still in its adolescence, there is something healthy about the kind of pluralism that abounds (Norcross and Wogan, 1983). Just as a foreclosed identity does not serve the adolescent well, neither does premature rejection of ideas, theories, models, and methods serve a young professional discipline. On the other hand, I certainly approve of the movement to discover "converging themes" (Goldfried, 1982) in counseling and psychotherapy, because such a movement places service to clients above the dogmas of any particular school and above the techniques of any particular approach. I prefer theories of helping that are integrative rather than "over against" other theories (see Staats, 1981).

I have tried, at least in a modest way, to further an interdisciplinary approach to helping (Egan & Cowan, 1979; Egan, 1984). Psychology in general and counseling and psychotherapy in particular are less rich than they might be due to the walls between academic disciplines and between human-service professions. In the helping field we have much to learn from applied sociologists, applied anthropologists, those who study and work with the politics of everyday life, and even consultants to organizations and institutions. The unifying principle in the debate between the two cultures is the client, the human being who comes for help.

Problem-solving or problem-management approaches to helping are growing in popularity; in this edition, I have further developed the three-stage helping model, clarifying each step at each stage of the helping process. Additionally, I have emphasized the nonlinearity of the helping process and the overlap among the stages and steps of helping. There is an increased focus on goals—the valued outcomes of counseling and therapy—in terms of the development of preferred scenarios. There is a greater emphasis on creativity in helping. I express my growing concern about what I view as an overemphasis on the first stage of helping, problem definition and insight. For the first time I have added some graphics for those of us who visualize things better than we conceptualize them.

This edition, like the one it succeeds, has benefited greatly from the suggestions of those who have used the second edition as a classroom tool. I would like to thank John Shack and Richard McGourty, both of Loyola University, for their helpful comments. I am also grateful to Donald Soule, a Loyola graduate student, for saving me from the temptation to add a fourth stage to the model by suggesting that I place evaluation at the center of each stage. Finally, I would like to thank my editor, Claire Verduin, for her help and gentle persuasion over the last 15 years. She and all the others at Brooks/Cole have made the life of this author a joy. Monica Kuchera, my graduate assistant for the past three years, deserves a special note of thanks for her meticulous work on the manuscript.

I would like to thank Dennis B. Anderson, Southern Illinois University at Carbondale; Terry Anderson, Frazer Valley College, Abbotsford, B.C., Canada; William M. Barkley, Vanderbilt University, Nashville, Tennessee; John W. Bloom, Northern Arizona University at Flagstaff; David F. Bush, Villanova University; Carol J. Erdwins, George Mason University, Fairfax, Virginia; Basil A. Fiorito, California Polytechnic State University, San Luis Obispo; Margaret T. Fong, University of Florida at Gainesville; Arleen C. Lewis, University of Arkansas at Fayetteville; W. Brendan Reddy, University of Cincinnati; Linda Seligman, George Mason University, Fairfax, Virginia; Linda Sherman, University of Oregon at Eugene; Jerry Venn, Mary Baldwin College, Staunton, Virginia; and Donald R. Welti, Northern Kentucky University at Highland Heights, for their reviews of the original manuscript. Their comments were most helpful.

I would like to reiterate my debt of gratitude to my students at Loyola—with a special bow to those from other countries—and to those who have participated in workshops on counseling in the United States, Australia, Canada, Germany, New Zealand, Tanzania, and the United Kingdom. Their enthusiasm for experiential learning, and their feedback, have ensured that I remain a learner. For this I am deeply grateful.

Gerard Egan

Contents

Six   Stage I: Step I-B Focusing: Helping Clients Develop Leverage and Clarity   156

Seven   Stage I: Step I-C Challenging: New Perspectives at the Service of Action   183

Third Edition

The Skilled Helper

A Systematic Approach to Effective Helping

Part One

Introduction

One

Introduction

■

While the topics treated in this introductory chapter are important, they may be more fully appreciated once the basic dimensions of the helping model outlined in this book are understood. Therefore, some readers might want to begin with the overview of that model in Chapter Two and then return to the topics treated here.

■ The Helping Professions: Who Needs Helping Models and Skills?

Throughout history there has been a deeply embedded conviction that, under the proper conditions, some people are capable of helping others come to grips with problems in living (Frank, 1973). In more recent times, that conviction has become institutionalized in a variety of formal helping professions. Counselors, psychiatrists, psychologists, and social workers are expected to help people manage their social-emotional problems.

However, there is a second level of professionals who often deal with clients in times of crisis: consultants, dentists, doctors, lawyers, ministers, nurses, police, probation officers, teachers, and the like. In fact, priests and ministers are often the first to be sought out by people in trouble. Second-level helpers are specialists in their own professions, but additionally must meet the expectation that they can help their clients manage the social-emotional dimensions of problem situations. At best, they help clients manage problems and crises in a holistic way. For instance, dentists care for clients' teeth and gums, but can also help them overcome their fears of being treated or resistance to oral hygiene programs. Teachers teach English, history, and science, but as their students are people who are growing physically, intellectually, socially, and emotionally—and therefore struggling with normative developmental tasks and crises— they can also help them, in direct and indirect ways, to explore, under- stand, and deal with these tasks and crises. And, of course, parents may be the most important level-two helpers.

Furthermore, as Cowen (1982) notes, there is a third-level set of professionals such as managers, supervisors, bartenders, and hairdres- sers. Many of them perceive themselves as interpersonal helpers—and as competent helpers, at that. For instance, bartenders frequently en- counter people in crisis. They may listen carefully to their clients, provide support and advice, and generally help them to cope with problems of greater or lesser severity. Third-level helpers are often proud of the services they provide.

A fourth level of helpers would include everybody else who tries to help relatives, friends, acquaintances, or even strangers come to grips with some kind of problem. In summary, the world is filled with informal helpers and only a small fraction of the help provided comes from level-one professionals. Levels two, three, and four usually receive no formal training as interpersonal helpers, and the amount and quality of training of level-one helpers varies greatly.

Since interpersonal helping is such a common human experience, one wonders whether some kind of training in helping shouldn't be as common as training in reading, writing, and math. Therefore, although this book focuses specifically on counselors, social workers, ministers, psychologists, and psychiatrists, it is assumed that training in helping skills could benefit all interpersonal helpers: parents, in managing marital problems and in helping their children grow and develop; friends, in helping loved ones in times of trouble; and individuals, in helping themselves to cope more creatively with the problems of life.

■ The Ongoing Crisis in Helping: Does Helping Really Help?

Before embarking on a career in counseling or psychotherapy, you should know that a debate about the usefulness of these professions has been going on for at least 30 years (Hariman, 1984). The disturbing question "Does formal helping really help?" is still being asked. Some answer this question with a resounding "yes." For instance, Smith, Glass, and Miller (1980), through an analysis of hundreds of outcome studies, found convincing evidence of the efficacy of psychotherapy. However, the validity of the methodology they used, called meta-analysis, has been debated ever since their first report (see Rosenthal [1983] and others in the *Journal of Consulting and Clinical Psychology, 51* [1]). The American Psychiatric Association Commission on Psychotherapies (1982) draws a guarded conclusion from a complex study of the helping process when it says the following:

> Although research in psychotherapy is still plagued by many problems connected with assignment of patients, use of statistics, outcome measures, and experimental design, the data have shown empirically that psychotherapy is effective with some populations with some problems [p. 226].

Others express serious doubts about the helping industry as a whole, some even claiming that helpers are taking money under false pretenses (see Eysenck, 1984; Gallo, 1978; Mansfield & Busse, 1977; Presby, 1978; Rimland, 1979; Tennov, 1975). Cowen (1982) expresses the problem with literary flair.

Once upon a time, mental health lived by a simple two-part myth. *Part 1:* People with psychological troubles bring them to mental health professionals for help. *Part 2:* One way or another, often based on verbal dialogue, professionals solve these problems and the people live happily ever after.

And sometimes the cookie does indeed crumble according to the myth. But events of the past several decades suggest that the "marriage-in-heaven" script is *not* nature's only, or even most frequent, way. In real life the idyllic myth breaks down at several key points.

Let's talk first . . . about Part 2. Heresy though it may have been 20 years ago, it is not permissible to say that not all problems brought to mental health professionals are happily adjudicated. How much of the shortfall is due to the imprecision of our professional "magic," or even to the lack of skill of our magicians, and how much to the selectively refractory nature of the problems that professionals see remains unclear. Much clearer is a sense of mounting dissatisfaction with the reach and effectiveness of past traditional ways, a dissatisfaction that has powered active new explorations toward a more promising tomorrow in mental health [p. 385].

A number of helping professionals claim that the problem lies not with the helping process itself but with the number of inept helpers currently engaged in providing counseling and psychotherapy (Lambert, Bergin, & Collins, 1977; Strupp, Hadley, & Gomes-Schwartz, 1977). Because of inept helpers, some clients—their number is disputed—get *worse* from treatment (see Bergin, 1980; Mays & Franks, 1980, for a discussion of this issue). Bergin (1971, 1980; Bergin & Lambert, 1978) and Carkhuff and his associates (Carkhuff, 1969a, 1969b; Carkhuff & Berenson, 1976; Carkhuff & Anthony, 1979) have long claimed that helping is never neutral, that it is always "for better or for worse."

Helping is a powerful process that is all too easy to mismanage. Unskilled and unprincipled helpers can do a great deal of harm. Ellis (1984) cites evidence that indicts the competence of many helpers. He claims that many helpers are ineffective and that many who are effective in some sense of that term are *inefficient,* "using methods that are often distinctly inept and that consequently lead these clients to achieve weak and unlasting results, frequently at the expense of enormous amounts of wasted time and money" (p. 24). There is also growing evidence that clients are joining the consumer movement and expressing dissatisfaction with the so-called help they receive (Laungani, 1984; Lebow, 1982).

Since studies on the efficacy of counseling and psychotherapy do not usually make a distinction between high-level and low-level helpers, and since the research on deterioration effects in therapy suggests that there are a large number of low-level or inadequate helpers in the world, the negative results found in many studies are predictable. However, in the hands of skilled and socially intelligent workers—people whom Gilbert (1978) and Carkhuff (1985) call "exemplars"—helping can do a great deal of good.

In summary, it would be unfair to tell those thinking of a career in the helping professions that all is well in Camelot. It is not. You are encouraged to acquaint yourself with the ongoing debate concerning the efficacy of helping. After reading the research, the discussions, and the summaries, you may well shake your head and repeat what Carl Rogers said in 1958: "[I have] never learned much from controlled studies of therapy" (in Rubenstein & Parloff, 1959, p. 313). Research findings are often so tentative and contradictory that it is difficult to formulate a coherent approach to practice based on them. However, study of this debate is not meant to discourage you, but to help you (1) appreciate the complexity of the helping process, (2) acquaint yourself with the issues involved in evaluating the outcomes of helping, (3) appreciate that helping, poorly done, can actually harm others, (4) become reasonably cautious as a helper, and (5) motivate yourself to become a high-level helper, learning and using practical models, methods, skills, and guidelines for helping. Since the needs of clients are urgent, the practice of both formal and informal helping will always move ahead of its empirical research base. To my mind (Egan, 1984; Egan & Cowan, 1979), the best formal helpers are "translators," people who stay abreast of the best in current theory and research and who constantly update their practical helping through ongoing, action research with their clients.

In a more positive vein, Norman Kagan (1973) has suggested that the basic issue confronting the helping professions is not validity—whether helping helps or not—but reliability.

> Not, can counseling and psychotherapy work, but does it work *consistently*? Not, can we educate people who are able to help others, but can we develop methods which will increase the likelihood that *most* of our graduates will become as effective mental health workers as only a rare few do? [p. 44].

More effective training programs for helpers are needed. The studies just mentioned suggest that while there are many professionals with the proper credentials, many of them do not have the essential skills. Carkhuff (1971a) calls helpers "functional" professionals if they have the skills needed for effective helping. There is a great need for functional helpers, whether they are "credentialed" or not. The helping model presented in this book, together with the skills and techniques that make it work, is designed precisely to increase both the validity and the reliability of the helping process.

■ Models of Helping: Richness or Clutter?

Even the slightest investigation will reveal that the number of models or approaches to helping is staggering. For instance, if you were to read the sections of the *Annual review of psychology* that deal with approaches to helping, leaf through books that are compilations of the different approaches to counseling and psychotherapy (Braswell & Seay, 1984; Corey, 1986; Corsini, 1984; Jurjevich, 1973; Lichtenstein, 1980; Patterson, 1986—to name but a few), or keep abreast of the fairly steady stream of new approaches, you would soon discover a bewildering number of schools, systems, approaches, and techniques, all of which are proposed with equal seriousness and all of which claim success. Is this richness, clutter, or a bit of both? We are justified in believing it to be richness, as long as helpers have an integrative model or framework helping them to organize and borrow from all the models. Helpers, especially beginning helpers, need a practical, working model of helping that tells them the following:

- What to do to help people facing problems in living
- What stages and steps make up the helping process
- What communication skills they need to help clients move through that process
- What techniques they must master to help clients cope with problems in living
- How they can acquire those skills and techniques
- What resources and skills clients need to collaborate in the helping process and to manage their problems more effectively
- How clients can acquire those skills and develop those resources
- How to determine whether the helping is effective or not.

Furthermore, the model of choice is one that will help the counselor organize and make sense of the reams of helping literature. To my mind, a flexible, humanistic, broadly based *problem-management* model or framework meets all of those requirements.

■ A Problem-Management Approach to Helping

Let us say your intention is to become a manager in or consultant to organizations and institutions. You decide you need some training. You look at the training programs available and notice that just about every one of them includes problem solving as a skill to be learned. Then, while reviewing the professional literature on managing and consulting, you notice there are dozens of problem-solving and decision-making models, most of them elaborations of a basic problem-solving model that has been around for centuries. You quickly surmise that if you are to be helpful to your clients, whether they are individuals or institutions, you must become adept at problem solving: individual problem solving, group problem solving, collaborative problem solving, creative problem solving, and so forth.

Common sense suggests that problem-solving models, techniques, and skills are important, not just for managers and consultants, but for all of us, since all of us must grapple daily with great or small problems in living. Ask anybody whether problem-solving skills are important for day-to-day living and the answer is inevitably "certainly." Bruner (see Hall, 1982) says, "One of the big changes in educational psychology over the past decade is a shift to 'metacognition'—teaching kids how to think about their own thinking, how to think about problem solving, how to attack problems" (p. 59). Talk about the importance of problem solving is everywhere. However, review the curricula of our primary, secondary, and higher-level schools and you will find that talk outstrips practice.

There are those who say the reason that formal courses in problem-solving skills are not found in our schools is that such skills are picked up through experience. To a certain extent, this is true. However, if problem-solving skills are so important, I wonder why, with relatively few exceptions, society leaves the acquisition of those crucial skills to chance. The whole world may be a laboratory for problem solving, but the skills needed to optimize learning there should be taught; a problem-solving mentality should become second nature to us. You will soon discover that most of the clients you counsel are ineffective problem solvers.

The model of helping used in this book is, broadly speaking, a problem-management model, a cognitive-behavioral approach to counseling and psychotherapy. Mahoney and Arnkoff (1978) recognized the value of such an approach when they said

> Among the cognitive learning therapies, it is our opinion that the problem-solving perspectives may ultimately yield the most encouraging clinical results. This is due to the fact that—as a broader clinical endeavor—they encompass both the cognitive restructuring and the coping skills therapies (not to mention a wide range of "noncognitive" perspectives). With the problem-solving approaches, clients are not only taught specific coping skills, but also the more general strategies of assessment, problem definition, and so on [p. 709].

The value of problem-management approaches to helping is being recognized more and more as more helpers, either implicitly or explicitly, adopt a problem-management approach (Burke, Haworth, & Brantley, 1980; Carkhuff & Anthony, 1979; Dixon and others, 1979; D'Zurilla & Goldfried, 1971; Goldfried & Davidson, 1976; Held, 1984; Heppner, 1978; Heppner & Petersen, 1982; Ivey & Matthews, 1984; Jacobson, 1977; Janis, 1983b; Jones, 1976; Livneh, 1984; Mahoney, 1977; Mahoney & Arnkoff, 1978; Prochaska & Norcross, 1982; Schwebel, Schwebel, & Schwebel, 1985; Scott, 1979; Searight & Openlander, 1984;

Wagman, 1979, 1980a, 1980b; Wasik & Fishbein, 1982; Watson & Tharp, 1985; Wheeler & Janis, 1980; Zins, 1984). Most crisis-intervention models have a strong problem-solving component (Janosik, 1984). A problem-management model in counseling and psychotherapy can take advantage of the vast amount of research that has been done on the problem-solving process itself, much of which focuses on human problem solving. The model, techniques, and skills outlined in this book tap into that research base.

■ Using the Problem-Management Model to Organize the Contributions of Different Approaches to Helping: A Systematic and Integrative Eclecticism

Although many counselors and psychotherapists like to consider themselves "eclectic" (Garfield & Kurtz, 1974, 1977), there is some confusion among them as to just what eclecticism means (Brabeck & Welfel, 1985; Patterson, 1985; Rychlak, 1985; Swan, 1979; Thorne, 1973a, 1973b). An effective eclecticism must be more than a random borrowing of ideas and techniques from here and there. Helpers need a conceptual framework (Dimond, Havens, & Jones, 1978; Ward, 1983) that enables them to borrow ideas, methods, and techniques systematically from all theories, schools, and approaches and integrate them into their own theory and practice of helping (Brabeck & Welfel, 1985). The problem-solving framework presented here is placed against a larger, people-in-systems model (Egan, 1984; Egan & Cowan, 1979) that takes into consideration the following:

- Developmental factors: clients' developmental stages and stage-related tasks together with the normative developmental crises they experience over the life span
- Social-system factors: the resources and obstacles that the range of social settings in which clients "live and move and have their being" contributes to those developmental processes
- The life skills related to physical, mental, and moral development: learning how to learn, interpersonal living, problem solving and decision making, functioning in small groups, and participating actively in the social settings of life.

These two models provide the conceptual framework for an integrative (Brammer & Shostrom, 1977) or systematic eclecticism. Held (1984) views the problem-solving treatment sequence—assessment, goal setting, intervention, and evaluation—as central to what she calls a "strategic eclecticism." In her approach biological, intrapsychic, and interpersonal levels of human functioning are addressed within the problem-solving framework.

A comprehensive problem-solving or problem-management model can be used to make sense of the vast literature in counseling and psychotherapy in at least three ways: organizing, mining, and evaluating.

Organizing. The principles, methods, and techniques discussed in the literature can be located in the "geography" of the problem-management model. That is, any given principle or technique contributes to the work to be done in one or more of the stages or steps of the model. For instance, a number of contemporary therapies have elaborated excellent techniques for helping clients identify blind spots and develop new perspectives on their problem situations. Those techniques can be organized, as we shall see, in Step I-C under the "new perspectives" task of the problem-management model. Using an integrative framework helps reduce the amount of clutter found in the literature.

Mining. Helpers can use the problem-management model in a more active way to mine or "dig out" what is useful in a school or approach without having to accept everything offered. Helpers can use the problem-solving model as a tool to go searching for methods that will fit their own styles and the needs of their clients. I routinely read books and articles through the comprehensive filters provided by the problem-management and people-in-systems models.

Evaluating. Since the problem-management model is pragmatic, and since it focuses on the *outcomes* of helping, it can be used to evaluate the numerous helping techniques that are constantly being devised. The model poses the question, "In what way does this technique or method contribute to the bottom line—that is, therapeutic outcomes?"

Still, the problem-management model is an open-systems model, not a dogma. Although it takes a stand on how counselors may help their clients, it is open to being corroborated, complemented, and challenged by any other approach, model, or school of helping.

> Like the scientific method itself, efficient therapy remains flexible, curious, empirically-oriented, critical of poor theories and results, and devoted to effective change. It is not one-sided or dogmatic. It is ready to give up the most time-honored and revered methods if new evidence contradicts them. It constantly grows and develops; and it sacredizes no theory and no methodology [Ellis, 1984, p. 33].

The needs of clients—not the egos of model builders—must remain central to the helping process.

■ The Training of Helpers

The skills you will need to develop in order to become an effective helper will be discussed in the separate chapters dealing with the stages of the problem-management process. They include establishing working relationships, basic and advanced communication skills, helping clients challenge themselves, problem clarification, goal setting, program development, program implementation, and ongoing evaluation. Your skill development will have four phases:

1. *Conceptual understanding.* Reading this book, reviewing examples, and listening to lectures will give you a conceptual or cognitive understanding of the skills.
2. *Behavioral-based feeling.* By watching instructors model the skills and by doing the exercises in the manual that accompanies this book, you will develop a behavioral rather than just a conceptual feeling for the skills.
3. *Initial mastery.* You will begin to master the skills by practicing them with your fellow trainees under the supervision of a trainer.
4. *Further mastery.* You will improve your command of the skills by using them in practicum or internship experiences under the supervision of skilled and experienced helpers.

Competency-based training in counselor-education programs is essential. Hatcher and others (1978) report that of over 400 counselor-education programs surveyed in 1977, 76.1% of those responding reported a commitment to competency-based training. That's the good news. The bad news is that only about 7% had actually made the shift to a practical implementation of that goal.

Acquiring competence in a helping model and the methods and skills that make it effective are only one part of a complete counselor-training program, however. Effective helpers also develop further working knowledge and skills such as the following (see Egan, 1984; Egan & Cowan, 1979; Larson, 1984; Marshall & Kurtz, 1982).

Applied developmental psychology.   You need to learn the developmental stages, tasks, and crises of the clients with whom you work. This will help you distinguish between the normal developmental problems all of us face over a life span and more serious social-emotional problems and disorders. A solid working knowledge of applied developmental psychology will help you become an effective developmental counselor in all your interactions with clients.

Specific problems.   You will soon discover a rich literature dealing with the whole gamut of problems that women and men face—alcoholism, child abuse, phobias, learning disabilities, drug abuse, marital and family problems, sexual disorders, dying and bereavement, religious problems, delinquency, mental retardation, the problems associated with physical rehabilitation, the social-emotional dimensions of medical problems— the list is endless. People who have worked with specific problems share their wisdom with us in excellent books and articles. While it is true that the helping model to be outlined in the pages of this book can be used to help people manage any kind of problem, your ability to use the model effectively is enhanced by your working knowledge of specific disorders.

The social settings of life.   Many people find themselves mired down in problem situations that have their primary origin not in their own internal psychology but in the social settings of life. The more you learn about how people's daily lives are affected by the organizations, institutions, and communities to which they belong, the more intelligently you will help them devise action programs to cope with problems whose origins are in those settings.

The power of culture.   Culture refers to beliefs, values, and norms that give rise to patterns of behavior, both in individuals and in organizations, institutions, and communities. Culture in this sense is rightly called the largest and most controlling of the systems. Individual and system cultures provide and impose "blueprints" (Bronfenbrenner, 1977) on behavior, blueprints that may be enhancing or limiting. Culture, as described here, refers not just to cross-cultural realities such as an older, middle-class Black helper dealing with a younger, socially-deprived Hispanic client, although the impact of cross-cultural factors in that traditional sense is critical. But culture in the sense discussed here affects all interactions, even those between identical twins. Since no two individuals grow up having exactly the same set of beliefs, values, and norms, even interactions between identical twins have a cross-cultural dimension to them. A working knowledge of the power of culture is a relatively new tool for helpers (see Egan, 1985).

■ Client Self-Responsibility: A Guiding Value

Client self-responsibility is one of the principal values in the approach to helping taken here. However, clients are clients often because they have problems with self-responsibility. The list of ways in which we avoid responsibility is endless; some categories are passivity, learned helplessness, and disabling self-talk.

Passivity.   Early in the history of modern psychology, William James remarked that few people bring more than about 10% of their human potential to bear on the problems and challenges of human living. Others since James, although changing the percentages somewhat, have said substantially the same thing, and few have challenged their statements (Maslow, 1968). It is probably not an exaggeration to say that unused human potential constitutes a more serious social problem than do emotional disorders, as it is more widespread. Maslow (1968) suggests that what is usually called "normal" in psychology "is really a *psychopathology of the average,* so undramatic and so widely spread that we don't even notice it ordinarily" (p. 16, emphasis added). Many of your clients, beside having more or less serious problems in living, will probably be chronic victims of the psychopathology of the average.

Schiff (1975) discusses four kinds of passivity: (1) doing nothing—not responding to problems and options; (2) overadaptation—uncritically accepting the goals and solutions suggested by others; (3) random or agitated behavior—acting aimlessly; and (4) becoming incapacitated or violent—shutting down or blowing up. How often people shake their heads when some "nice" person engages in an act of violence—"He was such a quiet, unassuming fellow." Passivity is one of the most important ingredients in the generation and perpetuation of the psychopathology of the average (Oblas, 1978); it represents the failure of people to take responsibility for themselves in one or more developmental areas of life or in various life situations that call for action.

■

When Zelda and Jerry first noticed small signs that things were not going right in their relationship, they did nothing. They noticed certain incidents, mused on them for a while, and then forgot about them. They lacked the interpersonal skills to engage each other immediately and to explore what was happening, but they were also victims of their own learned passivity.

■

They had both *learned* to remain passive in the face of the little crises of life, not realizing how much their passivity would ultimately contribute to their downfall (see Egan, 1985, pp. 167–170).

Learned helplessness. Seligman's (1975) concept of "learned helplessness" and its relationship to depression has received a great deal of attention (*Journal of Abnormal Psychology,* No. 1, 1978). Clients (and to an extent all of us) can learn to believe from an early age that there is nothing they can do about certain life situations. Obviously there are degrees in feelings of helplessness. Some clients feel minimally helpless (and minimally depressed) and come to a helper primarily because they believe that getting help will be a more effective or efficient way of facing some problem or difficulty. Other clients feel totally helpless and over-whelmed by the difficulties of life and fall into a deep, almost intractable depression.

Disabling self-talk.   Ellis (1974, 1977a, 1977b, 1979; Ellis & Harper, 1975) and others (Grieger & Boyd, 1980) have shown that people often talk themselves into passivity. They tell themselves such things as:

"I can't do it."
"I can't cope."
"I don't have what it takes to engage in that program; it's too hard."
"It won't work."

Clients get into the habit of engaging in disabling "self-talk." Such self-defeating conversations with themselves get people into trouble in the first place and then prevent them from getting out. Ways of helping clients to manage disabling self-talk will be discussed in Chapters Seven and Eight.

Approaches to Client Self-Responsibility

Brickman and his associates (1982) indicate that different forms of coun-seling and psychotherapy make different assumptions about client re-sponsibility (see also Halleck, 1982). Some see clients as responsible for their problems, some for the solutions to these problems, some for nei-ther, and some for both. Such assumptions contribute to the way helping takes place. Weisz, Rothbaum, and Blackburn (1984; also see Rothbaum, Weisz, & Snyder, 1982; Weisz, 1983) discuss the cultural bias found in North America with regard to people's ability to control their destinies.

> There are at least two general paths to a feeling of control. In *primary* control, individuals enhance their rewards by influencing existing realities (e.g., other people, circumstances, symptoms, or behavior problems). In *secondary* control, individuals enhance their rewards by accommodating to existing realities and maximizing satisfaction or goodness of fit with things as they are. American psychologists have written extensively about control, but have generally de-fined it only in terms of its primary form [p. 955].

The position taken here is this: whether clients are victims of their own doings, the doings of others (including the social settings of their lives), or some combination of the two, they must take an active part in managing their problems, including the search for solutions and efforts toward achieving those solutions. In some cases this will involve primary control. For instance, a woman might convince her spouse to go with her to a counselor and there work actively toward creating a more sat-isfactory marriage. In other cases it will involve secondary control. For instance, a man might be dissatisfied with his marriage, but estimate the probability of his wife's working with him to renew the marriage as very low. He sees a counselor, but most of his effort goes into coping with and making the best of marital realities as they are. This is not the same as passivity.

The ideal is for clients to take the lead in problem management even though others, including counselors, may help in a variety of ways. The function of helpers is not to remake the lives of their clients but to help them handle problems in living and refashion their lives according to their own values.

Self-efficacy. The opposite of passivity is "agency" (Egan, 1970), "assertiveness," or "self-efficacy" (Bandura, 1977a, 1977b, 1980, 1982; Bandura & Schunk, 1981; Clifford, 1983; Lee, 1983). Bandura suggests that people's expectations of themselves have everything to do with their willingness to put forth effort to cope with difficulties, the amount of effort they will expend, and their persistence in the face of obstacles. People tend to take action if two conditions are fulfilled:

1. They see that certain behaviors will most likely lead to certain desirable results or accomplishments (outcome expectations).
2. They are reasonably sure that they can successfully engage in such behavior (self-efficacy expectations).

For instance, Yolanda not only believes that engaging in a job-search program will produce good results—that is, get her a job (an outcome expectation)—but she also believes that she has whatever it takes to engage in the job-search program (a self-efficacy expectation). Thus, she joins the program. On the other hand, Yves is not convinced that a weight-loss program will really help him lose weight (a negative outcome expectation), so he does not participate, while Xavier is convinced that the program will work but does not feel that he has the will power to engage in it (a negative self-efficacy expectation). People's sense of self-efficacy can be strengthened in a variety of ways:

- *Success.* They act, and see that their behavior actually produces results. Often success in a small endeavor will give them the courage to try something more difficult.
- *Modeling.* They see others doing what they are hoping to do, and are encouraged to try it themselves.
- *Encouragement.* Others exhort them to try, challenge them, and support their efforts.
- *Reducing fear and anxiety.* If people are overly fearful that they will fail, they generally do not act. Therefore, procedures that reduce fear and anxiety can heighten a person's sense of self-efficacy.

As a helper, you can do a great deal to help people develop a sense of agency or self-efficacy. First, you can help them challenge self-defeating beliefs and attitudes about themselves and substitute realistic beliefs about self-efficacy. This includes helping them reduce the kinds of fears and anxieties that keep them from mobilizing their resources. Second, you can help them develop the working knowledge, life skills, and resources they need to succeed. Third, you can challenge them to take reasonable risks and support them when they do.

Although an important goal of helping is to encourage clients to develop more and more responsibility, this does not mean that they will move away from passivity and dependency toward aggressiveness and fierce independence. With some clients forms of primary control might be possible, but with others forms of secondary control might be the only realistic option. Our clients, like ourselves, have limitations. Like us they are, in many, many ways, not captains of their own fates. It is assumed here that the problem-management model presents a framework for helping clients develop realistic and self-enhancing degrees of agency and self-efficacy. This includes helping clients to actively participate in and "own" the helping process itself. It is extremely rewarding to see clients use problem-solving and decision-making skills they have learned in counseling in order to become "change agents" (Remer & O'Neill, 1980) in their own lives.

■ Helping as a Social-Influence Process

A full consideration of client responsibility must take into account social influence in the helping process. History, both ancient and recent, provides ample evidence of people suffering from a variety of emotional disturbances and a variety of physical ailments of psychogenic origin who have been "cured" by their belief in the curative powers of a helper (Frank, 1973). Very often such cures have taken place in religious contexts, but they have not been limited to such contexts. Typically, people come to perceive a certain person as a healer with great powers. That person might be a tribal shaman or a psychiatrist with a good reputation. People hear that such healers have cured others with ailments similar to theirs, and believe them to be acting not in their own interests but rather in the interests of the afflicted who come to them. That belief enables the afflicted person to place great trust in the healer. Finally, in a ceremony that is often public and highly emotional, the healer in some way touches the afflicted person and the person is "healed." The tremendous need of the afflicted person, the reputation of the healer, and the afflicted person's trusting belief in the healer all heighten the person's belief that he or she will be cured. In fact, if such afflicted persons are not cured, they are often charged with a lack of belief or some other evil within them (for instance, possession by a demon, or poor motivation); to their afflictions is added a loss of face in the community (as outcasts, "crazies"). This state is worse than the first: the afflicted person is not only ill but also an object of opprobrium.

The dynamics of successful "cures" are hard to explain empirically. It is obvious that elements of the healing process help marshal the emotional energies and other resources of the afflicted: they experience hope and other positive emotions that they perhaps have not experienced for years. The situation also places a demand on them to be cured. It presents the afflicted person with an opportune, acceptable, favorable, legitimate time to leave his or her old way of life behind and take up a new one. The power of suggestion in such cases can be great, even overwhelming. Skilled helpers are aware of and have a deep respect for such "arational" factors in the helping process.

What Frank describes is a process of social influence. Different forms of social influence are a fact of everyday life—we are constantly influencing one another in many different ways, though not always in the dramatic ways discussed by Frank. It will be helpful to review what is currently being said about social influence in counseling and psychotherapy.

Current Views of Social Influence in Counseling and Psychotherapy

In 1968 Stanley Strong wrote what proved to be a landmark article on counseling as an interpersonal-influence process. The word *landmark* is used because the article has stimulated much writing and research. Overviews of this research can be found in Corrigan, Dell, Lewis, and Schmidt (1980), Dorn (1984), and Strong and Claiborn (1982). Corrigan and his associates outline the main points of Strong's argument.

> Strong postulated that the extent to which counselors are perceived as expert, attractive, and trustworthy would reduce the likelihood of their being discredited [by clients] . . . . From these hypotheses, Strong suggested a two-stage model of counseling. In the first stage, counselors *enhance* their perceived expertness, attractiveness, trustworthiness, and clients' involvement in counseling. In the second stage, counselors *use* their influence to precipitate opinion and/or behavior change in clients [p. 396].

In this view, helpers establish a power base and then use that power to influence clients to do whatever is necessary to manage their lives more effectively.

Goldstein (1980) describes the social-influence process in helping in a way that is complementary to Strong's. First, he calls behaviors by means of which helpers establish an interpersonal power base with their clients "relationship enhancers." He suggests that there are various ways of establishing the base: by providing clients with the kind of structure that enables them to give themselves more easily to the helping process (for instance, by setting up a clear client-counselor contract), by modeling the kinds of behaviors expected of clients so that they can imitate those behaviors (for instance, the kinds of behaviors associated with respect and genuineness), by attending to clients and to what they are saying, by expressing appropriate warmth, by communicating understanding, by sharing their own experiences, and the like. Second, these behaviors, if carried out skillfully, lead to mutual liking, respect, and trust. Third, this kind of relationship helps clients become more willing to engage in dialogue with helpers, reveal themselves more deeply, and open themselves to the different kinds of direction helpers can provide throughout the helping process. Finally, because of all this, the probability that clients will change their behaviors in self-enhancing ways is increased. Constructive behavioral change on the part of the client is always the "bottom line" of the influence process.

Applying Social-Influence Theory to the Problem-Management Model of Helping: The Client's Experience of Helping

Let's take a closer look at social influence as it takes place in the helping relationship in terms of attractiveness, trustworthiness, and competence. We are especially interested in the experiences or perceptions of the client—that is, the client's experience of the helper and his or her behavior both before and during the helping process. Before beginning, however, it is important to note that different clients will experience the same helper in different ways. A complex web of factors goes into any given person's perception of another. Therefore, it must be said that by engaging in the behaviors outlined below there is some probability that you will appear attractive, trustworthy, and competent to clients, but outcomes will vary from client to client. It should also be noted that attractiveness, trustworthiness, and competence, even though presented separately here, are often interrelated in the client's perception. For instance, if you are experienced as competent, then you well might be experienced as trustworthy.

What attractiveness means.   Strong (1968) suggests that clients' perceptions of counselor attractiveness are based on "perceived similarity to, compatibility with, and liking for" the helper (p. 216). For instance, if the client is young and the helper is also at least relatively young, the perceived similarity might help the client to be attracted to the helper. If the client is an addict and the helper is a reformed addict who talks about his or her own experience of addiction, this self-sharing might help the client see the counselor as similar to and compatible with himself or herself. It might also happen that a client is spontaneously attracted to a helper because of a "package" of things such as friendliness, accepting behavior, and the like. When asked to identify the reasons, the client might say "I don't know, I just like her."

The sources of perceptions of attractiveness.   You may appear attractive to clients because of physical characteristics and general appearance (you are good-looking or well-groomed), because of your particular helping role (counselor, psychologist, doctor, nurse, minister), because of your reputation (others have told a prospective client that you are a friendly, understanding person), and/or because of your behavior. Behavior will be emphasized because there is usually little that can be done about the other categories, even though you know they are affecting a client. For instance, some clients might find ministers more attractive helpers than psychologists, but if you are a psychologist you would hardly become a minister for that reason.

What trustworthiness means.   Strong suggests that a helper's perceived trustworthiness is based on his or her "(a) reputation for honesty, (b) social role, such as physician, (c) sincerity and openness, and (d) lack of motivation for personal gain" (p. 217). It can mean a number of things:

- *Confidentiality:* The client can say, "If I tell this person about myself, she will not tell others."
- *Credibility:* "Interpersonal trust is defined . . . as an expectancy of help by an individual or a group, that the word, promise, verbal or written statement of another individual or group can be relied on" [Rotter, 1971, p. 444]. The client can say "I can believe what he tells me."
- *Consideration in the use of power:* The assumption here is that the helper is perceived as having power and as being the kind of person who will not misuse it. The client can say "If I entrust myself to this person, she will be careful with me."
- *Understanding:* The client can say "If I tell this person about myself, he will make an effort to understand me."

The sources of trustworthiness.   The sources of trustworthiness are the same general sources as those of attractiveness. Someone might see you as trustworthy—or untrustworthy—because of your physical appearance ("I just don't trust him; he reminds me of a used-car salesman who once did me in."); because of your reputation ("Ira says that she doesn't talk about any of her clients, even in general terms."); because of role ("I can trust him because he's a priest."); and/or because of your actual behavior. You may increase your trustworthiness in the eyes of your clients if you

- Strike a contract with the client and live up to its provisions
- Maintain confidentiality
- Manifest respect in the ways outlined earlier in this chapter
- Are sensitive to the needs and feelings of the client
- Demonstrate genuineness, sincerity, and openness in the ways outlined earlier in this chapter
- Are realistic but optimistic about the client's ability to come to grips with his or her problems in living
- Are willing to give the client information or feedback that might benefit him or her
- Use whatever social-influence power you have carefully and in the interests of the client
- Are open to feedback and reasonable social-influence attempts on the part of the client
- Avoid behavior that might imply such ulterior motives as voyeurism, selfishness, superficial curiosity, personal gain, or deviousness.

What competence means. In the literature on social influence this is usually called "expertness," but I prefer the term *competence,* which, at least for me, has a broader meaning. It takes little experience in life to realize that people who are called "experts" are not always competent— and you can draw this inference without being cynical. Generally, clients believe that the counselor has some information, skill, or ability to help them; that he or she possesses "answers" to their problems or information that will enable them to come up with their own answers. In any case, they believe that such information will enable them to live less painfully or more effectively. Strong (1968) goes on to say that this belief is influenced by "(a) objective evidence of specialized training such as diplomas, certificates, and titles, (b) behavioral evidence of expertness such as rational and knowledgeable arguments and confidence in presentation, and (c) reputation as an expert" (p. 216). That is, like attractiveness and trustworthiness, there are three general sources of perceived competence: role, reputation, and behavior. Let's take a closer look at each of these.

- *Role-competence.* Role-competence refers to the fact that helpers belong to some profession (they are counselors, psychotherapists, ministers, social workers, and the like) and that they have a variety of credentials (degrees or certificates) attesting to the fact that they are experts. Other role-related factors that can suggest competence are such things as offices, nameplates, and titles. Clients see helpers as "credentialed" professionals.
- *Reputation-competence.* This means that clients are aware of some direct or indirect testimony that the helper is an expert or is competent. This testimony may come from those who have actually been helped by the

counselor, or it may come from other helpers who consider their colleague to be a good helper. Helpers' reputations may also come from being associated with prestigious institutions. Obviously, helpers' reputations may or may not be deserved: a reputation is not an absolute indication of competence. But a reputation for expertness does have at least an initial impact on the client.

- *Behavior-competence.* Some people let themselves be influenced by helpers because the behaviors in which the helpers engage have at least the aura of competence. Helpers are seen as competent because they are active, because they listen intently, because they talk intelligently, because they exude a quiet confidence as they offer suggestions to their clients, because they are understanding, genuine, and respectful. However, the appearance of acting competently does not mean a helper is actually competent; competence is found not in appearances but in outcomes. Still, clients can be beguiled by this or that set of behaviors that seem to be indications of competence, and trust helpers who engage in those behaviors. I suggest a more radical kind of expertness or competence, something that can be called "accomplishment-competence."
- *Accomplishment-competence.* In my estimation, accomplishment-competence (Gilbert, 1978) represents the "bottom line" of social influence. If helpers are perceived to be attractive, trustworthy, and/or competent (in the sense that they engage in behaviors that seem competent to the client) and then, in the long run, do not actually help, this second state is worse than the first. Clients' reasonable expectations are not met and they lose confidence in the helping process itself.

CLIENT: It's just no use. I went to this guy; he was actually a nice guy. I trusted him. He was a doctor and everything. But we got no place. It seemed that we went 'round and 'round and nothing got any better.

Of course, there can be no automatic assumption that most of the fault lay with the helper, but the fact remains that being perceived by the client as attractive, trustworthy, and competent, even though it might have opened the client up to influence, did not accomplish anything.

Therefore, helpers must be able to *deliver* what is promised by the helping contract, whether that contract is explicit or only implicit. According to Gilbert (1978), competence does not lie principally in behaviors but in the *accomplishments* toward which those behaviors are directed. If Brenda comes to a helper with persistently high levels of free-floating anxiety, then "anxiety reduced" is one of the hoped-for accomplishments of the helping process. If a year later she is still as anxious as ever despite weekly visits to a professional helper, that helper's attractiveness, trustworthiness, and competence based on role and reputation go for naught. Trust in a helper can evaporate quickly if little or nothing is accomplished through the helping sessions. And yet, too often it would seem, clients persist in trusting helpers even though they fail to demonstrate competence through verifiable accomplishments. Role, reputation, and behavior beguile them even in the face of problem situations that remain unmanaged.

The problem-solving approach to helping does much to avoid this impasse. Problem situations are translated into solution-related goals, action programs are devised and implemented to achieve those goals, and the entire process is shared with the client to the degree that it is possible. The process is open to continual evaluation: since goals are identified, it is possible to monitor whether or not they are achieved.

Strong (1968) suggests that one source of competence is the confidence counselors have in the theory and model they use in helping others. Such confidence implies more than blind faith in a particular system. Counselors who work hard to make any particular theory or model their own manifest their investment in their attitudes and behaviors. They speak and act enthusiastically and confidently. More than that, they work hard with their clients. The problem-management model provides the impetus for such behavior.

Some of the Ways in Which Clients Influence Helpers

Even a cursory examination of the helping process reveals that clients can affect helpers in many different ways. Here are a few of them.

Attraction.   Helpers are affected by physical and other forms of attractiveness in their clients. Once they are aware that they perceive any given client as attractive, unattractive, or somewhere in between, they are in a position to monitor their reactions to the client. For instance, they may realize that they will tend to be less demanding of attractive clients and more prone not to listen well to unattractive clients.

Reacting to clients' distortions of helpers.   Some clients trip over their own distorted views of their helpers. For instance, a young woman who has had serious problems in her relationship with her mother might begin to act toward the woman who is her helper in unproductive ways similar to the ways in which she acts toward or reacts to her mother. Skilled helpers realize the potential for such behavior and therefore are better prepared for it when it happens. Unskilled helpers can get caught up in the game, as it were. They follow clients' leads instead of understanding and, in due time, challenging distorted views.

Problem similarity.   It may happen that clients will bring up problem situations similar to those currently being experienced by their helpers. For instance, Ingrid might discuss her impending divorce with Elsa, who sees herself as headed for divorce. If this so affects Elsa that she cannot work effectively with Ingrid, a referral to another therapist is in order. Ideally helpers are striving to become "effective," (Carkhuff 1969a, 1969b), "intentional" (Ivey, 1980), "transparent" (Jourard, 1971b), "self-actualized" (Maslow, 1968, 1971), and capable of "I-Thou" relationships (Buber, 1937). This means, in part, that they are capable of applying the problem-solving model being discussed in these pages to the management of their own lives. They might do this on their own or take counsel with others. If they are successful, the problem situations they are facing will not interfere with their ability to help others faced with similar problems. However, if problem similarity does interfere with their ability to help, they know that a referral is in order.

This hardly exhausts the list. These examples are meant to help you start thinking of the mutuality of the influence process.

■ Client and Helper Collaboration in the Helping Process: Reconciling Self-Responsibility and Social Influence

Both Frank (1973) and Goldstein (1980) describe "unilateral" processes of social influence.

> The *unilateral* aspect of the helping relationship reflects the fact that the participants agree that one person is defined as the helper and the other as the client. It is also agreed, explicitly or implicitly, that the focus of the relationship and all its activities is on solving the problems of the client. In this respect, the change process is unlike most other interpersonal interactions. The personal problems, the private affairs, the worries, and the wishes of one person, the helper, are intentionally not focused upon. Treatment, therapy, or whatever the helping relationship may be called, is one-sided and concentrates exclusively on the client [Goldstein, 1980, p. 2].

However, whereas social influence is a fact of everyday life and a fact of the helping process, it need not be unilateral. Helping can be dangerous if it actually increases clients' feelings of powerlessness (Stensrud & Stensrud, 1981).

Helpers as Consultants versus Helpers as Agents of Social Influence

If client self-responsibility and self-efficacy are important values, then helpers can be viewed as consultants hired by clients to help them more effectively face problems in living.

> The therapist serves as a consultant and expert who negotiates with the client in how to go about change and to what end. The interactions are future

oriented in that they focus on the development of general repertoires for dealing with problem situations [Kanfer, 1980, p. 336].

Consultants in the business world adopt a variety of roles: they listen, observe, collect data, report observations, teach, train, coach, provide support, challenge, advise, offer suggestions, and even become advocates for certain positions. *But the responsibility for running the business remains with those who hire the consultant.* Therefore, even though some of the activities of the consultant can be seen as quite directive, the decisions are still made by managers. Consulting, then, is a social-influence process, but it is a collaborative one, which does not rob managers of the responsibilities that are theirs.

Kanfer (1980) sees helping at its best as a participative, rather than directive, model.

> A *participant* model emphasizes the importance of client responsibility in treatment. It represents a shift from the provision of a protective treatment environment toward the offering of rehabilitative experiences in which the client accepts increasing responsibilities for his or her own behavior, for dealing with the environment, and for planning the future. The therapeutic environment is viewed as a transitory support system that prepares the client to handle common social and personal demands more effectively [p. 334].

Therefore, helper social influence and client self-responsibility are by no means contradictory terms. Client collaboration is to be encouraged at every stage and step of the helping process (Evans, 1984).

The Resource-Collaborator Role

Tyler, Pargament, and Gatz (1983) describe client-helper collaboration under the rubric of the "resource-collaborator role."

> In sum, the paradox facing psychologists [helpers] in their relationships with others arises from the presumption that one can teach, study, elicit, or develop expertise, independence, or autonomy in others through relationships that ignore or exclude those characteristics in the potential beneficiaries [clients] [p. 388].

They focus on the reciprocity that characterizes—or should characterize—the helping process. Freire (1970) points out that helping the oppressed is often another, though sometimes more subtle, form of oppression. Tyler and his associates see both helper and client as people with defects. Either can approach the other to initiate the helping process. They have equal status in defining the terms of the relationship, in initiating action within the relationship, and in evaluating the relationship. In the best cases, positive change occurs in both parties.

Consultants and empowerment. Carkhuff (1969a, 1969b) has claimed that helping is *for* the client, but is *on the terms of* the helper, since the helper is the "more knowing" or more potent part in the relationship. Consultants, on the other hand, take clients as they are and try to use their resources to *empower* their clients. The notion of *empowerment* in human-services professions is a powerful one (Berger & Neuhaus, 1977; Egan, 1984; Egan & Cowan, 1979; Kanter, 1983; Rappaport, 1981). Rappaport notes that "Prevention suggests professional experts; empowerment suggests collaborators" (p. 24). I firmly believe that helpers should seek out every opportunity to help clients empower themselves to manage their lives more effectively.

For consultants working with systems, I have devised a triadic consultation model in which the consultant works not directly with the group whose behavior is to be changed (the target group), but with a mediator or mediator group who represents and will work with the target group directly (Egan, 1978, 1985). This model is illustrated in Figure 1–1. I use the same model in working with individual clients. Since there are only two of us, I cannot talk in the same way about a triadic model. However, I view the client from two different perspectives. As shown in Figure 1–2, the "mediator" is now that person "inside" the client who wants or needs to manage his or her life more effectively. I deal with the mediator part of the client, but my expectation is that the mediator part will "talk to" the client and that the client, the "target," will act.

The Client as Problem Solver

When people are presented with the basic steps of a problem-solving model, they tend to say "Oh yes, I know that." Recognition of the logic of problem solving, however, is a far cry from *using* that logic.

> In ordinary affairs we usually muddle ahead, doing what is habitual and customary, being slightly puzzled when it sometimes fails to give the intended outcome, but not stopping to worry much about the failures because there are still too many other things still to do. Then circumstances conspire against us and we find ourselves failing where we must succeed—where we cannot withdraw from the field, or lower our self-imposed standards, or ask for help, or throw a tantrum. Then we may begin to suspect that we face a problem.... *An ordinary person almost never approaches a problem systematically and exhaustively*

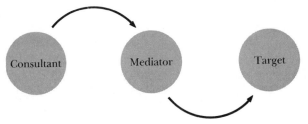

Figure 1–1. Triadic consultation model

Figure 1–2. Triadic helping model

unless he has been specifically educated to do so [Miller, Galanter, & Pribram, 1960, pp. 171, 174, emphasis added].

During the past few years there has been a great deal of interest in the problem-solving abilities of people in general and of clients in particular (Alpert & Rosenfield, 1981; Baucom, 1982; Black & Scherba, 1983; Bransford & Stein, 1984; Dixon, Heppner, Petersen, & Ronning, 1979; Heppner, Baumgardner, & Jackson, in press; Heppner, Hibel, Neal, Weinstein, & Rabinowitz, 1982; Heppner, Neal, & Larson, 1984; Heppner & Petersen, 1982; Heppner & Reeder, in press; Heppner, Reeder, and Larson, 1983; Hussian & Scott, 1981; Leichenbaum, 1980; Phillips, Pazienza & Ferrin, 1984; Robin, 1981; Scott, 1979; Voss, in press). Furthermore, problem solving has been a useful approach not only with adults but also with children, and the technology for training children in problem-solving skills has been developed (Shure & Spivack, 1978; Spivack, Platt, & Shure, 1976; Spivack & Shure, 1974, Urbin & Kendall, 1980). Clients tend to be poor problem solvers—or whatever problem-solving ability they have tends to disappear in times of crisis. The function of the helper is to get clients to apply problem solving to their current problem situations and to increase the probability that clients will take problem-solving approaches to future problems in living. Since you will be using a problem-management approach to helping clients, you are in an excellent position to coach clients in the unlocking and development of their own problem-solving styles.

■ The Contract between Helper and Client

Both implicit and explicit contracts govern the transactions that take place between people in a wide variety of situations, including marriage (where some but by no means all of the provisions of the contract are explicit) and friendship (where most of the provisions are implicit).

The observation that human beings relate to one another in an orderly, patterned way over a period of time is nothing new or startling. This kind of observation is readily made by layman or behavioral scientist. . . . I have found in my own practice that conceptualizing human relationships in contract terms has been most helpful to my clients in clarifying expectations and negotiations which go on in the interpersonal drama [Shapiro, 1968, p. 171].

One way of helping clients who are having difficulties in interpersonal relationships is to review with them the implicit interpersonal contracts that exist between them and the significant others in their lives. Often enough these implicit contracts have provisions that are self-defeating. For instance, during the first four years of marriage a couple might enter into an implicit contract with a provision that "the man makes all the major decisions." This might work for a while, but eventually will cause friction.

The notion of contract is also relevant to the helping process itself, since "virtually all counseling is governed by implicit contracts that define both the treatment goals and procedures and the client-counselor relationship" (Goodyear & Bradley, 1980, p. 512). Typically, therapists fail to tell their clients much about the therapeutic process (Goldstein, Heller, & Sechrest, 1966), even though "ethical principles assert that therapists should inform clients about the purpose and nature of therapy and that clients have freedom of choice about their participation" (Hare-Mustin and others, 1979, p. 7). In a sense, clients are often expected to buy a pig-in-a-poke without much assurance that it will turn out to be a succulent pig. In view of the importance of client self-responsibility, this book urges what Coyne and Widiger (1978) call a "participatory model" of helping (see also Kanfer, 1980). The helping process must be "owned" by helper and client alike, and there should be a basic understanding of the major goals to be pursued and procedures to be used in the helping process so that both persons own the same thing. An explicit contract, whether verbal or written, between helper and client can help achieve this. Wollersheim and her associates (1980) show that contracts make clients more willing to enter counseling and help them develop a more accurate understanding of the requirements of treatment.

The contract need neither be too detailed nor too rigid. It should provide a structure for the relationship and the work to be done without frightening or overwhelming the client.

Written or at least explicit verbal contracts can do much to clarify mutual expectations as to goals and methods, but inflexibility and irrevocable commitment to initial goals need to be avoided. An optimal form of contracting would involve making explicit mutual expectations, while allowing for periodic reassessment and revision [Coyne & Widiger, 1978, p. 707].

Establishing the helping contract is quite important; it is a practical issue that deserves a more thorough treatment than can be given here. You are encouraged to read the cited articles at your leisure. Once you become familiar with the helping process and with effective practitioners and trainers, it will be easier for you to determine what should be in the contracts between you and your clients. Clients are consumers who have the right to know whether they can expect their needs to be met (Laungani, 1984).

■ Portrait of a Helper

We will end this chapter with a brief portrait of what ideal helpers might look like. Ideally, they are first of all committed to their own growth—physical, intellectual, social-emotional, and spiritual—for they realize that helping often involves modeling the patterns of behavior their clients hope to achieve. They know that they can help only if, in the root sense of the term, they are "potent" human beings—that is, people with both the resources and the will to act. Since action needs direction, they work at formulating and reformulating the values that enable them to provide that direction.

They show respect for their bodies through proper exercise and diet. They make their bodies work for them rather than against them. They realize that helping is hard work and that if they are to give themselves effectively to this work they need a high level of energy. Physical fitness, to their minds, is a source of the energy they need.

Helpers have adequate basic intelligence, are aware of their own intellectual possibilities, and have respect for the world of ideas. Since ideas are important to them, they read and discuss what they read with others. They often read actively and hungrily, for they are eager to expand their view of the world. They respect good literature, for it is rich in human experience, and they respect the world of myth and metaphor, for they sense that there are dimensions of human life that can be reached only through symbol, myth, allegory, and metaphor. They respect good theory and good research for the ways in which they can nourish enlightened practice. They are practical people, "translators," who make what they read work for them. They can turn good theory and good research into practical programs that enable them to help others more effectively, and they have the action-research skills to evaluate those programs.

Even more important, they have good common sense and good social intelligence. They are at home in the social-emotional world: both their own and that of others. They have developed an extensive repertory of social-emotional skills that enable them to respond spontaneously and effectively to a wide range of human needs. For instance, they are not afraid of deep human emotions: their own or others'. They work at making such skills second nature to them.

Good helpers know that helping is a great deal of work, but they also know that working smart is just as important as working hard; that is, they are more interested in accomplishments than in behavior. They attend to their clients both physically and psychologically. They know what nonverbal messages they send their clients and can read those sent to them. They listen intently to clients, but know that the fruits of listening are gathered through effective responding. They see helping as a goal-oriented, accomplishment-oriented dialogue. And so they respond frequently to clients, for they are working hard at understanding them. They respond within their clients' frames of reference, for they can see the world through their clients' eyes. But they also listen to their clients in context, realizing that their points of view are sometimes distorted and need to be challenged.

They respect their clients and express that respect by being available to them, working with them, not judging them, trusting the constructive forces found in them, and ultimately by placing the expectation on them to do whatever is necessary to handle their problems in living more effectively. They genuinely care for those who have come for help. They are nondefensive, spontaneous, and always willing to say what they think and feel, provided it is in the best interests of their clients. Good helpers are concrete in their expressions, dealing with actual feelings and actual behavior rather than vague formulations, obscure psychodynamics, or generalities. Their speech, while caring and human, is also lean and to the point.

Skilled helpers are integrators. They help clients explore the world of experience, feeling, and behavior. As clients produce data about themselves, helpers assist them to integrate that data in a way that helps clients understand themselves and their behavior. They also realize that insight and understanding are not to be pursued or prized for themselves but rather to the extent that they help clients set problem-managing goals and move toward constructive behavioral change. Counselors in this process are not afraid to share themselves and their own experiences if they see that it will advance the helping process. They are not afraid to challenge clients—with care—and to help clients place demands on themselves, provided that these demands arise from the experience of the client and not from the needs of the helper. They are not afraid to deal openly with their own relationships with their clients to the degree that it helps clients understand their own behavior and interpersonal style and helps them move toward goals and action. But counselors do all these things with caution and respect, remembering that helping is for the client.

Effective helpers are people of imagination. They try to be imaginative in their approach to helping, while avoiding fads. They realize that clients are often mired down in their problem situations because they are no longer in touch with their own imaginal resources. And so they do whatever they can to help clients reawaken their imaginations. They stimulate their clients to envision futures that are better and more creative—without being pollyana-ish. And they do this while remaining aware of the personal and environmental constraints of individual clients.

Action is important to good helpers. Since they are agents in their own lives—that is, people who seize life rather than submit to it—they are capable of helping their clients set goals and elaborate action programs that lead to constructive behavioral change. They know that self-understanding is not enough and that the helping process is not complete until clients act on their understandings. Skilled helpers are pragmatists: they will draw on all possible helping resources to enable clients to achieve their goals. Indeed, they realize that the process of helping is developmental—that is, that the entire process is leading to the constructive management of clients' problems in living. Because of their wide repertory of response, skilled helpers can approach a problem from many different vantage points and help clients see alternatives. They are not bound to any single course of action. They may use a variety of techniques in the counseling process, but are the masters of the techniques they use. They follow a comprehensive helping model, but are not rigid in its applications. The model is not central; clients are. The model is seen as an instrument for helping clients live more effectively.

Good counselors are at home with people, both in one-to-one situations and in groups. They are not afraid to enter the world of others and to confront the distress of that world. However, the intimacy of the counseling process is not substitutive for them; they are not people who need people with problems to help. Although they do not help others in order to satisfy their own needs, they know that "when they make it possible for others to choose life they increase their own possibilities of continuing to choose life" (Carkhuff, 1969a, I, xii). They can handle crises: they can mobilize their own energies and help others mobilize their own in order to act forcefully and decisively. They realize that it is a privilege to be allowed to enter the life of another person, and they respect that privilege.

Skilled helpers have their own human problems, from which they do not retreat. They explore their own behavior and know who they are. They know what it means to be helped and have a deep respect for the helping process and its power—for better or for worse. Even though they are living effectively, they also know they are in process, that each stage of life has its own developmental tasks and crises.

This, then, is one version of the ideal. It goes without saying that we do not live in an ideal world. The best of helpers can fall short of the ideal in different ways at different times.

Two

Overview of the Helping Model

■

The starting point
The goal of helping
The stages and steps of the helping process
Stage I: Identifying and clarifying problem situations and unused opportunities
        Step I-A: Helping clients tell their stories
        Step I-B: Focusing: The search for leverage
        Step I-C: Blind spots and new perspectives
Stage II: Goal setting: Developing and choosing preferred scenarios
        Step II-A: Constructing a new scenario
        Step II-B: Evaluating new-scenario goals
        Step II-C: Choice and commitment
Stage III: Action: Moving toward the preferred scenario
        Step III-A: Discovering strategies for action
        Step III-B: Choosing strategies and developing a plan of action
        Step III-C: Action—Implementing plans and achieving goals
The helping relationship: The steps of the helping process as ways of "being with" clients
Humanizing the helping process: Flexibility in meeting the needs of clients
Overcoming awkwardness as a beginning helper
The foundations of helping: Core values
Respect: Translating values into behaviors
Genuineness: Translating values into behaviors
Some final considerations and cautions
An open model: Learning from other approaches
Sharing the helping model with clients

A helping model or framework is like a map that helps you know where to go in your interactions with clients. Given the intensity of your interactions with clients, you will need such an aid to orient yourself, to understand "where you are" with the client and what work still needs to be done.

■ The Starting Point: Clients with Problem Situations and Unused Opportunities

Clients' problem situations, as well as their unused opportunities or potential, constitute the starting point of helping.

Problem situations.   First of all, clients enter counseling because they have crises, troubles, doubts, difficulties, frustrations, or concerns. These are often called—generically—*problems,* but they are not problems in a mathematical sense because emotions often run high and there are usually no clear-cut solutions. Clients face not problems but *problem situations* (D'Zurilla & Goldfried, 1971)—that is, often complex and messy difficulties in living that they are not handling well. And so they come for help. Or third parties believe that potential clients are not coping well and send them to get help. Although even those who come on their own may be resistant to help, involuntary clients—who "may well account for the majority of caseloads throughout the land" (Dyer & Vriend, 1975, p. 102)—are especially difficult to deal with since they are both reluctant and resistant. Truant students may not see their truancy as problematic, but their parents and school officials do. Helpers need to find ways of dealing with reluctant and resistant clients.

Missed opportunities and unused potential.   Unused opportunities and potential constitute a second starting point for helpers. Unused potential refers not to what is going wrong but to what could be done better. It has often been said that we use only a fraction of our human potential; therefore, we should be capable of dealing much more creatively with ourselves, with our relationships with others, and with the social settings of our lives. Counselors can help their clients empower themselves by encouraging them to identify and develop unused or underused opportunities and potential.

In the model outlined in these pages it is assumed that most clients are both grappling with difficulties and failing to take advantage of opportunities. Even when clients talk about specific problems, effective helpers listen for missed opportunities and unused potential. A woman filled with self-doubt because of her background, her upbringing, and the obstacles presented by a male-dominated culture is probably also a woman who has missed opportunities and failed to develop many of her own resources. She may well be a victim of society, but she is probably also a victim of her own unexploited potential.

■ The Goal of Helping

If clients become clients because—either in their own view or that of others—they are involved in problem situations that they are not handling well, they need ways to come to terms with, solve, or transcend those situations. In other words, they need to *manage* their problems in living more effectively. Problem situations arise in our interactions with ourselves, with others, and with the organizations, institutions, and communities of life. Being hounded by self-doubt, being intelligent and yet failing in school, having to face life after being told that one has cancer, being burdened by uncontrolled thoughts and feelings, being abusive to one's children, being involved in a failing marriage, being a nuisance to one's neighbors, being unemployed because of a faltering economy, being dissatisfied with one's job, being victimized by racism—these are all problem situations that move people to seek help or move others to send them for help.

Helpers are effective if they help their clients to *manage* the problem situations of their lives. Even devastating problem situations can be handled more effectively. Consider the following example.

■

Fred was thunderstruck when the doctor told him that he had terminal cancer. He was only 52; death *couldn't* be imminent. He felt disbelieving, bitter, angry, and depressed all at the same time. After a period of angry confrontations with doctors and members of his family, he finally, in despair, talked to a clergyman who had on a few occasions gently and nonintrusively offered his support. They decided to have some sessions together, but the clergyman also referred him to a counselor who had a great deal of experience with the terminally ill. With their help Fred gradually learned how to manage the ultimate problem situation of his life. He came to grips with his religious convictions, put his affairs in order, began to learn how to say good-bye to his family, and the world he loved so intensely, and, with the help of a hospice, set about managing his physical decline. There were some outbursts of anger and some brief periods of depression and despair, but generally, with the help of the clergyman and counselor and with the support of his family and the hospice workers, he managed the process of dying much better than he thought he could.

■

This case demonstrates in a dramatic way that the goal of helping is not to make everything all right. Fred did die. Some problem situations are simply more unmanageable than others. Helping clients discover what kind and degree of problem management is possible is, as we shall see, a central part of the helping process.

But clients are also clients because they miss opportunities or fail to develop their resources. In that case, the identification and development of opportunities are the valued outcomes of helping.

■

After ten years as a helper in several mental health settings, Carol was experiencing burnout. In the opening interview with a counselor, she berated herself for not being dedicated enough. When asked when she felt best about herself, she said it was on those relatively infrequent occasions when she was asked to help another mental health center to get started or reorganize itself. The counseling sessions helped her explore her potential as a consultant to human-service organizations and to make a career adjustment. Carol stayed in the helping field but developed a new focus with a new set of skills.

■

In this case the counselor helped the client manage her problems (burnout, guilt) more effectively and at the same time develop her potential more fully.

■ The Stages of the Helping Process

The helping framework used in this book has three major stages. Each is considered from the point of view of what needs to be accomplished in it.

Stage I. Clients' problem situations and/or opportunities are explored and clarified.   Clients can neither manage problem situations nor develop opportunities unless they identify and understand them. Initial exploration and clarification of problems and opportunities takes place in Stage I. As indicated in Figure 2–1, Stage I deals with a state of affairs or "scenario" that the client or those who send the client for help find unacceptable: problem situations are not being managed and opportunities are not being developed.

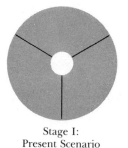
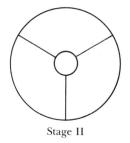
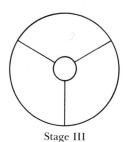

Stage I:
Present Scenario

Stage II

Stage III

Figure 2–1. Stage I

Stage II. Goals based on an action-oriented understanding of the problem situation are set. Once clients understand either their problem situations or opportunities for development more clearly, they may need help in setting goals—that is, help in determining what they would like to change. Involuntary clients need to understand the changes others are demanding of them. As indicated in Figure 2–2, Stage II deals with the preferred scenario.

Stage III. Action: Strategies for reaching goals are devised and implemented. Finally, clients need to act on their new understandings; that is, they have to work at turning the preferred scenario into reality. Involuntary clients especially need to see that it is in their own interest to act and be helped to act. Figure 2–3 adds the action stage to the helping model. Stage III is a transition stage, moving from the current, unacceptable scenario to the preferred scenario.

This model can be called developmental in that it is systematic and cumulative. The success of Stage II often depends on the quality of work in Stage I, and that of Stage III on the quality of work in both Stages I and II. Just why this is so will become clear as we move through the model.

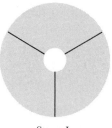
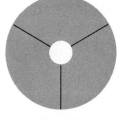
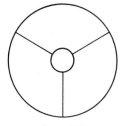

Stage I:
Present Scenario

Stage II:
Preferred Scenario

Stage III

Figure 2–2. Stages I and II

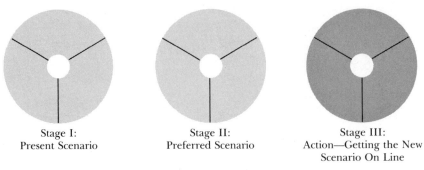

Stage I:
Present Scenario

Stage II:
Preferred Scenario

Stage III:
Action—Getting the New
Scenario On Line

Figure 2–3. Stages I, II, and III

Each stage of the model, as we are about to see, has three "steps." I put the word *steps* in quotation marks for at least two reasons. First, the problem-management and opportunity-development process is not as clean, clear, and linear in practice as the stages and steps described here. Second, some steps—for instance, the "step" of helping clients manage blind spots and develop new perspectives—refer to processes that apply to the entire model. More will be said about the flexibility needed to use this model later in the chapter. This overview presents a reasonably detailed model of the helping process with a succession of stages and steps as part of that model. The model is a framework or map to help you find your way. It is also an outline of this book.

■ Stage I: Identifying and Clarifying Problem Situations and Unused Opportunities

Helpers cannot be of service to clients if the latter fail to develop an understanding of the difficulties and possibilities in their lives. Most people handle most problems in living, whether successfully or unsuccessfully, by themselves or with the informal help of family and friends. They live without professional help. On the other hand, people who find that they are not coping with their problems in living and either do not want to share them with family and friends or feel that family and friends are not competent enough to help them might turn to some kind of professional or paraprofessional helper: a member of the clergy, teacher, coach, supervisor, doctor, counselor, social worker, nurse, psychologist, psychotherapist, psychiatrist, and the like. They will often turn to such a person (1) if the problem is serious or disturbing enough, (2) if they are seriously committed to their personal development, and (3) if they believe that the person to whom they are turning can actually help them.

As indicated in Chapter One, client self-responsibility is central to the view of helping espoused in this book. Clients should "own" as much of the helping process as possible. The steps of this model are actually tasks that clients need to accomplish, with the help of counselors. Some will need more direction than others; some will need to be challenged more than others. But helpers can provide both direction and challenge without clients abdicating their self-responsibility. There are three steps in Stage I.

Step I-A: Helping clients tell their stories. First of all, as indicated in Figure 2–4, clients need to tell their stories—that is, reveal their problem situations and their missed opportunities. Some clients are quite verbal, while others may be almost mute. Some clients easily reveal everything that is bothering them, while others are quite reluctant to do so. You need only examine your own experience to discover how reluctant you are at times to share your own problems with others. Involuntary clients often prefer to talk about the failings of those who sent them. Therefore, helpers need to develop a set of communication skills that enable clients to tell the "real" story and to support them as they do so. As we shall see, these communication skills are central to the entire helping process. The outcome of Step I-A, then, is "story told," whether it all comes out at once or only in bits and pieces over the entire helping process.

Relationship building is also central to the entire process. A good working relationship is one that contributes to productive outcomes in the counseling sessions. Therefore, different kinds of relationships will probably be established with different clients. For example, while all relationships, as we shall see, need to be based on respect, not all will involve the same degree of warmth. Some clients are helped by a closer, more intimate relationship, while others are helped by one that is more matter-of-fact. Some clients need a closer relationship as part of a program of social-emotional re-education. Through the helping relationship they learn or relearn such things as how to relate to others and how to prize rather than despise themselves. As you listen to a client telling his

Stage I: Present Scenario

Figure 2–4. Step I-A: Telling the story

or her story, you pick up clues about the kind of relationship that best suits his or her needs.

Highlights from an actual case will be used to illustrate each step of the model. For the sake of clarity, a relatively easy case has been chosen: for instance, the client is voluntary and verbal. The case has also been simplified. It is presented here in bare outline form and in a linear way to illustrate the stages and steps of the helping model.

■

Ray, 41, is a middle manager in a manufacturing company located in a large city. He goes to see a friend of his, an older woman whom he trusts and who happens to be a counselor, because he is experiencing a great deal of stress. She is supportive and helps Ray tell his story, which proves to be somewhat complex. He is bored with his job, his marriage is lifeless, he has poor rapport with his two teenage children, he is drinking heavily, his self-esteem is low, and he has begun to steal things—small things—not because he needs them but because he gets a kick out of it. He tells his story in a rather disjointed way, skipping around from one problem area to another. His agitation in telling the story reflects the anxiety he is experiencing. The counselor's non-judgmental attitude and facilitative communication style help Ray overcome the unease he is experiencing in talking about himself and his problems. Since Ray is a talented person, the counselor assumes that missed opportunities for growth also form part of the overall picture, even though he does not talk about this directly.

■

Since Ray is quite verbal, a great deal of the story comes tumbling out in a spontaneous way and its telling is merely supported by the helper. However, involuntary clients, clients with poor verbal skills, or clients who are hostile, confused, ashamed, or highly anxious provide a much greater challenge for helpers in this first step.

As helpers listen to their clients tell their stories, they are not judging but rather assessing their clients. They are assessing such things as the nature and severity of the problem situation, hints at further problems not being discussed, the impact of the client's environment on his or her problems, the personal, interpersonal, and environmental resources to which the client has access, and the ways in which problems might be, paradoxically, opportunities (as in the Zen saying, "The obstacle is the path"). Assessment, as we shall see later, is not limited to Stage I.

Step I-B: Focusing: In Figure 2–5 the term *focusing* is used as the general name of Step I-B, although this step actually includes screening, focusing, and clarifying. First, since helping is an expensive proposition,

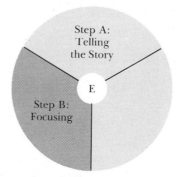

Stage I: Present Scenario

Figure 2–5. Step I-B: Focusing

both financially and psychologically, some kind of *screening* is called for: is the problem situation, at least as stated, worth the time and effort that is about to be spent in managing it? Second, if clients, in telling their stories, reveal a number of problems at the same time or if the problem situation discussed is complex, some criteria are needed to determine which concern is to be dealt with first. This is the point of *focusing*. In other words, counselors help clients search for some kind of leverage in dealing with complex problem situations. For instance, they help them work on a problem that, if managed successfully, will contribute to the management of a number of other problems. Counselors are most useful when they help clients handle issues that make a difference in their lives. If one of the themes that underlies or runs through a number of a client's problems is a lack of discipline, self-discipline might well be an issue with leverage. Finally, once an issue is chosen for further exploration, counselors need to help clients *clarify* the problem, issue, or concern in terms of specific patterns of experiences, behaviors, and feelings. The process of clarification can help clients determine which patterns need to be changed. In Step I-B it is especially important to help clients clarify their concerns from *their* point of view, even though it might eventually have to be challenged.

■

It is obvious from the beginning that Ray's problems and unused opportunities merit serious consideration. However, the counselor listens carefully for cues indicating Ray's degree of commitment to working with those issues. The counselor asks Ray which of the concerns he has mentioned bothers him most and which he would like to work on. After some discussion, Ray decides he would like to tackle the job problem, and makes some vague comments about needing to manage his drinking better. The counselor, through a combination of careful listening, empathic responding, and judicious probing helps Ray spell out concretely his concerns about his job and, to a lesser degree, about his drinking, since he is somewhat reluctant to talk about the latter. The counselor makes sure she understands Ray's point of view, even though she feels at times that it needs to be challenged, supplemented, or transcended. Some of the principal issues clarified are that Ray is in a dead-end job—that is, one in which there is no chance for promotion; he feels on reflection that he has always been underemployed, that his talents have never been significantly utilized; his dislike for his job is contaminating his interpersonal relationships at work and adding to his stress; he feels that his negative feelings about his job probably carry over into his home life; he has been in the same job for 14 years and has never thought about changing; he believes that he is too far "over the hill" to get a different job. Furthermore, he thinks he drinks "a bit too much" as a way of handling his stress and frustration, but does not see it as a central problem. However, it is evident to the counselor that Ray is sometimes uncomfortable with what he hears himself saying. That is, he is beginning to understand that he needs to challenge himself.

■

It is important to understand the client's frame of reference or point of view even when it is evident that it needs to be challenged. Helping clients translate vague situations, experiences, behaviors, and feelings into ones that are clear and specific is a form of challenge in itself.

Step I-C: Blind spots and new perspectives.   One of the most important things counselors can do is help clients identify blind spots and develop new, more useful perspectives on both problem situations and unused opportunities. As shown in Figure 2–6, this is the final step of Stage I.

Stage I: Present Scenario
Figure 2–6. Step I-C: New perspectives

Most clients need to move beyond their initial subjective understanding of their problem situations. Many people fail to cope with problems in living or to exploit opportunities because they do not see them from new perspectives; old and often comfortable frames of reference keep them locked into self-defeating patterns of thinking and behaving. It is at this point that helpers begin to tap the *imaginal resources* of their clients. Helping clients to place their imaginations at the service of problem management and opportunity development is one of the major ways in which this helping model empowers them. Challenging blind spots is not the same as telling people what they are doing wrong; it is rather helping people see themselves, others, and the world around them in more creative ways. At this "step"—one that may be used throughout the entire helping process—helpers ideally invite their clients to develop the kinds of alternate frames of reference that lead to problem-managing and opportunity-developing action.

■

The counselor asks Ray to describe his drinking behavior a bit more fully. Ray, pointing out that his drinking is "problematic" rather than a problem in itself, does so only reluctantly. With a bit of probing, the counselor soon discovers that Ray drinks not only excessively but also secretly. When he complains that she is accusing him of being an alcoholic, she replies that she isn't interested in labels but in lifestyle. Together they explore the impact his drinking has on him, on his relationships with others, on his work, and on his leisure. It is soon evident that his drinking is far more than problematic. He is an alcoholic who is reluctant to admit his alcoholism. In the course of their dialogue he does admit that his drinking is far more problematic than he had thought. Furthermore, the counselor helps him confront the discrepancy between his view of himself as underemployed and, at the same time, "over the hill." Ray has always disliked people he perceives as overly ambitious, but now he begins to see himself at the other end of the continuum—underambitious in self-defeating ways.

■

The counselor is very supportive as Ray explores these issues. She realizes that support without challenge is often superficial and that challenge without support can be demeaning and self-defeating. Challenge in the service of new perspectives, though presented here as a "step," is best woven into the fabric of the entire helping process: into storytelling, screening, focusing, clarifying, and beyond.

These three steps constitute Stage I. If they are done well, the problem situation or parts of it, in addition to overlooked or unexploited opportunities, can be identified and explored to the point where it makes sense to look beyond the present unacceptable scenario to a preferred scenario.

EVALUATION

In many helping models, evaluation is presented as the last step in the model. However, if the process is evaluated only at the end, it is too late. Therefore, in Figure 2–7, an E is placed in the center of Stage I to indicate that the helping process needs to be evaluated at every step along the way, including the first. Evaluation is not the last step; it is an ongoing process. At each step helpers and clients need to ask themselves, "Is what we are doing here contributing substantially to problem management and opportunity development?" Ongoing evaluation will be explored in a later chapter.

■ Stage II: Goal Setting—Developing a More Desirable Scenario

Steps A, B, and C are all related to problem/opportunity identification and clarification, but once that has been done, it is time to move on to the more imaginative stages of the helping process, as indicated in Figure 2–8. Counseling is successful only to the degree that it leads to *problem-managing action*. Assessment for the sake of assessment, exploration for the sake of exploration, and insight for the sake of insight are close to useless. Steps A, B, and C are successful to the degree that they enable clients to construct more desirable scenarios in terms of realistic problem-managing goals or objectives.

Step II-A: Constructing a new scenario.   If a client's current state of affairs is problematic and unacceptable, he or she needs to be helped to envision a new one. This is the first step in Stage II, as indicated in Figure 2–9. A new scenario is not a wild-eyed, idealistic state of affairs, but rather a conceptualization of what the situation would be like if improvements were made. For instance, for a couple whose marriage is

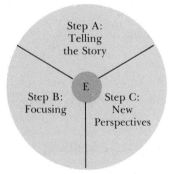

Stage I: Present Scenario

Figure 2–7. Evaluation as an integral part of each stage and step

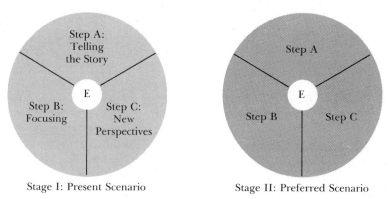

Stage I: Present Scenario   Stage II: Preferred Scenario

Figure 2–8. Developing a preferred scenario and setting goals

coming apart and who fight constantly, one of the elements of the new scenario might be fewer and fairer fights. In Step II-A, helpers, against the background of problem identification and clarification of Stage I, help clients develop either a range of scenarios or a range of elements for a new scenario. These scenarios or scenario elements constitute the *goals* of the helping process—that is, more constructive patterns of behavior. For instance, in career counseling, a range of new scenarios would be different kinds of jobs for which the client might be suited. In marriage counseling, the standard new scenario would be a better marriage. Some of the elements of this better marriage might be greater mutual respect, fewer fights, more openness, more effectively managed conflicts, a more equitable distribution of household tasks, the elimination of extramarital encounters, doing more things together, surrendering past animosities, greater mutuality in sexual relationships, more effectively managed emotions—especially jealousy and hurt—decreased game playing, and so forth. Let us return to our case.

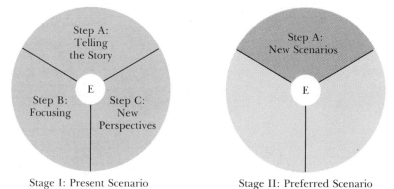

Stage I: Present Scenario   Stage II: Preferred Scenario

Figure 2–9. Step II-A: Developing new scenarios

■

First, Ray decides to get a new job. The counselor helps him review the kinds of jobs he might like. Ray identifies five or six different possibilities and even some of the companies in which they might be found. He wants to work for a different and smaller company, where he would be challenged but would have a sense of camaraderie with his fellow workers. If he does move to a different kind of job, he still wants one in which he can use his experience. Second, although Ray still does not admit he is an alcoholic, he does think he should stop drinking. Otherwise, he says, it will interfere with the work that needs to be done to get a new job. The counselor thinks it is a good sign that Ray says it "*will* interfere," instead of merely saying that "it could" or "it might." Therefore, Ray's new scenario includes a new, more satisfying job and an alcohol-free lifestyle.

■

Galbraith (1979) suggests that one of the reasons (but hardly the only or even the principal one) poor people remain mired in their poverty is that they get caught up in what he calls the "culture" of poverty. That is, they accept themselves as poor and do not even imagine themselves as not poor. In my estimation, this failure to imagine scenarios different from the present one contributes greatly to clients remaining mired in their problem situations. In Step I-C and especially in Step II-A, helpers empower clients by helping them liberate their conceptual and imaginal resources.

Step II-B: Critiquing the new scenario. Once a variety of scenarios or a number of scenario elements, which constitute the goals or desired outcomes of the helping process, have been generated, it is time to help clients critique them. Figure 2–10 adds this step to the helping model. Goals, if they are to be translated into action, need to be clear, specific,

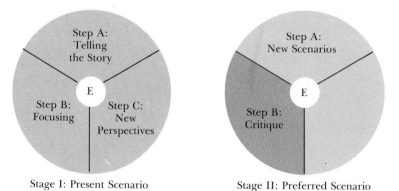

Stage I: Present Scenario   Stage II: Preferred Scenario

Figure 2–10. Step II-B: Evaluating new scenarios

realistic, adequately related to the problem situation, in keeping with the client's values, and capable of being accomplished within a reasonable time frame.

For instance, if a couple wants "better communication" as part of the renewal of their marriage, they need to spell out specifically what better communication means in that context. Precisely what undesirable patterns of communication are now in place? Precisely what patterns of communication are preferred? For example, a couple might say, "When we experience small annoyances in our relationship, we tend not to share them with each other. We think we swallow them but in reality we save them up and let them eat away at us inside. It seems that we could discuss our annoyances as they arise, and do so without being petty or playing the game of putting each other down. If we were to manage little problems better, we could avoid the bigger ones." Such a statement is at least a beginning at spelling out what "better communication" means. Often helpers need to challenge clients to make vague goals more specific. If a client says "I guess I should be a better father in a lot of ways," the counselor should ask "What are some of those ways?"

Part of the critiquing process is to help clients set priorities by reviewing the *consequences* of possible choices. For instance, if a client sets her sights on a routine job with minimally adequate pay, it might well take care of some of her immediate needs but turn sour in the long run. Helping clients foresee the consequences of their choices may not be easy. I remember one woman with cancer who felt she was no longer able to cope with the sickness that came with her chemotherapy treatments. She decided abruptly one day to end them, saying she didn't care what happened. Eventually, when her health deteriorated, she had second thoughts about the treatments, but it was too late.

■

The counselor helps Ray expand his checklist and then apply it to each of the five or six jobs he identified in Step II-A. She encourages him to imagine each of these possibilities in some detail. Ray is a bit impatient in discussing the pros and cons of each job, but she challenges him to do so, helping him see the consequences of making a poor choice at this juncture. While applying the checklist to specific jobs, Ray soon realizes that at least three of the jobs do not meet his criteria. Ray is less enthusiastic about exploring his tentative decision to stop drinking. He refers to it somewhat guardedly as an "experiment." He is still having trouble seeing himself as a problem drinker and resists discussing his drinking.

■

Note that challenge is not relegated to Step I-C. Critiquing alternate scenarios or scenario elements is often difficult for clients because it involves painful choices or painful self-revelation. For instance, truants may have to choose between going back to a school they hate or being locked up in a detention center. Even before they are sent for counseling, they probably suspect that their options are limited; this contributes to their reluctance to come and their resistance to the helping process if they do come.

Step II-C: Choice and commitment. In the last step of Stage II, some clients may need help in making a final choice of goals based on their priorities and in committing themselves to that choice. Figure 2–11 adds this step to the helping model. Effective helpers leave responsibility for the choice to their clients. However, while they realize they are not responsible for their clients' sense of commitment, they can help clients commit themselves by guiding them in the search for *incentives* for commitment. Such guidance is especially needed when the choices are hard to make. How are truants with poor home situations to commit themselves to returning to school? What are the incentives for such a choice? Ray, too, must face the issue of choice and commitment.

■

Ray commits himself to getting a new, more challenging job. Having reviewed the possibilities, he now concentrates on his top priority, a middle-management job in a high-tech company. If it proves that this kind of job is not available, he will move to the second choice on his list. His incentives include a strong desire to get rid of the pain he is currently experiencing and a more positive desire to develop some of his talents that have lain dormant over the past years. A third incentive is his conviction that getting a more fulfilling job will lead to managing his home life better. A final incentive is his need to regain his self-esteem. He also decides to stop drinking—cold turkey. His desire to get a different job and his need for self-esteem are both incentives to do so. He also realizes that stopping drinking will give him a new

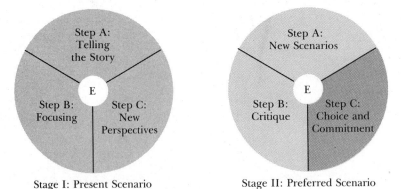

Stage I: Present Scenario   Stage II: Preferred Scenario

Figure 2–11. Step II-C: Choice and commitment

image at home and give him the kind of credibility he will need to start managing his home life better.

■

If Stage II is done well, clients will have a clear idea of *what* they would like to accomplish without necessarily knowing *how* they will accomplish it. Once Ray says, "I want a middle-management job in a high-tech firm," he must figure out just how he is going to get one. The goal is clear; the means to achieve the goal need to be developed. This brings us to Stage III of the helping process.

■ Stage III: Action—Moving toward the Preferred Scenario

Helping is not just talking and planning. Clients must ultimately act if they are to live more effectively. Stage III gets the preferred scenario on line; it implements decisions and accomplishes goals. Figure 2–12

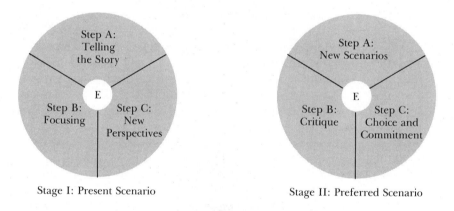

Figure 2–12. Action—Getting the new scenario on line

adds this final stage to the process. One reason that most of us fail to cope with problems in living or to exploit unused opportunities is that we simply fail to act. When Kate says at a New Year's Eve party, "I'm going to lose twenty pounds this year," but finds herself five pounds heavier a year later, she has made several errors. First of all, it would have been better for her to say, "I'm going to change my eating habits this year in such a way that I will lose twenty pounds and then maintain that weight." The real goal is optimal weight maintenance, not just losing pounds. Second, she does not evaluate the issue of commitment. Third, she does not indicate how she is going to accomplish her goal; that is, she does not set up a program. Goals left to chance ordinarily are not attained. Finally, she does not act: she does little or nothing to lose weight and to substitute a new set of eating habits. Stage III includes three steps: helping clients discover *strategies* for action, helping clients choose the options that make most sense for them and turn them into a *plan,* and providing support and challenge as clients actually *implement* goal-directed programs.

Step III-A: Discovering strategies for action.   Options for action are simply the means chosen to implement goals. Figure 2–13 adds this step to the helping model. A goal is an *end,* while a strategy is a *means* for achieving a goal. Strategies can be very simple or they can be long and relatively complicated. In the latter case, a goal is ordinarily divided into a sequence of related subgoals, and each subgoal has its own set of strategies. This process can lead to seemingly amazing and virtually impossible achievements, such as placing a person on the moon or salvaging an apparently hopeless marriage. In the first part of Stage III, counselors help their clients develop a list of concrete, realistic options for action that will lead to the realization of the scenario or the achievement of the goal set in Stage II.

One reason people fail to achieve goals is that they do not explore the different ways in which the goal can be reached. They choose one means or strategy without a great deal of exploration or reflection, try it, and when it fails, conclude that they just can't achieve that particular goal. Coming up with as many ways of achieving a goal as possible increases the probability that one of them or a combination of several will suit the resources of a particular client. At this stage of the problem-managing process, as many means as possible, within time and other constraints, should be uncovered. At first, time need not be wasted criticizing the options for action already discovered. Even seemingly outlandish strategies can provide clues for realistic action programs. Techniques such as brainstorming and fantasy are often very useful in identifying different ways of achieving goals. Let us return to Ray.

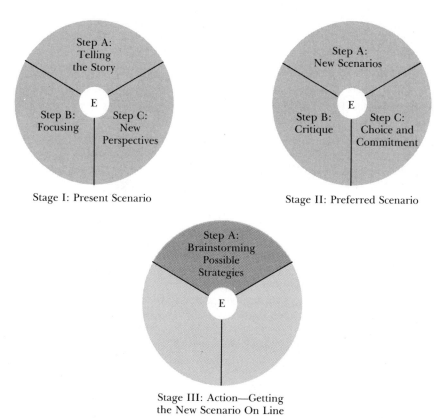

Stage I: Present Scenario

Stage II: Preferred Scenario

Stage III: Action—Getting
the New Scenario On Line

Figure 2–13. Step III-A: Brainstorming possible strategies

■

Since Ray has been in the same job for so long, he is not familiar with the ways people look for new jobs. The counselor gives him a short article on career development that includes a section titled "Fifty-Four Ways to Get a Job." He finds the article very useful. He checks the ways that make sense to him, adds some of his own, and combines some of them into innovative groups. Just being aware of so many possibilities gives him a sense of freedom and hope. However, he is still somewhat defensive about his drinking problem. He says that the only way to stop drinking is to stop drinking. He indicates that he is not at all interested in any of the groups such as Alcoholics Anonymous that deal with drinking problems. The counselor challenges him a bit. He need not go to any group, but it might help to review some of the strategies people have used to stop drinking, just as he has reviewed ways of getting a job. She gives him a photocopy of a page from a book that outlines about two dozen ways to stop drinking and asks him to use his imagination to expand the list. He does this in private. He admits to himself that reviewing the list and adding to it give him a feeling for the pitfalls facing a person who has been drinking heavily and some strategies to cope with them. He still thinks he can cope with his drinking on his own.

■

Some counselors never get to Stages II or III with their clients, assuming that those stages are the client's responsibility. It is true that some clients, once they have a clear idea of what is going wrong or a clear picture of some undeveloped opportunity, set goals, devise programs, and act. However, many do not do so on their own and therefore can profit from the support and challenge helpers can provide.

Step III-B: Choosing strategies and devising a plan of action. Once a number of different options for action have been identified, client and helper collaboratively review them and try to choose either the best single option or the best combination. "Best" here means the single strategy or combination of strategies that best fits the client's needs, preferences, and resources, and the one that is least likely to be blocked by factors in the client's environment. That is, strategies should be evaluated in terms of their realism. The options chosen must also be in keeping with the values of the client. For instance, even though one of the ways a young woman can afford to stay in college for the coming year is to accept a gift from a close relative, she might reject that option because developing a healthy independence of her family may be more important to her. In that case, she will either have to put off going to school this year or find other sources of finance.

Next, the strategies that are chosen need to be translated into a step-by-step plan. Clients are more likely to act if they know what they are going to do first, what second, what third, and so forth. Realistic time frames for each of the steps are also essential. Figure 2–14 adds this step to the helping model. Part of the challenge of this helping model is the demand for discipline that it places on clients. Let's see how this applies to Ray.

■

Ray takes a critical look at his short list of "ways to get a new job" and eliminates some of the options because of their lack of realism, because of time constraints, or because they do not fit his style. He puts an asterisk next to the options that seem to have the greatest potential for success. These include such things as joining a job-search group, making use of business contacts he has made over the years, telling

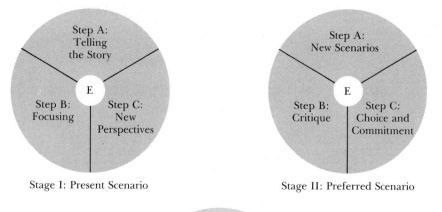

Stage I: Present Scenario

Stage II: Preferred Scenario

Stage III: Action—Getting
the New Scenario On Line

Figure 2–14. Step III-B: Formulating a plan

selected friends of his availability, getting copies of the professional journals that list the kinds of jobs he is looking for, cold canvass by telephone—that is, calling employers to identify organizations with appropriate vacancies, and so forth. Second, he draws up an overall plan. For instance, now that he has sorted out his priorities with regard to the kind of job he wants, the first order of business is to draw up a resume. He does this on a word processor so that he can easily tailor it to the specific organization and the specific job in question. He outlines the steps in the job-search process—canvassing, getting interview offers, choosing among the offers, preparing for interviews, engaging in the interviews, follow-up, and so forth—and sets up a flexible schedule. For instance, he outlines the kinds of canvassing he will do, the order in which he will do it, and the time frame he will allow for it. Ray is not nearly so systematic in setting up a program for keeping away from alcohol. After all, he says, he *has* stopped drinking. One thing he instinctively does, however, is to begin a moderate exercise program. He says to himself that he might be old-fashioned, but that in his view physical fitness and heavy drinking do not go together.

■

Self-responsibility is still a key value in Stage III. Goals must be the client's goals, strategies must be the client's strategies, and action plans must be the client's plans. The helper's job is to stimulate the client's imagination and to help him or her in the search for incentives.

Step III-C: Action—Implementing plans and achieving goals. The function of planning is to institute and give direction to action. Figure 2–15 adds this final step to the helping model. First, counselors can help clients in their immediate preparations for action. This may be called the "forewarned-is-forearmed" phase. Effective counselors help clients foresee difficulties that might arise during the actual implementation of

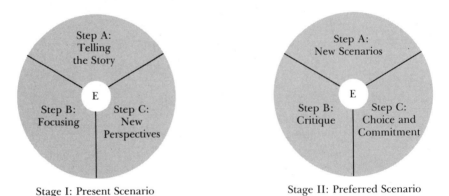

Stage I: Present Scenario

Stage II: Preferred Scenario

Stage III: Action—Getting
the New Scenario On Line

Figure 2–15. Step III-C: Action

their plans. There are two extremes to beware of here. One is pretending that no difficulties will arise. The client launches into a program quite optimistically then runs headlong into obstacles and fails. The other extreme is spending too much time anticipating obstacles and figuring out ways of handling them. This can be just another way of delaying the real work of problem management and opportunity development.

A reasonable consideration of obstacles that might well arise during the implementation of a program can be most useful. One way of doing this is to consider the principal "facilitating forces" and the principal "restraining forces" that will most likely be operative in the client's environment, including the client's inner environment of thoughts, feelings, imaginings, attitudes, and the like. For instance, if a person is trying to stop smoking, one facilitating force is thinking about the increased amount of aerobic energy that will be available for sports and exercise programs. A principal restraining force will probably be the longing that arises during withdrawal from a pleasurable habit. Another will be the envy the person will experience when in the company of his or her friends who are still smoking.

Second, helpers can also provide support and challenge for clients as they act. Clients need both to support and challenge themselves and to find support and challenge from others. For instance, when a client feels inadequate and discouraged as he or she moves through a program, the counselor can provide understanding. The counselor can also challenge the client to mobilize whatever resources are needed to stick to a program. If a wife unilaterally institutes a program of more decent communication with a husband who refuses to see the counselor either with his wife or alone, she may have a rough time in the beginning. She may find it extremely discouraging when he does not appreciate her attempts at a more caring kind of communication and even makes fun of them. But if there is a reasonable probability that her patience will eventually pay off, she needs support and challenge to stick to the program. This can come from herself, from her friends, and from the counselor. Helpers at this point of the process do not act for clients but rather help them mobilize their resources in order to increase the strength of facilitating forces and decrease the strength of restraining forces. How does this refer to Ray?

■

Ray draws up a resume and implements his plan of canvassing for a job. The counselor asks him two questions as he launches his program. "In what ways might this plan fall apart?" "What incentives and resources are available to keep you working at it?" Ray discusses some possible pitfalls. One he views as quite serious: he wants something to happen quickly. He fears if results are not quick in coming, he might get frustrated and quit trying. He might also begin drinking again. He and the counselor discuss ways of handling this possible pitfall. One of his best resources is his feeling of having a new lease on life. It is too sweet to let slip out of his hands. He contracts with the counselor to call her when he first begins to feel frustrated, even though he would prefer to "tough it out" himself. Ray's spirits have been raised by this entire process. He and his wife go to a party at a neighbor's house and he lets his guard down. He tells himself that it will be all right to have a couple of drinks to be sociable and to celebrate the new course he is on. He gets drunk, and out of shame and desperation the next day gets drunk again. On Sunday morning he calls the counselor. They decide to take a closer look at his "problematic" drinking.

■

The example of Ray's case is necessarily sketchy and perhaps overly sanguine; that is, it may make the helping process, which takes a great deal of work and certainly has its frustrating moments, seem too pat. The sole purpose of the example, however, is to give you a glimpse of the model in action and some idea of how you can use it to give direction to the entire process. In the best of worlds, Ray will get a more challenging job and manage his drinking problem more effectively and then move on to renewing his home life. But we do not live in the best of worlds. Clients may disappoint helpers and helpers may disappoint clients; they may both disappoint themselves. In my experience, the best helpers maintain an optimism tempered by realism.

■ The Steps of the Helping Model as Ways of "Being With" Clients

Helping, at its best, is a deeply human venture. Models, techniques, and skills are tools at the service of that venture. They are not meant to "overtechnologize" the process. The relationship between helper and client is extremely important, but it is a relationship of service, not an end in itself. The nine steps of the helping model offer ways in which helpers can "be with" their clients humanly and productively.

1. I can be with clients by helping them tell their stories, especially when those stories are difficult to tell.
2. I can be with clients by helping them find starting points in complex problem situations, by helping them find signs of hope, and by helping them clarify problem situations from their own point of view.

3. I can be with clients by helping them identify and overcome blind spots, by helping them reconceptualize problems and opportunities, and by helping them develop the kinds of new perspectives that serve action.

4. I can be with clients by helping them see and develop hopeful alternatives to their problem situations; I can be with them by helping them tap into their conceptual and imaginal resources for the creation of new scenarios.

5. I can be with clients by helping them distinguish between what is possible and what is not; I can be with them by helping them stretch themselves realistically.

6. I can be with clients by helping them make choices and by helping them find the incentives that enable them to commit themselves to those choices.

7. I can be with clients by helping them brainstorm options for action; I can help them stimulate their imaginations in the search for strategies that lead to the accomplishment of goals.

8. I can be with clients by helping them turn viable strategies into meaningful plans.

9. I can be with clients by providing both support and challenge for them as they act to accomplish goals.

Helpers will not be with all clients in each of these ways, because they will tailor their active, involving, caring presence to the needs of their clients. Genuineness and respect will characterize the spirit of their being with, but what they do depends on what their clients need.

■ Flexibility in the Application of the Model

The beginner, or even an experienced but unskilled helper, can apply this model too rigidly. Helping is for the client; the model exists only as an aid in the helping process. *Flexibility* is the key word.

One kind of rigidity is a mechanical progression through the stages of the model. As indicated earlier, counseling does not always happen as neatly as the overview of the model and the example used to illustrate it might suggest. As Heppner, Reeder, and Larson (1983) note:

> Although stage sequential models seem to effectively prescribe problem-solving activities within a training format, they are less useful in describing what actually happens when a client is faced with a problem. Perhaps as researchers are able to describe the real-life problem-solving process in greater detail and as models of applied problem solving are developed, we will be closer to developing a technology for helping clients solve their personal problems more effectively [p. 543].

The phases of helping are not always as differentiated and sequential as they are presented in this book. For instance, since clients do not always present all their problems at once, it is impossible to work through Stage I completely before moving on to Stages II and III. New problems must be explored and understood whenever they are presented.

Logic versus literature.   What is presented in the overview is the *logic* of the model. The *literature* of the model—that is, the model in actual use—is not as neat and clean. The problem-solving model gives form and direction to the helping process, but it must also respond to the realities of the particular helping situation. This means that helpers will often enough find themselves moving back and forth in the model.

> But the process is not that simple! We know that we do not follow such a simple linear or one-way procedure—we double back and repeat ourselves many times. Indeed, we cannot truly separate the processes at times. Sometimes we seem to be doing two of the functions simultaneously [Robertshaw, Mecca, & Rerick, 1978, p. 3].

For instance, a client might actually try out some program before the problem situation is adequately defined and a definite goal has been set. Action sometimes precedes understanding. If the action program is not successful, then the counselor helps the client return to the tasks of clarifying the problem situation and setting some realistic goals.

Overlap of both stages and steps.   In practice, both the stages and the steps overlie and mingle with one another, as illustrated in Figure 2–16. Clients set goals and choose goal-achieving strategies at the same time. New and more substantial concerns arise while goals are being set, and the process moves back to an earlier exploratory stage. Step I-C, which involves challenge, can overlie and mingle with all the other steps.

Time flexibility.   Another kind of rigidity is trying to predetermine the amount of time to be spent in any one stage or step. A general rule is that the helper should move as quickly as the resources of the client

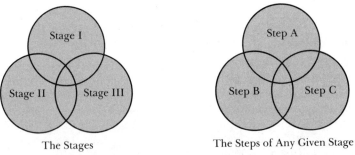

The Stages   The Steps of Any Given Stage

Figure 2–16. Overlap of stages and steps

permit. The client should not be penalized for the helper's lack of skills in Stages II and III. Beginning helpers often dally too long in Stage I, not merely because they have a deep respect for the necessity of empathic understanding and problem clarification, but because they either do not know how to move on or fear doing so. High-level clients may be able to move quickly to action programs. The helper, obviously, should be able to move with them. Sometimes clients will drag their feet. Then they need to be challenged.

Effective helpers are like good ballplayers who have learned both standard skills and individual "moves" that tailor those skills to the current situation. They can use the model to give definition to the helping process, but they also develop techniques that enable them to individualize each of its steps.

The "stage-specific" specialist. Some counselors tend to specialize in the skills of a particular step or stage of the model. Some specialize in basic empathy and problem exploration; others claim to be good at confrontation; others want to move to action programs immediately. Helpers who specialize like this are usually not very effective even in their chosen specialties. For instance, the counselor whose specialty is confrontation is often an ineffective confronter. The reason for this is obvious. The model is organic; it fits together as a whole. Confrontation is ill-judged if it is not solidly based on an empathic understanding of clients. The most effective counselors are those who have the widest repertory of responses and can use them in a socially intelligent manner. Such a repertory enables them to respond spontaneously to the wide variety of client needs. Counseling is for the client; it is not a virtuoso performance by the helper.

■ Overcoming Awkwardness

As a beginner, you can expect to experience some awkwardness as you learn to use the model and the skills and techniques it calls for. You need both practice and experience to be able to put all the elements of the model together smoothly. The following will help you achieve this integration.

1. *Modeling of extended counseling sessions by skilled helpers.* It helps to watch someone who can "put it all together." Live sessions, training films, and videotapes all help. You can read and listen to lectures about the helping process, but you then need to watch someone actually doing it. Modeling gives you the opportunity to have an "ah-hah" experience in training; that is, as you watch someone competent, you say to yourself "Oh, *that's* how it's done!"

2. *Step-by-step supervised practice.* Watching someone else do it well will help you develop a behaviorally-based feeling for the model and its skills, but it will not, of itself, dispel your feelings of awkwardness. The next step is to learn and practice the stages, steps, and skills under some kind of supervision. A supervisor, in this instance, is someone who can tell you what you are doing right, so that you can keep on doing it and celebrate your success, and what you are doing wrong, so that you can correct it. If you have a clear understanding of the requirements of the helping process, you can also give yourself feedback and get it from your fellow trainees. Once you learn basic skills, you can begin to practice short counseling sessions with your fellow trainees. As you become more and more self-assured, the length of those mutual helping sessions can be increased.

3. *Extended practice in individual skills outside the training sessions.* The problem-management model and the skills you will be learning are the skills needed for effective living in everyday life. Perhaps a violin-lesson analogy can be used here. If you were taking violin lessons from an instructor, you would be introduced gradually and systematically to the skills of playing during the lesson itself. There would also be some time for practice during the lesson, because the instructor would want to make sure you had the right idea about each technique. However, once you learned the basics during each lesson, it would be essential to go off and practice intensively in order to master what you had learned. It would be a waste of time to return for a second lesson without having practiced what you learned in the first one. The same holds true in learning how to be a helper. In the classroom or training group you will learn the basics of the model and the skills and techniques that make it operative, and you will have time for some practice. However, since the skills you will be learning are skills important for everyday living and relating, you will, if you so desire, have ample opportunity to practice them outside the training sessions themselves. For instance, you can sincerely and genuinely practice the communication skills that serve the model in your daily interactions with others, and you can do so without making yourself obvious as an amateur psychologist. Furthermore, since planning and problem solving are part of everyday life, you will have ample opportunity to practice the stages and steps of the model. With enough practice, this model and its skills can become second nature and your feelings of awkwardness will lessen. They will be part of your humanity rather than something tacked onto it.

4. *Supervised practice of the entire model.* Learning microskills is a segmental process. The skills of helping are not helping itself. They all have to be integrated into that human encounter called helping, counseling, or psychotherapy. Supervised practicum experience is an essential step toward such integration.

■ The Foundations of Helping: Core Values

Helping at its best is a deeply human process based on a core of human values. Since the entire helping process rests on those values, they can be called the foundations of helping. Some of these core values are summarized here under the headings *respect* and *genuineness* (see the May 1980 issue of the *Personnel and Guidance Journal*, which deals with values and the counselor). Figure 2–17 shows the helping process resting on these two sets of values. Raths, Harmin, and Simon (1960) describe a value as something a particular person prizes and cherishes, is committed to publicly, chooses freely from alternatives after considering the consequences of those alternatives, and *acts* upon. Although respect and genuineness are values rather than skills, they need to be translated into and permeate skillful behaviors if they are to make a difference.

RESPECT: A BEHAVIORAL APPROACH

Harre (1980), in a book on the social nature of human beings, contends that the deepest human need is that for respect. Respect can be considered an attitude or a moral quality, a way of looking at and prizing people. Respect is such a fundamental notion that, like most fundamental notions, it eludes definition. The word comes from a Latin root that includes the concept of "seeing" or "viewing." Indeed, respect is a particular way of viewing other people. Respect means prizing others simply because they are human beings.

Respect, if it is to make a difference, cannot remain *just* an attitude, *just* a way of viewing human beings. As Mayeroff (1971) put it, "caring is more than good intentions and warm regards" (p. 69). Respect makes

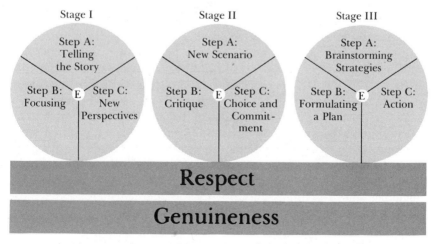

Figure 2–17. Foundation values of the helping process

a difference only when it becomes a value—that is, an attitude expressed behaviorally. In helping situations, respect is not often communicated directly in words. Actions literally speak louder than words. For instance, the helper seldom if ever says "I respect you because you are a human being." Respect is communicated principally by the ways in which helpers orient themselves toward and work with clients.

Orientation toward. "Orientation toward" refers to the attitudes that, once translated into concrete behaviors, comprise respect. Some of these attitudes are the following:

- *Being "for" the client.* The counselor's manner indicates that he or she is "for" the client simply because the client is human. This is not a tender or sentimental attitude. The helper is a caring person in a down-to-earth, nonsentimental sense. As a sign of this, respect ultimately involves placing demands on clients or helping them place demands on themselves. This "being for," then, refers to clients' basic humanity and to their potential to be more than they are right now. Respect is both gracious and tough-minded.
- *Being willing and able.* Respectful helpers can say "Working with this client is worth my time and energy." They are ready to commit themselves to their clients and are available to them in reasonable ways. But willingness is not enough. Helpers' respect for clients is found also in their skill to deliver their part of what the helping contract promises.
- *Regard for the client as unique.* Respect means prizing the individuality of clients. This means that helpers are committed to supporting each client in his or her uniqueness and to helping each develop the resources that make him or her unique. Effective helpers are not committed to making clients over in their own image or likeness. Respect means personalizing: tailoring the helping process to the needs, capabilities, and resources of this particular client.
- *Regard for the client's self-determination.* The helper's basic attitude is that clients do have the resources to manage their lives more effectively. Those resources may be blocked in a variety of ways, or they may just be lying fallow. The counselor's job is to help clients liberate and cultivate those resources; it is also to help clients assess them realistically so that aspirations do not outstrip resources. Ultimately, if clients choose to live less effectively than they might, counselors, after helping clients challenge such choices, can only respect their clients' rights to determine their own fates. Effective helpers do not manipulate their clients. It may be that the client's values so differ from those of the helper that it is impossible to work together; in such a case, respect and genuineness would call for the termination of that helping relationship.

- *Assuming the client's good will.* Respectful helpers proceed on the assumption that clients want to work at living more effectively. They continue with this assumption until it is demonstrated false. The reluctance and resistance of involuntary clients is not evidence of ill will— respect means entering their world in order to understand the resistance, followed by a willingness to help them work through it. The best helpers ask themselves whether *they* are contributing in any way to the failure of the counseling relationship. It is all too easy for counselors to abandon "unmotivated" clients.
- *Maintaining confidentiality.* Clients have the right to assume that what happens between them and their helpers is not discussed with others unless they give permission to do so.

Working with the client.   In working with clients, helpers express respect in a variety of ways:

- *Attentive physical presence.* As we shall see later, respect can be demonstrated through attentive physical presence. It says, behaviorally, "I am with you. I am committed to your interests. I am available to help you live more effectively. It is worth my time and effort to help you." Poor physical presence can say such things as, "You are not worth my time. What you say is not worth listening to. I am not really committed to working for your interests."
- *Suspending critical judgment.* In Stage I, respect takes the form of suspending critical judgment of the client. Rogers (1961, 1967), following Standal (1954), calls this kind of respect "unconditional positive regard," meaning that "the therapist communicates to his client a deep and genuine caring for him as a person with potentialities, a caring uncontaminated by evaluations of his thoughts, feelings, or behaviors" [1967, p. 102]. Consider the differences in the following counselors' remarks.

> CLIENT: I am really sexually promiscuous. I give into sexual desires whenever they arise and whenever I can find a partner. This has been the story for the past three years at least.
> COUNSELOR A: Immature sex hasn't been the answer, has it? Ultimately it's just another way of making yourself miserable.
> COUNSELOR B: So letting yourself go sexually is also part of the total picture.

Counselor B neither judges nor condones. She merely tries to communicate understanding to the client (understanding is obviously not synonymous with approval) so that both counselor and client can begin to see the total picture. She believes that the client's approach to life needs to be understood. But she is not naive. She realizes that some of the client's experiences must be transcended and that some of his behaviors must change, but she still respects him as the subject of those experiences and behaviors. She gives him room to move, room to explore himself. She sees her function in Stage I as helping the client explore both his behavior and the values from which that behavior springs, and she realizes that judgmental behavior on her part might well cut such exploration short.

In my view, respect, even at Stage I, is not completely unconditional. Respect includes a regard for clients' resources. At Stage I it means a regard for clients' abilities to commit themselves initially to the helping process and to engage in self-exploration. Clients might well find this process painful, but counselors show respect by helping them through their pain, not by letting them avoid it. In other words, respect includes an assumption on the part of the counselor that the client, even at Stage I, will pay the necessary price in order to begin to live more effectively. Respect, then, places a demand on the client at the same time that it offers him or her help in meeting the demand. For instance, let's assume that a voluntary client has been manifesting a great deal of resistance. He talks about superficial issues or issues that are serious but unrelated to the real problem situation; he changes the subject when the helper's responses bring him face to face with more crucial issues. Finally, the helper says something like this:

COUNSELOR: I'd like to share with you my perception of what's happening between you and me and get your reaction. The way I see it, you come close to discussing problems that are quite important for you, but then draw back. It's almost as if you were saying, "I'm not sure whether I can share this part of my life here and now." My hunch is that exploring yourself and putting all the cards on the table is extremely painful. It's like writing a blank check: you don't know how high a figure is going to be written in.

This counselor's deeper understanding is gently demanding. It demonstrates that challenge, in practice, is not limited to Step I-C.

- *Communicating understanding.* In Stage I, one of the best ways of showing respect is by working to understand clients: their experiences, their behavior(s), their feelings. People generally believe that people respect them if they spend time and effort in trying to understand them.
- *Helping clients cultivate their own resources.* Helping clients cultivate their own resources follows from the helper's esteem for the uniqueness, the individuality, of the client. Skilled helpers help clients search for resources. Effective helpers do not act for the client unless it is absolutely necessary, and then only as a step toward helping the client act on his or her own. Consider the following example.

CLIENT: There are a lot of things I find really hard to talk about. I would rather have you ask questions. That would be easier for me.

COUNSELOR A: Okay. You mentioned that you got in trouble in school. What kind of trouble was it? How did it all start?

COUNSELOR B: Well, let's talk about that for the moment. I feel that if I ask a lot of questions, I'll get a lot of information that *I* might think important, but I'm not convinced that it would be important for you. Putting yourself on the line like this is really new to you, and it seems you're finding it quite painful.

Counselor B assumes that the client does have, somewhere, the resources necessary to engage in self-exploration. She expresses her own feelings and tries to understand the client's blocking. She is willing to help the client work through his pain in order to get the work of Stage I done in a way that promotes the self-efficacy of the client.

• *Expressing reasonable warmth.* Gazda (1973) sees warmth as the physical expression of understanding and caring, which is ordinarily communicated through nonverbal media such as gestures, posture, tone of voice, touch, and facial expression. Warmth is only one way of showing respect. It is not necessarily the best way and can be misused. The helper can express initial warmth through friendliness, which is not the same as either "role" warmth (standard counselor warmth) or the warmth he or she would accord a good friend. The client is simply not a good friend.

• *Being genuine in the helping relationship.* Being genuine in one's relationship with another is a way of showing the other respect. Therefore, the behaviors listed under "genuineness" in the next section also constitute ways of showing respect.

GENUINENESS: A BEHAVIORAL APPROACH

Genuineness, as discussed here, refers, like respect, to a value expressed in a set of counselor behaviors. Rogers and Truax (1967) describe genuineness under the rubric "congruence" and relate it to therapy:

> In relation to therapy, [congruence] means that the therapist is what he *is*, during the encounter with the client. He is without front or facade, openly being the feelings and attitudes which at the moment are flowing in him. It involves the element of self-awareness, meaning that the feelings the therapist is experiencing are available to him, available to his awareness, and also that he is able to live these feelings, to be them in the relationship, and able to communicate them if appropriate. It means that he comes into a direct personal encounter with his client, meeting him on a person-to-person basis. It means that he is *being* himself, not denying himself [p. 101].

Genuine people are at home with themselves and therefore can comfortably be themselves in all their interactions. This means that they do not have to change when they are with different people; that is, they do not constantly have to adopt new roles in order to be acceptable to others or acceptable to themselves when they are with others.

Being genuine has both positive and negative implications; it means doing some things and not doing others.

Refusing to overemphasize role.   Genuine helpers do not take refuge in the role of counselor. Relating deeply to others and helping are part of their lifestyle, not roles they put on or take off at will. Gibb (1968, 1978) suggests that helping at its best is role-free. He says that helpers should learn how to do the following:

- Express directly to another whatever they are presently experiencing
- Communicate without distorting their own messages
- Listen to others without distorting their messages
- Reveal their true motivation in the process of communicating their messages
- Be spontaneous and free in their communications with others rather than use habitual and planned strategies
- Respond immediately to another's need or state instead of waiting for the "right" time or giving themselves enough time to come up with the "right" response
- Manifest their vulnerabilities and, in general, the "stuff" of their inner lives
- Live in and communicate about the here-and-now
- Strive for interdependence rather than dependence or counterdependence in their relationships with clients
- Learn how to enjoy psychological closeness
- Be concrete in their communications
- Be willing to commit themselves to others.

In my estimation, what Gibb espouses in no way makes counselors "free spirits" who inflict themselves on others. Indeed, "free spirit" helpers can even be dangerous to their clients (see Lieberman, Yalom, & Miles, 1973, pp. 226–267). Being role-free is not taking license; freedom from role means that counselors should not use the role or facade of counselor to protect themselves, to substitute for effectiveness, or to fool the client. Gibb is suggesting that credentialed professionals who are at the same time functional do not overemphasize their credentials. Being professional and being role-free in Gibb's sense are not contradictory.

Being spontaneous.   Genuine people are spontaneous. Many of the behaviors suggested by Gibb are ways of being spontaneous. Effective helpers, while being tactful (as part of their respect for others), do not constantly weigh what they say to clients. They do not place filters between their inner lives and what they express to others. Rogers (1957) notes that being genuine does not mean verbalizing every thought to the client. For instance, he suggests that helpers express negative feelings to clients only if such feelings persist or if they are interfering with their ability to move with the client through the helping process.

Being assertive. Genuine counselors are assertive in the helping process without being aggressive. I find that a cardinal problem of many trainees in the helping professions is that they are afraid to assert themselves. Some want to settle for a caricature of "nondirective counseling" as a helping model, not necessarily because they espouse the theory underlying it but because that is the approach with which they are most comfortable. They end up practicing a counterfeit form of nondirective counseling. Since they do not move out and meet others spontaneously in their day-to-day lives, to do so in counseling seems foreign to them. Many trainees, therefore, need a kind of counselor training program that will teach them experientially that it is all right to be active, spontaneous, free, and assertive.

Avoiding defensiveness. Genuine helpers are nondefensive. They know their own strengths and deficits and are presumably trying to live mature, meaningful lives. When clients express negative attitudes toward them, they try to understand what they are thinking and feeling and they continue to work with them. Consider the following example.

CLIENT: I don't think I'm really getting anything out of these sessions at all. Things are going just as poorly at school. Why should I waste my time coming here?

COUNSELOR A: I think you are the one wasting time. You just don't want to do anything. Have you thought of that?

COUNSELOR B: Well, that's your decision.

COUNSELOR C: As you see it, there's been no payoff for you here. It seems like a lot of dreary work with nothing to show for it.

Counselors A and B are both defensive. Counselor C enters into the experience of the client, giving the client the opportunity to get at the issue of responsibility in the helping process. Since genuine helpers are at home with themselves, they can allow themselves to examine negative criticism honestly. Counselor C, for instance, would be the most likely of the three to ask himself or herself whether he or she is contributing to the stalemate that seems to exist.

Being consistent. Genuine helpers are not constantly running afoul of significant discrepancies in their interactions with clients. They do not think or feel one thing and say another—or at least they are able to identify the discrepancies, especially those affecting their ability to help others, and are willing to deal with them.

CLIENT: Frankly, I don't think you like me. I think you're working hard with me, but I still don't think you like me.

COUNSELOR A: I'm not sure how liking or not liking relates to what we're doing here.

COUNSELOR B: I'm not sure that makes any difference ... (Pause) ... Wait a minute. Last time we talked about your being more assertive in our relationship. I think that right now you are being more assertive with me, and I'm brushing you aside. You seem to be saying that it's time we take a look at how we're relating to each other here. My seeming not to like you even though I work hard with you bothers you.

Counselor A brushes aside the client's challenge as irrelevant. Counselor B catches herself in a discrepancy. She wanted the client to be more assertive toward her and now realizes that she has to take the client's demands seriously.

Being open.   Genuine helpers are capable of deeper levels of self-disclosure. They do not see self-disclosure as an end in itself, but they feel free to reveal themselves intimately when it is appropriate. Since genuineness in the form of helper self-disclosure or self-sharing is part of Step I-C, it will be dealt with in greater detail in a later chapter.

These, then, are some of the values that undergird the helping process (see Box 2–1). I am sure that you can examine your own values in relating to others and add to this list.

■ Some Final Considerations and Cautions

Everything written here will become clearer as you watch others model the helping process and try it yourself. But before we leave this overview, here are a couple of final suggestions.

AN OPEN MODEL: LEARNING FROM OTHER APPROACHES TO COUNSELING AND PSYCHOTHERAPY

While the helping model presented here represents a solid introduction to becoming a helper, it does not pretend to be "all you've ever wanted to know about counseling"; it does not exhaust the ways of helping. It does, however, set forth the basic tasks and goals of the helping process. Therefore, once you learn it, it can become a tool or framework that helps you read the literature on counseling and psychotherapy critically and organize other approaches to helping around the basic tasks and goals of each of the stages and steps of this helping framework. This model will help you mine techniques from other approaches to help you accomplish each of the basic tasks. While it presents a way of approaching any human problem situation, you will also want to acquire specialized

---

■ Box 2–1. A Summary of Respect and Genuineness

Respect

The value of respect is manifested in both your attitudes toward and the ways in which you work with clients.

ATTITUDE
Your attitude toward clients is respectful if you

- Care about the welfare of your clients
- Consider each client to be a unique human being rather than a case
- View clients as capable of determining their own fates
- Assume the good will of clients until this assumption is demonstrated to be wrong.

BEHAVIOR
Your attitude becomes respectful behavior when in working with clients you

- Develop competence in helping and use it
- Attend and listen actively
- Suspend critical judgment
- Communicate empathic understanding
- Express reasonable warmth or friendliness
- Help clients identify and cultivate their own resources
- Provide encouragement, support, and appropriate challenge
- Help clients get the work of each relevant step of the helping process done.

Genuineness

You are genuine in your relationship with your clients when you

- Do not overemphasize your professional role and avoid stereotyped role behaviors
- Are spontaneous but not uncontrolled or haphazard in your relationships
- Remain open and nondefensive even when you feel threatened
- Are consistent and avoid discrepancies—between your values and your behavior, and between your thoughts and your words in interactions with clients—while remaining respectful and reasonably tactful
- Are willing to share yourself and your experience with clients if it seems helpful.

---

information and skills to deal with specialized problems: juvenile delinquency, alcoholism, sexual deviation, psychosis, mental retardation, family problems, problems associated with aging, and so on. The best helpers call upon all available resources—their own experience, other approaches to helping, research, developing theories—to clarify, modify, refine, and expand the model. Any model is useful only to the degree that it produces results.

SHARING THE HELPING MODEL WITH CLIENTS AS PART OF THE CONTRACT

Up to this point, much has been said about the counselor's knowledge and use of the model as a cognitive map to give direction to his or her interactions with the client. But how much should the client know about the counseling model being used? Goldstein, Heller, and Sechrest (1966) suggest that "giving patients prior information about the nature of psychotherapy, the theories underlying it, and the techniques to be used will facilitate progress in psychotherapy" (p. 245). Some counselors are reluctant to let the client know what the process is all about. Others seem to "fly by the seat of their pants" and can't tell clients what it's all about simply because *they* don't know what it's all about. Still others seem to think that a knowledge of helping processes is secret or sacred or dangerous and should not be communicated to the client.

In my opinion, clients should be told as much about the model as they can assimilate. Obviously, highly distressed clients should not be told to contain their anxiety until helpers have taught them the helping model. But, generally speaking, clients should be given some kind of cognitive initiation into the model, either all at once or gradually, so that they can participate in it more actively. The theory is that if they know where they are going they will get there faster. Like helpers, clients can use the model as a cognitive map to give themselves a sense of direction. This helps to ensure that helping, even though it remains a social-influence process, is still a collaborative one. Chapter One suggested that you make the contract between yourself and your clients as explicit as possible before helping begins. Sharing the model with the client can be part of the contract.

Part Two

Basic Communication Skills

The next two chapters explain and illustrate the basic communication skills helpers need in order to interact effectively with clients at every stage and step of the helping process. These skills are not the helping process itself, but are essential human tools for developing relationships with clients and helping them move toward managing their problems in living.

There are four basic helping skills. Chapter Three deals with the skills of attending and listening.

1. *Attending* refers to the ways in which helpers can effectively orient themselves toward and be with their clients, both physically and psychologically.
2. *Listening* refers to the ability of helpers to capture and understand the messages transmitted by clients: verbal or nonverbal, vague or clear.

Chapter Four deals with the skills of basic empathy responding and of probing.

3. *Empathy* refers to the helper's ability to communicate to clients that he or she understands what they are saying. Central to empathy is letting clients know that their viewpoints have been listened to and understood.
4. *Probing* refers to the counselor's ability to help clients identify and explore experiences, behavior(s), and feelings that will help them engage more constructively in any of the steps of the helping process.

A second set of communication skills related to helping clients identify blind spots and develop new perspectives will be presented in Chapters Seven and Eight.

Three

Attending and Listening

∎

Attending: Orienting yourself to the client
    Level 1: Microskills
    Level 2: The body as a means of communication
    Level 3: The quality of your presence to clients
Active listening
    Listening to and understanding nonverbal communications
    A framework for listening to and understanding verbal
    messages
    Integration: Listening to and understanding clients themselves
Basic empathic listening and understanding
Advanced empathic listening and understanding
Listening to and understanding client-related realities beyond
empathy
Identifying and managing bias in listening
    Inadequate listening
    Evaluative listening
    Filtered listening
    Sympathetic listening
Becoming productively self-conscious in the helping process

Two sets of communication skills are essential to the helping process. The first, which concerns helping clients explore and clarify issues, is the focus of this chapter and the next. The second, which concerns challenging clients' perspectives and behavior, is dealt with in Chapters Seven and Eight. Both are commonly used throughout the helping process in all stages and steps, but, as we shall see later, the second set derives much of its efficacy from the first. The first set includes the following skills: attending, listening, responding with empathic understanding, and probing.

Communication skills are not ends in themselves, but means or instruments that must be placed at the service of helping *outcomes* in order to be meaningful. Certainly helpers need to become adept at these skills, but mere competence in communication skills does not automatically make for effective helping.

There has been a growing concern about the overemphasis of communication microskills and techniques in both communication-skills training (Mahon & Altman, 1977; Plum, 1981) and in the helping process. Rogers (1980), while admitting that an analysis of precisely what counselors do to help clients provides fruitful information—"We became expert in analyzing, in very minute detail, the ebb and flow of the process in each interview, and we gained a great deal from that microscopic study" (p. 138)—decries what he calls the "appalling consequences" (p. 139) of an overemphasis on the microskills of helping. Helping, instead of being a fully human endeavor, then gets reduced to its bits and pieces. Hills (1984) discusses an "integrative" versus a "technique" approach to training in communication skills. An integrative approach to both training in helping and helping itself means several things:

- Helpers need to find *personal meaning* in communication skills and helping techniques. That is, skills and techniques must be extensions of the helper's humanity and not just bits of helping technology. The "discovery of personal meaning" (Combs, 1965, p. 2; see also Combs, 1982, and Mahon & Altman, 1977) leads to more integrated learning.
- Communication skills and helping techniques must serve the larger helping process—that is, the helping *outcomes* described in Stages I, II, and III of our model. Helping does not take place when helpers communicate well; it takes place when clients manage their lives more effectively.
- Communication skills and helping techniques need to be permeated by the *values* discussed under the headings of respect and genuineness.

This integration must begin in helper training programs if it is to be found in the helping process. Communication skills learned, practiced, and used in a fully human way at the service of a helping relationship and a helping process is the goal of the communication-microskills training. Ivey and Gluckstern (1984) suggest that a post-training phase is needed to provide for the transfer and integration of microskills. Otherwise communication skills can drive rather than serve the helping process. Practicum and internship experiences provide forums for such transfer and integration.

In sum, the skills we are about to describe and analyze need to be placed in the context of the full helping framework, of the humanity of clients to be helped, and of the humanity of helpers themselves.

■ Attending: Orienting Yourself to the Client

At some of the more dramatic moments of life, just being with another person is extremely important. For example, if a friend of yours is in the hospital, your presence there may make a difference, even if conversation is impossible. Similarly, your being with someone whose wife or husband or child or friend has just died can be very comforting to that person, even if little is said. Human presence is important. Erikson (1964) speaks of the effects of both inattention and negative attention on the child:

> Hardly has one learned to recognize the familiar face (the original harbor of basic trust) when he becomes also frightfully aware of the unfamiliar, the strange face, the unresponsive, the averted . . . and the frowning face. And here begins . . . that inexplicable tendency on man's part to feel that *he has caused the face to turn away* which happened to turn elsewhere [p. 102, emphasis added].

Perhaps the averted face is too often a sign of the averted heart. At any rate, most of us are sensitive to others' attention or inattention to us. Given that fact, it is paradoxical how insensitive we can be at times about attending to others. The ways in which you are present to clients are extremely important, for they easily read the cues that indicate the quality of your presence to them.

Before helpers can respond to clients and their concerns, they must first pay attention to them and listen carefully to what they have to say. Effective helpers are, above all, perceptive helpers; most of the skills discussed in this book are based on the ability of helpers to be astute observers of clients and of themselves in their interactions with them. Therefore, good helpers attend carefully to both the verbal and nonverbal messages of clients.

Attending and listening seem to be concepts so simple to grasp and so easy to do that you may wonder why they are being given such explicit treatment here. But simple as they seem, it is amazing how often people fail to attend to and listen to one another. Consider how many times you've heard the statement "You're not even listening to what I'm saying!" directed toward someone who is caught not attending well. When the person so accused answers, almost predictably, "I am too, I can repeat everything you've said," the reply seems of little comfort to the accuser. What people look for in attending and listening is not someone's ability to repeat their words; a tape recorder could do that perfectly. People want more than physical presence in human communication; they want the other person to be fully there, meaning *psychological* or *social-emotional* presence.

Helping—and other deep interpersonal transactions—demands a certain intensity of presence. That presence, that "being with" the client, is what is meant by attending, in its deepest sense. Collaborative problem solving involves both establishing a working *relationship* with clients and helping them use their resources to identify, clarify, and manage problem situations. Attending, or the way you orient yourself physically and psychologically to clients, contributes to both those goals. Your nonverbal behavior and the many messages you communicate through it influence clients for better or worse. It can invite them to trust you, open up, and explore the significant dimensions of their problems, or it can promote their distrust and lead to a reluctance to reveal themselves to you. Furthermore, the quality of your attending, both physical and psychological, influences the quality of your perceptiveness. If you attend poorly to clients, you will most likely miss data relevant to clarifying the problem situation. Effective attending, then, does two things: it lets clients know you are with them and therefore helps establish good rapport, and it puts you in a position to be an effective listener. Attending is now considered by many to be a basic and important helping skill, and research into its meaning and use is continuing (Carkhuff & Anthony, 1979; Claiborn, 1979; Fretz and others, 1979; Genther & Moughan, 1977; Gladstein, 1974; Haase & Tepper, 1972; Ivey & Authier, 1978; Lacrosse, 1975; Smith-Hanen, 1977; Tepper & Haase, 1978).

Attending can be considered from three different perspectives or successively deeper levels: (1) the microskills involved in attending, (2) the cues and messages helpers send through their bodies, and (3) the quality of the helper's presence to the client.

Level 1: Microskills

Consider the following five ways in which you can make sure you are physically present to a client. While the microskills level is the most superficial level of attending, it does serve as a starting point. The microskills can be summarized in the acronym SOLER.

S: Face the client Squarely, that is, adopt a posture that indicates involvement. In North American culture facing another person "squarely" is often considered a basic posture of involvement. It usually says, "I'm available to you; I choose to be with you." Turning your body away from another person while you talk to him or her can lessen your degree of contact with that person. Even when people are seated in a circle, they usually try in some way to turn toward the individuals to whom they are speaking. By directing your body toward the other person in some way that is meaningful to you, you say "I'm with you right now." The word *squarely* here may be taken literally or metaphorically. *What is important is that the bodily orientation you adopt conveys the message that you are involved with the client.* If, for any reason, facing the person squarely is too threatening, then an angled position may be called for. The point is the quality of your attention.

O: Adopt an Open posture. Crossed arms and legs can be signs of lessened involvement with or availability to others, while an open posture can be a sign that you're open to the client and to what he or she has to say. In North American culture an open posture is generally seen as nondefensive. It can say "I'm open to you right now." Again, the word *open* can be taken literally or metaphorically. If your legs are crossed, it doesn't mean you are not involved with the client. But it is important to ask yourself, "To what degree does my present posture communicate openness and availability to the client?"

L: Remember that it is possible at times to Lean toward the other. Watch two people in a restaurant booth who are intimately engaged in conversation. Very often they are both leaning forward over the table as a natural result of their involvement. Remember that the upper part of your body is on a "hinge"; it can move toward a person and also back away. In North American culture a slight inclination toward a person is often interpreted as saying, "I'm with you; I'm interested in you and in what you have to say." Leaning back (the severest form of which is a slouch) can be way of saying "I'm not entirely with you" or "I'm bored." Leaning *too* far forward or doing so too soon may frighten a client. It can be perceived as a demand on the other for some kind of closeness or intimacy. Effective helpers are not rigid, but can move back and forth naturally according to what is happening in the dialogue. In this sense, *leaning* means a kind of bodily flexibility or responsiveness that enhances your communication with a client.

E: Maintain good Eye contact. In North American culture fairly steady *eye contact* is not unnatural for people deep in conversation. It is not the same as staring. Again, watch two people talking seriously in a restaurant. You will be amazed at the amount of direct eye contact. Maintaining good eye contact with a client is another way of saying "I'm with you; I want to hear what you have to say." Obviously this principle is not violated if you occasionally look away, but if you catch yourself looking away frequently, it may be a clue to your reluctance to be with and to get involved with the person. Alternatively, it may tell you something about your discomfort with closeness in general.

R: Try to be relatively Relaxed while engaging in these behaviors. This means two things. First, it means not fidgeting nervously or engaging in distracting facial expressions. This can cause the client to wonder what's making you nervous. Second, it means becoming comfortable with using your body as a vehicle of contact and expression. Once you feel natural in engaging in the behaviors listed here, you will find that they help you to focus your attention on the client and to "punctuate" your dialogue nonverbally.

These "rules" should be followed cautiously. People differ both individually and culturally in the ways in which they show attentiveness. The main point is that an internal "being with" a client might well lose its impact if the client does not see that attitude reflected in the helper's nonverbal communication. It is not uncommon for helpers in training to become overly self-conscious and awkward about their attending behavior, especially in the beginning and perhaps even more if they are not used to attending carefully to others. However, the SOLER rules should not be taken as absolute dictums to be applied rigidly in all cases. They are rather *guidelines* to help you orient yourself physically to the client. In a filmed therapeutic interview, Carl Rogers, a master at being with clients in a concerned human way, can be seen following all these "rules"—but he followed them before they were invented; that is, the behaviors stemmed naturally from his concern for his clients. That concern taught him how to orient himself to them. He is both intense *and* relaxed; that is, he is natural, "himself."

Level 2: The Body as a Vehicle of Communication

Much more important than a mechanical application of the SOLER guidelines is an awareness of your body as a source of communication. Through your body you are *always* communicating cues or messages to clients. Effective helpers are, first of all, mindful of what cues and messages they are sending as they interact with clients; that is, they are in touch with and capable of "reading" their own nonverbal behavior during the interview. For instance, if you feel your muscles tensing as a client talks, you can say to yourself, "I'm getting anxious here. What's causing my anxiety? And what cues am I sending the client?" Once the messages are read, you can use your body to communicate appropriate messages, or even to censor messages you feel are inappropriate. For instance, if the client says something that triggers instinctive anger in you, you can control the external expression of anger (for instance, a grimace or frown) to give yourself time to reflect. It may be that you heard the client wrong, or that expressing your anger toward the client would not be helpful at this point.

This second level of attending does not mean that you become preoccupied with your body as a source of communication. It means rather that you learn to use your body instinctively as a means of communication.

Level 3: The Quality of Your Presence to Your Clients

What is most important is the quality of your presence to your clients. You are present through what you say and what you do. If you care about your clients and feel deeply committed to their welfare, it is unfair to yourself to let your nonverbal behavior convey a contradictory message. On the other hand, if you feel indifferent to them and your nonverbal behavior suggests commitment, you are not being genuine. Effective helpers stay in touch with how they are present to clients, without becoming preoccupied with it. They ask themselves such questions as

- What values are operative in my interactions with clients?
- What are my attitudes toward this particular client?
- Am I experiencing some kind of conflict in terms of my values or attitudes right now? Am I indifferent to this client?
- How would I rate the quality of my presence to this client right now?
- How are my values and attitudes being expressed by my nonverbal behavior?
- How are my values and attitudes being expressed in my verbal behavior?
- How might I be more effectively present to this person?

Obviously, helpers are not constantly asking themselves these questions as they interact with clients. However, effective helpers are habitually aware of the quality of their presence to their clients.

Thus far, attending has been considered insofar as it is a relationship-enhancement skill (Goldstein, 1980)—that is, insofar as it affects rapport between you and your clients. But since attending also includes observing, it also means gathering or helping clients to gather the kind of data needed to explore and define problem situations. Box 3–1 summarizes, in evaluation question form, the main points related to attending. Attending is related to your presence, and one of the ways in which you are present is as a *listener*.

■ **Box 3–1. Attending—Evaluation Questions**

- Does the client experience me as effectively present and working with him or her?
- Does my nonverbal behavior reinforce my internal attitudes?
- In what ways am I distracted from giving my full attention to this client?
- What am I doing to handle these distractions?

■ Active Listening

Good attending enables the helper to listen carefully to what clients are saying, both verbally and nonverbally. Total or complete listening involves three things: (1) observing and reading the client's nonverbal behavior—posture, facial expression, movement, tone of voice, and the like; (2) listening to and understanding the client's verbal messages; and (3) listening in an integrated way to the person in the context of both the helping process and everyday life.

The goal of listening is understanding. As we shall see later, sharing your understanding with clients can help them understand themselves more fully and put them in a better position to act constructively. The art of listening has three parts: (1) listening to and understanding nonverbal behavior; (2) listening to and understanding verbal messages; and (3) listening to and understanding the person.

Listening to and Understanding Nonverbal Behavior

We are only beginning to realize the importance of nonverbal behavior and to make a scientific study of it. The face and body are extremely communicative. We know from experience that even when people are together in silence, the atmosphere can be filled with messages. Knapp (1972) defines nonverbal behavior as "all human communication events which transcend spoken or written words" (p. 20). Sometimes the facial expressions, bodily motions, voice quality, and autonomic physiological responses of a client communicate more than words.

Mehrabian (1971) reports on research he and his associates did in the area of nonverbal behavior and inconsistent messages. The research reported here involves the way one person expresses liking for another.

One interesting question now arises: Is there a systematic and coherent approach to resolving the general meaning or impact of an inconsistent message? Indeed there is. Our experimental results show:

Total liking equals 7% verbal liking plus 38% vocal
liking plus 55% facial liking

Thus the impact of facial expression is greatest, then the impact of the tone of voice (or vocal expression), and finally that of the words. If the facial expression is inconsistent with the words, the degree of liking conveyed by the facial expression will dominate and determine the impact of the total message [p. 43].

If you say to a client, "It's hard talking about yourself, isn't it?" and she says, "No, I don't mind at all," but speaks hesitatingly while looking away and grimacing a bit, the real answer is probably in her nonverbal behavior.

In Mehrabian's research the exact percentages are not important, but the role of nonverbal behavior in the total communication process is. Effective helpers learn how to listen to and "read" the following: (1) bodily behavior such as posture, body movements, gestures; (2) facial expressions such as smiles, frowns, raised eyebrows, twisted lips, and the like; (3) voice-related behavior such as tone of voice, pitch, voice level, intensity, inflection, spacing of words, emphases, pauses, silences, fluency; (4) observable autonomic physiological responses such as quickened breathing, the development of a temporary rash, blushing, paleness, pupil dilation; (5) physical characteristics such as physique, height, weight, complexion, and the like; and (6) general appearance such as grooming, dress, and so forth.

If you notice that a client has developed a temporary rash or reddening of the neck while talking to you, it probably means that he or she feels some kind of pressure. Taking account of such cues is most important. A person's nonverbal behavior has a way of "leaking" messages to others (Ekman, 1982; Ekman & Friesen, 1969).

Nonverbal behaviors are generally more spontaneous than verbal behaviors. "Words can be selected and monitored before being emitted. . . . Nonverbal behaviors, on the other hand, are not as easily subject to control" (Passons, 1975, p. 102). Clients' nonverbal expressions can constitute a kind of royal route into their inner life.

Besides being a channel of communication in itself, nonverbal behavior—through facial expressions, bodily motions, voice quality, and autonomic physiological responses—can punctuate verbal messages in much the same way that periods, question marks, exclamation points, and underlinings punctuate and give emphasis to written language. Nonverbal behavior can punctuate or modify interpersonal communication in the following ways (see Knapp, 1978, pp. 9–12).

Confirming or repeating. Nonverbal behavior can confirm or repeat what is being said verbally. For instance, if you do your best to communicate understanding to a client and her eyes light up (facial expression) and she leans forward a bit (bodily motion) and says animatedly (voice quality), "Yes, I think you've hit it right on the head!" then her nonverbal behavior confirms her verbal message to you.

Denying or confusing. Nonverbal behavior can deny or confuse what is being said verbally. If a client tells you he is not upset by the way you have challenged him, yet he blushes (autonomic physiological response), his voice falters a bit (voice quality), and his upper lip quivers (facial expression) as he says so, his nonverbal message seems to deny what he is saying verbally. Or if one member of a counseling group tells another that she is quite angry with him but smiles while doing so, her nonverbal behavior contradicts her verbal message and may confuse the other person. Her smile might mean, "I'm angry with you, but I don't want to hurt or alienate you," or it might mean, "I'm angry, but I'm very uncomfortable trying to tell you about it."

Strengthening or emphasizing. Nonverbal behavior can strengthen or emphasize what is being said. If a counselor suggests that a client discuss a certain issue with his wife (who is not present) and he responds by saying, "Oh, I don't think I could do that!" while slouching down and putting his face in his hands, his nonverbal behavior underscores his verbal message. Nonverbal behavior does much to add emotional color or intensity to verbal messages. If a client tells you she doesn't like to be confronted without first being understood, and then stares at you fixedly and silently with a frown on her face, her nonverbal behavior tells you something about the intensity of her emotion. If she then proceeds to stalk out of the room, her nonverbal behavior underscores even further the intensity of her anger and hurt.

Controlling or regulating. Nonverbal cues are often used in conversation to regulate or control what is happening. If, in group counseling, one participant looks at another and gives every indication that she is going to speak to him or her, she may hesitate or change her mind if the other looks away or frowns. Skilled helpers are aware of the ways in which clients send controlling or regulating nonverbal cues.

READING NONVERBAL BEHAVIOR

The word *reading* is used here instead of the word *interpreting* to stress that caution must be taken to discover the meaning of what clients are saying verbally and nonverbally, without reading more into their behavior than is there. Recall that listening is in the service of understanding, not dissecting, the client. There is no simple program available for learning how to read and interpret nonverbal behavior. Once you develop a working knowledge of nonverbal behavior and its possible meanings, you must learn through practice and experience to be sensitive to it and to read its meaning in any given situation (Cormier & Cormier, 1979, Chapter 3; Gazda, 1973, pp. 89ff; Gladstein, 1974; Knapp, 1978; Mehrabian, 1971; Passons, 1975; Stone & Morden, 1976; Sue & Sue, 1977). Nonverbal behaviors can often mean a number of things—how, then, do you know which? The key is *context*. Effective helpers listen to the entire context of the helping interview and do not become overly fixated on details of behavior. Effective helpers are aware of and use the nonverbal communication system, but they are not seduced or overwhelmed by it.

The earlier caution about integrative versus technique approaches to helping is worth repeating here. The helping process is presented in these chapters in bits and pieces, as it were. Sometimes novice helpers will fasten selectively on this bit or that piece. For example, they will become intrigued with nonverbal behavior and make too much of a half-smile or a frown on the face of a client. They will seize upon the smile or frown and, in the interpretation (or overinterpretation) of it, lose the person. A failure to keep nonverbal behavior in context distorts their reading of the client and the client's problem situation. Skilled helpers, through practice and experience, learn to integrate all the pieces of the helping process. They do not become victims of their own microskills.

Listening to and Understanding Verbal Messages: A Practical Framework

What follows is a simple microskills framework for listening to, organizing, and understanding clients' verbal messages. Other, more integrative frameworks will be mentioned in later chapters. Clients talk about their

- *Experiences*—that is, what happens *to* them. If a client tells you she was fired from her job, she is talking about her problem situation in terms of an experience.
- *Behaviors*—that is, what they do or fail to do. If a client tells you he has sex with underage boys, he is talking about his problem situation in terms of his behavior.
- *Affect*—that is, the feelings and emotions that arise from or are associated with either experiences or behavior. If a client tells you how depressed she gets after drinking bouts, she is talking about the affect associated with her problem situation.

This listening framework is concerned with helping clients clarify their problem situations and their unused opportunities. A problem situation is clear if it is seen and understood in terms of specific experiences, specific behaviors, and specific feelings and emotions. As you listen to clients, you can first communicate understanding to them in terms of their experiences, behaviors, and feelings, and then, if these are sketchy or vague, you can help them explore and clarify in terms of further or clearer experiences, behaviors, and feelings. Let's take a closer look at each of these three categories.

First, an example. A client says to a counselor in the personnel department of a large company, "I had one of the lousiest days of my life yesterday." The counselor knows that something went wrong and that the client feels bad about it, but she knows relatively little about the specific experiences, behaviors, and feelings that made the day a horror for the client. However, let us say the client continues, "Toward the end of the day my boss yelled at me for not getting my work done [an experience]. I lost my temper [emotion] and yelled right back at him [behavior]. He blew up [emotion] and fired me [an experience]. And now I feel awful [emotion] and am trying to find out if he had the authority to do that [behavior]." Now the problem situation is much clearer because it is spelled out in terms of specific experiences, behaviors, and feelings related to specific situations.

LISTENING TO THE CLIENT'S EXPERIENCES

Most clients spend a fair amount of time talking about what happens *to* them.

> "I get headaches a lot."
> "My ulcers act up when family members argue."
> "My wife doesn't understand me."

They often talk about what other people do or fail to do, especially when it affects them adversely:

> "She doesn't do anything all day. The house is always a mess when I come home from work."
> "He tells his little jokes, and I'm always the butt of them."

Clients often see themselves, whether rightly or wrongly, as victims of forces beyond their control. If those forces are described as *outside* them, they can be called *external* or *overt* experiences:

> "He treats me like dirt."
> "Company policy discriminates against women."
> "The way the economy is right now, I just can't get a job."
> "There's an unwritten rule here that an innovative teacher is considered suspect."

Or those forces may be described as *covert* or coming *from within:*

"These feelings of depression come from nowhere and seem to suffocate me."
"No matter what I do I always feel hungry."
"I just can't stop thinking of her."
"It's the way I was educated. I was always taught to think of Blacks as inferior and now I'm just saddled with those feelings."

One reason that some clients are clients is that they see themselves as victims. Other people, the immediate social settings of life, society in its larger organizations and institutions, or cultural prescriptions affect them adversely. They feel that they are no longer in control of their lives. Therefore, they talk extensively about these experiences. This kind of talk can include statements about the forces by which they feel victimized.

"He treats me like dirt. But that's the way he is. He just doesn't care about people and their feelings at all. He's totally self-centered."
"I just can't get a job. The politicians run the economy for their own benefit. They talk about the common people in public, but in the back rooms they are all dealing with big business."
"I can't control my appetite. I've heard that some people are just like that. They have a different sort of metabolism. I must be one of them."
"I keep hearing voices. They tell me to harm myself. I think they're coming from the devil."

Careful listening is critical since helping, as we shall see more fully later on, starts with the frame of reference of the client. Even though this frame of reference may need to be transcended, it is still the starting point and needs to be understood. That kind of understanding is impossible unless you first listen to the client's experiences in as unbiased a way as possible.

LISTENING TO THE CLIENT'S BEHAVIORS

Some clients talk freely about their experiences but are much less willing to talk about their behaviors—that is, what they do and don't do. The reason for this is rather simple and applies to most of us. While we may not feel accountable for our experiences—what happens *to* us—we realize at some level that we are responsible for our behaviors—what we do and refrain from doing—or at least we sense that accountability is more of an issue when it comes to behavior.

"When he ignores me, I go off by myself and cry."
"I haven't even begun to look for a job. I know there are none in this city."

"When I feel the depression coming on, I take some of the pills the doctor gave me."

"When I get bored with my studies, I close the books and go lift a few beers with my friends."

Behaviors, too, can be overt (external) or covert (internal). Overt behavior is that which can be witnessed by others, whether it is actually witnessed or not. Here are some examples of overt behavior:

"When he called me a name, I punched him."

"I haven't told my husband that they found cancer."

"I find release by going to pornography stores."

Covert behavior refers to the inner life of the person, which cannot be seen directly by others. Here are some examples of covert behavior:

"When he called me a name, I began thinking of the ways I could get back at him. And I told myself that I would."

"I like to daydream about having a child."

"I never let myself think bad of another person."

Covert behaviors include thoughts, fantasies, daydreams, attitudes, imaginings, decisions, memories, plans, and the like that people feel they have some control over.

"When she left me, I decided I'd find some way of getting back at her."

"I try not to let thoughts of sex enter my mind."

"I have every intention of looking for a job this month."

If a person feels that he or she has little or no control over what is going on inside, I tend to interpret this as covert experience—that is, as something that is happening *to* the person—rather than covert behavior.

"I try to get into my work, but I just can't stop thinking of her and how she played me for a fool."

"Sexual fantasies seem to keep popping up all the time. I just don't seem to have any control."

"I know I get depressed and cry when I think of John on his deathbed, but I can't help thinking of him."

Part of the counseling process is to help clients realize that they often have more control over their experiences, especially internal or covert ones, than they had thought.

LISTENING TO THE CLIENT'S AFFECT

This means listening to the feelings and emotions that proceed from, accompany, underlie, give color to, or lead to a client's experiences and behaviors.

"I finished the term paper that I've been putting off for weeks and I feel great!"

"I've been feeling sorry for myself ever since he left me."

"I yelled at my mother last night and now I feel pretty ashamed of myself."

"I've been anxious for the past few weeks, but I don't know why. I wake up feeling scared and then it goes away but comes back again several times a day."

Of course, clients often *express* feelings without talking about them. A client who is talking listlessly and staring down at the floor may not say in so many words "I feel depressed." A dying person might express feelings of anger and depression without talking about them. Some clients feel deeply about things but do their best to repress those feelings. But usually there are cues or hints, whether verbal or nonverbal, of the feelings inside.

Some clients imply that their emotions have a kind of life of their own and that they can do little or nothing to control them. This includes describing others as the cause of their emotions:

"Whenever I see him with her, I feel hurt."

"She can get my goat whenever she wants. She's always making me angry."

"I can't help crying when I think of what they did to her."

As we shall see later on, people *can* learn how to control their emotions. Part of the helping process consists in showing people how to get out from under the burden of disabling feelings and emotions. On the other hand, they can also learn how to express emotions as part of their humanity, as a way of enriching their interactions with themselves and others.

Listening to and Understanding Clients Themselves

People are more than the sum of their verbal and nonverbal messages. Listening in its deepest sense means listening to the *person* of clients as influenced by the contexts in which they "live, move, and have their being." Total listening to the person involves (1) basic empathic listening and understanding, (2) advanced empathic listening and understanding, and (3) listening to and understanding realities that lie beyond empathy: "trans-empathic" realities, if you will, related to clients' problem situations and unused opportunities.

BASIC EMPATHIC LISTENING AND UNDERSTANDING

Empathy as a form of human communication involves both listening and understanding *and* the communication of that understanding to the client. Empathy that remains locked up in the helper contributes little to the helping process. Here we address empathic listening and understanding. The communication of empathy is dealt with later in this chapter.

A helper cannot communicate an understanding of a client's world without getting in touch with that world. Therefore, a great deal of the discussion on empathy centers around the kind of attending, observing, and listening—the kind of "being with" the other—needed in order to develop an understanding of the client and his or her world. In other words, empathy is primarily a mode of human contact. Mayeroff (1971) sees this mode of contact as essential to caring.

> To care for another person, I must be able to understand him and his world as if I were inside it. I must be able to see, as it were, with his eyes what his world is like to him and how he sees himself. Instead of merely looking at him in a detached way from outside, as if he were a specimen, I must be able to be *with* him in his world, "going" into his world in order to sense from the "inside" what life is like for him, what he is striving to be and what he requires to grow [pp. 41–42].

Huxley (1963) notes, however, that it is metaphysically impossible to get inside another in such a way as actually to experience reality as the other does:

> We live together, we act on, we react to, one another; but always in all circumstances we are alone. . . . Sensations, feelings, insights, fancies—all these are private and, except through symbols and second hand, incommunicable.

Yet he, too, believes that empathy is both possible and necessary in human relationships.

> Most island universes are sufficiently like one another to permit inferential understanding or even empathy or "feeling into." . . . To see ourselves as others see us is a most salutary gift. Hardly less important is the capacity to see others as they are themselves [pp. 12–13].

Huxley, then, describes empathy as an attempt to penetrate the metaphysical aloneness of the other.

Empathy in its most fundamental sense, primary accurate empathy, involves understanding the experiences, behaviors, and feelings of others as *they* experience them. It means that helpers must, to the best of their abilities, put aside their own biases, prejudices, and points of view in order to understand as clearly as possible the points of view of their clients. It means entering into the experience of clients in order to develop a feeling for their inner world and how they view both this inner world and the world of people and things around them.

Rogers (1980) talks about basic empathic listening, being with, and understanding as "an unappreciated way of being" (p. 137) because, despite its usefulness in counseling and therapy, even so-called expert helpers either ignore it or are not skilled in its use. Rogers defines basic empathic listening or being with in the following manner:

> It means entering the private perceptual world of the other and becoming thoroughly at home in it. It involves being sensitive, moment by moment, to the changing felt meanings which flow in this other person, to the fear or rage or tenderness or confusion or whatever that he or she is experiencing. It means temporarily living in the other's life, moving about in it delicately without making judgments . . . [p. 142].

It becomes clear that empathy flows from the foundation values of respect and genuineness discussed in the last chapter.

ADVANCED EMPATHIC LISTENING AND UNDERSTANDING

The second level, although based on the first, cuts a bit deeper. Helpers, in the intensity of their listening and being with, and without going beyond the experience of their clients, sometimes see more clearly what clients only half see and hint at. This deeper kind of empathy involves "sensing meanings of which the client is scarcely aware" (Rogers, 1980, p. 142). For instance, a client talks about his anger at his wife, but as he talks, the helper hears not just anger but also hurt. It may be that the client can talk with relative ease about his anger but not about his feelings of hurt. Advanced empathic listeners ask themselves, at least implicitly, such questions as, "What is this person only half saying?" "What is this person hinting at?" "What is this person saying in a confused way?" "What messages do I hear behind the explicit ones?" Note that advanced empathic listening deals with what the client is actually saying or expressing, however confusedly, not with interpretations of what the client is saying.

Effective helpers listen for the *resources* deeply buried in clients and often forgotten by them. Cummings (1979) gives an example of this kind of listening in his work with addicts.

> The therapist must start with the full realization that the client does not really intend to give up drugs as a way of life. During the first half of the first session the therapist must listen very intently. Then, somewhere in midsession, using all the rigorous training, therapeutic acumen, and the third, fourth, fifth, and sixth ears, the therapist discerns some unresolved wish, some long-gone dream that is still residing deep in that human being, and then the therapist pulls it out and ignites the client with a desire to somehow look at that dream again. This is not easy, because if the right nerve is not touched, the therapist loses the client [p. 1123].

It is not just a question of managing problems but of developing or, in this case, reigniting and redeveloping, opportunities.

**LISTENING TO AND UNDERSTANDING CLIENT-RELATED REALITIES
BEYOND EMPATHY**

A client's vision of and feelings about himself, others, and the world is something quite real and can be understood, but this does not mean that it is all of reality. Helpers' understanding of clients, as a result of attending, listening, and being with their clients, is not limited to getting a feeling for the world of their clients—even the half-experienced world addressed by advanced empathic listening. For instance, if a client believes herself to be ugly when in reality she is beautiful, her experience of herself as ugly is real and needs to be listened to and understood. But her experience of herself, however important as a subjective reality, does not square with *what is*. The latter, too, needs to be listened to and understood.

Since it is probably impossible to set one's own critical faculties aside completely, empathic listening is most often a question of emphasis. That is, the emphasis is on listening for understanding rather than listening for evaluation. Furthermore, basic empathic listening and understanding is called basic because it lays the groundwork for other kinds of understanding. In the example above, listening to and understanding the woman's experience of herself as ugly has priority. The client's experience is the starting point of the helping process.

Identifying and Handling Bias in Listening

Listening is not as easy as it sounds (Wills, 1978). Large corporations not known for spending their money readily on psychological education and training currently spend a great deal training their employees to be better listeners, because they believe good listening contributes to productivity. One company gives the following reasons for its extensive program:

> Good listeners think more broadly—because they hear and understand more facts and points of view. They make better innovators. Because listeners look at problems with fresh eyes, and combine what they learn in more unlikely ways, they are more apt to hit upon truly startling ideas. Ultimately, good listeners attune themselves more closely to where the world is going—and the products, talents, and techniques it needs to get there.

They claim that helping the members of their organization become more effective listeners has (1) improved the quality of working life, (2) helped to increase productivity, and (3) helped the members of the organization become more creative. In a word, these organizations appreciate the contributions good listening makes to *creativity*, a factor that is critical to effective helping. However, there are obstacles to good listening. Here are some of the principal forms of defective listening.

Inadequate listening.   In conversation it is easy for us to be distracted from what other people are saying. We get involved in our own thoughts or begin to think about what we are going to say in reply to the other. Then, as discussed in Chapter Two, we may get the "You're not listening to me!" complaint. Suffice it to say that the various forms of inadequate listening are part and parcel of everyday life.

Helpers can become preoccupied with themselves and their own needs in ways that keep them from listening fully to their clients. Consider the following possibilities:

- *Attraction.* You find a client either quite attractive or quite unattractive. You pay more attention to what you are feeling about the client than to what the client is saying.
- *Physical condition.* You are tired or sick. Without realizing it, you tune out some of the things the client is saying.
- *Concerns.* You are preoccupied with your own concerns. For instance, you keep thinking about the argument you've just had with your spouse.
- *Overeagerness.* You are so eager to respond that you listen to only a part of what the client has to say. You become preoccupied with your responses rather than with the client's revelations.
- *Similarity of problems.* The problems the client is dealing with are quite similar to your own. As the client talks, your mind wanders to the ways in which what is being said applies to you and your situation.
- *Differences.* The client and his or her experience is very different from you and your experiences. This lack of communality is distracting.

You can probably think of other ways in which you might be distracted from listening. The point is that listening fully is not as easy as it seems. Since there are so many ways in which you can be distracted, you must work at listening.

Evaluative listening.   Most people, even when they listen attentively, listen *evaluatively.* That is, as they listen they are judging the merits of what the other person is saying in terms of good/bad, right/wrong, acceptable/unacceptable, like/dislike, relevant/irrelevant, and so forth. They might also be making similar judgments about the *person* of the speaker. Helpers are not exempt from this universal tendency, but they best realize that they, too, are prone to judge and are able to develop a habit of nonevaluative listening.

This is not to say that all evaluation of what the client says and does is dysfunctional. Understanding the client's point of view is not the same as accepting it. Indeed, judging that a point of view, once understood, needs to be expanded or transcended or that a pattern of behavior, once appreciated, needs to be altered can be a productive form of evaluative listening. For instance, helpers might "hear" patterns of unused or underused resources as they listen to clients tell their stories. We will return to this point when challenging the client is discussed, in Step I-C.

Filtered listening.   It is probably impossible to listen to other people in a completely unbiased way. Through socialization we develop a variety of filters through which we listen to ourselves, others, and the world around us. Hall (1977) notes: "One of the functions of culture is to provide a highly selective screen between man and the outside world. In its many forms, culture therefore designates what we pay attention to and what we ignore. This screening provides structure for the world" (p. 85). As he indicates, this process has a positive function: we need filters to provide a structure for ourselves as we interact with the world. But personal, familial, sociological, and cultural filters also introduce various forms of bias into our listening—and do so without our being aware of it.

The stronger the cultural filters, the greater the likelihood of bias. For instance, a White, middle-class helper probably uses White, middle-class filters in listening to others. This may make little difference if the client is also White and middle-class, but if the helper is listening to a well-to-do Oriental with high social status in his or her community, to a Black person from an urban ghetto, or to a poor White person from a rural area, the helper's cultural filters might introduce biases that would impede his or her ability to listen and understand.

Prejudices, whether conscious or not, are dysfunctional filters. You may harbor some kind of prejudice toward the client. You pigeonhole him or her because of gender, race, sexual orientation, nationality, social status, religious persuasion, political preference, lifestyle, and the like.

Psychological theories, models, and constructs can also constitute dysfunctional filters. For instance, if my sole assessment model suggests that all problems in living are ultimately interpersonal problems (however important such problems may be), my listening can be truncated. I don't hear valuable, even essential, information. If you are being trained as a counselor or clinical psychologist, it is quite likely that you have taken or will take at least one course in psychopathology or abnormal human behavior. The models or frameworks for understanding deviant behavior that you are taught add to the "filters" through which you listen to others, especially to clients. Unless you are careful, "psychopathology" filters can play too strong a role in your listening; you can begin to interpret too much of what you hear as abnormal human behavior. What you have learned may help you to organize what you hear but may also distort your listening. Effective helpers realize that even otherwise useful filters can distort the messages of others.

On the other hand, helpers can develop filters in terms of frameworks to help them listen in more focused ways. For instance, developmental frameworks dealing with the normative stages, tasks, and crises of life can help counselors to understand more easily and fully clients' concerns. Although such frameworks are not the subject matter of this book, some of them will be reviewed briefly in the next chapter.

Sympathetic listening.   Often clients are people in pain or people who have been victimized by others or by society itself. Such clients can arouse feelings of sympathy in helpers, sympathy strong enough to distort the stories being told. For instance, there is something intrinsically human about feelings of sympathy (not to mention anger) that arise in a helper as he or she listens to a woman's story of marital abuse. But sympathy is a two-edged sword that can blind a helper to nuances in the story that need to be understood if the client is to be helped. This is especially true because the abusing party is not there. Helping this client means helping her understand her part in the overall problem situation and helping her set problem-managing goals and choose goal-oriented means that are under her control. Sympathy has an unmistakable and ineradicable place in human transactions, but its "use"—if that doesn't sound too inhuman—is limited in helping. It cannot take the place of empathy.

Becoming Productively Self-Conscious in the Helping Process

To be an effective helper, you need to listen not only to the client but also to yourself when you are with a client. This helps you identify what is standing in the way of your being with and listening to the client. It is a positive form of self-consciousness. For instance, some years ago a friend of mine who had been in and out of mental hospitals for a few years and whom I had not seen for over six months showed up unannounced one evening at my apartment. He was in a highly excited state. A torrent of ideas, some outlandish, some brilliant, flowed nonstop from him. I sincerely wanted to be with him as best I could. I started by more or less naturally following the "rules" of attending outlined earlier in this chapter, but I kept catching myself at the far end of the couch on which we were both sitting, with my arms and legs crossed. I think that I was, almost literally, defending myself from this torrent of ideas. I would untwist my arms and legs only to find them crossed again ten minutes later. It was hard work being with him. And, in retrospect, I realize I was concerned for my own security. Rogers (1980) makes the point clearly:

> In some sense it [empathic listening and being with] means that you lay aside your self; this can only be done by persons who are secure enough in themselves that they know they will not get lost in what may turn out to be the strange and bizarre world of the other, and that they can comfortably return to their own world when they wish [p. 143].

This ability to focus almost exclusively on a client while forgetting oneself and then to return to productive self-consciousness comes with both experience and maturity.

Skilled helpers ask themselves from time to time during helping sessions whether there is anything affecting their ability to be with and listen to their clients. They listen to their own verbal and nonverbal behavior for hints of bias, self-preoccupation, and distraction. Once they discover the ways in which they are being distracted, they do what is necessary to be with and listen to clients more fully.

■

Tracy was a new counselor at the high school. He was from a White, middle-class background. He found himself somewhat disoriented the first time he counseled a Black student. After the first session, he spent some time with Art, a Black counselor, who helped him identify what was preventing him from being with and listening to the student. What he discovered was that he was afraid. He was afraid that his own background would keep him from doing a good job. He was also afraid that the Black student might resent being counseled by a White. Once he worked through his fears, he was in a much better position to be with and listen to Black students.

■

Skilled helpers monitor the quality of their attending and listening. They also realize that probably no one can listen to another in a completely unbiased and undistracted way. Box 3–2 summarizes, in evaluation question form, the main points related to effective listening.

■ Box 3–2. Listening—Evaluation Questions

- Am I reading the client's nonverbal behaviors and seeing how they modify what he or she is saying verbally?
- Am I careful not to overinterpret this or that facial expression or gesture?
- Am I listening carefully to what the client is saying verbally, noticing the mix of experiences, behaviors, and feelings discussed?
- Am I listening carefully to the client's point of view, even when I sense that this point of view needs to be challenged or transcended?
- Do I move beyond empathic listening, carefully noting the ways in which the client exaggerates, contradicts himself or herself, misinterprets reality, holds things back, and so forth?
- Do I engage in such transempathic listening without prejudice to my empathic understanding of the client and his or her perceived world?
- Am I aware of my biases and how they affect my ability to listen?
- Do I listen to what is going on inside myself as I interact with the client?
- What distracts me from listening more carefully and what can I do to manage these distractions?

Four

Empathy and Probing

∎

■ Basic Empathy as a Communication Skill

Empathy is the ability to enter into and understand the world of another person and to communicate this understanding to him or her. There are three levels of empathy. At its deepest, it is a "way of being" (Rogers, 1975, 1980), a way of "being with" others, a way of appreciating the nuances and complexities of their worlds. Second, it is an extremely useful mode of professional presence, a mode of professional contact with clients. Clients are complex, they can *be* in many different ways. Mature helpers develop a sensitivity to this complexity without letting it overwhelm them. Third, it is a communication skill that can be learned and used but the technology of communicating empathy will be hollow unless it is an expression of the helper's way of being.

A great deal has been written about empathy in the field of therapeutic psychology and the training of helpers (for instance, Barrett-Lennard, 1981; Berger, 1984; Clark, 1980; Gladstein, 1983; Gladstein & Feldstein, 1983; Hackney, 1978; Rogers, 1975; Scott, 1984). Gladstein (1983), in a stimulating article, reviews the literature and suggests applications to the field of helping; he finds two kinds of empathy discussed. *Emotional empathy* is the ability to be affected emotionally by another person's state. For instance, I become sad, to a greater or lesser degree, when I become aware of the misfortunes and sadness of others. On the other hand, *role-taking empathy* is the ability to understand another person's state, condition, frame of reference, or point of view. But there is yet a third way of looking at empathy: as a *communication skill*, it is the ability to communicate one's community of feeling (emotional empathy) and/or the understandings that flow from role taking (role-taking empathy).

The ongoing debate about whether and to what degree empathy is useful in the helping process is due, at least in part, to confusing those three ways of looking at empathy. In this book, role-taking empathy is emphasized as critical to the helping model, though the ability to be affected by clients' states and conditions is not excluded. There is a kind of natural flow in which role-taking empathy becomes emotional empathy. After reviewing the literature on empathy and his own 30 years of counseling experience, Gladstein concludes that role-taking empathy is helpful in initiating the helping process, establishing rapport and developing closeness, helping clients identify problems, and helping them explore themselves and their problem situations. Tyler, Pargament, and Gatz (1983) summarize the centrality of empathy to the helping process when they say, "In fact, professionals may be unable to bring their perspectives to bear until they understand their clients' perspectives" (p. 391).

Everything said here about empathy as a communication skill pre-supposes the deeply human issues discussed under the topics of attending and listening. Helper-technicians could deliver the mechanics of basic empathy, but without empathy as a "way of being" would run the risk of being the "hollow men" of T. S. Eliot's poem. Empathy is far more than a communication technique: it is as rich or as poor as its foundations. It demands maturity of the person who uses it in terms of patience or control of impulsiveness. Gladstein and Feldstein (1983) talk of "cognitive suspension," while Berger (1984) talks about the "ability to tolerate a state of puzzlement." Effective helpers know that understanding a client is a qualitative rather than a quantitative experience.

If attending and listening are the skills that enable helpers to get in touch with the world of the client, empathy is the skill that enables them to communicate their understanding of that world to the client. Since it is a skill, it is something that can be learned. However, communicating understanding does not necessarily mean putting it into words. Given enough time, people can establish what I call "empathic relationships" with one another in which understanding is communicated in a variety of rich and subtle, but nonverbal, ways. A simple glance across a room as one spouse sees the other trapped in an unwanted conversation can communicate worlds of understanding. The glance says, "I know you feel caught. I know you don't want to hurt the other person's feelings. I can feel the struggle going on inside. I know you'd like me to rescue you, if I can do so tactfully." People with empathic relationships express empathy through actions. An arm around the shoulders of someone who has just suffered a defeat can convey both support and empathy. I was in the home of a poverty-stricken family when the father came bursting through the front door shouting "I got the job!" His wife, without saying a word, went to the refrigerator, took out a bottle of beer with a makeshift label reading "champagne," and offered it to her husband. Beer never tasted so good.

Empathic participation in the world of another obviously admits of degrees. As a helper, you must be able to enter the world of a client deeply enough to understand his or her struggle with problem situations or search for opportunities at a deep enough level to make your partic-ipation in problem management and opportunity development valid and substantial. If your help is based on an incorrect or invalid understanding of the client, your helping may lead him or her astray. If your under-standing is valid but superficial, you might miss the central issues of the client's life.

Some people do enter caringly into the world of another and are "with" him or her, but are unable to communicate understanding, especially through words. Others develop the skill or technology of communicating empathic understanding but have little to communicate because their experiencing of or with the other person is superficial. It is unfortunate, but the direct communication of empathy in conversation is, in my experience, an improbable event. Helpers need both the depth of human contact and understanding *and* the ability to communicate it in both verbal and nonverbal ways. The following discussion of the microskills needed for the communication of empathy is based on the assumption that the helper enters the world of the client through attending, observing, listening, and "being with" at a deep enough level to make a difference.

The Three Dimensions of Communication Skills in the Helping Process

The communication skills involved in responding to and engaging in dialogue with clients have three components or dimensions: awareness, technical ability, and assertiveness.

Awareness. Empathy, probing, and the different forms of challenging all have an awareness dimension. They are based on your *perceptions* of the experiences, feelings, and behaviors of the client and of your own experiences, feelings, and behaviors as you interact with the client. By attending, observing, and listening, you gather the data you need to respond intelligently to clients. If your perceptions are inaccurate, your communication skills are flawed at their root.

■

Jenny is counseling Frank in a community mental health center. Frank is scared about what is going to happen to him in the counseling process, but he does not talk about it. Jenny realizes his discomfort but does not identify it as fear. She finally says, "Frank, I'm wondering what's making you so angry right now." Since Frank does not feel angry, he says nothing. He's startled by what she says and feels even more insecure. Jenny takes his silence as a confirmation of his "anger." She tries to get him to talk about it.

■

As we have seen, attending and active listening are the bases of the kind of perceptiveness needed in helping skills. Helpers who fail to attend and to listen well or who, though they do attend and listen, fail to understand the client may command the two dimensions described below, but because of their lack of perceptiveness their responses are impaired.

Technical ability. Once you are aware of what skill is called for in the helping process, you need to be able to deliver it. For instance, if you are aware that a client is anxious and confused because this is his first visit to a helper, it does little good if your understanding remains locked up inside you.

■

Frank and Jenny end up arguing about his "anger." Frank finally gets up and leaves. Jenny, of course, takes this as a sign that she was right in the first place. Frank goes to see his minister. The minister sees quite clearly that Frank is scared and confused. But he in turn does not know what to do with his understanding. He does not have the know-how to translate his perceptions into meaningful interactions with Frank. As Frank talks, his minister nods and says "uh-huh" quite a bit. He is fully present to Frank and listens intently, but he does not know how to respond.

■

You need to *know how* to communicate your perceptions to clients so as to facilitate their participation in the helping process. Accurate perceptions are useless without the skill of delivering them to the client.

Assertiveness.   High-level awareness and excellent technical ability are meaningless unless they are actually used when called for. Certainly, to be assertive in the helping process without awareness and without know-how is to court disaster. For instance, Jenny confronted Frank in a punitive, heavy-handed way (lack of know-how), challenging behavior that she did not fully understand (lack of awareness), and, as a result, her intervention did more harm than good. On the other hand, if you see that a client needs new perspectives on his or her problem situation, and you know how to present these new perspectives in a responsible way, yet you fail to do so, you are deficient in the third dimension of your communication skills.

■

Edna, a young helper in the Student Development Office, is in the middle of her second session with Aurelio, a graduate student. It soon becomes clear to her that he is making sexual overtures to her. In her training she did quite well in challenging her fellow trainees. The feedback she got from them and the trainer indicated that she challenged others directly and caringly. But now she feels immobilized. She does not want to hurt Aurelio or embarrass herself. She tries to ignore his seductive behavior, but Aurelio takes silence to mean consent.

■

In this case awareness and technical ability are both wasted due to a lack of assertiveness. In my experience, this lack of assertiveness is a critical issue for many people while training to be helpers.

The Technology of Basic Empathy as a Communication Skill

Since empathy is not only a way of being with others, as Rogers notes, but also a communication skill, the "technology" of the skill needs to be understood. Basic empathy involves listening carefully to the client and then communicating understanding of what the client is feeling and of the experiences and behaviors underlying those feelings. This skill is useful in every stage and step of the helping process. It's the helper's way of saying, "I'm with you, I've been listening carefully to what you've been saying and expressing, and I'm checking to see if my understanding is accurate." Basic empathy is not an attempt to dig down into what the client might be only half-saying or saying implicitly. Since that kind of advanced empathy often has a challenging edge to it, it will be discussed in a later chapter on challenging. Here are a few examples of basic empathy.

A single, middle-aged woman who has been unable to keep a job shares her frustration with a counselor.

CLIENT: I've been to other counselors and nothing has ever really worked. I don't even know why I'm trying again. But things are so bad—I just have to get a job. I guess something has to be done, so I'm trying it all over again.

HELPER: You're here with mixed feelings. You're not sure that our sessions will help you get a job and keep it, but you feel you have to try something.

CLIENT: Yes, "something," but I don't know what the something is. What can I get here that will help me get a job? Or keep a job?

A woman on public assistance seeking a divorce and needing legal assistance has been told that counseling is a prerequisite for receiving assistance.

CLIENT: I need a lawyer. You're not a lawyer. Everybody gives you the runaround. I know what I want. Do these people think I'm crazy to want a divorce? I'd be crazy not to want a divorce!

HELPER: Since you know you want a divorce, a lawyer would seem to make much more sense than a counselor.

CLIENT: It's certainly stupid to me. Maybe you know something that I don't. If you do, you'd better tell me now.

A young woman visits the student services center at her college.

CLIENT: And so here I am, two months pregnant. I don't want to be pregnant. I'm not married, and I don't even love the father. To tell the truth, I don't even think I like him. Oh Lord, this is something that happens to other people—not me! I wake up thinking this whole thing is unreal.

HELPER: You're still so amazed that it's almost impossible to accept that it's true.

CLIENT: Amazed? I'm stupefied! And yet I have no one to blame but myself. Maybe that's it. I feel so alone in all of this.

In these interchanges the helper says what could have been said by the client. Each response stays within the immediate frame of reference of the client. The client's response to the helper's empathy is given to underscore the fact that there is no such thing as an empathic response that is good in itself. The purpose of empathy is both to help the client feel understood and to help the client move on.

The technology of basic empathy involves translating your understanding of the client's experiences, behaviors, and feelings into a response that shares that understanding with the client. For instance, if a student comes to you, sits down, looks at the floor, hunches over, and haltingly tells you that he has just failed a test, that his girlfriend has told him she doesn't want to see him anymore, and that he might lose his part-time job because he has been "goofing off," you might respond to him by saying something like this:

HELPER: You feel pretty miserable right now because you've been deserted and because you've done yourself in on your job.
CLIENT: I keep kicking myself because I've been so blind and stupid. Damn!

You see that he is both agitated and depressed (affect) and you understand in an initial fashion what has happened to him (experiences) and what he has done (behaviors) to contribute to the problem situation, and then you communicate to him your understanding of his world. This is basic empathy. If your perceptions are correct, it can be called *accurate* empathy. In this example the client's story contains all three elements: experience, behavior, and feeling.

Or let us say that a client, after a few sessions with you spread out over six months, says something like this:

CLIENT (talking in an animated way): I really think things couldn't be better. I'm doing very well at my new job and my husband is not just putting up with it—he thinks it's great! He and I are getting along better than ever, even sexually, and I never expected that. We're both working at our marriage. I guess I'm just waiting for the bubble to burst.
HELPER: Things are going so well, especially with your job and in your marriage, that it seems almost too good to be true.
CLIENT: I can make it be true. I can see now that it's not just a question of luck. I used to think that most of life was a question of luck.

This client, too, talks about experiences and behaviors and expresses feelings, the flavor of which the helper captures in her empathic response. The response seems to be a useful one, because the client moves on.

THE CORE MESSAGE

In order to respond empathically, you can ask yourself as you listen to the client: *What is the core message or messages being expressed* in terms of feelings and the experiences and behaviors that underlie these feelings?

Once you feel you have identified the core messages, you check out your understanding with the client. The formula, "You feel . . . because . . ." (used in the first of the two examples above) gets at the heart of the technology in the communication of basic empathy.

Feelings. "You feel . . . " is to be followed by the correct family of emotions and the correct intensity. For instance, the statements "You feel hurt," and "You feel relieved," and "You feel great" specify different families of emotion, while the statements "You feel annoyed," "You feel angry," and "You feel furious" specify different degrees of intensity within the same family.

The emotions a client expresses in the interview may or may not be the ones associated with the problem situations. For instance, in the interview a client may express anger over the fact that he gives in to fear when talking with his father. If your empathic response picks up the fear but not the anger, the client may feel misunderstood. "You feel angry because you let fear get the best of you in your interactions with your father" is the correct response. There is a difference between clients' *talking about* feelings and emotions that took place in the past and their *expressing* feelings and emotions in the interview.

Experiences and behaviors. The "because . . . " is to be followed by an indication of the experiences and/or behaviors that underlie the client's feelings. "You feel angry because he stole your course notes and you let him get away with it" specifies both the experience and the behavior (in this case, a failure to act) that give rise to the feeling.

> "You feel sad because moving means leaving all your friends."
> "You feel anxious because the results of the biopsy aren't in yet."
> "You feel frustrated because the social services center keeps making you do things you don't want to do."
> "You feel annoyed with yourself because you didn't even reach the simple goals you set for yourself."
> "You feel hopeless because even your best efforts don't seem to help you lose weight."
> "You feel relieved because sticking to the regime of diet and exercise means that you probably won't need the operation."
> "You feel angry with me because I keep pushing all the responsibility onto you."

Of course, the exact words of the formula are not important; they merely provide a framework for communicating understanding to the client. Though many people in training use the formula to help themselves communicate understanding of core messages, experienced helpers tend to avoid formulas and use whatever wording best communicates their understanding. As Berger (1984) notes, empathy is contextual and integrating. Any given empathic response is not based solely on the client's words and nonverbal behavior. It takes into account everything that has happened in the helping relationship up to this point; everything that "surrounds" a client's statement.

Reasons for Becoming Good at Empathy

In interpersonal communication, empathy is a tool of civility. Making an effort to enter the frame of reference of another transmits a message of respect. Empathy is also an unobtrusive tool for helping clients to explore themselves and their problem situations. The understood client is influenced to move on, to explore more widely or more deeply. Empathy can play an important part in establishing rapport with clients, and since it is a way of staying in touch with clients and their experiences, behaviors, and feelings, it can provide support throughout the helping process. It is never wrong to make sure that you are in touch with the frame of reference of the client. Finally, empathy acts as a kind of a communications lubricant; it encourages and facilitates dialogue.

There are certain criteria for judging the quality of empathic responses. First, they are effective if they help develop and maintain a good working relationship with the client. Second, they are effective if they help the client explore the problem situation in terms of relevant experiences, behaviors, and feelings more fully. Consider the following interchange between a trainee and her trainer.

TRAINEE: I don't think I'm going to make a good counselor. The other people in the program seem brighter than I am. Others seem to be picking up the knack of empathy faster than I am. I'm still afraid of responding directly to others, even with empathy. I have to reevaluate my participation in the program.

TRAINER: You're feeling pretty inadequate and it's getting you down, perhaps even enough to think of quitting.

TRAINEE: And yet I know that giving up is part of the problem, part of my style. I'm not the brightest, but I'm certainly not dumb either. The way I compare myself to others is not very useful. I know that I've been picking up some of the skills; I do attend and listen well. I'm perceptive, even though at times I have a hard time sharing my perceptions with others.

When the trainer "hits the mark," the trainee moves forward and explores her problem a bit more fully. Empathy as a way of "being with" others is a human value and needs no justification, but empathy as a communication skill is instrumental—that is, good—to the degree it helps a client persist in the helping process and move on toward problem management.

In most of the examples given so far, the helper has responded to both affect and content; to both feelings *and* the experiences and behaviors underlying the feelings. While this might ordinarily be the best kind of response, helpers may want to emphasize feelings *or* experiences *or* behaviors. Consider the following example.

CLIENT: This week I tried to get my wife to see the doctor, but she refused, even though she fainted a couple of times. The kids were out of school, so they were underfoot almost constantly. I haven't been able to finish a report my boss expects from me next Monday.

COUNSELOR: It's been a lousy week.

CLIENT: When things are lousy at home and at work, there's no other place for me to relax. I'm beginning to see why some men have mistresses. It's not just the sex: it's a haven.

Here the counselor chooses to emphasize the feelings of the client because she believes that what is uppermost in his consciousness right now are his feelings of frustration and irritation. The emphasis with another client might be quite different:

CLIENT: My dad yelled at me all the time last year about how I dress. But just last week I heard him telling someone how nice I looked. He yells at my sister about the same things he ignores when my younger brother does them. Sometimes he's really nice with my mother and other times he's just awful—demanding, grouchy, sarcastic.

COUNSELOR: It's his inconsistency that bothers you.

CLIENT: Right, it's hard for all of us to know where we stand. I hate coming home when I'm not sure which "dad" will be there.

In this response the counselor emphasizes the client's experience of his father, for she feels that this is the core of the client's message. The point is that effective helpers use a variety of empathic responses to help clients explore themselves more thoroughly. The principal question to address is always what the client's core message is.

If the client is easily threatened by a discussion of his or her feelings, Hackney and Cormier (1979) suggest that, in responding, the helper start by emphasizing experiences and behaviors and proceed only gradually to a discussion of feelings. Furthermore, the authors suggest that one potential way of getting at such a client's feelings is to have the helper say what he or she might feel in similar circumstances.

CLIENT: My mother is always trying to make a little kid out of me. And I'm in my mid-thirties! Last week, in front of a group of my friends, she brought out my rubber boots and an umbrella and gave me a little talk on how to dress for bad weather.

COUNSELOR: If she had treated me that way, I think I probably would've been pretty angry.

CLIENT: It's hard for me to get angry with her . . . or, at least it's hard to talk about getting angry with her.

Since this client does not feel she has been accused of being angry with her mother, she is better disposed to talk about her more sensitive feelings.

For some clients, fear of intimacy is part of the problem situation. This can include the kind of intimacy involved in the helping process. Since empathy is a kind of intimacy, too much empathy too soon can inhibit rather than facilitate helping. Warmth, closeness, and intimacy are not goals in themselves. The goal of Stage I is to help clients explore themselves and their problems. If empathy, or too much empathy too soon, stands in the way of this goal, it should be avoided.

Empathy is important for the *movement* it brings to the helping process. If it is used well by helpers, clients explore their experiences, behaviors, and feelings, and better understand the relationships among all three. Figure 4–1 indicates this movement both when helpers are on the mark and when they fail to grasp what the client has expressed. If the helper's empathic response is accurate, the client often tends to confirm its accuracy by a nod or some other nonverbal cue or by a phrase such as "that's right" or "exactly." This is followed by a further, usually more specific, elaboration of the problem situation.

HELPER: So the neighborhood in which you live pushes you toward a whole variety of behaviors that can get you in trouble.
CLIENT: You bet it does! For instance, everyone's selling drugs. You not only end up using them, but you begin to think about pushing them. It's just too easy.

When the helper again responds with empathy, this leads to the next cycle. The problem situation becomes increasingly clear in terms of specific experiences, behaviors, and feelings.

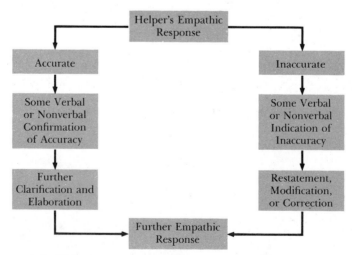

Figure 4–1. The movement caused by accurate and inaccurate empathy

When the helper is less than accurate, all is not lost. A similar cycle can take place, but this time the client first indicates in some verbal or nonverbal way that the helper has not hit the mark, modifies or corrects what the helper has said, and finally elaborates. In the following example, the client is a survivor of a flash flood that destroyed his home.

HELPER: So you don't want to do a lot of things you used to do before the flood. For instance, you don't want to socialize much any more.

CLIENT (pausing a long time): Well, I'm not sure that it's a question of wanting to or not. I mean that it takes much more energy to do a lot of things. It takes so much energy to phone others to get together. It takes so much energy sometimes being with others that I just don't try. It's as if there's a weight on my shoulders a lot of the time.

A client says that it is not a question of motivation but one of energy. The difference is important. If you are empathic in the way you present yourself to clients, they will not be put off by occasional inaccuracies on your part.

Some Hints for Improving the Quality of Empathy

Give yourself time to think.   Beginners sometimes jump in too quickly with an empathic response when the client pauses. "Too quickly" means that they do not give themselves enough time to reflect on what the client has just said in order to identify the core message being communicated. As mentioned earlier, Carl Rogers (Rogers, Perls, & Ellis, 1965), who pioneered the use of accurate empathy in the helping process, uses basic empathy masterfully in one of his training films. In his interactions with the client, he always gives himself time to assimilate and reflect on what the client says before responding. Since he attends and listens carefully and then gives himself time to formulate a response, his responses are most thoughtful.

You may not find it easy to pause and reflect before responding. During the pause, you can ask yourself, "What feelings is this person expressing?" "What is the core message?" This does not mean losing your spontaneity. You should speak up any time you think you can help, even if it means "interrupting" the client. In the film, Rogers gives the client some sign, either verbal or nonverbal, that he would like to respond. For instance, he says "Let me see if I've got what you're saying."

Use short responses.   I find that the helping process goes best when I engage the client in a *dialogue,* not when I make speeches or allow the client to ramble. In a dialogue the helper's responses are relatively frequent but they should also be lean and trim. In trying to be accurate, the beginner may become longwinded, sometimes speaking *longer* than the client in trying to elaborate an adequate response. This often happens when the helper tries to respond too quickly.

CLIENT: I have never been very spontaneous in social situations. Since I'm shy, I kind of stand off to the side and wait to see how I can get into the conversation. As a result, the conversation often passes me by when I'm ready to say something. Then I'm not even at the same place in the conversation as the others. I've been inside myself and don't know what's been going on.

COUNSELOR (jumping in right away): You're really shy and that cuts down on your spontaneity. It shows up especially when a group is standing around talking. You are listening all right: you know what people are saying. But then you begin to ask youself, "What should I say? I shouldn't stand around here dumb." But by the time you think of what to say, it's just too late. No, it's worse than that. Now you've lost the thread of the conversation and it's twice as hard trying to get back in. Your shyness backfires on you in more than one way.

CLIENT: Uh, yeah. . . . I guess that's it. . . .

This response might be accurate, but it is probably not very facilitative. It places the focus on the counselor's attempts to understand rather than on the client's self-exploration. The result is that the client is smothered by all that the helper has to say, becomes lost and confused, and finds it difficult to move forward. The client can even end up trying to understand the helper. Again, the question "What is the core of what this person is saying to me?" can help you make your responses short, concrete, and accurate. Note, however, that since you cannot respond to everything the client says and since you are making a judgment as to what the central messages are, you are providing direction in the helping process. That is, even in your empathic responses you are providing social influence. This underscores how important it is to listen carefully and stay close to the experience of the client.

Gear your response to the client.   If a client speaks animatedly with the helper, telling her of his elation over various successes in his life, and she replies accurately, but in a flat, dull voice, her response is not fully empathic. This does not mean that helpers should mimic their clients. It means that part of being with the client is sharing in a reasonable way in his or her emotional tone. Helpers are also more empathic when their language is in tune with the language of the client. Consider the following somewhat extreme example.

TEN-YEAR-OLD CLIENT: My teacher started picking on me from the first day of class. I don't fool around any more than anyone else in class, but she gets me anytime I do. I think she's picking on me because she doesn't like me. She doesn't yell at Bill Smith and he acts funnier than I do.

COUNSELOR: You're perplexed. You wonder why she singles you out for so much discipline.

The counselor's response is accurate in a sense, but it is not the kind of language that communicates understanding to a 10-year-old. The following response would have have much more meaning for the child:

COUNSELOR: You're mad because she seems unfair in the way she picks on you.

The helper's choice of words reflects his or her ability to assume the client's frame of reference. However, use caution: helpers should not adopt language far from their own just to be on the client's wavelength. Imagine a middle-class probation officer responding in the following manner to a client who is tempted to steal in order to pay off a debt to someone he fears.

HELPER: Unless you find some bread, man, that cat's going to get you wasted.

Helpers can use informal language without adoping dialects that are simply not their own.

Some Common Problems in Communicating Basic Accurate Empathy

Though many of the following problems affect the beginning helper, they are not restricted to beginners.

USING POOR SUBSTITUTES FOR EMPATHY

There are a number of poor substitutes for empathy. Peter, the client in the next example, is a college freshman. This is his second visit to a counselor in the student services center. After talking about a number of concerns, he says

PETER (speaking in halting voice as he looks at the floor and clasps his hands tightly between his knees): What seems to be really bothering me is a problem with sex. I don't even know whether I'm a man or not and I'm in college. I don't go out with women my age. I don't even think I want to. I may . . . well, I may even be gay. . . . Uh, I don't know.

The following are examples of poor responses.

- *No response.* First of all, the counselor might say nothing. Generally, if the client says something significant, respond to it, however briefly. Otherwise the client might think that what he or she has just said doesn't merit any kind of response.
- *A question.* The counselor might ask something like, "How long has this been bothering you, Peter?" This response ignores the emotion Peter is experiencing. Since a question elicits further information, it implies that Peter has not said anything worth responding to. Probing is in order only after significant messages have been understood.
- *A cliché.* The counselor might say, "Many people struggle with sexual identity throughout their lives." This is a cliché. It completely misses the feelings of the client and deals only with the content of his statement, and even then only in the vaguest way. The impact of such a

response is "You don't really have a problem at all—at least not a serious one."

- *An interpretation.* A counselor might say something like, "This sexual thing is probably really just a symptom, Peter. I've got a hunch that you're not really accepting yourself." This is a poor and misplaced attempt to offer advanced empathy. The counselor fails to respond to the client's feelings and also distorts the content of the communication. The response implies that what is really important is hidden from the client.
- *Moving to action.* Another counselor might say, "There are a few videotapes on sexuality during the college years that I'd like to have you take a look at." This counselor also ignores Peter's feelings and jumps to an action program in sex education. It well may be that Peter could use some good input on sexual development, but this is neither the time nor way to do it.

All of these responses are poor substitutes for empathy. A more skilled counselor might have said something like this:

COUNSELOR: You've got a lot of misgivings about just where you stand with yourself sexually, but it's not easy to talk about it.
PETER: I'm having a terrible time talking about it. I'm even shaking right now.

This counselor responds with basic empathy. It gives the client the opportunity to deal with his immediate anxiety.

COUNTERFEITS OF ACCURATE EMPATHY

Some responses look something like basic empathy but are really distortions of it.

Inaccurate empathy.   Sometimes helpers' responses are simply inaccurate because they fail to attend and listen well. Consider the following response to Peter.

COUNSELOR: You're eager to start exploring your sexual preferences and make some decisions.

Peter is not eager and has said nothing about making decisions. All helpers can be inaccurate at times. If any given response is inaccurate, the client often lets the counselor know in a variety of ways: he or she may stop dead, fumble around, go off on a new tangent, tell the counselor "That's not exactly what I meant," or even try to provide empathy for the counselor and get him or her back on the track. Even the best helpers can miss the mark. What can counselors do about inaccuracy? They must learn to pick up cues from their clients that indicate that they have been inaccurate and then work to get back "with" the client.

Pretending to understand. Sometimes helpers find it difficult to understand what their clients are saying even when they are attending fully and listening intently. Clients are sometimes confused, distracted, and in a highly emotional state; all those conditions affect the clarity of what they are saying about themselves. On the other hand, counselors themselves might become distracted and fail to follow the client. If that happens, it is best not to feign understanding; that's phony. Genuineness demands that they admit they are lost and then work to get back on the track again. "I think I've lost you. Could we go over that once more?" If the counselor is confused, it is all right to admit his or her confusion. "I'm sorry. I don't think I got what you just said. Could we go through it a bit more slowly?" Such statements are signs that the counselor thinks it is important to stay with the client. They indicate respect and caring. Admitting that one is lost is infinitely preferable to such clichés as "uh-huh," "ummmm," and "I understand."

If helpers feel that they do not quite understand what clients are trying to express, they should be tentative in their responses and give their clients room to move. In the following example, the helper is tentative and so the client, a teacher having trouble in the classroom, feels free to correct her and give her a clearer picture of what he means.

COUNSELOR: You seem to be saying that your students don't trust you because your emotions change so much from day to day. Is it something like that?

CLIENT: Well, that's partly it. But I also think that the mood of the class changes from day to day, so there are many days when my emotions and theirs just don't seem to mix.

This client feels that he has room to move. The counselor's tentative response helps him clarify what he means. Brammer (1973) calls this process of checking with the client whenever you are confused or unsure "perception checking" (p. 86).

Parroting. Accurate empathy is not mere parroting. The mechanical helper corrupts basic empathy by simply restating what the client has said.

CLIENT: I feel pretty low because all my children have left home and now I'm lonely, with nothing to do.

COUNSELOR: You feel low because the children are gone, you're all alone, and you have nothing to do.

The effective counselor is always looking for the core of what is being expressed by the client; he or she becomes expert in ferreting out that core and communicating it to the client. Empathy, then, is not mere repetition. The effective counselor tries to communicate *understanding* rather than simply mirror what the client has said.

Many people use the terms *empathy* and *reflection* or *rephrasing* inter-changeably. While rephrasing is not the same as parroting, I see a distinction between rephrasing and empathy. When I listen to a client and keep asking myself such questions as "What is this person's point of view?" and "What are the core messages in what this person is saying?" I am engaged in a process that is more than mere reflection. When I am empathic, I am sharing a part of myself—that is, my understanding of the other person. This is not to say that rephrasing and reflection are not useful forms of communication. But empathy, in the sense that Rogers (1980) uses the term, is something more.

It seems that there are individual differences in the role-taking abilities that are central to empathy (Epstein, 1972; Ham, 1980; Hogan, 1969). That is, all people are not equal in the *awareness* dimension of this skill.

> [I]t seems quite reasonable to expect that some counselors' role-taking em-pathic abilities are more "childlike" than "adultlike." Although they may have the intellectual capacity . . . they are still energetically egocentric. In this sense they are acting like young children. Assuming this to be true, it should not surprise us that some therapists are not easily able to learn empathic responses [Gladstein, 1983, p. 477].

This squares with my own experience. However, even those who have moved beyond egocentricity will not learn the skill well unless it becomes part of their day-to-day communication style. Doing the exercises in the manual that accompanies this book and practicing in counselor-training groups can help, but is not enough to incorporate empathy into one's communication style. Empathy that is trotted out, as it were, for helping encounters runs the danger of having a hollow ring to it.

As important as the communication skill of empathy is, it is only one among a number of skills. If overused, it can contribute to the client's reviewing the same issues over and over again. Ideally, helpers are people who appreciate empathy as a "way of being" and who incorporate it into their professional lives. The actual use of the communication skill is geared to the needs of the client. Box 4–1 summarizes the essential uses of basic empathy.

■ Probes

In most of the examples used in the discussion of empathy, clients have demonstrated willingness to explore themselves and their behavior rather freely. Obviously, this is not always the case. While it is essential that helpers respond empathically to their clients when they do reveal themselves, it is also necessary at times to encourage or prompt clients to explore problem situations when they fail to do so spontaneously. Therefore, the ability to use prompts and probes well is another important

---

■ **Box 4–1. Suggestions for the Use of Basic Empathy**

1. Remember that empathy is, ideally, a "way of being" and not just a professional role or communication skill.
2. Attend carefully, both physically and psychologically, and listen to the client's point of view.
3. Try to set aside your biases and judgments for the moment and walk, as it were, in the shoes of your client.
4. As the client speaks, listen for the core messages.
5. Listen to both verbal and nonverbal messages *and* their contexts.
6. Respond fairly frequently, but briefly, to the client's core messages.
7. Be flexible and tentative enough so that the client does not feel pinned down.
8. Be gentle, but keep the client focused on important issues.
9. Respond to the main features of core messages—experiences, behaviors, and feelings—unless there is reason for emphasizing one over the others.
10. Gradually move toward the exploration of sensitive topics and feelings.
11. After responding with empathy, attend carefully to cues that either confirm or deny the accuracy of your response.
12. Determine whether your empathic responses are helping the client remain focused, while developing and clarifying important issues.
13. Note signs of client stress or resistance. Try to judge whether these arise because you are inaccurate or because you are too accurate.
14. Keep in mind that the communication skill of empathy, however important, is a tool to help clients see themselves and their problem situations more clearly with a view to managing them more effectively.

---

skill. Prompts and probes are verbal tactics for helping clients talk about themselves and define their problems more concretely and specifically. As such, they can be used in all the stages of the helping process. They can take different forms.

STATEMENTS THAT ENCOURAGE CLIENTS TO TALK AND CLARIFY

Some people think that all prompts and probes are questions. This need not be the case at all. Too many questions can give a client the feeling of being "grilled." Statements and requests can be used to help clients talk and clarify relevant issues. For example, an involuntary client may come in and then just sit there and fume.

HELPER: I can see that you're angry, but I'm not entirely sure what it's about.

Such statements of their very nature make some demand on the client either to talk or to become more specific. They can relate to the client's experiences, behaviors, feelings, or any combination of the three.

Again, clients' *experiences* are what they see as happening *to* them.

HELPER: I realize now that you often get angry when your mother-in-law stays for more than a day, but I'm still not sure what she does that makes you angry.

HELPER: You feel trapped in the ghetto and want to get out. Maybe you could tell me what it is about living there that gets to you the most.

In these examples the helper's statements place a demand on the client to clarify the experiences that give rise to certain behaviors and feelings. Clients' *behaviors* are what they *do* or *refrain from doing*:

HELPER: The Sundays your husband exercises his visiting rights with the children end in his taking verbal pot shots at you and you get these headaches. I've got a fairly clear picture of what he does when he comes over, but it might help if you could describe what you do.

HELPER: When the diagnosis of cancer came in two weeks ago, you said that you were both relieved, because you knew what you had to face, and depressed. You've mentioned that your behavior has been a bit chaotic since then. Tell me what you've been doing.

In these instances the helper encourages clients to describe their behavior as a way of bringing greater clarity to the problem situation.

Affect refers to the *feelings* and *emotions* clients experience.

HELPER: So *he* got the job you worked your tail off for, and you suspect that your being a woman has a lot to do with it. I imagine that a number of feelings have been bouncing around inside you this past week.

HELPER: When you talk about your wife and what she does, you use fairly positive emotions. For instance, you "appreciate" it when she points out what you do wrong. I haven't heard any negative or fixed feelings yet; maybe it's because there are none.

The helper provides these clients with an opportunity to discuss the feelings that arise from their experiences and behaviors.

QUESTIONS THAT HELP CLIENTS TALK MORE FREELY AND CONCRETELY

Notice that the statements in the previous section could have been put in the form of questions. For instance, "I imagine that a number of feelings have been bouncing around inside you this past week" could have been, "What kinds of feelings have been bouncing around inside you this past week?" The following guidelines can be used when asking questions.

First, when clients are asked too many questions, it can interfere with the *rapport* between helper and client.

I feel certain that we ask too many questions, often meaningless ones. We ask questions that confuse the interviewee, that interrupt him. We ask questions the interviewee cannot possibly answer. We even ask questions we don't want the answers to, and, consequently, we do not hear the answers when forthcoming [Benjamin, 1981, p. 71; the author devotes an entire chapter to the question, its uses, and his misgivings about it].

Turning questions into statements such as those in the previous section helps. Statements are gentler forms of probes than questions, but even probing statements should not be overused.

Second, remember that the goal of questioning is to help the client get clear information that is *related* to the step of the helping process involved. Some helpers use questions to amass information, much of which proves to be irrelevant. Helpers who ask too many questions are often meeting their own needs or working under the assumption that information so amassed will lead in and of itself to more effective management of the problem situation.

Third, when you feel that a question is called for, generally ask *open-ended* questions—that is, questions that require more than a simple "yes" or "no" or similar one-word answer. Not, "Now that you've decided to take early retirement, do you have any plans?" but, "Now that you've decided to take early retirement, what do you plan to do?" Counselors who ask closed questions to which clients respond with one-word answers find themselves asking more and more questions. This is often a problem for beginners. Of course, if a specific piece of information is needed, then a closed question may be used: "How many jobs have you had in the past two years?" Such a question could provide essential background information in a career-counseling session. The point here is not questions in and of themselves but how they can promote or hinder the overall helping process. Too many questions can turn the helping interview into a boring question-and-answer session. One possibility is to have clients ask relevant questions of themselves.

COUNSELOR: What are some of the questions you need to ask yourself if you're to understand what's happening between you and your husband a little better?"

CLIENT: Hmmm. I think I'd have to ask myself, "What do you do that makes him want to drink all the time?" That's a scary question for me.

You can help clients ask relevant, even "impertinent" questions of themselves.

Questions are useful when you are not following what the client is saying.

HELPER: I didn't follow the last part. Could you go over it once more?

HELPER: Could you describe how you feel once more? I'm not sure that I understand.

Some helpers, embarrassed by the fact that they have not understood the client, pretend that they have. Such an approach is neither genuine nor practical. Obviously an overuse of requests for clarification is distracting and makes the helper look inept.

Hackney and Cormier (1979) suggest two other probe-type helper responses that can contribute to uncovering relevant information: the "accent" and "minimal prompts."

THE "ACCENT"

"The accent is a one- or two-word restatement that focuses or brings attention to a preceding client response" (p. 52).

CLIENT: My son and I have a fairly good working relationship now, even though I'm not entirely satisfied.
HELPER: Not *entirely* satisfied?
CLIENT: Well, I should probably say "dissatisfied," because . . .

CLIENT: At the end of the day with the kids and dinner and cleaning up I'm *bushed*.
HELPER: Bushed?
CLIENT: Tired, angry, hurt—he does practically nothing to help me!

In these cases the "accent" helps clients say more fully what they are only half saying.

MINIMAL PROMPTS

Hackney and Cormier (1979) also talk about the "minimal verbal activity" (p. 68) of the helper. This includes such things as "uh-huh," "mmm," "yes," "I see," "ah," "oh," and the like, which often serve as reinforcers or prompts and lead the client into further exploration. Part of Carl Rogers' approach to attending and listening, at least in his films, is a fairly steady use of such prompts.

CLIENT: There are a lot of things I don't like about this school. (Pause)
HELPER: Uh-huh.
CLIENT: For instance, the food in the cafeteria is lousy.

Minimal prompts can also be nonverbal.

CLIENT: He never lets me have my way. We always do what he wants. (Pause)
HELPER nods her head.
CLIENT: Well, I don't mean always, but when I want to do something my way, I have to fight for it. I go along with his suggestions most of the time, but

when I suggest something to do, it's like I have to prove to him that it's worth doing.

CLIENT: I don't know if I can tell you this. I haven't told anyone.
HELPER maintains good eye contact and leans forward a bit.
CLIENT: Well, my brother had sexual relations with me a few times a couple of years ago. I think about it all the time.

In the last chapter it was suggested that as a helper you become aware of the messages your nonverbal behavior communicates. Now you are encouraged to *use* nonverbal forms of communication to prompt the client to explore and concretize the problem situation.

Notice that minimal interventions on the part of counselors help clients use their *own* initiative to clarify what they mean.

Some Cautions in the Use of Probes

It is probably clear that prompts and probes, both verbal and nonverbal, can be overused to the detriment of both rapport and the gathering of relevant information. As noted in an earlier chapter, "self-efficacy" (Bandura, 1977a, 1982) or client self-responsibility is an ideal in the helping process. If you extort information from clients via a constant barrage of probes and prompts, they are unlikely to take more and more responsibility for the problem-solving and opportunity-development process. They are likely to see you as a demanding parent rather than a collaborative consultant. Keep in mind two general principles: (1) once you have used a prompt or probe, let the client take the initiative in exploring the information it yields if at all possible; (2) after using a probe, use basic empathy rather than another probe or series of probes as a way of encouraging further exploration. After all, if a probe is effective, it will yield information that needs to be listened to and understood. Carkhuff, in a workshop, suggested that if helpers find themselves asking two questions in a row, it might just be that they have asked two stupid questions. Box 4–2 is a checklist for effective probing.

■ Communication Skills: An Overall Caution

One of the reasons I have separated a discussion of the basic communication skills from the steps of the helping process is that I feel that helpers tend to overidentify the helping process with the communication skills that serve it. This is true not only of attending, listening, empathy, and probing, but also of the skills of challenging, which will be treated

---

■ Box 4–2. Suggestions For the Use of Probes

1. Keep in mind the goals of probing:
   a. To help nonassertive or reluctant clients tell their stories and engage in other behaviors related to the helping process;
   b. To help clients remain focused on relevant and important issues;
   c. To help clients identify experiences, behaviors, and feelings that give a fuller picture of the issue at hand;
   d. To help clients understand themselves and their problem situations more fully.
2. Use a mix of probing statements, open-ended questions, accents, and prompts.
3. Do not engage clients in question-and-answer sessions.
4. If a probe helps a client reveal relevant information, follow it up with basic empathy rather than another probe.
5. Use whatever judicious mixture of empathy and probing that is needed to help clients clarify problems, identify blind spots, develop new scenarios, search for action strategies, formulate plans, and review outcomes of action.
6. Remember that probing is a communication tool that is effective to the degree that it serves the helping process.

---

later on. Having good communication skills is not the same as being a good helper. An overemphasis on communication skills can make helping lots of talk and very little action: technique can replace substance. Communication skills are essential, of course, but they must always serve the outcomes of the helping process. Each of the chapters describing the steps of the helping process will begin with a review of the outcomes or accomplishments looked for in that step. Then ways of using communication skills to produce those outcomes will be illustrated.

Part Three

Stage I
The Present Scenario

■ Stage I: Helping Clients Define and Clarify Problem Situations

Clients come to counseling because they feel they need help in managing their lives more effectively. Stage I itemizes three ways in which counselors can help clients understand themselves and their problem situations with a view toward setting goals and taking action.

Step I-A: Helping clients tell their stories.   Each client has his or her story or set of stories—that is, the problem situation as he or she sees it. In this step the counselor establishes a relationship with the client and helps him or her tell the story in whatever detail is necessary. The skills helpers need to do this are outlined and illustrated.

Step I-B: Helping clients focus.   In this step counselors do three things. First they, in collaboration with the client, decide whether the concerns merit the kind of investment called for in counseling. Second, they help clients decide which part of a problem situation they would like to handle first. In doing so, they help clients find "points of leverage" in the problem situation. Third, they help clients make the problem situation as clear as possible in terms of specific experiences, specific behaviors, and specific feelings.

Step I-C: Helping clients overcome blind spots and develop new perspectives.   In this step counselors help clients see dimensions of themselves and the problem situation—dimensions that they are overlooking but that need to be explored if the situation is to be managed. All three steps may overlap and interact with one another and, as shall be seen, helping clients overcome blind spots and develop new perspectives is a skill that can be used throughout the helping process.

Five

Stage I: Step I-A
Helping Clients Tell Their Stories

■

Figure 5–1 highlights the first step in the helping process. Though "telling the story" may come first logically, it may not come first in time. As mentioned in Chapter Two, clients do not necessarily start at the beginning. For instance, I once spent one session with a man who had gone through all the steps in managing the problems involved with bypass heart surgery by himself. He sought my help only because a few things had not turned out as he had wanted. We spent a session fine-tuning his goals and action program and I never saw him again.

■ The Goals of Step I-A

Goals are desired outcomes—that is, those specific things you are trying to help your clients accomplish. Each step has its outcomes and a range of techniques or methods for achieving those outcomes. There are three principal achievements in this first step. If it is completed successfully, (1) clients tell their stories, (2) helpers make useful assessments of their clients, and (3) a working relationship between client and helper is established. Let us take a brief look at each of those outcomes.

Helping Clients Tell Their Stories

Using the communication skills outlined in Chapters Three and Four, counselors help clients tell their stories—stories about problem situations and unused opportunities. In the following example, the client is a 34-year-old woman separated from her husband and living in public housing in a large city in the Midwest. This is her first session with a social worker.

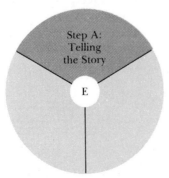

Stage I: Present Scenario

Figure 5–1. Step I-A: Telling the story

SOCIAL WORKER: You say that a lot of things are bothering you. What kinds of things?

CLIENT: Well, they don't take care of this building very well. It's actually dangerous to live here. I've got two children and I'm always worried about them. I worry about myself, too, but mostly about them.

SOCIAL WORKER: So things are so bad that you fear for the safety of your kids and your own safety. . . . What kinds of dangers bother you most?

CLIENT: Well . . . there's lots of things . . . but I think that elevators scare me the most. . . .

SOCIAL WORKER: In what ways?

CLIENT: Often they're broken down. But that's not the real scary part. . . . People that don't live here can get in and women have been raped. . . . I'm afraid the kids could get hurt. That's the real scary part. . . . And no one seems to do anything about it. This building's not at the top of anyone's list, I can tell you that.

SOCIAL WORKER: So the dangers to you and the kids are real, but the frustrating part is that no one seems to care.

Attending, listening, empathy, and probing are all used to help the client tell her story. If client and helper are successful in working together, the client will reveal the main features of the problem situation and, in telling the story, understand the problem situation more fully; the helper will develop an understanding of the client and his or her needs.

The counselor helps the client "draw a self-portrait" (Frey & Raming, 1979): "The therapist essentially acts as a facilitator as the client draws a self-portrait and then makes the requisite conclusions and changes" (p. 32). For instance, a client might say:

CLIENT: I'm the kind of person that waits for others to approach me. As a result I don't have the kind of friends I'd like to have and sometimes I'm lonely.

HELPER: So just waiting backfires on you.

CLIENT: I'm beginning to see just how passive I am in all sorts of different ways. Even when I'm with people I like I don't show any initiative. They call. They make the plans. They change the plans. I just go along. I wonder when I made the decision to be dull!

As the client is helped to draw a self-portrait, his dissatisfaction grows and the seed of change is planted.

Helpers are expected to deal with a wide variety of clients having a wide variety of concerns.

■

Martin, 24, asks a counselor for an appointment in order to discuss "a number of issues." Since Martin is both verbal and willing to talk, his story comes tumbling out in rich detail. While the helper uses the skills of attending, listening, empathy, and probing, she does so sparingly. Martin is too eager to tell his story.

Martin tells a rather full story. Although trained as a counselor, Martin is currently working in his uncle's business because of an offer he "could not turn down." Although he is doing very well, he feels guilty because service to others has always been a value for him. He both likes his job and feels hemmed in by it. A year of study in Europe has whetted his appetite for "adventure." He feels that he is nowhere near fulfilling the "great expectations" he has for himself.

He also talks about problems with his family. His father is dead. He has never gotten along well with his mother, and now that he has moved out of the house he feels he has abandoned his younger brothers, whom he loves very much.

Another topic is his relationship to a woman two years older than himself. They have been involved with each other for about three years; she wants to get married, but he feels he is not ready. He still has "too many things to do" and would like to keep the arrangement they have now.

This whole complex story comes tumbling out in a torrent of words. Martin feels free to skip from one topic to another. The way he tells his story is part of his impulsive style. At one point he stops, smiles, and says, "Boy, I didn't realize I had so much on my plate!" While all of these issues bother him, he does not feel overwhelmed by them.

■

Compare that example with the following one of a woman who comes to a local mental health center because she feels she can no longer handle her 9-year-old boy.

■

Edna is referred to the clinic because she is having trouble with her son. She has been divorced for about two years and is living on public assistance. After introductions and preliminary formalities have been taken care of, she just sits there and says nothing; she does not even look up. Since Edna offers almost nothing spontaneously, the counselor uses a relatively large number of probes to help her tell her story. Even when the little she says is responded to with empathy, she volunteers very little. Every once in a while, she begins to cry. When asked, she says she does not want to talk about the divorce. "Good riddance" is all she can say about her husband. Gradually, almost torturously, the story gets pieced together. She talks mostly about the "trouble" her son is getting into, how uncontrollable he seems to be getting, and how helpless she feels.

■

Consider a third example. Terry, a young woman in her late teens who has been arrested several times for street prostitution, is an involuntary client. She ran away from home when she was sixteen and is now living in a large city on the East Coast. Like many other runaways, she was seduced into prostitution by "a halfway decent pimp." Now she is pretty street smart: she is quite cynical about herself, her occupation, and the world. Terry is forced to see a counselor as part of the probation process.

■

As might be expected, Terry is quite hostile during the interview. She has seen other counselors and views the interview as a game. The counselor already knows much of the story from the court record.

■

CLIENT: I'm not going to talk about anything here. What I do outside is my business.

HELPER: You don't have to talk about what you do outside. You could talk about what we're doing here. I mean you and me.

CLIENT: I'm here because I have to be. You're here either because you're dumb and like to do stupid things or because you couldn't get a better job. You people are no better than the people on the street. You're just more "respectable." That's a laugh.

HELPER: So nobody could really be interested in you.

CLIENT: *I'm* not even interested in me!

HELPER: And if you're not, no one else could be, including me.

■

The counselor tries to help Terry tell, not the story "out there"—the story of the lifestyle that gets her into trouble—but rather the story that both of them are living right now "in here." Even though there are some explosive moments, Terry tells a story of her distrust of just about everyone, especially anyone connected with "the system." She emphasizes her contempt for the kind of people that try to "help" her.

■

Each client is different and will approach the telling of the story in different ways. Some of the stories you will help clients tell will be long and detailed, others short and stark. Some will be filled with emotion; others will be told coldly, even though they are stories of terror. Some stories will be, at least at first blush, single-issue stories—"I want to get rid of these headaches"—while others, like Martin's, will be multiple-issue stories. Some will be told readily, tumbling out with practically no help, while others will be told only haltingly or even begrudgingly. Some clients will tell the core story immediately, while others will tell a secondary story first in order to test the reactions of the helper. Some stories will deal with the inner world of the client almost exclusively—"I hate myself," "I hear voices"—while others will deal with the outer world of interpersonal problems and the social settings of life. Still others will present a combination of inner and outer concerns. The job of helpers is to be with their clients in such fully human and skillful ways that they are enabled to tell their stories. A story "out in the open" is the starting point for possible constructive change. Often the very airing of the story helps the client see it more objectively.

There are times when clients will speak at greater length—for instance, in the beginning, they may pour out their stories because it is the first time they have had the opportunity to do so. If the helper judges that it is best to let the client pour everything out at once, without much interaction, he or she should, while listening, concentrate on identifying the core experiences, behaviors, and feelings and the core themes running through the story. At the end, however, it is impossible for the helper to respond empathically all at once to everything the client has said. Therefore, the helper needs some way of getting back to the most salient issues and of helping the client explore them further. Expressions like the following can be used to help the client retell core parts of the story.

"There's a lot of pain and confusion in what you've just told me. Let's see if I've understood some of the main points you've made."

"You've said quite a bit. Let's see if we can see how all the pieces fit together."

Such comments let the client know you have been listening intently.

The telling of the story is not a goal in itself; it is a subgoal in the larger helping process. As such, it is a means to help clients manage their lives more effectively. Just as some helpers overidentify communication skills with helping, so others overidentify the telling of the story with helping. It is only a step on the way.

Assessment: Broad-Band versus Narrow-Band Filters

The second goal or achievement of Step I-A is assessment. I do not mean the kind of assessment arrived at through a battery of psychological tests; assessment in the sense meant here involves observing and listening to clients carefully in order to discover anything that might be of use to them. Assessment is what takes place through the kind of "trans-em-pathic" or reality-testing listening discussed in the last chapter. As helpers listen to clients, even as they listen in intensely empathic ways, they hear more than the client's point of view. For instance, it is possible to listen to the client's deep conviction that he is "not an alcoholic" and at the same time see the trembling hand, smell the alcohol-laden breath, and be struck by the desperate tone of voice. The purpose of such listening is not to place the client in the proper diagnostic category, but rather to be open to any kind of information or understanding that will enable you to help the client. For instance, Richardson (1984) has developed an empirically derived set of client categories in rehabilitation counseling that can help counselors tailor the helping process to the client's needs.

In the discussion of listening in Chapter Three, you were warned about the kinds of mental filters that tend to distort our perceptions of clients. However, it was also suggested that helpers can develop useful filters—that is, frameworks that help them listen in more focused ways to the stories of clients with a view to seeing patterns and organizing detail.

There are what I call *broad-band* and *narrow-band* filters or frameworks for listening and assessment. For instance, in my training in clinical psychology, assessment frameworks based on abnormal psychology were stressed. There were some unfortunate consequences of that emphasis. I, like other novices, tended to see psychopathological symptoms everywhere, both in myself and in others. When I interviewed clients and wrote reports based on diagnostic tests, I often focused on the category and missed the client. The very fact that clients were called "patients" made me look for illness; I was sensitized to illness, open to finding it wherever I could. I am not suggesting that books and courses on psychopathology, diagnostic frameworks, and batteries of tests designed to identify emotional illness cannot be of some service to clients. But I am convinced that most diagnostic procedures are narrow-band filters or frameworks that can actually distort listening to and assessing clients, unless they are tempered by broad-band filters or frameworks. Perhaps the most important broad-band filter is common sense. Some of the broad-band frameworks that I believe helpers should be sensitized to and trained in are frameworks based on client resources, developmental psychology, social settings, and the principles of behavior. A word about each follows.

A BIAS TOWARD RESOURCES

Low-level helpers concentrate on the deficits of clients. High-level helpers, as they listen to and observe clients, do not blind themselves to clients' deficits, but are also quick to spot resources, whether used, unused, or even abused (see Wright & Fletcher, 1982). These resources can become the building blocks in whatever action program the client ultimately undertakes. For instance, Terry, the street prostitute, has obvious deficits. She is engaged in a dangerous and self-defeating lifestyle. But the probation counselor, as she listens to Terry, discovers a range of resources. Terry is a tough, street-smart woman. The very virulence of her cynicism and self-hate, the very strength of her resistance to help, and her almost unchallengeable determination to go it alone are signs of resources. Many of her resources are currently being used in self-defeating ways, but they are resources nevertheless.

Helpers need resource-oriented mind sets in all their interactions with clients.

CLIENT: I practically never stand up for my rights. If I disagree with what anyone is saying—especially in a group—I keep my mouth shut. I suppose that on the rare occasion that I do speak up, the world doesn't fall in on me. Sometimes others do actually listen to me. But I still don't seem to have much impact on anyone.

COUNSELOR A: It's depressing for you to keep backing away from saying what's on your mind, but you've learned to accept it.

COUNSELOR B: Sometimes when you do speak up, you get a hearing. And so you're annoyed at yourself for getting lost in the crowd so often.

Counselor A misses the resource mentioned by the client. Although it is true that the client habitually fails to speak up, he does have some kind of impact when he speaks. Others do listen sometimes. And this is a resource. Counselor A emphasizes the deficit; Counselor B notes the asset. The search for resources is especially important when the story being told is bleak.

■

A counselor listened to a man's story, a story that included a number of crushing disappointments in life—a divorce, false accusations that led to his dismissal from a job, months of unemployment, serious health concerns, and more. The only emotion the man exhibited as he told the story was depression.

■

HELPER: Just one blow after another, grinding you down.

CLIENT: Grinding me down and almost doing me in.

HELPER: Tell me a little more about the "almost" part of it.

CLIENT: Well, I'm still alive, still sitting here talking to you.

HELPER: Despite all these blows you haven't fallen apart. That seems to say something about the fiber in you.

■

At the word "fiber," the client looked up and there seemed to be a glimmer of something besides depression in his face. The helper put a line down the center of a newsprint pad. On the left side he listed the blows the man had experienced. On the right he put the word "fiber" and said, "Let's see if we can add to the list on the right side." They came up with a list of the man's resources: his "fiber," his musical talent, his honesty, his concern for and ability to talk with others, and so forth. After about a half-hour, he smiled—just weakly, but he did smile.

■

Of course, a sensitivity to and search for resources is not limited to this step of the helping model. It belongs in every step.

A DEVELOPMENTAL FRAMEWORK

A developmental framework—one that deals with the normative stages, tasks, and crises of the entire life span—can help counter biases introduced by listening through narrow-band frameworks such as psychopathology (Levinson & associates, 1978; Newman & Newman, 1984). Recall the case of the man in his early forties discussed in Chapter Two.

■

He comes to a counselor complaining of a variety of ills. He is having trouble with his marriage, his teenage children seem to be more and more alienated from him, he is bored at work, depressed from time to time, drinking heavily, and has begun to steal things—just small things like candy bars and toothpaste—not because he doesn't have the money, but for the "kick" he gets from it. The helper listening through a framework of psychopathology might interpret what he is saying more negatively than a helper using primarily a developmental model or a combination of a developmental and a psychopathological model. The former sees a person who is falling apart and who perhaps is even a kleptomaniac! The latter sees a middle-class person in a normative mid-life crisis and listens to and interprets his behavior from that wider point of view. This helper might well feel that the client is in a relatively severe crisis and not handling it as well as he might, but the context is still primarily developmental.

■

Developmental *stages* refer to the fact that within particular societies important developmental events occur with some predictability during specific age-related phases of an individual's life. For instance, the years from 23 to 30 can be designated as the stage of early adulthood in North American society. This stage has its particular developmental *tasks,* which are the challenges that confront individuals and which demand new patterns of behavior as they move through life. For instance, late adolescence (18 to 22) brings challenges revolving around independent living, initial career decisions, the internalization of morality, and sustained intimacy. Normative developmental *crises* refer to significant decision points related to the stages of life. We can talk about the age-30 transition crisis and the mid-life crisis. These are often times when an individual's life is deeply affected for better or worse. These points are often, but not always, times of excitement, turbulence, and anxiety. The decisions made at these points are often critical for the individual's future. For instance, for older persons, one crisis revolves around the possibilities for continued meaning in life versus giving in to despair.

This is not the place for a short course in applied developmental psychology, but I am utterly convinced that training for helpers should include developing a solid working knowledge of the practical findings of research in the field. If a helper is dealing with a client who is ill, he or she must realize that serious illness is experienced differently at 20 than at 40 or 70. If your clients are spread across the life span, your working knowledge of developmental realities should also cover the life span. Understanding healthy development (Heath, 1980a, 1980b) is essential background for understanding and treating problems and deviations.

A PEOPLE-IN-SYSTEMS FRAMEWORK

Egan and Cowen (1979; Egan, 1984) have developed a broad-band "people-in-systems" model to help counselors do a number of things, including listen to their clients in focused ways with a minimum of bias. The model addresses the different levels of *social systems* or *settings* in which people live out their lives and in the context of which developmental events take place (see Conyne & Clack, 1981; Fine, 1985; Hiltonsmith & Miller, 1983; Stadler & Rynearson, 1981).

> Psychologists have long acknowledged that complete understanding of a given individual's behavior depends on knowledge of the attributes of both the individual and the setting in which that individual's behavior is occurring. This sounds simple enough in theory, yet in practice most professional psychologists appear to have gathered little information on the setting aspect of assessment [Hiltonsmith & Miller, 1983, p. 419].

Helpers need to listen to the ways in which their clients are being victimized by the social settings of their lives—from sexual abuse to problems stemming from a downturn in the economy. There is a difference between helping clients understand how the social systems of life can stand in the way of personal development and aiding and abetting them as they wallow in their roles as victims. We live in a society that tends to "blame the victim" (Caplan & Nelson, 1973; Ryan, 1971).

The people-in-systems model also addresses the kinds of *life skills* (Adkins, 1984; Gambrill, 1984; Gazda, 1984; Goldstein, Gershaw, & Sprafkin, 1984) people need to pursue developmental tasks and involve themselves in, contribute to, and cope with the various social systems of life. Part of assessment is helping clients identify their life-skills strengths and deficits. Clients often fail because they do not have the kinds of life skills needed to cope with the difficulties of life, from everyday problems to developmental crises. Then, as suggested in Chapter One, training in required skills needs to become part of the helping process.

A PRINCIPLES-OF-BEHAVIOR FRAMEWORK

Another useful assessment framework is the A-B-C model based on the principles of behavior. It deals with the antecedents (A) and the consequences (C) of behavior (B). The behavioral sequence is

$$\text{Antecedents} \rightarrow \text{Behavior-in-a-Situation} \rightarrow \text{Consequences} \rceil$$

The arrow from consequences back to antecedents and behavior indicates that in a number of ways behavior is controlled by its consequences, but generally, human behavior is stimulated by its antecedents and modified by its consequences. For instance, Alex's 6-year-old son, Toby, sees his father light up and enjoy a cigarette (A). The next day he sees a pack of cigarettes lying on the kitchen table, takes one out, and puts it in his mouth in imitation of his father (B). His mother comes into the kitchen and slaps the cigarette out of his mouth (C). The next day he sees the pack of cigarettes lying on the table, but he leaves them there.

Both self-enhancing and self-defeating patterns of behavior are governed by the principles of behavior. Antecedents include all relevant factors that precede the behavior. Consequences comprise the reinforcement, punishment, or lack of either reward or punishment that follows the behavior. Consequences contribute, often in complex ways, to the control of behavior through rewards and punishments, while antecedents contribute, also in complex ways, to the control of behavior by acting as stimuli or cues. For instance, Alex's opening the refrigerator door and looking at food (A) cues or signals that eating (B) will lead to an immediate reward (C). Antecedents can signal that a reward or punishment or neither is likely to follow a possible behavior.

Incentives are antecedents that "tell" us that a behavior or set of behaviors will lead to a reward. *Disincentives* are antecedents that tell us a behavior or set of behaviors will lead to no reward or even to some sort of punishment. Incentives and disincentives can have their origin in the client's past experiences. For instance, Bridget, who is thinking of having a gynecological examination, remembers the pain she experienced during the last one. Her present memory of a past event signals the possibility of punishment and she decides to put the examination off. All the present internal dispositions of the individual and the influences of the individual's environment can serve as cues. For instance, Brad witnesses the "bad trips" of two friends who experiment with hallucinogens. When offered some LSD, he declines because it signals possible punishment.

Helping clients maximize incentives and minimize disincentives for productive patterns of behavior is one of the most important tasks of the helping process.

If a client is engaging in some self-defeating or self-destructive pattern of behavior (for instance, alienating others by sarcasm or other rude and inconsiderate behavior; overeating and gaining weight even after a heart attack), the following questions can be asked:

- What, concretely, is the unacceptable pattern of behavior? What exactly does the client do or fail to do that is self-defeating?
- What antecedents, especially what incentives, within the individual and in the environment cue or stimulate the behavior?
- What consequences reinforce the behavior? Even though the behavior in question seems to be self-defeating, it must in some way be rewarding. What is the payoff?
- What disincentives are at work when a client avoids behavior that seems to be in his or her best interest?

Failure to understand and use the principles of behavior leads to what Cross and Guyer (1980) call "social traps."

> Put simply, a social trap is a situation characterized by multiple but conflicting rewards. Just as an ordinary trap entices its prey with the offer of an attractive bait and then punishes it by capture, so the social situations which we include under the rubric "social traps" draw their victims into certain patterns of behavior with promises of immediate rewards and then confront them with consequences that the victims would rather avoid. On the level of the individual person, examples are easy to think of. In the case of smoking . . . we find the cigarette smoker enjoying at first the repeated gratification of smoking, and only after a long delay, when it is much too late, does he find himself faced with the disagreeable consequences. . . . All [examples] involve individuals who use reinforcements like road signs, traveling in the direction of rewards and avoiding the paths marked by punishments. . . . Occasionally, these road signs lead to unfortunate destinations [pp. 4, 12–13].

Helpers usually meet these "victims" down the road, at their "unfortunate destinations." For instance, the married couple who continually reap the reward of avoiding small problems and annoyances may find themselves at an unfortunate destination sooner than they expected. We can see how persuasive social traps are simply by examining our own experiences.

There are a number of advantages to an assessment or listening framework based on the principles of behavior. Tryon (1976) calls it a "behavioral diagnosis" model and suggests these benefits:

Useful for all problems. According to Tryon, it can be used not only with "simple unidimensional problems that are thoroughly described from information obtained from the client in an interview setting," but also with problems that are "multidimensional, seemingly vague, and not well articulated by the client" (p. 495). It is a way of helping clients understand their stories.

Controlling antecedents.   Once the antecedents of self-defeating patterns of behavior are identified and clarified, there is the possibility that they can be changed. This is called "cue control" or "stimulus control." For instance, one of the reasons that Alex overeats is that he keeps the refrigerator full of appetizing food. Stimulus control could begin in the supermarket. He could buy not only smaller amounts of food but also less fattening and even less appealing food. This kind of stimulus control is easier than struggling with "will power" in the face of a refrigerator loaded with high-caloric, tasty food. In the case of his son, Toby, better modeling could be offered: his parents could refrain from engaging in undesirable behaviors in front of him. More positively, clients can be helped to identify incentives for engaging in self-enhancing behaviors.

Controlling consequences.   Once the consequences of a self-defeating pattern of behavior are identified, there is the possibility that they, too, can be changed. For instance, once a wife discovers that her husband actually enjoys the game of "uproar" they get into when they are discussing finances, she can refuse to play the game. That is, she can refuse to engage in their arguments, which are almost always associated with a discussion of finances. Once the reward disappears, it is likely that the behavior sustained by it will also disappear.

Training as treatment.   It is possible to teach clients to analyze their own behavior in terms of its antecedents and consequences and show them how to minimize antecedents that cue self-defeating behavior, maximize antecedents that cue self-enhancing behavior, minimize reinforcement for self-defeating behavior, and maximize reinforcement for self-enhancing behavior.

A few cautions are in order. The A-B-C assessment framework can be misused in at least two ways. First of all, it can be used too globally and superficially. A cursory analysis of a complicated problem situation in terms of some antecedents and consequences could well be a useless exercise. If helpers are to use this model, they need an adequate working knowledge of the principles involved and should be able to train clients in the rudiments of their use. The few remarks in these pages are no substitute for adequate training in the principles of behavior. Second, the A-B-C framework can be overused. It is possible to spend an excessive amount of time examining behavioral patterns so thoroughly that both helper and client get lost in detail. If you develop a good working knowledge of the principles of behavior and keep in mind the overall goals of helping and the valued accomplishments of each step, the A-B-C model can help you and your clients define problems not only clearly and concretely, but also in a way that suggests goals and courses of action for handling them.

There are, of course, other frameworks that can help you listen to clients in constructive ways. If the practical learnings from personality theory and psychopathology are added to the frameworks outlined above, the model illustrated in Figure 5–2 (see Hulse & Jennings, 1984) depicts the usefulness of filters in listening to clients and helping them identify and clarify problem situations. I also use frameworks drawn from other approaches to helping such as the Parent-Adult-Child framework of transactional analysis (Berne, 1964) and the A-B-C (activating event-belief-emotional consequence) framework of rational-emotive therapy (Ellis & Grieger, 1977; Ellis & Harper, 1975). I borrow frameworks freely from a wide variety of approaches to helping because problems in living cannot be tied down to neat categories.

> Our understanding of mental illness has been obstructed by the assumption that reality comes packaged in well-bounded categories waiting to be discovered. . . . It may be that whatever mental illness is, it will not be ameliorated until it is seen in ecological terms, connected to and continuous with other features of our biological, cultural, and social existence. And if it turns out that meaningful interventions take the form of efforts to reduce the stressors

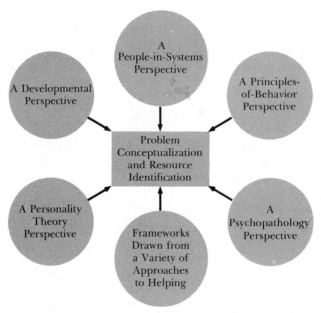

Figure 5–2. Using a variety of frameworks to help clients conceptualize problem situations and solutions

of urban-industrial life or create a healthy fetal environment or eliminate poverty, then we must become as informed and disciplined in those pursuits as we have been in . . . psychotherapy [Dumont, 1984].

Helping others is a profession for the open-minded and the broad-minded.

Assessment, as discussed in these pages, is not limited to Step I-A. It is an *ongoing* process, useful at every stage and step of the helping model. Effective counselors are always helping clients identify resources. They help clients see problems, new scenarios, strategies, plans, and action through the frameworks outlined above.

JUDGING THE SEVERITY OF PROBLEMS

One of the things you are doing as you listen to clients and help them tell their stories is estimating the severity of the client's problem situation. Clients come to helpers with problems of every degree of severity. Problems run, objectively speaking, from the inconsequential to the life threatening. Speaking subjectively, however, even a relatively inconsequential problem can be experienced as severe by a client. In that case, the client's tendency to "catastrophize," to judge a problem situation as more severe than it actually is, becomes in itself an important part of the problem situation. Then one of the tasks of the counselor will be to help the client put the problem in perspective or teach him or her how to distinguish between degrees of problem severity.

Mehrabian and Reed (1969) suggest that the following formula can be useful in determining the severity of any given problem situation:

$$\text{Severity} = \text{Distress} \times \text{Uncontrollability} \times \text{Frequency}$$

The "$\times$" in the formula indicates that these factors are not just additive. For instance, even low-level anxiety, if it is uncontrollable and/or persistent, can constitute a severe problem; that is, it can severely interfere with the quality of a client's life.

Let's consider a example in which two people react quite differently to the same external situation.

■

Andy and Joan, who work in the same office, are both dissatisfied with their jobs because they feel that the work they do is not rewarding, there is little opportunity for social contact with fellow workers, they have a couple of supervisors who are authoritarian and self-centered, and, even though there is some opportunity for advancement, office politics play a central role in the granting of promotions. These two workers experience the problem situation quite differently, however.

In Andy's case, the culture from which he comes has taught him that much of his identity depends on the kind and quality of work he does. Work for him is a primary value, and to be locked into an unrewarding job with supervisory personnel who see him as just another worker is demeaning. Joan, on the other hand, looks upon work as a necessary evil. She is willing to put up with 40 hours of pedestrian work as long as she gets enough satisfaction from the rest of the hours of the week. She does her work conscientiously enough, but is not interested in investing time and effort in improving her work situation. Whenever a supervisor gives her negative feedback, she listens to it for what it is worth and then is no longer bothered by it. When Andy gets even mildly negative feedback from a supervisor, he fumes about it for days.

∎

These two people can be compared using the three dimensions of Mehrabian and Reed's formula.

Distress. Andy experiences a great deal of distress in his work situation; he is highly anxious. Joan, while disliking her work, experiences relatively little distress on the job.

Frequency. Extremely distressing days at work are relatively infrequent for Joan, while for Andy the opposite is true. In fact, the number of distressful days have come to outnumber the ones of relative calm.

Uncontrollability. Joan finds a great deal of fulfillment in her social life, which is more important to her than work. Since this is the case, she finds she can control her adverse emotional reactions at work quite easily. In contrast, almost any kind of problem at work sets Andy on edge.

And so, when Joan is at work, she experiences what might be called the ordinary *stress* of everyday life. She can cope quite well with it. As Selye (1974) notes, the goal is not to rid life of all stress, for a life without any stress would be insipid. However, when increasing amounts of stress turn into *distress,* trouble is brewing. High levels of stress can literally begin to tear the body apart. For Andy it is not work that causes stress, but rather his dissatisfaction with his work. His continual, intense feelings of frustration and failure add up to a high degree of problem severity.

One way of viewing helping is to see it as a process in which clients are helped to control the severity of their problems in living. The severity of any given problem situation will be reduced if the stress can be reduced, if the frequency of the problem situation can be lessened, or if the client's control over the problem situation can be increased. Consider the following example.

■

Indira is greatly distressed because she experiences migraine-like headaches sometimes two or three times a week and seems to be able to do little about them. No painkillers seem to work. She has even been tempted to try strong narcotics to control the pain, but fears she might become an addict. She feels trapped. For her the problem is quite severe because distress, uncontrollability, and frequency are all high.

She is finally referred to a doctor who specializes in treating headaches. He is an expert in both medicine and human behavior. He first helps her to see that the headaches are getting worse because of her tendency to "catastrophize" whenever she experiences one. That is, the self-talk she engages in ("How intolerable this is!") and the way she fights the headache simply add to its severity. He helps her control her stress-inducing self-talk and teaches her relaxation techniques. Neither of these get rid of the headaches, but they help reduce the stress she feels when she has them.

Second, he helps her identify the situations in which the headaches seem to develop. They tend to come at times when she is not managing other forms of stress well—for instance, when she lets herself become overloaded and gets behind at work. He helps her see that, while her headaches constitute a very real problem, they are still part of a larger problem situation. Once she begins to control and reduce other forms of stress in her life, the frequency of the headaches begins to lessen.

Third, the doctor also helps her spot cues that a headache is beginning to develop. She finds that while she can do little to control the headache once it is in full swing, there are things she can do during the beginning stage. For instance, she learns that medicine having no effect when the headache is in full force does help if it is taken as soon as the symptoms appear. Relaxation techniques are also helpful if they are used soon enough. Indira's headaches do not disappear completely, but they are no longer the central reality of her life.

■

The doctor helps the client manage a very severe problem situation much better than she had been doing by helping her reduce distress and frequency, while increasing control.

Establishing a Working Relationship

The third objective of Step I-A is to develop a working relationship with the client. The relationship can be seen as the heart of helping people (Patterson, 1985; Perlman, 1979).

> Counseling or psychotherapy is an interpersonal relationship. Note that I
> don't say that counseling or psychotherapy *involves* an interpersonal relation-
> ship—it *is* an interpersonal relationship [Patterson, 1985, p. 3].

Patterson goes on to point out how central respect, genuineness, empathy, and specificity of communication (discussed in the next chapter)
are to the helping relationship. However, although all agree on the
importance of the relationship (Highlen & Hill, 1984), some "maintain
that a good relationship is important inasmuch as it provides the counselor leverage in applying procedures and techniques that themselves
are the central change agents" (Gelso & Carter, 1985). The position taken
here is that the helping relationship is extremely important and that the
objective of establishing a good working relationship with the client applies, of course, to all the stages and steps of the model. The relationship
that is developed early on must be sustained throughout the helping
process.

Greenson (1967) divides the helping relationship into three components: the working alliance, the transference relationship (I call this the
"shadow side" of the relationship), and the real relationship (I call this
the basic human relationship; also see Gelso & Carter, 1985). Different
approaches to counseling and therapy stress one over the others. A word
about each.

The working alliance.   This term appeals to me because it stresses part-
nership and thus underscores the responsibility of the client (the "resource-collaborator" notion mentioned in the introductory chapter).
Since the helping model in this book is, broadly speaking, a cognitive-
behavioral model, it stresses the notion of the working alliance and its
contributions to the client's practical learnings. Deffenbacher (1985) outlines what the helping alliance might look like from a cognitive-behavioral
perspective.

> A strong working alliance and at least moderate attention to real relationship
> parameters are important in dealing with complex client problems from a
> learning perspective. Good cognitive-behavioral therapists work to build rap-
> port, lessen interpersonal anxiety in the relationship, increase trust, and build
> an interpersonal climate in which clients can openly discuss and work on their
> problems. Their clients need to perceive that they have a caring, positive,
> hopeful collaborator in understanding and making changes in their world.
> Cognitive-behavioral therapists, like other therapists, use themselves and the
> interpersonal relationship with the client to achieve much of this. Good lis-
> tening in an open, nondefensive manner, careful attention and tracking of
> client concerns, direct, honest feedback, and the like are not only important
> for assessment, but also create the context in which further exploration and
> cognitive-behavioral strategies may be implemented. Clients of cognitive-be-
> havioral therapists need to be cared for, attended to, understood, and gen-
> uinely worked with if successful therapy is to continue [p. 262].

Deffenbacher suggests that many of the outcomes of the helping process, such as the development of goals and plans, can take place inadvertently as helper and client concentrate on the relationship. The central characteristic of the relationship as a working alliance is its focus on the collaborative *work* to be done in the management of problem situations. Hutchins (1984) suggests that matching counseling models, techniques, and strategies to clients can contribute substantially to effective working alliances.

The shadow side of the helping relationship. The helping relationship, like all others, has both its overt and its covert (or shadow) side. For instance, without even realizing it, clients can react to helpers as if they were people from their past lives. Novice helpers can be put off when they see clients well up with emotions toward them that they did nothing to cause. On the other hand, helpers, also without realizing it, may attempt to use the helping relationship to satisfy personal, but often buried, needs. These are the arational dimensions of the helping relationship that have as yet been insufficiently catalogued. It is not suggested here that you scrutinize every interchange between you and your clients. However, it is useful to know that more happens in these relationships than you or your clients intend. It is very helpful to explore with your supervisors what is happening between you and your clients below the surface. Even experienced helpers can benefit from similar dialogues with their colleagues. Helpers all too often blame clients for being resistant when the actual problem involves the interplay of covert dramas in which both helper and client play a part.

The basic human relationship. There is something unreal, or at least confusing, about the term "the real relationship" because both the helping alliance and the shadow side of the helping relationship are quite real. Therefore, I prefer to talk about the basic human relationship in the helping process. The relationship between client and helper is real because they are two human beings involved in a human encounter. But it is also *made* real when both give themselves openly and genuinely to each other in the work of helping.

> Both parties contribute to [the reality of the relationship] from the moment of their first exchange. The counselor does so through his or her genuineness, facilitation of the client's genuineness, and the abiding attempt to see and understand the client realistically. The client contributes to the real relationship likewise through his or her struggle to be genuine and perceive realistically [Gelso & Carter, 1985, p. 187].

In a sense, the real relationship is the human base or substrate on which the helping alliance is to be built. Since different helpers have different helping orientations, the helping alliance will look different from helper to helper but all need to be built on a solid foundation. Early in the relationship both helper and client can get a sense of what the other person is: "We would suggest . . . that clients and counselors are able very early in their relationship, perhaps immediately, to perceive in an undistorted fashion at least some of who the other person essentially is" (Gelso & Carter, p. 188). This enables both clients and helpers to challenge one another when they are not being authentic. Attending, listening, empathy, challenge, respect, and genuineness are all facets of the basic human relationship.

The existence of one perfect kind of helping relationship is a myth. Different clients have different needs and these needs are best met through different kinds of relationships. For instance, one client may work best with a helper who expresses a great deal of warmth, while another might work best with a helper who is more objective and business-like. Respect and genuineness can be expressed in different ways with different clients. For instance, as mentioned earlier, some clients arrive with a fear of intimacy. If helpers attend very carefully and communicate a great deal of empathy and warmth, these clients might be put off. Therefore, effective helpers use a mix of the various skills and techniques at the service of the kind of relationship that is best for any given client. Helping skills and techniques are important but secondary; helping relationships, outcomes, and values are primary.

SOCIAL-EMOTIONAL REEDUCATION

Effective helpers are capable of identifying the relationship needs of clients and of adapting their style to those needs. Their relationships are characterized by two elements that run through all effective helping: support and challenge, in whatever judicious mix of the two that meets the needs of any given client. The kind of social-emotional reeducation that takes place through the relationship between helpers and their clients is sometimes the most significant outcome of the helping process. Clients begin to care for themselves, trust themselves, and challenge themselves more because of what they learn through their interactions with helpers. Sometimes this critical outcome is overlooked and helpers, after a relationship is terminated, say to themselves, "Nothing much seemed to happen." But if such a helper were to examine both process and outcomes more carefully, he or she might say, "Because I trusted her, she trusts herself more; because I cared for her, she is now more capable of caring for herself; because I invited her to challenge herself and took the risk of doing so, she is now more capable of challenging herself. Because of the way I related to her, she now relates better to herself and is in a better position to relate to others more effectively. She is now more likely to tap into her own resources."

■ Blocks to Self-Disclosure

Even when helpers are skillful in Stage I-A, clients may find self-disclosure and self-exploration quite difficult for a number of reasons.

Fear of intensity.   If the counselor uses high levels of attending, accurate empathy, respect, concreteness, and genuineness, and if the client cooperates by exploring the feelings, experiences, and behaviors related to the problematic areas of his or her life, the helping process can be an intense one. This can cause both client and helper to back off. Skilled helpers know that counseling is potentially intense. They are prepared for it and know how to support a client who is not used to such intensity.

Concern about confidentiality.   Some clients find it very difficult to trust anyone, even a most trustworthy helper. They have irrational fears of being betrayed. In such cases, helpers must work at creating trust through the behavioral manifestations of respect and genuineness outlined in Chapter Two.

When counseling is done in a group, however, the question of confidentiality becomes more crucial. Especially if group members socialize with one another, worries about confidentiality will be more pressing. In this case, the question of confidentiality needs to be dealt with directly as one of the factors that affect the trust level of the group. More positively, the members need to develop a facilitative level of trust as quickly as possible. They can do this as the helper does it—that is, by being genuine, respectful, and understanding in the behavioral ways described in this chapter. Such behaviors, in conjunction with a willingness to take reasonable risks in self-disclosure, can do much to raise the trust level of a group.

Fear of disorganization.   Some people fear self-disclosure because they feel they cannot face what they might find out about themselves. This is a very critical issue. The client feels that, no matter how much energy must be expended to keep up the facade he or she has constructed, it is still less burdensome than exploring the unknown. Such clients often begin well but, once they begin to be overwhelmed by the data produced in the self-exploration process, retreat. Digging into one's inadequacies can lead to a certain amount of disequilibrium, disorganization, and crisis (Carkhuff, 1969a, 1969b; Piaget, 1954). But as Piaget suggests, disequilibrium is part of the price a child must pay to assimilate new stimuli into an existing schema: it is the price of growth. Carkhuff suggests, similarly, that growth takes place at crisis points. Skilled counselors realize that the self-exploration process might well be ineffective if it produces either very high or very low levels of disorganization. High disorganization immobilizes the client, while very low disorganization is often indicative of a failure to get at the central issues of his or her problem situation.

Shame.   Shame, a much overlooked experiential variable in human living (Egan, 1970; Lynd, 1958), is an important part of disorganization and crisis. The root meaning of the verb "to shame" is "to uncover, to expose, to wound," and therefore it is related to the process of self-exploration. Shame is not just being painfully exposed to another; it is primarily an exposure of self to oneself. Shame often has the quality of suddenness: in a flash one sees his or her heretofore unrecognized inadequacies, without being prepared for such a revelation. Shame is sometimes touched off by external or insignificant incidents, such as a casual remark someone makes, but it could not be so touched off unless, deep down, one was already ashamed. A shame experience might be defined as an acute emotional awareness of a failure *to be* in some way.

In a study by Talland and Clark (1954), clients judged the therapeutic value of 15 topics discussed during counseling. There was general agreement on the relative value of topics. Ratings showed a high correlation between the perceived helpfulness of a topic and its disturbing qualities. The topic called "shame and guilt" was identified as extremely upsetting, but discussion of it was considered most helpful. A group of psychologists also rated the same 15 topics on a scale of relative intimacy; there was a high correlation between what the psychologists deemed intimate and what the clients judged to be helpful. Self-exploration must eventually deal with intimate areas that are relevant to the client's problem situation. If this exploration entails disequilibrium, disorganization, shame, and crisis, those comprise the price that must be paid for growth. Effective helpers both provide support for such clients and help them mobilize supportive resources in their own environments.

Fear of change.   Some people are afraid of taking stock of themselves because they know, however subconsciously, that if they do they will have to change—that is, surrender comfortable (but unproductive) patterns of living, work more diligently, suffer the pain of loss, acquire skills needed to live more effectively, and so on. For instance, a husband and wife may realize at some level of their beings that if they see a counselor they will have to reveal themselves and that, once the cards are on the table, they will have to go through the agony of changing their style of relating to each other.

In a counseling group I once met a man in his sixties whose presenting complaint was a very high level of anxiety that was making his life quite painful. He told a story of being treated brutally by his father until he finally ran away from home. Over the years he had developed a peculiar logic that went something like this: "No one who grows up with scars like mine can be expected to take charge of his life and live responsibly." He had been using his mistreatment as a youth as an excuse to act irresponsibly at work (he had an extremely poor job record), in his life with himself (he drank excessively), and in his marriage (he had been uncooperative and unfaithful and yet expected his wife to support him). The idea that he could change, that he could take responsibility for himself even at his age, frightened him, and he wanted to run away from the group. But since his anxiety was so painful he stayed. He had to learn that a change in his style of living was absolutely necessary if he wanted to break out of the vicious cycle in which he was caught.

■ Self-Exploration

Since clients are being influenced in Stage I-A to talk about and explore themselves and their problem situations in terms of concrete and specific experiences, behaviors, and feelings, it is useful to take a closer look at self-disclosure as a human process. Psychologists have only just begun to study self-disclosing behavior scientifically (Chelune, 1979; Cozby, 1973). It is difficult, then, to place the kind of self-disclosure demanded by the helping process (Doster & Nesbitt, 1979) in a wider context of "normal" self-disclosing behavior.

Jourard (1971a, 1971b), among others, claims that responsible self-sharing is part of the normal behavior of the healthy, actualized person. According to him, people who cannot share themselves deeply are ultimately incapable of love. Some theoreticians, taking a commonsense approach to self-disclosure, have hypothesized that there is a curvilinear relationship between self-disclosure and mental health: very high and very low levels of self-disclosing behavior are signs of maladjustment, while moderate (and appropriate) self-disclosure is optimal. Overdisclosers can be exhibitionistic or, at least, preoccupied with themselves. Underdisclosers may be fearful of intimacy or feel that they have a great deal to hide. Underdisclosers can pour great energy into building and maintaining facades so that their real selves will not be discovered (see Mowrer, 1968a, 1968b, 1973a, 1973b for an interesting approach to underdisclosing behavior in counseling and psychotherapy). The overdiscloser reveals a great deal even when the situation does not call for it, while the underdiscloser remains silent even when the situation calls for self-disclosing behavior.

Self-disclosure, either within or without the helping relationship, is never an end in itself. To be growth-inducing, it must be appropriate to the setting (Egan, 1976). Derlega and Grzelak (1979) outline seven aspects of self-disclosure useful for identifying what is appropriate self-disclosure within a helping context.

1. *Informativeness.* This refers to both the quantity (breadth) and quality (depth or intimacy) of the information provided. In helping settings this covers, as we shall see, the experiences, behaviors, and feelings that need to be explored to define the problem situation adequately.

2. *Accessibility.* This refers to the ease with which information can be obtained from the client. Some clients need more help than others in getting at relevant experiences, behaviors, and feelings. As we have seen, empathy and probing are important skills in this effort.

3. *Voluntariness.* This refers to the willingness of the client to provide relevant information. Clients who are more fearful about revealing themselves need support and encouragement to do so.

4. *Reward value.* This refers to the extent that providing information promises positive (reinforcing) or negative (punishing) outcomes for the client. If you fail to listen to what a client is saying, or respond in a way that the client finds punitive, it is likely that the client's self-disclosing behavior will diminish. On the other hand, if you attend and listen well and deal carefully with revelations, self-disclosing behavior is likely to be maintained. The ultimate reward for self-disclosure, of course, is better management of the client's life.

5. *Truthfulness.* This refers to the extent to which the client's messages provide information about his or her actual psychological state. If you discover that the client is not telling you the truth, it may be that he or she is afraid of telling you or fears other punishing consequences. If this is the case, accusing clients of being "defensive" will not help. What is needed is both support and reasonable challenge.

6. *Social norms.* This refers to the extent to which what is disclosed conforms with or deviates from cultural expectations about appropriate disclosing behavior. Some clients are very low disclosers in their everyday lives—in fact, that may be part of the problem situation. It is sometimes hard for them to realize that the "rules" are different in the counseling setting. This is especially common in group counseling. Providing such clients with some kind of facilitative structure for self-disclosure can help (see Egan, 1986, *Exercises in Helping Skills*).

7. *Effectiveness.* This refers to the extent to which the messages revealed contribute to the client's goals. It makes little difference if clients talk intimately and at length about themselves if such disclosure does not contribute ultimately to the management of the problem situation. Through empathy, probing, and summaries you can help clients make their disclosures focused and goal directed.

No claims are made here that self-disclosure in itself "cures." However it should be noted that, as Mowrer demonstrates, in some cases self-disclosure can release powerful "healing" forces or resources in the client. For instance, it may help a client get out from under a burden of guilt. Therefore, adequate self-disclosing behavior has been one factor in predicting therapeutic outcome (Truax & Carkhuff, 1965).

> If we can find a way to expand the statement of a problem to a concrete list of specific behaviors which constitute it, one major obstacle to the solution of the problem will have been overcome. In other words, the initial ambiguity with which most people analyze their interpersonal problems tends to contribute to their feeling of helplessness in coping with them. Knowing which specific behaviors are involved, and thereby what changes in those behaviors will solve the problem, provides a definite goal for action—and having that goal can lend a great sense of relief [Mehrabian, 1970, p. 7].

Self-disclosure does not "cure," but it can contribute significantly to the overall process. More is said about helping clients talk concretely about their problem situations in the next chapter.

■ Do Some Clients Need Only Step I-A?

It would seem at first glance that some clients are "cured" in this first step of the helping process.

A declaration of intent and the mobilization of resources. For some clients, the very fact that they have approached someone for help seems to help them begin to pull together the resources needed to manage their problem situations more effectively. Going to a helper is then a declaration not of helplessness but of intent: "I'm going to do something about this problem situation." Once they begin to mobilize their resources, they manage their lives quite well and no longer need the services of a helper.

Getting out from under self-defeating emotions. Some clients come to helpers because they are incapacitated, to a greater or lesser degree, by feelings and emotions. It frequently happens that when such clients are shown respect, listened to, and understood in a nonjudgmental way, their self-defeating feelings and emotions subside. Once that happens, they are able to call on their own inner and environmental resources and begin to manage the problem situation that precipitated the incapacitating feelings and emotions in the first place. These clients, too, seem to be "cured" merely by telling their story. Once they get from under the emotions that have been burdening them, they can once more take charge of their lives. Such clients may even say something like, "I feel relieved even though I haven't solved my problem." Often they feel more than relieved; they feel empowered by their interaction, however brief, with a caring helper.

However, it goes without saying that not all clients fall into these categories. Most need further help. Skilled helpers are able to help clients discover what services they need beyond being helped to tell their stories.

■ Reluctant and Resistant Clients

All helpers encounter reluctant or resistant clients: those who do not seem to know what they want; who present themselves as not needing help; who, though unwilling, are forced to see a helper or come only at the urging of a third party; who feel abused; who are resentful; who only talk about safe or low-priority issues; who sabotage the helping process by being overly cooperative; who are directly or indirectly uncooperative; who set unrealistic goals and then use them as an excuse for not working; who unwarrantedly blame others or the social settings and systems of their lives for their troubles; who show no willingness to establish a relationship with the helper; who do not work very hard at changing their behavior; who play games with helpers; who are slow to take responsibility for themselves; who are either testy or actually abusive or belligerent. Resistance to helping is, of course, a matter of degree—not all those behaviors in their most virulent forms are seen in all resistant clients.

Resistance is hardly an uncommon phenomenon; there is probably some degree of resistance in every client. "Resistance is an unavoidable process in every effective treatment, for that part of the personality that has an interest in the survival of the pathology actively protests each time therapy comes close to inducing a successful change" (Redl, 1966, p. 216). Clients come "armored" against change to a greater or lesser degree. Resistance can even be seen as something positive, a sign of life and struggle rather than just another form of pathology. What follow are some considerations that will help you deal with reluctant clients or the resistance that is found in one degree or another in all clients. Researchers and practitioners are paying more and more attention to resistance (Anderson & Stewart, 1983; Cavanaugh, 1982; Chamberlain and others, 1984; Cormier & Cormier, 1985; Dyer & Vriend, 1975; Ellis, 1985; Kerr and associates, 1983; Larrabee, 1982; Lauver, Holiman, & Kazama, 1982; Manthei & Matthews, 1982; Paradise & Wilder, 1979; Ridley, 1984; Riordan, Matheny, & Harris, 1978; Smaby & Tamminen, 1979; Spinks & Birchler, 1982; Stream, 1985; Wachtel, 1982).

Reluctance versus Resistance

It is possible to make a distinction between reluctance and resistance, although the principles for handling both are basically the same.

Reluctant clients.   Reluctant clients are those who do not want to come in the first place; they are not self-referred. They come because they are more or less forced to come. For instance, in marriage counseling one of the clients might be there willingly while the other is there because he or she feels pressured by the helper, the spouse, or both to be there. Helpers can expect to find a large proportion of such clients in settings where clients are forced to see a counselor (for instance, in high schools, where students in trouble with teachers must go to a helper as a form of punishment) or where some reward can be achieved only on condition of being involved in a counseling process (for instance, when being counseled is part of getting a job—going to a counselor is the price that must be paid). Clients like these are found in schools, especially below college level, in correctional settings, marriage counseling (especially if court mandated), employment agencies, welfare agencies, court-related settings, and other social agencies. Paradise and Wilder (1979) discovered that reluctant clients, perhaps as a kind of self-fulfilling prophecy ("What am I doing here—they're not going to help me anyway"), found the helping process less satisfactory and improved less than those who were not reluctant; saw the agency as not geared to handle their kinds of problems; and tended to terminate the counseling process prematurely. Dyer and Vriend (1975, p. 102) suggest that reluctant clients constitute the majority of clients seen by helpers in North America.

The fact that a client is not self-referred does not automatically mean he or she is reluctant, even though evidence seems to indicate that most are. However, even if initial reluctance is overcome, it can be expected that, as in the case of self-referred clients, some greater or lesser degree of resistance will be found. If something is defined as a cooperative venture, Smaby and Tamminen (1979) wonder whether it makes sense to talk about "counseling" reluctant clients—perhaps not, until the problem of their reluctance is faced and resolved.

Resistant clients.   The fact that a client is self-referred does not automatically mean that he or she is ready to participate in the helping process wholeheartedly. Paradise and Wilder (1979) also studied a group of self-referred clients and found varying degrees of reluctance among them. Resistant clients are those who, insofar as can be judged, come more or less willingly or who, though initially reluctant, overcome their reluctance but still fail to give themselves adequately to the helping process at one or more points along the way. For instance, a client might explore a problem situation quite willingly, set some goals, and cooperate with the helper in devising a program, and then balk at the implementation of the program—or begin to implement it, but only halfheartedly.

Causes of Reluctance and Resistance

In order to work with reluctance and resistance, it is helpful first to understand some of their common causes. The following kinds of clients are likely to be reluctant and/or resistant:

- Those who see no reason for going to a helper in the first place.
- Those who resent third-party referrers (parents, teachers, agencies), and whose resentment carries over to the helper.
- Those who fear the unfamiliar. They do not know what counseling is or they have misconceptions about it.
- Those who do not know how to participate effectively—that is, how to be "good" clients.
- Those who have a history of being rebels against systems. They rock the boat, and boat-rockers are more likely to become involuntary clients.
- Those who see the goals of the helper or the helping system as different from their own. For instance, the goal of counseling in a welfare setting might be to help clients become financially independent, whereas some clients might be satisfied with the present arrangement. The goal of helping in a mental hospital might be to help clients get out, whereas some clients might feel quite comfortable there.
- Those who have developed negative attitudes about helping agencies and who harbor suspicions about helpers. Helpers are referred to in derogatory and inexact terms ("shrinks").
- Those who believe that going to a helper is the same as admitting weakness, failure, and inadequacy. They feel they will lose face by going. By resisting the process, they preserve their self-esteem.
- Those who feel that counseling is something that is being done to them. They feel that their rights are not being respected.
- Those who feel that helpers have not invited them to be participants in the decisions that are to affect their lives, including expectations for change and decisions about procedures to be used in the helping process.
- Those who feel a need for personal power and find it through resisting a "powerful" figure or agency. "I may be relatively powerless, but I still have the power to resist." Riordan, Matheny, and Harris (1978) suggest that this can be a healthy sign in that "clients are grasping for a share in the control of their destiny" (p. 8).
- Those who are testing the helper's level of support and competence.
- Those who dislike their helpers, but do not discuss it with them.

- Those who see no payoffs for change.
- Those who, during the helping process, discover that the price of behavioral change is higher than they expected.
- Those who remain ambivalent about change.
- Those whose conception of the degree of change desired differs from that of the helper.

This list, as you will learn, is not exhaustive. Many sociopsychological variables such as sex, prejudice, race, religion, social class, upbringing, cultural and subcultural blueprints, and the like can play a part in resistance. For instance, a man might instinctively resist being helped by a woman, and vice versa. A Black might instinctively resist being helped by a White, and vice versa. A person with no religious affiliation might instinctively think that help coming from a minister will be "pious" or will automatically include some form of proselytizing. Different schools or approaches to counseling and psychotherapy identify causes of resistance that are derived from the theory of the particular school or approach (see Stream, 1985; Wachtel, 1982).

Unhelpful Responses to Reluctance and Resistance

Helpers, especially beginning helpers who are unaware of the pervasiveness of resistance, are disconcerted by it and face unexpected feelings and emotions in themselves when they encounter it. For instance, they feel confused, panicky, irritated, hostile, guilty, hurt, rejected, meek, or depressed. Distracted by these feelings, they can react in ways that are not helpful. For instance:

- They accept the guilt and try to placate the client.
- They become impatient and hostile and manifest it either verbally or nonverbally.
- They do nothing and hope that the resistance will disappear.
- They lower their expectations of themselves and proceed with the helping process, but in a halfhearted way.
- They try to become warmer and more accepting, hoping to win the client over by love.
- They blame the client and end up in a power struggle with him or her.
- They allow themselves to be abused by the client, playing the role of scapegoat.
- They lower their expectations of what can be achieved by counseling.
- They hand the direction of the helping process over to the client.
- They give up and terminate counseling.

In short, when helpers meet resistance they experience stress, and some give into dysfunctional "fight or flight" reactions.

The source of the stress is not just the behavior of the clients; it also comes from the helper's own self-defeating attitudes and assumptions about the helping process. Some of these are as follows:

- All clients should be self-referred and adequately committed to change before appearing at my door.
- Every client must like me and trust me.
- I am a consultant and not a social influencer; it should not be necessary to place demands on clients or even to help them place demands on themselves.
- Every unwilling client can be helped.
- No unwilling client can be helped.
- I alone am responsible for what happens to this client.
- I have to succeed completely with every client.

Effective helpers neither court resistance nor are surprised by it.

Productive Approaches to Dealing with Reluctance and Resistance

In a book like this it is impossible to identify every possible form of resistance, much less provide a set of strategies for managing each. What is suggested here is a general way of approaching reluctance and resistance in whatever form they take. Here are some suggested principles or steps for managing the kinds of resistance you may face.

See some resistance as normative.   Help clients see that they are not odd because they are reluctant or resistant. Beyond that, help them see the positive side of resistance. It may well be a sign of their affirmation of self.

See resistance as avoidance.   Reluctance and resistance can be viewed as forms of avoidance not necessarily tied to client ill will. Therefore, you need to understand the principles and mechanisms underlying avoidance behavior (which is often discussed in texts dealing with the principles of behavior; see Watson and Tharp, 1985). If clients are avoiding counseling because they perceive it as punishing—or, at least, as lacking in suitable rewards—helpers have to demonstrate to them in concrete and specific ways that engaging in the helping process can be rewarding rather than punishing and that change can be more rewarding than maintaining the status quo. Effective helpers realize that motivation usually has more to do with *incentives* than with "motives" locked away in the hearts of clients (Gilbert, 1978). Ask youself such questions as, "What incentives move this client to engage in this form of resistance?" "What incentives does this client need to move beyond resistance?"

Explore your own resistance.   Examine resistance in your own life. Intensive training in the models, methodologies, and skills of helping provides you with an opportunity to examine more or less at your leisure the ways in which you yourself resist growth and development. If you are in touch with the various forms of resistance in yourself and are finding ways of overcoming them, you are more likely to help clients deal with theirs. Note how difficult it is at times for you to move beyond your own resistance to managing problem situations.

Examine the quality of your interventions.   Without giving in to unwarranted guilt, examine your helping behavior. See if you are doing anything to elicit resistance from the client. For instance, you may have become too directive without realizing it. Furthermore, take stock of the emotions that are welling up in you because of the client's resistance, and of the ways in which they are being communicated to the client. Do not deny those feelings; rather, own them and find ways of coming to terms with them. For instance, do not *overpersonalize* the client's resistance. If you are allowing a hostile client to get under your skin, you are probably reducing your effectiveness.

Accept and work with the client's resistance.   This is a central principle. Start with the client's frame of reference. Accept both the client and his or her resistance. Do not ignore it or be intimidated by it. Let clients know how you experience it and then explore it with them. Model openness to change. Be willing to explore your own negative feelings. The skill of direct, mutual talk (called *immediacy* and discussed in Chapter Eight) is extremely important here. Help clients work through the emotions associated with resistance. Avoid moralizing. In some sense of the term, *befriend* the resistance.

Be realistic and flexible.   Remember that there are limits to what a helper can do. Know your own personal and professional limits. If your expectations for growth, development, and change exceed the client's, you can end up in an adversarial relationship with him or her. As Cormier and Cormier (1985) note, "Some of what gets labeled 'client resistance' is nothing more than the inflexibility of the therapist" (p. 577).

Prize client self-responsibility.   Even though a client's resistance has some legitimacy, he or she is still ultimately responsible for coping with it. Do not take responsibility for the client's resistance except insofar as you see yourself contributing to it. Teach clients how to involve themselves effectively in the helping process and show them how doing so can serve their self-interest.

Establish a "just society." Very often reluctant and resistant clients feel like victims. Therefore, provide in the helping relationship what Smaby and Tamminen (1979) call a "two-person just society" (p. 509). Establish as much mutuality as is consonant with your helping goals. A just society is based on mutual respect and shared planning—recall what was said in Chapter One about the resource collaborator role.

Invite participation. Invite resistant clients to participate in every step of the helping process and in all the decision making. Share expectations. Discuss and get reactions to helping procedures. With the client, design a minicontract that covers only the first couple of sessions.

Help clients identify resistance-supporting incentives. Help clients see and appreciate the roots and even the legitimacy of their resistance. If they discover the payoff that is associated with and helps maintain their resistance, they may be open to finding other ways of getting the same kinds of payoff. Use challenging skills (discussed in Chapter Eight) to help clients develop new perspectives on their resistance.

Search for incentives for moving beyond resistance. Help clients find incentives for participating in the helping process. Use client self-interest as a way of identifying these. Use brainstorming (see Chapter Ten) as a way of discovering possible incentives. For instance, the realization that he or she is going to remain in charge of his or her own life may be an important incentive for a client.

Begin with small goals. Begin with moderate, realizable goals that have been set cooperatively. Do not let the client use perfectionism in the form of unrealistic short-term or long-term goals as a cop-out. Help the client experience some kind of real success in the helping process as soon as possible. Help clients choose goals that will improve their lives from their perspective.

Tap significant others as resources. Do not assume you are the only helper in your clients' lives. Engage significant others such as peers and family members in helping clients face their resistance. For instance, lawyers who belong to Alcoholics Anonymous might be able to deal more effectively than you can with another lawyer's resistance to joining a treatment program.

Employ clients as helpers. If possible, find ways to get resistant clients into situations where they are actually helping others. The change of perspective involved can help them come to terms with their own resistance. One person who did a lot of work for Alcoholics Anonymous had a resistant alcoholic go with him on his city rounds, which included visiting hospitals, nursing homes for alcoholics, jails, flophouses, and down-and-out people on the streets. The alcoholic saw through all the lame excuses other alcoholics offered for their plight. After a week he joined AA himself. Another, more immediately usable form of this approach to resistance is role reversal. In the interview, take the role of the client and manifest the same kind of resistance he or she displays. Have the client take the counselor role and help you overcome your resistance. Group counseling, too, is a forum in which clients become helpers.

In summary, do not avoid dealing with resistance, and do not reinforce it; work with it, and become inventive in finding ways of dealing with it. Cormier and Cormier (1985) offer a range of strategies based on client variables, environmental variables, and helper variables (see Chapter Twenty in their book). As you will see in the last section of this chapter, a review of how either you or the client or both of you are resisting should be part of the ongoing evaluation process at every stage and step of the model.

A Model for Dealing with Helping-Process Problems, Including Resistance: Process versus Content Problems

Resistance is one of the most common problems to occur in counseling interactions, but not all helping-process problems concern resistance. For instance, there may be a value gap or culture gap between you and a client that makes the interaction difficult. A client may not like you; you may dislike a client. Or you might feel sexually attracted to a client. Or you both might find yourselves involved in aimless interactions. With a little experience, you will be able to extend the list quite easily.

I call the problems clients come to discuss *content* problems, simply because they ordinarily constitute the content of your dialogues with them. On the other hand, I call problems related to the helping process itself, such as resistance or incompatibility, *process* problems. The key point is that *the three-stage helping process is just as applicable to process problems as to content problems.* Instead of coming up with hints to help you manage all forms of resistance and the whole range of other process problems, I suggest that you quickly learn to apply the basic model to all the problems, concerns, and difficulties generated in helping encounters. For instance

> *Current scenario:* The client is avoiding talking concretely about the principal issues in her problem situation.
> *Preferred scenario:* The client talks more freely and accurately about her principal concerns.
> *Getting to the preferred scenario:* Brainstorm strategies for helping the client talk more freely and implement the best-fit strategies. For instance, the client might respond to a direct approach: "The issues

you're talking about are very sensitive and I appreciate how difficult it may be for you to talk about them in any detail. Is there anything that I can do to help you do this more easily?" The list of possible strategies can be as long as your imagination is fertile.

Sometimes in our frustration or even our panic we can fail to use our own medicine in managing the problems we encounter as helpers. In training counselors, I encounter both what-if questions—"What if the client does X, Y, or Z, then what do I do?"—and the very real problems that arise in practicum and internship situations—"The client did X and I didn't know what to do." When the trainee is challenged to apply the three-stage model to the process problems, almost inevitably she or he comes up with a viable approach. In classroom situations, trainees can brainstorm a whole range of strategies.

■ Ongoing Evaluation

The "E" in the center of each of the stages of the helping process reminds us that Evaluation should be built into the entire model. Appraisal that comes at the end of a process is often quite judgmental: "It didn't work." Ongoing evaluation is much more positive. It helps both client and helper learn from what they have been doing, celebrate what has been going well, and correct what has been going poorly. Therefore, a series of evaluation questions will be listed for each step of the helping model (see the Summary Box for Step I-A). In the beginning, you might well ask yourself these questions—at least the relevant ones—explicitly. If you do so, you will come to a point where the questions do not have to be asked explicitly at all because you will have developed an *evaluative sense*. That is, some part of you will always be monitoring your interactions with your clients in an unobtrusive and constructive way. It is this sense that will prompt you at times to stop the interaction and say something like, "Let's stop a moment and take stock of how well we're doing here." Evaluation questions or topics are included for each of the nine steps of the helping process (see Summary Box that follows). These questions serve as a summary of the main points of the chapter.

Once the helping sessions have ended, is follow-up necessary as a part of the evaluation process? Nicholson and Berman (1983) reviewed the follow-up literature and discovered that follow-up often added little to what was already known by the end of therapy. Their conclusion: "The findings highlight the general durability of gains during psychotherapy, suggesting that costly follow-up procedures may be used more selectively" (p. 261). If your sessions with a client end in an unsettled way, then scheduling a follow-up session may be in order. Whenever possible, leave the scheduling of follow-up sessions to the responsibility of the client.

■ Evaluation Checklist for Step I-A: Helping Clients Tell Their Stories

How effectively are you doing the following?

THE TELLING OF THE STORY

- Using a mix of attending, listening, empathy, and probing to help clients tell their stories
- Understanding blocks to client self-disclosure and providing a mix of support and challenge for clients having difficulty talking about themselves.

ONGOING ASSESSMENT

- Getting a sense of where the client is in the problem-management process in order to meet his or her needs as a client, rather than your own as a helper
- Noting resources both in clients themselves and in their environments
- Seeing clients in terms of their developmental stages and the normative tasks and crises of those stages
- Seeing clients contextually; that is, in terms of the social settings of their lives
- Assessing the life skills clients have and which ones they lack
- Understanding clients in terms of the principles of behavior, such as incentives, disincentives, punishment, avoidance behavior, shaping, and the like
- Using frameworks drawn from other approaches to helping that fit this client
- Judging the severity of a client's problems and his or her ability to handle them, as well as your own.

ESTABLISHING A WORKING RELATIONSHIP

- Being genuine and respectful in the behavioral ways outlined in Chapter Two; seeing the relationship as two-way
- Establishing a working alliance with the client that is outcome oriented
- Not doing for clients what they can do for themselves

- Providing a climate in which the social-emotional reeducation of the client is possible
- Becoming aware of and managing the inevitable "shadow side" of the relationship, the undercurrents arising from past history, current prejudices, personal needs, faulty interpersonal development, individual differences, failures in mutual understanding, and the like.

MANAGING CLIENT RELUCTANCE AND RESISTANCE

- Understanding your own resistance to growth and not being surprised by client resistance
- Accepting client resistance and working with it rather than against it
- Seeing resistance and other difficulties in the helping process as problems in their own right and using the problem-solving approach to address them.

Six

Stage I: Step I-B
Focusing: Helping Clients Develop
Leverage and Clarity

■

The goals of Step I-B
    Screening
    Focusing: The search for points of leverage
    Focusing: Exploration and clarification of problems and
    opportunities
Probing for missing experiences, behaviors, and feelings
Summarizing as a focusing skill
Writing approaches to the clarification of problem situations
Common problems in Step I-B
Is focusing enough?
Evaluation questions for Step I-B

As indicated in Figure 6–1, Step I-B is called *focusing*, but includes three processes: screening, focusing, and exploration and clarification. There are goals or outcomes associated with each of these processes.

■ The Goals of Step I-B

Although the following goals can be distinguished conceptually, in practice they often overlap. Furthermore, Step B itself can overlap and intermingle with Step A.

1. *Screening.* A judgment needs to be made as to whether the problems or missed opportunities revealed in the telling of the story merit serious consideration. The first goal, then, is to decide whether or not to continue. If the story being told has little substance, a decision may be made to probe for a more substantive story.

2. *Focusing.* Since all the concerns in a complex problem/opportunity situation cannot be dealt with at once, a second goal is to help clients decide what they would like to deal with first. Even problems that are told as single-issue stories—"I'd like to get rid of these headaches"—when examined often become multiple-issue problem situations. For instance, the headaches are a symptom of overwork, poor interpersonal relationships, and financial worries.

3. *Exploration and Clarification.* Once an issue is focused upon, it needs to be explored and clarified in terms of relevant experiences, behaviors, and emotions. The third goal of this step is to help clients spell out their concerns with the kind of specificity needed to set goals and develop

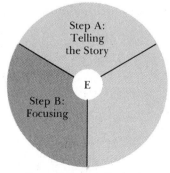

Stage I: Present Scenario

Figure 6–1. Step I-B: Focusing

problem-managing strategies. The desired outcome is a clear under-standing on the part of the client of the issue or issues chosen for attention.

Screening

Counseling and psychotheraphy are expensive in terms of both financial and human costs; neither should be undertaken lightly. Relatively little is said in the literature about screening—that is, making a decision as to whether any given problem situation or opportunity deserves attention—and the reasons are obvious. Helpers are urged to take their clients and their clients' concerns seriously. They are also urged to adopt an opti-mistic attitude, an attitude of hope, about their clients. Finally, they are schooled to take their profession seriously and are convinced that their services can make a difference in the lives of clients. For those and other reasons, the first impulse of the average counselor is to try to help clients no matter what the problem situation might be.

There is something very laudable in this. It is encouraging to see helpers prize people and express interest in their concerns. It is reward-ing to see helpers put aside the almost instinctive tendency to evaluate and judge others and to offer their services to clients just because they are human beings. However, helping, like other professions, can suffer from the "law of the instrument." A child, given a hammer, soon discovers that almost everything needs hammering. Helpers, once equipped with the models, methods, and skills of the helping process, can see all the human problems as needing their attention. There is a film series (Rog-ers, Perls, & Ellis, 1965) in which the same client is counseled by three different helpers with different orientations. After showing students the films, I ask whether the client needs counseling. The immediate answer is "yes." Then I ask a second question. "If this woman needs counseling, how many people in our society need counseling?" Since the woman's concerns are not unlike those of millions of other people, including the students' own, they are forced to rethink their answer to the first question. Counseling may be a *useful* intervention in many cases and yet be a luxury whose expense cannot be justified. The problem-severity formula dis-cussed in Chapter Five is a useful tool for screening.

Frances, Clarkin, and Perry (1984) discuss under the rubric of "dif-ferential therapeutics" ways of fitting different kinds of treatment to different kinds of patients. They also delineate the conditions under which "no treatment" is the recommendation of choice.

> Now that we have considered methods of selecting a therapeutic setting, format, technique, [and the] frequency and duration [of treatment], and have

also described somatic treatment and ways of combining different kinds of treatment, we are better prepared to discuss what may be the most difficult choice for the consultant, a choice that is in fact all too often totally overlooked: Is psychiatric treatment advisable at all or would no treatment be the preferred recommendation [p. 213].

They consign to the latter category such borderline clients as patients with a history of treatment failure or who seem to get worse from treatment; criminals trying to avoid or diminish punishment by claiming to be suffering from psychiatric conditions ("We may do a disservice to society, the legal system, the offenders, and ourselves if we are too willing to treat problems for which no effective treatment is available" [p. 227]); malingering patients with a fictitious illness, chronic nonresponders to treatment, patients likely to have spontaneous improvement, healthy patients with minor chronic problems, and oppositional patients refusing treatment. While a decision needs to be made in each case, and while some might dispute the categories proposed, the possibility of no treatment deserves serious attention.

Frances, Clarkin, and Perry suggest some of the benefits that may follow from a no-treatment decision. No treatment may do the following:

1) protect the patient from iatrogenic harm, especially by interrupting a sequence of destructive treatments;
2) protect the patient and clinician from wasting time, effort, and money;
3) delay therapy until a more propitious time;
4) protect and consolidate gains from previous treatments;
5) provide the patient an opportunity to discover that he or she can do without treatment; and
6) avoid a semblance of treatment when no effective treatment exists [p. 248].

Currently, a no-treatment decision on the part of helping professionals is countercultural and therefore difficult to make.

Seeking professional help is not the only avenue open to people wanting or needing to manage their problems in living more effectively. In a TV talk show, Melina Mercouri, once an actress and now a member of the government of Greece, was asked whether there were a lot of psychologists and psychiatrists in Greece. She threw her head back, laughed her infectious laugh, and said, "Oh no, we have to make do with our friends!"

It goes without saying that screening, or helping clients screen their stories, can be done in a heavy-handed way. Statements such as the following are not useful:

"Your concerns are actually not that serious."
"You should be able to work that through without help."
"I don't have time for problems as simple as that."

Whether such sentiments are expressed or merely implied, they obviously indicate a lack of respect and constitute a caricature of the screening process. Helpers are not alone in grappling with this problem. Doctors, too, face clients day in and day out with problems that run from the life-threatening to the inconsequential. Statistics suggest that more than half of the people who come to doctors have nothing physically wrong with them. And so doctors have to find ways to screen their patients and their complaints. I am sure that the best find ways to do so that preserve the dignity of their patients.

Screening, poorly executed, can lead to premature judgments about the seriousness of a client's problems. As mentioned earlier, some clients discuss relatively inconsequential problems as a way of putting their toe in the water, to test the humanity of the helper. A student talks about study habits when his real concern is his sexual identity. A woman talks about boredom when her real concern is aging and the normative "integrity versus despair" crisis people face as they grow older. At one end of the continuum is a willingness on the part of helpers to work with clients no matter how small their concerns. At the other end is the demand that clients come with serious problems and that they prove they are in need of and will benefit from help. Virtue lies somewhere in the middle.

A second screening issue involves the commitment of clients to do something about their problem situations. This means that there is some reasonable hope that a client is willing to do more than merely talk about his or her concerns. Or it means that there is some reasonable hope that a client will become productively involved in the helping process. Again, at one end of the continuum is a willingness on the part of helpers to work with clients who give little or no evidence of a commitment to working for change. At the other end is a tendency to ignore the understandable hesitancies of clients to commit themselves to change and to throw down the gauntlet,"Come back when you want to do something about it." Such an approach is meaningless in settings in which reluctant clients are the norm.

Experienced helpers opt for the end points of neither of these continuums. Because they are empathic, they stay close to the experience of clients and develop hypotheses about both the substance of problems and the commitment of clients, and test them in a humane way. If clients' problems seem inconsequential, they probe for more substantive issues. If clients seem reluctant, resistant, and unwilling to work, they challenge clients' attitudes and help them work through their resistance. But in both cases they realize that there may come a time—and it may come fairly quickly—to judge that further effort is uncalled for because of lack of results.

In summary, I think that helpers should make a *decision* to involve themselves in the concerns of clients, rather than doing so automatically. Screening is an activity that can overlap other steps. Whenever a helper sincerely committed to the interests of a client comes to realize that either substance or willingness or both are missing, he or she has the right or even the obligation to share these concerns with the client. Such a challenge may come early or late in the helping process, but whenever it comes, it needs to be handled with the skill necessary to carry off any kind of challenge. (Challenging skills are discussed in the next chapter.) Clients with relatively minor concerns might be better off in some other forum such as a self-help group or problem-management skills-training group. This would be a more efficient use of expensive helper resources, would provide a forum in which clients' concerns could be dealt with, and would empower clients to manage similar concerns on their own or in conjunction with friends and acquaintances.

Focusing: The Search for Points of Leverage

Clients often need help to get a handle on complex problem situations. A 41-year-old depressed man with a failing marriage, a boring job, deteriorating interpersonal relationships, health concerns, and a drinking problem cannot work on everything at once. There needs to be a focus in the helping process around which the resources of the client can be mobilized. Lazarus (Rogers, Shostrom, & Lazarus, 1977), in a film on his multimodal approach to therapy (Lazarus, 1976, 1981), employs a focusing technique I find useful. He asks the client to use just one word to describe her problem. She searches around a bit and offers a word. Then he asks the client to put the word in a simple sentence that would describe her problem. It is a simple way to begin, but it can greatly facilitate the focusing process.

If the problem situation has many dimensions to it, the helper and client are faced with the quandary of where to start.

■

Andrea, a woman in her mid-thirties, is referred to a neighborhood mental health clinic by a social worker. During her first visit she pours out a story of woe both historical and current: brutal parents, teenage drug abuse, a poor marriage, unemployment, poverty, and the like. Andrea is so taken up with getting it all out that the helper can do little more than sit and listen.

■

As we have seen, assessment frameworks can be used by helpers to listen in a focused way and to organize what clients are saying, but, as in the case of Andrea, helpers also need principles that will help determine what to do next.

Helpers can use the principles of focusing to guide their clients in choosing what issue or issues to focus on first. These principles are interrelated, so that more than one might apply at the same time.

- If there is a crisis, first help the client manage the crisis.
- Focus on issues that the client sees as important.
- Begin with a problem that seems to be causing the client pain.
- Focus on an issue that the client is willing to work on, even if it does not seem important to you.
- Begin with some manageable subproblem of a larger problem situation.
- Begin with a problem that can be managed relatively easily, one that shows promise of being successfully handled by the client.
- Begin with a problem that, if handled, will lead to a general improvement in the client's overall condition.
- When possible, move from less severe to more severe problems.
- Focus on a problem for whose solution the benefits will outweigh the costs.

Counselors use these principles to help clients discover points of leverage in the management of problem situations and the development of opportunities. Underlying all these principles is an attempt to make clients' initial experiencing of the helping process rewarding so that they will have the incentive they need to continue to work. Examples of the use and abuse of these principles follow.

If there is a crisis, first help the client manage the crisis.   While crisis intervention is usually seen as a special form of counseling (Baldwin, 1979; Janosik and others, 1984), it can also be seen as a rapid application of the three states of the helping process to the most distressing aspects of a crisis situation.

■

Principle violated.   A resident-hall assistant (RA), a graduate student, meets an obviously agitated undergraduate student, Zachary, in the hall. The student says he has to talk to him. They go to the assistant's office to talk. The student sits down but is literally shaking. He finds it extremely difficult to talk. The problem is a case of attempted homosexual rape. Once the student blurts it out, the RA begins asking questions such as, "Has this ever happened before?" "Do you think you did anything to make him think you were interested?" "How do you feel about your own sexual orientation?" "Do you think you should press charges?" and the like.

Principle observed.   Zachary talks with the RA for a few minutes and then explodes: "Why are you asking me all these stupid questions?" He stalks out and goes over to a friend's house. His friend, seeing his agitation, says something like, "Good grief, Zach, you look terrible. Come in. What's going on?" He listens to Zachary's account of what has just happened, interrupts very little, just a word here or there to let his friend know he is with him, just sits with him when he falls silent or cries a bit, and then slowly and reassuringly "talks Zach down," engaging in an easy dialogue that gives his friend an opportunity gradually to find his composure again.

■

The friend's instincts are much better than those of the RA. He does what he can to defuse the immediate crisis.

Focus on issues that the client sees as important.   The client's frame of reference can be a point of leverage. Given the client's story, *you* may not think she has chosen the most important issues for initial consideration, but helping clients choose issues that are important to them sends an important message: "I am working with you in *your* interests."

■

Principle violated.   A woman comes to a counselor complaining about her relationship with her boss. She believes that he is sexist and there are hints of sexual overtones. After listening to her story, the counselor believes that she probably has some leftover developmental problems with her father and that this affects her attitude to older men. He pursues this line of thinking with her. The client is confused and feels put down. When she does not return for a second interview, the counselor says to himself that she is not motivated to do something about her problem.

Principle used.   A dying patient talks to a pastoral counselor about his concern for his wife. As she listens to the patient, the counselor picks up indications that the patient has strong feelings and unresolved attitudes about his own dying that he is not admitting to. However, for the present she does not address these issues. She helps him deal with his concern about his wife's pain. She will look for an opportunity to help him come to grips with his concern about himself later on.

■

It may well be that the immediate frame of reference of a client needs broadening. But helping at its best starts with the frame of reference of the client.

Begin with the problem that seems to be causing pain.   Clients usually come to helpers because they are hurting. Their hurt, then, becomes an incentive, a source of leverage. Their pain also makes them vulnerable. This means they are open to influence from helpers and even to manipulation. If it is evident that they are open to influence because of their pain, seize the opportunity, but move cautiously. Their pain may also make them demanding. They can't understand why you cannot help them get rid of it immediately. This kind of importunity may put you off but it, too, needs to be understood. Such clients are like patients in an emergency room, each one seeing himself or herself as needing immediate attention. The demands for immediate relief may well signal a self-centeredness that is part of the client's character and therefore part of the problem situation but unidentified by the client. It may be that the pain, in your eyes, is self-inflicted and it well may be that you will have to challenge the client. But pain, whether self-inflicted or not, is still pain. Part of your respect for clients is your respect for them as vulnerable, while helping them use their own distress as a motivating force.

■

Principle violated.   Rob, a man in his mid-twenties, comes to a counselor in great distress because his wife has just left him. The counselor quickly sees that Rob is an impulsive, self-centered person with whom it would be difficult to live. The counselor immediately challenges him to take a look at his interpersonal style and the ways in which he alienates others. Rob seems to listen but he does not return.

Principle used.   Rob goes to a second counselor who also sees a number of clues indicating self-centeredness and a lack of maturity and discipline. However, she listens carefully to his story, even though it is one-sided. Instead of adding to his pain by making him come to grips with his selfishness, she focuses on the future, Rob's preferred scenario. Of course, his wife's return is the principal element in this scenario, but she helps him describe in some detail what life would be like once they got back together. His hurting provides the incentive for working with the counselor on the future scenario. Once the preferred scenario is outlined, she helps him explore what he needs to do, ways in which he might need to change, to get the preferred scenario on line. He is now in a better position to see how he has contributed to his wife's leaving him.

■

The helper's focusing on a better future responds to Rob's need. This future, then, becomes the stepping-stone to challenge. What is Rob willing to do to create the future he says he wants?

Focus on an issue, however important, that the client is willing to work on.   The client's willingness to work on an issue can be a point of leverage. It is important to elicit the client's cooperation early in the helping process. Making premature demands on clients to explore and clarify highly sensitive issues may only alienate them.

■

Principle violated.   A college student in the initial presentation of his concerns talks about a variety of issues: doing poorly in his courses, inconsistent relationships with friends, fights with his parents, and misgivings about his sexuality. The counselor believes that sexual conflicts may be central and begins by probing the young man's sexual concerns. The client shows a fair amount of reluctance to talk about sex so quickly, but the counselor persists.

Principle used.   A woman describes the disastrous interactions that characterize the relationship between her husband and herself. She talks about his faults readily, but is much more reluctant to talk about the ways in which her behavior contributes to their difficulties. The counselor notices this reluctance immediately but, without taking sides, helps her focus on her husband's behavior and, perhaps more importantly, her reactions to his behavior. He knows that this frame of reference needs to be transcended, but he does not immediately challenge the client to do so.

■

While the more painful issues are often the more critical, they call for the most sensitivity on your part. If you first help clients deal with the pain, they are likely to trust you enough to reveal some of its roots.

Begin with some manageable subproblem of a larger problem situation.   Large, complicated problem situations remain vague and unmanageable. Dividing a problem up into manageable bits can provide a point of leverage. Most larger problems can be broken down into smaller, more manageable subproblems.

■

Principle violated.   Carl and Carla arrive for marriage counseling. The history of their marriage is a stormy one. Both of them have been saving up their grievances and now want to pour them out to the counselor and, if possible, force her into the role of judge. They both work; each has good friends they do not share with the other; both have been married before. There are problems with sex, child care, communication, and finances. The counselor takes a somewhat passive, understanding role, so that for all practical purposes they are in charge of the sessions. They argue, jump from issue to issue, and generally involve themselves in the same kind of chaos they generate at home. The counselor continues to use basic empathy as her principal approach.

Principle used.   Lisa, a single woman in her mid-thirties, has not held a job for more than a year or two. Though intelligent and talented, she has been laid off several times. Two of the companies, when laying her off, talked about "general cutbacks," but a third said that she did not fit in with the other personnel. Lisa is seen by most people as "difficult." Her abrasive ways tend to alienate people who come into close contact with her. The counselor, too, finds her an abrasive person with little insight into how demanding she is. Lisa is presently between jobs and is seeking career counseling. The counselor does not immediately deal with her abrasiveness. Rather he suggests that one practical step is to help her see how she comes across in interviews. He videotapes a couple of role-playing sessions and helps her critique what she sees.

In the second case the counselor does not leap into the more complicated issue of interpersonal style. Rather he starts with the need of the client— getting a job—and focuses on one dimension of the job-seeking process— the interview—in which she expresses some dimensions of her style. Having the client critique her own performance in an interview is more manageable than dealing with the entire area of interpersonal style.

Begin with a problem that can be managed relatively easily, one that shows promise of being successfully handled by the client.   Starting with a simple problem can be a point of leverage. If clients are helped to manage some relatively easy part of a problem situation, the reinforcement they experience may well empower them to attack more difficult areas.

Principle violated.   Elmer has been through bankruptcy twice because of his mismanagement of two small businesses. Now on the verge of his third bankruptcy, he has been told by the court that he must see a counselor. The counselor has Elmer explore his entire history of financial mismanagement. He wants him to spot what goes wrong so that he can avoid making the same mistakes in the future. They soon get lost in long discussions about accounting procedures and about his managerial techniques and style.

Principle used.   Since they seem to be getting nowhere, the counselor refers Elmer to a self-help group made up of individuals with similar financial problems. In this group Elmer is first helped to explore how he manages his personal rather than his business finances. He learns what he is doing well and what he is doing poorly and makes some changes. Then he is helped to transfer that information to business situations.

■

Bobbe and Schaffer (1968) talk about "breakthrough projects."

> Success in carrying out change . . . even a rather moderate success—almost always reveals new opportunites for further change not visible before. These successes also produce new confidence and know-how about change. . . . That is why we call these success experiences "breakthrough projects," because they not only produce immediate progress but also generate the ingredients for additional, accelerating progress [p. 7].

In some cases an initial experience of success with a simple problem can release a flood of unused resources.

Begin with a problem that, if handled, will lead to a general improvement in the client's overall condition. Some problems, when addressed, yield results beyond what might be expected. Improvement in one area sometimes generalizes to other areas.

■

Principle violated. Jeff, a middle-aged carpenter, comes to a community mental health center with a variety of complaints including insomnia, excessive drinking, and temptations toward exhibitionism. He also has an intense fear of dogs, something that every once in a while affects the work he does. The counselor sees the latter problem as one that can be managed through the application of behavior modification methodologies. They spend a fair amount of time on the desensitization of this phobia. However, most of the client's other complaints remain. His phobia is not related closely enough to his principal life concerns.

Principle used. Cassie, a high-school senior, is having a number of developmental problems: a poor relationship with her parents, failure in school, conflicted peer relationships, low self-esteem, and bouts with both anxiety and depression. The counselor notes that a lack of self-discipline is a thread running through many of Cassie's problems. Although she is not an athlete, she is interested in physical fitness. The counselor helps her get involved in a simple physical fitness program as a way of putting some discipline into her life. Cassie enjoys seeing herself make steady, measurable progress. Other areas of her life begin to improve. Then, with the counselor's help, she begins to bring discipline to her schoolwork and interpersonal relationships in more direct ways.

∎

Effective counselors help clients find these leverage themes and capitalize on the resources they already have.

When possible, move from less severe to more severe problems. This is especially important when the more serious problems are chronic and do not currently constitute a crisis. Moving gradually can be a point of leverage.

∎

Principle violated. Ted has spent years in a state mental hospital. Several years ago he was diagnosed as schizophrenic and has since been leading a rather colorless life in an open ward. He practically never interacts with his fellow patients unless he absolutely has to. Recently he has been having some problems with his work assignments. He asks to see the therapist because he thinks she can do something about his work situation. The therapist, new to the hospital, decides to use this opportunity to deal with his refusal to socialize. Ted returns for a second session but then refuses to see the helper anymore.

Principle used. Mildred, a patient discharged from a state mental hospital to a halfway house, has spent a good deal of time in group sessions learning simple social skills including grooming, interacting with other patients, doing chores around the house, and using the city bus system. Now that she has achieved a certain degree of success in those tasks, the therapist thinks of other possibilities—for instance, some kind of work in a sheltered workshop.

∎

The helper in the first case misuses the principle of leverage. She tries to force an issue rather than look for a point of leverage for the client. As we shall see in the next chapter, helping clients place demands on themselves is a very important strategy, but helpers need to understand clients well enough to know when to use it.

Focus on a problem for whose solution the benefits will outweigh the costs. This is not an excuse for failing to tackle difficult problems. If you demand a great deal of work from both yourself and the client, basic laws of behavior suggest that there be a reasonable payoff for both of you.

∎

Principle used. Angie, a middle-aged homemaker, feels locked into the house. As she tells her story, it soon becomes clear that she is the victim of her own lack of assertiveness. She grew up as a "nice," compliant girl; womanhood and marriage have not changed the picture very much. Angie spends some time in a consciousness-raising, assertiveness-training group for women. The benefits far outweigh the costs. She begins to develop a rewarding life outside the home that complements her life as homemaker.

■

The economics of helping can be too easily overlooked. Currently, hospitals faced with being paid only a certain amount of money by the government for a particular kind of illness are quickly learning to deliver services with greater efficiency.

The principles of leverage, used together judiciously, can help counselors shape the helping process to meet the needs and resources of clients. However, helpers must avoid using those same principles to water down or retard the helping process. Ineffective helpers

- Begin with the framework of the client, but never get beyond it
- Don't push clients to consider significant issues they are avoiding
- Allow the client's pain and discomfort to mask the roots of his or her problems
- Fail to build on clients' successes
- Continue to deal with small, manageable problems and don't help clients face more demanding problems in living
- Fail to help clients generalize learning in one area of life—for instance, self-discipline in a fitness program—to other, more difficult areas of living—for instance, self-control in close interpersonal relationships.

In a word, ineffective helpers are afraid of making reasonable demands of clients or influencing clients to make reasonable demands of themselves. Even the supportive efforts of such helpers become empty when not complemented by challenge. Challenging is discussed and illustrated in Chapters Seven and Eight.

The search for leverage is not restricted to Step I-B. The larger question is: Given the entire helping model, what parts of it will provide the most leverage in helping the client manage the problem situation or develop an opportunity more effectively? This is an ongoing, collaborative search on the part of both helper and client.

Exploration and Clarification of Problems and Opportunities

Once clients decide on what they would like to focus, the next goal is *exploration and clarification*. Problems that are effectively defined and formulated are easier to manage (Nezu & D'Zurilla, 1981). Problem situations are clarified if they are spelled out in terms of specific and relevant experiences, behaviors, and feelings; the simple framework suggested in the discussion of listening (Chapter Three). Hutchins (1979, 1982) has developed a thoughts-feelings-actions matrix that can help counselors and clients to focus on high-priority areas. Once an issue has been chosen for exploration, the basic communication skills of attending, listening, empathic responding, and probing are the principal instruments counselors use to help clients explore and clarify it. Box 6–1 summarizes the elements of concreteness—experiences, behaviors, and feelings related to clarifying problem situations.

■ **Box 6–1. The Elements of Concreteness in Clarifying Problem Situations**

When clients talk about themselves, they do so in terms of *experiences* (the things that happen to them), *behaviors* (what they do or fail to do), and *affect* (the feelings and emotions that accompany and relate to experiences and behaviors).

Experiences: the things that happen *to* clients.
    Overt: those capable of being seen by others.
    "He keeps telling other people that I'm dishonest."
    "I've been fired three times in the last five years."
    Covert: experiences within the client that cannot be seen by others.
    "I have high blood pressure and I get headaches a lot."
    "I often hear voices when I'm alone."
Behaviors: the things clients do or refrain from doing.
    Overt: those capable of being seen by others.
    "I beat my child when I get angry with her."
    "When she says I'm not a real man, I just keep quiet."
    Covert: behaviors within the client that he or she directs in some way.
    "Inside my head I rehearse everything I say to him."
    "Everyday I think about getting back at her."
Affect: the feelings and emotions that precede, accompany, underlie, and give color and intensity to experiences and behaviors.
    Overt: feelings and emotions the client expresses outwardly or talks about.
    "I laugh out loud when he says he loves me."
    "I get depressed when she doesn't call me."
    Covert: feelings and emotions that clients experience but that they try to suppress or keep to themselves.
    "When he shows off, I fume inside."
    "She hurts me a lot, but I don't let on."
    "What do you mean 'What am I feeling'? Nothing much, I suppose."

A problem situation is clear when it is spelled out in terms of the clients' specific experiences, behaviors, and feelings, whether overt or covert, that are relevant to the problem situation.

In the following example, a young man talks to a counselor because he is shy.

CLIENT: My problem is that I'm shy. I'm just too shy for my own good.
HELPER: And you'd like to do something about it.
CLIENT: Yeah. . . . But I don't know what.
HELPER: Shyness is different for different people. Could you tell me a little bit more about yours?
CLIENT: Well some of it has to do with girls. I'm very shy around girls. That's one of the worst.
HELPER: So though your shyness is not limited to girls, that causes you a lot of difficulty.
CLIENT: Yeah, like when I'm at a dance. I tend to stand around and talk with the guys. I want to be noticed by girls and I don't want to be noticed. I get butterflies if I think someone is going to walk up and talk with me.
HELPER: Because of the butterflies, you sort of do things to make sure that you're not available. And yet you want to be available.
CLIENT: Yeah, I'm my own worst enemy. You know, I think that I'm not really a bad guy. . . . People can . . . well . . . sort of like me when they're with me.
HELPER: But girls don't get that chance. . . . Hmmm. What lousy things will happen if you make yourself a little more available to girls? I mean what goes on in your head when you see a girl headed toward you—besides the butterflies?
CLIENT: Oh, that she won't see me as important enough. You know, one of the big guys. . . . And I'm not that good-looking. Or that she'll think I'm a drip, you know, not with it.
HELPER: You have quite a conversation with yourself before she even gets there!

Attending, listening, empathy, and probes: all directed to helping the client get a clearer picture of the problem situation so that he can eventually say, though not in so many words, "Now that I understand what I'm experiencing, doing, and feeling, I'm beginning to get some idea of what I have to change or what I'd like to change." Shyness is a trait that cannot be managed until it is translated into

• What the person's internal and external experiences are. For instance, this client has not experienced much rejection, but has imagined a lot.
• What the person's internal and external behaviors are. For instance, this client has self-defeating conversations with himself.
• What the person's feelings and emotions are. For instance, this client feels afraid, ambivalent, and frustrated.

At first you help clients clarify problems in terms of experiences, behaviors, and feelings as they see them—that is, from their frame of reference. As you do this, you or the two of you may see that the frame of reference being used is too narrow to get the kind of objective understanding of the problem needed to develop alternate scenarios. If the point of view is too narrow or limited, the client needs to be invited to challenge and expand it. At this point Step I-C begins to overlap Step I-B. When helpers need to probe for "missing" or unidentified experiences, behaviors, and feelings, a bridge between Step I-B and Step I-C is being established.

■ Probing for Missing Experiences, Behaviors, and Feelings

What do you do if you feel there are significant experiences, behaviors, and feelings relevant to the problem situation but unidentified or undiscussed by the client? You can act on your hunches and gently probe for what you think might be missing. This kind of probing, together with the use of summaries to be discussed later in this chapter, constitutes a bridge between Step I-B and the challenging you will do in Step I-C.

In this first example, a woman is discussing the ups and downs of a relationship she is having with a married man. The client talks a great deal about her devotion to him and her deep feelings for him, but says relatively little about how he reciprocates. The counselor helps her take a closer look at the *experiences* that seem to be missing.

HELPER: You say that there is a great deal of mutuality in the relationship. I'm curious about a number of things. For instance, how you get in touch with each other. What you do when you're together. Things like that.

CLIENT: Well, actually he never calls me. It's sort of taken for granted that I'll call him. But he's usually pleasant when I call.

HELPER: So for the most part you take the initiative to get in touch with him, but, as you say, that's part of your arrangement. You say he's "usually" pleasant. Tell me a little bit more about the "usually" part.

CLIENT: Well, sometimes—not too often—he sounds a bit cross, maybe just a bit on edge, when I call. It could be that I'm reading something into it.

The helper is both empathic and probing. Of course, care needs to be taken on the part of the helper not to gather information to support some preconception. For instance, in the case at hand, if the helper has the preconception that the woman is being treated poorly, he may slant his probing to confirm his hypothesis. Ideally at this point, however, the helper is merely trying to fill out the picture.

In the following example the client is talking about a relationship that seems to be going sour. He keeps discussing what is going wrong in terms of experiences; what the other person does to him. He seldom talks about his own *behaviors*.

CLIENT: I don't know why she acts the way she does. One day she will be chattering away on the phone in the most engaging way. She's carefree and tells me all that's happening. She's great when she's in that mood. But at other times she's actually rude to me and moody as hell—and it seems so personal. I mean not just that she's in a bad mood in general, but that it is somehow directed at me.

COUNSELOR A: It seems unfair when she makes you a victim of her moods.

CLIENT: Right. For instance, it was only yesterday when she . . .

COUNSELOR B: It seems unfair when she makes you a victim of her moods. But since, as you say, her moods seem to be directed at you, you may begin to wonder what's going on in her mind. I wonder what she thinks you do that makes her want to get at you. Any guesses?

CLIENT (after a pause): Well, it's hard to read her mind, but maybe she thinks that, well, I'm a bit selfish, you know, always pushing what I want to do when we're together. Maybe it's something like that. I do get my way a lot, but in a very good-natured way. For instance, yesterday . . .

Counselor A at this stage might well, by the continued use of basic empathy, merely reinforce the client's sense of being victimized. Counselor B, by probing for the client's missing behavior in a nonaccusatory way, elicits the kind of exploration that could help the client understand *his* part in the deteriorating relationship. Box 6–2 reviews what is meant by problematic behaviors. Sometimes it is a question of what the client is doing, sometimes what he or she is not doing.

■ Summarizing

Summarizing can be used to help clients explore their problem situations in a more focused and concrete way. As such, it is a way of helping clients move from Step I-B, focusing and clarifying, into Step I-C, developing new perspectives. It is a "bridging" response.

Brammer (1973) lists a number of goals that can be achieved by the judicious use of summarizing: "warming up" the client, focusing scattered thoughts and feelings, bringing the discussion of a particular theme to a close, and prompting the client to explore a theme more thoroughly. Notice how these contribute to both helping clients clarify the problem situation from their own perspective and helping them develop new perspectives. Often, when scattered elements are brought together, the client sees the "bigger picture" more clearly. And so summarizing can lead to new perspectives or alternate frames of reference.

In the following example a trainer is giving a counselor-trainee feedback in the form of a summary.

TRAINER: Let's see how all these pieces fit together. Overall you see yourself on the way to becoming an effective helper, but besides your obvious strengths, you see some weaknesses. Your strengths include being an enthusiastic

■ **Box 6–2. Problematic Behavior**

Problem situations involve problematic behavior. A problematic behavior is one that:

- prevents an individual from *attaining some goal,* such as having a close relationship with a person of the opposite sex;
- causes the individual significant *personal pain* or discomfort; for instance, Tess is making it through school but she is always extemely anxious;
- results in *undesirable consequences for others;* for instance, Jamie's failure to control his temper causes suffering for his wife and children; Wayne's uncontrolled sexual appetites and penchant for violence make him a menace to women.

Problematic behaviors can involve behavioral excesses or behavioral deficits. Here are some examples of excesses:

■

Alex has a good sense of humor, but sometimes he does not know when enough is enough and he ends up annoying his friends rather than entertaining them. He is a problem for others.

■

Francine used to let people walk all over her. She always gave in to what others wanted. Now she has gone to the opposite extreme: she is not assertive but aggressive. For instance, at the office she demands that everything be done her way. Her coworkers have become uncooperative and she is not meeting her deadlines. She is experiencing personal pain and she is also a problem for others.

Here are some examples of deficits:

■

Carl avoids conflict whenever possible. This means that both at work and at home some of his legitimate needs are not met. For instance, at work he gets more than his share of overtime. This prevents him from pursuing goals outside the office.

■

Judy has nothing good to say about herself in her interactions with others. She does not put herself down, but she does not appreciate herself. As a result, she is less than she might be with her family, friends, and coworkers. Her interpersonal life is flat. Enjoyment of interpersonal relationships eludes her.

If clients are to manage their problems and develop opportunities, they must change self-defeating internal and external behaviors. Ultimately clients need to be helped to challenge themselves to act.

learner, caring deeply about others, and being good at the basic communication skills. And yet you bog down when it comes to inviting clients to challenge themselves. You feel uncomfortable in, well, *intruding* into others' lives.
You're somewhat fearful of saying things that might make clients feel uncomfortable. At that point you feel tied up in yourself and sometimes you
retreat back into exploring the same problem over again. Is this a fair picture?

TRAINEE: That's it. I keep telling myself I'm intruding. And I keep telling myself
that it's awful for the client to feel discomfort.

The trainer, using a summary, pulls together the highlights of the trainee's self-exploration and lets them speak for themselves. A good summary
is not a mechanical pulling together of a number of facts; it is a systematic
presentation of *relevant* data. The helper makes some decisions as to what
is relevant, but bases that decision on having listened to and understood
the client. So summaries, too, are social-influence processes.

In this example the trainer, by means of the summary, helps the
trainee focus more concretely on her misgivings about "intrusiveness"
(a fairly common problem for trainees and novice helpers). She has
learned and feels comfortable with the basic communication skills, but
challenging skills, while making sense conceptually, are more difficult
for her to learn and put into practice. They *are,* to some degree, intrusive,
but it is an intrusiveness called for by the helping contract and carried
out with the collaboration of the client. The trainer's response helps her
focus on her feelings of intrusiveness. She can explore this theme a bit
more and decide how she wants to cope with it.

Let's take a look at another summary that helps a client understand
himself more fully and see the need for action. The client is a 52-year-
old man who has revealed and explored a number of problems in living
and is concerned about being depressed.

COUNSELOR: Let's take a look at what we've seen so far. You're down—not just
a normal slump; this time it's hanging on. You worry about your health, but
you check out all right physically, so that seems to be more a symptom than
a cause of your depression. There are some unresolved issues in your life.
One that you seem to be stressing is the fact that your recent change of job
has meant you don't see much of your old friends anymore. Since you're
single, you don't find that easy. Another issue—one you find painful and
embarrassing—is your struggle to stay young. You don't like facing the fact
that you're getting older. A third issue is the way you—to use your own word—
overinvest yourself in work, so much so that when you finish a long-term
project your life is suddenly empty. That is, a number of factors in your
lifestyle seem to contribute to your depression.

CLIENT: (Pause) It's painful to hear it all that baldly, but that about sums it up.
I've suspected I've got some screwed-up values, but I haven't wanted to stop
long enough to take a look at them. Maybe the time has come. I'm hurting
enough.

This client, in the self-exploratory phase, produces data that point to certain painful conclusions: he is immature in some respects (for example, in his overvaluing youth), he is "out of community" (his interpersonal life is at a low ebb), and he is trying ineffective solutions to his problems (dealing with loneliness by a flight into work). The counselor's summary hits home—somewhat painfully. The client draws his own conclusion. He seems ready to consider the kinds of new perspectives that will help him establish problem-managing goals. Perhaps this summary would have been more effective had the helper also summarized some of the strengths of the client, to provide a more positive context for developing alternative frames of reference. Effective helpers listen for resources and help clients identify unused resources.

Summaries, if effective, help a client focus more intensively on some important issue. Ineffective summaries—mere rehashes of many of the things clients have said—can distract rather than help focus. Summaries, though they can be used at any time to give focus and direction to the helping process, are especially useful at certain times: at the beginning of a new session, during a session when a client seems to be rambling, and when a client seems to have exhausted everything he or she has to say on a particular topic.

At the beginning of a new session. When summaries are used at the beginning of a new session, especially when clients seem uncertain as to how to begin, they prevent clients from merely repeating what has been said before. They put clients under pressure to move on. In the following example the client is a 65-year-old widower who has just retired.

COUNSELOR: Last week you talked about your loneliness and your fears of dying. You mentioned how these feelings are particularly intense in the evening and on weekends. You also talked quite a bit on how much you depended on your wife and how much you defined yourself through your job. At the end of the session you were discussing your feelings about being too old to do anything about all of this. I'm wondering if this is how you saw our last session and whether you want to add anything to it.

Such a summary serves several purposes. It shows the client that the helper listened carefully to what he had to say and that she had reflected on it after the session. It gives the client a jumping-off point for the new session. It gives the client an opportunity to add to or modify what was said. It places the responsibility for moving on with the client. The client might well need help to move on, but it gives him the opportunity of exercising initiative. Summaries have a kind of "well, now what?" quality about them. They are part of the social-influence process: they provide gentle pressure to move on. As such, they can be used during any step of the helping process.

Sessions that are going nowhere.   A summary can be used to give focus to a session that seems to be going nowhere. In the following example, a young, White ghetto resident who has had several run-ins with the police is talking to a Black counselor associated with the probation office. The client is jumping from one topic to another and the counselor is having a hard time pulling it all together.

COUNSELOR: I'm not sure where we're headed here. Here's what I think I do understand. You're angry because your probation officer made you come see me. You feel it's a waste of time talking to me because I'm Black. And you feel that we can't do much for you here. Talking about your problems doesn't make any sense when the whole system's got you boxed in.

CLIENT: You got it. Where do we go from here?

The counselor presents the central issues as he thinks the client sees them. It doesn't produce any magical change, but it does stop the rambling process and gives both of them a chance to say "What do we do now?"

When a client gets stuck.   Summaries can be used when clients seem to have exhausted everything they have to say about a particular issue. A summary of the principal points they *have* made can help them see the "bigger picture" more clearly and help them move on. In the following example a young woman has been talking about her difficult relationship with her father. She has revealed a great deal about the history of that relationship and now stops dead and seems frustrated and confused.

COUNSELOR A: It's hard to pull all of this together. You feel you don't really have much more to say about your relationship with your father.

CLIENT: Yeah, that's about where it stands. (She remains silent.)

COUNSELOR B: Let's see if I can pull this together. Your father never had a good word for you when you were a kid, just criticism when you did something wrong. When you went to college, he seemed to resent it—perhaps because you, a woman, were getting more education than he did. He ridiculed the idea. Then his divorcing your mother was, for you, the last straw. Since you saw him as pretty much in the wrong, you were very angry and hurt, so you cut off all communication with him. That was over three years ago. Now he's gotten in contact with you once more. He seems to want to reestablish a relationship, almost as if nothing had happened. He's taking a let-bygones-be-bygones approach, but that doesn't satisfy you at all.

CLIENT: No, I have to get all of this off my chest to him. I don't know whether he knows why I stopped talking to him. This is like a rock on my chest.

Counselor A makes the wrong choice here: his use of basic empathy does not help. Counselor B, on the other hand, sees that this is a good time for a summary. She pulls together the salient facts in the client's experience with her father. Her response indicates something that she feels she needs to *do*. That is, the summary helps her see the need for some kind of action. Later in the counseling session the counselor role-played the client's father and had the client say directly what she wanted to say. This "rehearsal" was part of an action program that culminated in the client's speaking directly to her father.

Summaries can be instrumental in helping the client to take greater ownership of the helping process. Once the counselor presents a summary, the ball is in the client's court. The client can choose where to move. Even better, helpers can invite clients to summarize.

COUNSELOR (at the beginning of a new session): You probably have thought a bit about what you said last session. I wonder whether you could briefly outline what you think were the most important points you made last week.

Both empathy and probing on the part of the counselor can help the client get through the summary.

Brammer (1973; see p. 94 for his guidelines for using summaries) says that the main purpose of summarizing is to give the client a feeling of movement. This movement, in terms of the problem-management model, is toward the kind of problem clarification that leads to goal setting.

■ Writing Approaches to Problem Clarification

Sometimes questionnaires, diaries, checklists, logs, time-and-motion studies, tests, and other forms of writing can help clients clarify their concerns. For instance, one client said she was overworked at home and had no idea where her time went. For two weeks she kept a kind of time-and-motion log that she would fill in once in the middle of each day and once at the end. She did not evaluate *how* she spent her time, but merely collected the data needed to give her a clear picture of *what* she did. Once the data were collected, the counselor helped her put them into categories and probe the implications of what she discovered.

Another client was having difficulty relating to others, but could not put his finger on what was going wrong. The counselor had him draw up an "interpersonal check list" (LaForge, 1977) and then used it to probe specific interpersonal situations at home, at work, and with friends.

There are an endless number of tests and checklists that can be used informally with clients to help them probe specific areas of their experience. I sometimes have clients keep logs of what is happening in the counseling process itself. Clients keep a written account of what they are doing to reach the goals of each step of the process. In this one simple way clients are encouraged to "own the helping process themselves; it also contributes to concreteness. For instance, if a client writes a vague behavioral analysis of some difficulty, the counselor can help him or her learn how to move from vagueness to specificity.

■ Common Problems in Step I-B

Moving too quickly.   Counselors can retard the helping process by getting ahead of themselves, moving on too quickly to the third step before adequately doing the work of the first two steps. For instance, they challenge too soon or without laying down a base of understanding and support, thus confusing or threatening the client. Or they give advice. These premature responses can indicate a lack of respect for the client ("I want to move ahead at a pace that pleases me, not one that is good for the client").

Moving too slowly.   On the other hand, counselors sometimes feel very comfortable in the problem identification and exploration stage and tend to remain there. They encourage clients to explore themselves further and further until self-exploration no longer contributes meaningfully to the helping process. In that case, helping can degenerate into a game of "insight hunting." Insights into one's experiences, behaviors, and feelings certainly play an important part in the helping process, but searching for insights should never be allowed to become an end in itself.

Client rambling.   One reason helpers may be moving too slowly in this second step is that they are allowing their clients to ramble. Rambling destroys the concreteness, the focus, and the intensity of the helping experience. If the helper punctuates the client's ramblings with nods, "uh-huhs," and the like, the rambling is merely reinforced. Monologues on the part of either helper or client are ordinarily not helpful. Therefore, the counselor should respond relatively frequently to the client, without interrupting what is important or making the client lose his or her train of thought. Frequent use of accurate empathy and timely use of probes give a great deal of direction to the counseling process.

Spending too much time and energy probing the past and looking for causes.   In helping clients probe their experiences, behaviors, and feelings, helpers would do best to focus on the who, what, where, when, and how of the problem situation. Trying to find out *why* things are the way they are is, in my estimation, often an unfruitful pursuit because it does not lead to the kind of clarification of the problem situation that helps clients act in their own behalf. For instance, if a helper asks a married couple, "Why did you two start fighting?" he or she might well be opening the floodgates of endless hypothesizing.

CLIENT: Well, I don't know exactly. I don't think she ever got along well with her father. And her mother and I never really got along either. On the surface things seemed to be all right, but they never were.

Answers to "why?" questions are usually too speculative to be of any use. The causes of things, especially the remote causes, are seldom evident. To ask clients to come up with such causes is often inviting them to whistle in the wind. Clients can talk endlessly about causes, but such talk usually does not produce the kind of insight that leads to effective action programs. Insight-seeking in counseling is not the same as self-exploration. The former deals with the causes of things and the reason behind things, while the latter deals with experiences, behaviors, and feelings in actual situations. Furthermore, to know the cause of something (assuming that one can get to the real cause) does not necessarily help a client act.

CLIENT: I think I am the way I am with my husband mainly because of some of the things that happened when I was a child. My husband is a lot like my father was, and I did like my mother better.

Such talk is a bottomless pit. Clients can hypothesize forever on the causes of behavior leading to ineffective living. Deutsch (1954) notes that it is often almost impossible, even in carefully controlled laboratory situations, to determine whether event B, which follows event A in time, is actually *caused* by event A. In no way does this mean that a person's past does not influence his or her present behavior, however.

This is not to deny the significance of the past in indirectly affecting behavior. However, even though the past can create a certain condition which carries over into the present, it is, nevertheless, the *present* condition which is influential in the present. Strictly considered, linking behavior with a past is an extremely difficult undertaking; it presupposes that one knows sufficiently how the past affected the psychological field at that time, and whether or not in the meantime other events have again modified the field [p. 186].

Carl Rogers (1951) had already applied such thinking to therapeutic situations:

It should also be mentioned that in this concept of motivation all the effective elements exist in the present. Behavior is not "caused" by something which occurred in the past. Present tensions and present needs are the only ones which the organism endeavors to reduce or satisfy. While it is true that the past experience has served to modify the meaning which will be perceived in present experiences, yet there is no behavior except to meet a present need [p. 492].

The past, insofar as it is alive and operative in the present, is important. Certain schools of psychotherapy, such as psychoanalysis, put great emphasis on in-depth investigations of the past. In the problem-management model, while the past need not be avoided if it contributes in some substantial way to clarifying the problem situation and making it more amenable to management, it should probably never become the principal focus of the client's self-exploration. When it does, helping often "loses the name of action."

The temptation to stop.   Some counselors seem to have the skills needed to be effective in this second step of the helping model, yet do not seem to help the client move on to the third step or to Stage II and, especially, Stage III. In such cases, self-exploration becomes an end in itself and ceases to be useful. One sign of this problem is what can be called "circular" counseling: counselors, and often their clients, too, begin to realize that they are going over and over the same territory. This kind of "going around the mulberry bush" is, unfortunately, all too common. The summary box that follows suggests issues to be considered in evaluating your progress in Step I-B.

As suggested earlier, in actual helping situations Steps I-A and I-B often overlap and mix with each other. Clients tell bits of their story, some of it gets clarified, it gradually becomes clearer which parts of a more complex situation are critical, more of the story gets told, and revisions are made with respect to what needs to be dealt with first or in greater depth. Both steps contribute to the overall goals of Stage I: developing the kind of clarity and objectivity in the exploration of problems and opportunities that is needed to move on to goal setting and strategy development.

■ Is Focusing Enough?

Some clients seem to need only Step A and B of Stage I. They come in feeling confused about their problems in living. However, once they understand the critical dimensions of their problem situations in terms of specific experiences, behaviors, and feelings related to specific situations—that is, once they see the problem situation clearly—they know what they need to do and go out and do it. Or once they are helped to see points of leverage, their needs are met. Your job is not to deliver as many services as possible to clients, but to help them discover what they need and help them meet those needs.

■ Evaluation Checklist for Step I-B: Focusing

How well are you doing the following?

GENERAL

- Making sure that this is the step in which the client needs your help
- Not challenging the client too soon
- Maintaining a sense of movement and direction in the helping process
- Knowing where you are headed.

SCREENING

- Making some assessment of how substantial the concerns of the client are
- Making a preliminary determination of the commitment of the client to work on his or her problems
- Taking the client's concerns seriously
- Coming to a contractual working arrangement with the client.

FOCUSING

- Guiding the client in choosing which issues to focus on first
- Discovering points of leverage in helping the client make the choice.

EXPLORATION AND CLARIFICATION

- Helping clients explore and clarify relevant issues in terms of specific experiences, behaviors, and feelings
- Using probes to help clients surface experiences, behaviors, and feelings that belong to an adequate clarification of the problem
- Using summaries or getting the client to summarize as a way of remaining concrete and of keeping the client from rambling
- Not unnecessarily extending the problem identification and exploration stage
- Not spending too much time and energy focusing on the past
- Understanding the client's perspective even when you think his or her perspective needs to be transcended
- Using communication skills, especially probing, to make sure that the client gets a fuller understanding of the problem situation.

Seven

Stage I: Step I-C
Challenging: New Perspectives
at the Service of Action

■

The goals of challenging
    Helping clients interpret and understand experiences, behaviors, and feelings
    Helping clients explore the consequences of their behavior
    Helping clients move to action
Self-challenge as the ideal
Challenging clients to own their problems and opportunities
Principles underlying effective challenging
Reluctance to challenge: The "MUM effect"
The response of the client who is challenged
Evaluation topics for Step I-C

Recall that in the discussion of listening in Chapter Three it was suggested that effective helpers engage in both empathic listening—listening geared to the client's experience and point of view—and also listening for "what is," even when the "what is" goes beyond or even contradicts the client's point of view. While effective helpers are committed to understanding clients and the ways in which they experience themselves and the world, they are also reality testers. Reality-testing listening forms the basis of challenging. Challenge addresses the discrepancies between clients' experience of themselves and their world and the way things really are. Very often helpers experience clients differently from the ways in which clients experience themselves (Berenson & Mitchell, 1974). For instance, a client experiences himself as a victim, while the helper experiences him as a person who fails to use the resources he possesses in order to cope with the "slings and arrows" of everyday life.

In this chapter, the process of challenging and its place in helping are discussed. In Chapter Eight, the communication skills needed for challenging are discussed and illustrated. Note Figure 7–1, which adds the final step to Stage I of the helping process.

Some writers suggest that the power of challenge in counseling and psychotherapy tends to be overlooked or underestimated.

[I]t has been our experience that the client will move towards positive psychosocial behavior if presented with a non-overwhelming challenge with which he is forced to cope and unable to avoid. If the challenging provokes a self annoyance that leads to a decision to change, therapeutic progress can begin and be rapid indeed [Farrelly & Brandsma, 1974, p.37].

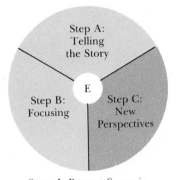

Stage I: Present Scenario

Figure 7–1. Step I-C: New perspectives

These same authors outline a number of challenge-related hypotheses that fit well with my own experience.

- Clients can change if they choose.
- Clients have more resources for managing problems in living and developing opportunities than they or most helpers assume.
- The psychological fragility of clients is overrated both by themselves and by others.
- Maladaptive and antisocial attitudes and behaviors of clients can be significantly altered no matter how severe or chronic they may be.

Current writers who emphasize helping as a social influence process (Dorn, 1984; Strong & Claiborn, 1982) consider challenge to be central to the counseling experience.

Once Steps A, B, and C of Stage I are carried out, in whatever sequence and pattern of overlap called for, the problem or opportunity should be defined, explored, and clarified to the point at which goals can be set. This chapter and the next explore ways in which challenge can contribute to problem and/or opportunity identification, exploration, and clarification.

■ The Goals of Challenging

Effective challenge focuses both on clients' *awareness or understanding* of their experiences, behaviors, and feelings and on the *actions* that flow or should flow from that awareness: actions that are needed to manage problems or develop opportunities. If challenge is successful, (1) clients are influenced to overcome blind spots and develop new perspectives that are action related, and/or (2) they are influenced to act.

It is especially important to clarify the goals of Step I-C for at least four reasons. First, it is a step that can overlap all other steps. There is no step in which some form of challenge may not be used. For instance, challenge is often used in the very first step with involuntary clients. Second, the challenging skills that serve this step are sometimes "strong medicine" and need to be used carefully and with direction—that is, at the service of outcomes that are in the best interests of the client. Third, challenge needs to be carried out in such a way that clients preserve their self-responsibility. Helping clients engage in self-challenge is the ideal. Fourth, some helpers tend to specialize in confrontation, taking a "technique" and segmental rather than integrative approach to helping. Since challenge tends to be effective to the degree that it is based on an understanding of the client, specializing in confrontation distorts the helping process. Empathic "being with" a client, on the other hand, contributes to both the validity and the impact of any given challenge.

The target of challenge can be any one or any combination of the following:

- Clients' lack of awareness of relevant experiences, behaviors, and feelings
- Clients' faulty or incomplete interpretation or understanding of experiences, behaviors, and feelings
- Clients' lack of understanding of the consequences of their behavior
- Discrepancies in clients' lives
- Clients' hesitancy or unwillingness to act on their understandings.

The first of these—probing for missing experiences, behaviors, and feelings needed to clarify the problem or opportunity in question—was discussed in Chapter Six. The other four are discussed here.

Helping Clients Interpret and Understand Experiences, Behaviors, and Feelings

Often enough clients fail to manage problem situations and develop opportunities because of the ways in which they interpret or understand their experiences, behaviors, and feelings. They either fail to see the meaning embedded in them or see a meaning that is "faulty" in that it does not lead them to constructive, problem-managing behavior. Clients' noninterpretations, misinterpretations, or mislabeling of experiences, behaviors, and feelings can keep them from managing their lives more effectively. For instance, a competent person may be unaware of her competence, see herself as incompetent, or label her competence as "pushiness" when it is not.

As Levy (1968) notes, if counselors see the world only as their clients do, they will have little to offer them. The client's implicit interpretation of the world is in some ways distorted and unproductive, at least in the problem areas of his or her life. Helpers assume, however, that clients have the resources to perceive reality, especially the reality of their own behavior, in an undistorted or less distorted way and to act on those perceptions. Since blind spots and distortions are so common in human experience, Strong and Claiborn (1982) see challenge, especially in terms of promoting attitude change and cognitive restructuring, as central to counseling and therapy.

Therefore, though the ultimate goal of challenge is problem-managing and opportunity-developing *action*, clients may need to be helped to develop the kinds of *awareness* or understanding that lead to action. On the other hand, awareness can be overstressed and can stand in the way of action: the search for insight can become a goal in itself. Awareness counts for little if clients do not act on what they have come to understand. The clarification of problem situations is not a goal in itself. They need to be clarified before something can be done about them. Most clients, in reviewing their concerns, doubts, difficulties, and problems, have blind spots that keep them from the kind of clarity that would enable them to act as fully as possible in their own interest. Blind spots contaminate the analysis of the problem situation and therefore contaminate the actions people take to manage them. As helpers listen carefully to clients, they spot cues that indicate the existence of such blind spots.

THE MANY NAMES OF AWARENESS STIMULATION

There are useful phrases to describe the process of helping clients develop the kinds of awareness and understanding that help them act to manage problems and develop opportunities: *seeing things more clearly, getting the picture, getting insights, developing new perspectives, spelling out implications, perception transformation, developing new frames of reference, looking for meaning, perception shifting, seeing the bigger picture, framebreaking, developing different angles, seeing things in context, rethinking, getting a more objective view, interpreting, overcoming blind spots, analyzing, second-level learning, double-loop learning* (Argyris, 1982), *reframing, thinking creatively, reconceptualizing, discovery, having an "ah-hah" experience, developing a new outlook, getting rid of distortions, relabeling, making connections,* and others. All of these imply some kind of understanding or awareness that did not exist previously and that is necessary or useful for engaging in situation-improving action. But just as creativity is useful only insofar as it leads to innovation, so new perspectives are useful only insofar as they lead to changed patterns of behavior toward self, others, and the environment.

EXAMPLES OF AWARENESS STIMULATION

Here are some examples of counselors helping clients develop new perspectives on their experiences, behaviors, and feelings.

The first set focuses on clients' external experiences. In the first example the client is a single, middle-aged man engaged in an affair with a married woman. The helper is getting the feeling that the client is being used but does not realize it.

HELPER: How often does she call you?
CLIENT: She doesn't. I always contact her. That's the way we've arranged it.
HELPER: I'm curious why you've arranged it that way.
CLIENT: What do you mean?
HELPER: Well, in mutual relationships, people are eager to get in touch with each other. I don't sense that in your relationship, but I could be wrong.
CLIENT: Well, it's true that in some ways I'm more eager. Maybe more dependent, but. . . .

The helper is inviting the client to explore the relationship more fully. The danger, of course, is arousing suspicions without justification. That is why it is critical to base challenge on the client's experience.

In the next example, a student is talking to a school counselor about a teacher.

CLIENT: I've had it with her. She has it in for me. She keeps making me toe the mark. I'd like to tell her where she can go.
HELPER: Does she single you out for special attention?
CLIENT: Well . . . not particularly.
HELPER: I was wondering whether making you toe the mark might be her way of showing she respects you—you know, of looking for the best in you?
CLIENT: Maybe. . . . But I still don't like it!

Note that clients can be blind to resources as well as to deficits.

The next example deals with internal experiences. A middle-aged man who has just been fired from his job is talking with a counselor.

CLIENT: I knew I was going to get fired. I've been expecting it for about a year now. There's hardly a day that I didn't think about it. I even dreamed about it.
HELPER: It sounds like actually getting fired was just the period at the end of the paragraph.
CLIENT: Exactly!
HELPER: Sometimes when I let negative thoughts flood in on me and get the better of me, I end up in self-fulfilling prophecies. Does that ever happen to you?
CLIENT: You're not telling me I got myself fired, are you?
HELPER: I'm just wondering how you handle it when negative thoughts begin bombarding you.
CLIENT: Well . . . I think that sometimes I get waylaid . . . by a bit of self-pity.

It may be that this client's internal life contributes to self-defeating behavior.

Counselors can also help clients develop new perspectives on their behavior. Helping clients find messages and meaning, especially in *patterns* of behavior, can be the first step toward behavioral change. The first set of examples focuses on internal behavior. In the first example the 83-year-old client, a resident of a nursing home, is talking to one of the nurses.

CLIENT: I've become so lazy and self-centered. I can sit around for hours and just reminisce . . . letting myself think of all the good things of the past . . . you know, the Old Country and all that. Sometimes a whole morning can go by.
NURSE: You mean you're worried about getting so much into yourself?
CLIENT: I guess so . . . I don't know if it's right.
NURSE: Sounds to me like reminiscing could be a form of meditation for you.
CLIENT: You mean like a prayer?
NURSE: Yes . . . like a prayer.

The nurse offers an alternative perspective that might help this woman interpret her internal behavior more constructively.

In the second example, the client is a divorced woman who has been talking about her ex-husband and his failure to meet child payments.

CLIENT: Oh, he's going to pay for all this. I'm planning ways to make sure he does. I've got lots of plans.

HELPER: He's gone, but he's still getting to you.

CLIENT: And I'm going to be getting to him.

HELPER: The planning you talk about. I wonder if it's possibly another way he's getting to you.

CLIENT: What do you mean?

HELPER: If I hear what you're saying, your planning keeps the bitter feelings you have, no matter how justified, very much alive. And you're the one who stays miserable.

CLIENT: You mean I'm still letting him get to me . . . but now in a kind of backhanded way?

The helper does not directly challenge her to stop engaging in what may well be a self-defeating pattern of behavior, but rather invites her to see her "planning" from a different angle.

In the following set the focus is on external behavior. The first example deals with a client who is having trouble with interpersonal relationships. She is a woman with a somewhat abrasive style.

CLIENT: I have a right to be myself. I have a right to my own style. Why can't people let me be myself?

HELPER: You feel that they have a right to their style and you have a right to yours.

CLIENT: Exactly.

HELPER: How would you describe your style?

CLIENT: Well, it's humorous. I speak with a fair amount of irony at times. And sometimes a bit cynically.

HELPER: It's not uncommon for people to mistake irony and cynicism for sarcasm. And then they may take it personally. It could be that they're seeing you as sarcastic.

The helper invites her to stand outside herself for a moment and get a look at her behavior from a different angle.

In the next example a man is talking about his visits to his elderly father, who is living on his own.

CLIENT: He gets so cantankerous. He puts me down constantly. I wonder why I keep going. Maybe it's just dumb.

HELPER: Could it be anything else besides dumb?

CLIENT: Well, he *is* my father . . . but he doesn't let you care for him much.

HELPER: So visiting him could also be a way of caring. . . . It sounds like caring for him might take a bit of pluck at times.

CLIENT: How often I have to screw up my courage just to go!

It is obvious that visiting his father is frustrating for this man, but a complementary perspective is that it is a form of caring that involves courage.

Counselors can also help clients develop new perspectives on their emotions. In the following example the client is a woman in her late 50's who is going to have an operation for cancer. The helper is a woman, about the same age, who is a minister from the patient's church.

PATIENT: I'm just so scared. I've never been so scared in my life.
(The minister holds her hand tightly.)
PATIENT: I never thought I could be so desperate, so desperately scared.
MINISTER: You sound desperate for life.

The minister suggests that she isn't just being consumed by fear. It's also a very human grasping for life.

The next example involves a woman who was extremely sensitive to whatever she perceived as criticism. I asked her if it would be all right to videotape one or two of our sessions, so that she could get a better feeling for her style. To my surprise, she said yes. After the session we played about ten minutes of the tape. She asked me to stop the tape, turned to me, and said, "I'm so angry! I would never have believed it. Where is all of it coming from?"

There has been some speculation (see Beck & Strong, 1982; Claiborn, 1982) about what makes interpretation effective. One possibility is that interpretation is effective only when it "hits the mark," when it is "correct." The client is moved by the truth of the challenge. A second possibility is that to some extent the content of the interpretation is not that important. What is important is that interpretation is being used as an instrument by the helper to express concern, care, and involvement. The client is moved to become more deeply committed to the helping process because the relationship is enhanced. A third possibility is that the content of the interpretation is not as important as the fact that the very act of interpreting stimulates a self-challenging process in the client. A fourth possibility is that interpretations provide frameworks that enable clients to better understand their experiences, behaviors, and emotions. Of course, none of these possibilities need exclude the others. It may be that they all contribute to the effectiveness of helpers challenging clients to develop new perspectives.

Awareness need not always precede action. Sometimes clients need to act in order to develop awareness.

■

Woody, a college sophomore, came to the student counseling services with a variety of interpersonal and somatic complaints. He felt attracted to a number of women on campus, but did very little to become involved with them. After exploring this issue briefly he said to the counselor, "Well, I just have to go out and do it." Two months later he returned and said that his experiment had been a disaster. He had gone out with a few women, but none of them really interested him. Then he did meet someone he liked quite a bit. They went out a couple of times, but the third time he called she said she didn't want to see him anymore. When asked why, she muttered vaguely about his being too preoccupied with himself and ended the conversation. He felt so miserable that he returned to the counseling center. He and the counselor took another look at his social life. This time, however, he had some questions to probe. He wanted to explore his being "too preoccupied with himself."

This student put into practice Weick's (1979) dictum that chaotic action is sometimes preferable to orderly inactivity. Some of his learning was painful, but now there is a chance of examining his interpersonal style much more concretely. One of the assumptions of Alcoholics Anonymous is that people sometimes need to act themselves into new ways of thinking rather than think themselves into new ways of acting. For instance, a person does not realize the degree to which alcohol has been controlling his or her life until he or she stops drinking.

Helping Clients Explore the Consequences of Their Behavior

One way of helping clients get new and more creative perspectives on themselves and their behavior is to help them explore the consequences of patterns of behavior currently "in place." A counselor is talking to a man who has lost his home in a flood. A couple of months have gone by, but he keeps returning to the site.

CLIENT: I've been out there four times this week. It's like I just can't believe it happened. I've got to go out there and make sure. I know it sounds crazy.
HELPER: It sounds like what people do when they're in mourning.
CLIENT: Like when your wife dies? . . . That's exactly it! It's like going to a grave.
HELPER: What else are you doing from day to day?
CLIENT: Nothing much. Filled in a few insurance forms. That sort of stuff.
HELPER: Sometimes people get so into mourning that they can't get back to their lives. You know, picking up the pieces and moving on.
CLIENT: . . . I know a guy who's still not right. And his wife died a couple of years ago. . . . You mean I might be headed down the same road?
HELPER: Well, maybe that's a good question to ask yourself.

The counselor is not telling the client what to do. Rather she is asking him to look at the possible consequences of a pattern of behavior that has developed.

In the next example the client is in a rehabilitation unit after a serious accident. She has been doing a variety of exercises, but progress is slow.

CLIENT: Sometimes I think that the courageous thing to do is just to chuck all this stuff, admit that I'm a cripple, and get on with life. I don't want to delude myself that I'm going to be a whole human being again. I'm not. And I'm not a hero.

COUNSELOR: So the depression's at you again.

CLIENT: It's not at me. . . . It's got me by the throat.

COUNSELOR: I wish I had a videotape.

CLIENT: Of what?

COUNSELOR: Of the way you could, or rather couldn't, move that left arm of yours six weeks ago. . . . Move it now.

CLIENT (moving her arm a bit): You mean people can notice a difference? . . . These damn exercises are making a difference?

COUNSELOR: Sure. . . . You know it, but you hate the snail's pace.

Helping the client look at the consequences of her behavior—in this case the exercises—is a supportive gesture on the part of the helper. This mild challenge is mingled with empathy.

Helping Clients Move to Action

The ultimate goal of challenging can be stated in one word: action. New perspectives and heightened awareness must serve action. Action includes the following:

- *Starting* activities related to managing problems and developing opportunities
- *Continuing and increasing* activities that contribute to problem management and opportunity development
- *Stopping* activities that either cause problems, limit opportunities, or stand in the way of problem management and opportunity development.

These activities can be either internal, external, or a combination of both.

Internal activities, as we have seen, are those things we do "inside" ourselves and that cannot be seen by others. They include thinking, understanding, judging, expecting, imagining, planning, wondering, deciding, and talking to oneself. If problems are to be managed and opportunities developed, some of these need to be started, some continued or increased, and some stopped. For instance, if I am going to manage interpersonal conflict between myself and a friend, I might need to

- *Start* thinking of her as an equal in our relationship, start understanding her point of view, and start imagining what an improved relationship with her might be like

- *Continue* exploring with myself the ways I contribute to the difficulties we are having and *increase* the number of times I tell myself not to jump to conclusions about her behavior
- *Stop* telling myself that she is the one with the problem, stop seeing her as the offending party when conflicts arise, and stop telling myself there is no hope for the relationship when I feel hurt.

That is, I have to put my internal life in order and begin to mobilize internal resources.

External activities are those that others can see or at least could see if they were present. Again, if problems are to be managed and opportunities developed, some activities need to be started, some continued or increased, and some stopped. For instance, if I am going to do my part in developing a better relationship with my friend, I might need to

- *Start* spending more time with her, start sharing my feelings with her, and start engaging in mutual decision making
- *Continue* visiting her parents with her and *increase* the number of times I go to church with her
- *Stop* criticizing her in front of others, stop canceling meetings with her at the last moment, and stop making fun of friends of hers whom I don't like.

I can challenge myself to do all of this, I can ask for my friend's help in challenging me, or I can ask a third party for help.

Thus clients, if they are to manage problem situations and develop opportunities, need to start, continue, increase, and stop certain behaviors, both internal and external. If they do not do these things on their own, counselors can help them challenge themselves to do what needs to be done or counselors can do the challenging themselves. Challenge to action focuses on critical or useful problem-managing or opportunity-developing behaviors, internal or external, that are currently not in place and on dysfunctional behaviors, internal or external, that are currently in place. Since challenge to action focuses on missing or dysfunctional behaviors, Step I-C can overlap or interpenetrate all the other steps of the helping process. That is, clients can be challenged to do the following:

- Talk about their problems when they are reluctant to do so
- Clarify problem situations in terms of specific experiences, behaviors, and feelings when they are being evasive
- Develop new perspectives on themselves and their behavior when they cling to their blind spots
- Review new scenarios, critique them, choose goals, and commit themselves to goals when they keep looking to the past instead of the future
- Search for ways of achieving goals when they despair of doing so
- Spell out problem-managing and opportunity-developing plans when they take a scattered, hit-or-miss approach to action

- Persevere in the implementation of those plans when they are tempted to give up.

In the following example the client, a 50-year-old man, wants to check himself into a mental hospital. The therapist views this as just one more step in a pattern of running away from problems instead of coping with them. Checking into the hospital is a program with no goal.

HELPER: What will checking into the hospital accomplish? I thought we had reached the conclusion that you're not sick.
CLIENT: I'll be safe there. . . . Won't harm myself or others.
HELPER: I could see that, if harming yourself or others had been an issue. It hasn't.
CLIENT: Well . . . I'll be safe there.
HELPER: Tom, you're safe out here . . . but you're not comfortable. In fact, you are extremely uncomfortable.
CLIENT: Okay! . . . I'm looking for a safe place, a refuge. I just want to get away.
HELPER: Tom, what's the distinction in your mind between getting away and giving up? Is the hospital a place to step back and regroup? What is it, really?
CLIENT: What the hell's so bad about giving up!
HELPER: Let's see if we can find ways of staying out and still getting the sense of peace you're looking for.

The helper has seen too many clients use a trip to the hospital as the beginning of the end. Her relationship with this client justifies the kind of challenge she engages in.

■ Self-Challenge as the Ideal

As we have observed, one of the values promoted here is client self-responsibility. It sometimes happens that when people are listened to, understood, and helped to explore problem situations from their own frames of reference, they move naturally to challenging themselves.

CLIENT (a 38-year-old woman who is coming to counseling because she has recently had a mastectomy): I can't believe what I've been learning here. When we began to look at how much support I have in terms of family and friends, it was the first time in my life that I had reviewed my relationships with others so explicitly. I never realized how selfish and self-serving I can be. I control how others relate to me: we do things when I want to do them, we spend as much time as I want to spend. And now I could just see me using this operation as another tool to get what I want. Don't get me wrong; I don't want to exaggerate. And I don't think I'm a lousy human being. But there are some things about the ways I relate to others that need changing.

This woman makes some discoveries about herself, owns them, and begins to translate them into goals. This kind of self-challenging is refreshing, perhaps because most of us see so little of it (even in ourselves).

Helpers who wait for clients to make this move on their own may wait a long time. Therefore, it is often necessary to invite clients to move beyond their own limited frames of reference. However, since the ideal still remains self-challenge rather than being challenged, it can be useful to teach clients how to challenge themselves (training as treatment) in reasonable ways.

Here are a number of instances of self-challenge. You can determine the likelihood of their taking place.

CLIENT A: I'm losing out on most of my life by being so mousy. It's very hard for me to be assertive with others, especially with men. But I've had it; I can't be like this—especially if I'm interested in a human-services profession. I just have to find ways to reach out to others.

CLIENT B: What a revelation this group experience has been! I had no idea how manipulative I can be. As I look back now, I see that I even got better grades than I deserved in school by the way I cultivated my teachers. And I'm still trying to do the same thing now that I'm out of school. I control my whole social life. At one time I actually thought it was altruism—I mean the way *I* would always be the one to seek others out. But now I see that it was just my way of controlling my involvement with others: I want to control whom I see and whom I don't see. (She turns to the group leader.) I even tried to manipulate you into counseling me the way I wanted to be counseled, but you won't play my game.

CLIENT C: I've been a clown so long that I'm not sure there's a solid me left underneath for others to interact with. My blustering, my so-called wit, my bull-in-the-china-shop relationships with others: all a cover-up. I tried to be just me this past week—no stream of jokes, no putting others down—and I was disoriented and even scared at times. I didn't know what to do and my friends didn't seem to know how to interact with a serious me.

As you probably have noted, all of these clients are quite verbal and nondefensive. Helpers can hardly expect this kind of behavior from involuntary and resistant clients. However, even reluctant clients can be nudged toward self-challenge.

■ Challenging Clients to Own Their Problems and Opportunities

One of the first things many clients need to be challenged to do is to *own* the problem situation. Many unwittingly get locked into seeing themselves as victims of their environment. Here is the experience of one counselor who had responsibility for about 150 young men in a youth prison.

I believe I interviewed each of the inmates. And I did learn from them. What I learned had little resemblance to what I had found when I read their files containing personal histories, including the description of their crimes. What I learned when I talked with them was that they didn't belong there. With almost universal consistency they reported a "reason" for their incarceration *that had little to do with their own behavior.* An inmate explained with perfect sincerity that he was there because the judge who sentenced him had also previously sentenced his brother, who looked very similar; the moment this inmate walked into the courtroom he knew he would be sentenced. Another explained with equal sincerity that he was in prison because his court-appointed lawyer wasn't really interested in helping him.

Many of them reported the stories of their crimes, which usually involved the heavy influence of "the other guys." ... I used to wonder what would happen to the crime rate if only we could have caught those mythological "other guys" who were responsible for all those young people being behind bars [Miller, 1984, pp. 67–68].

This is not to deny that we can be victimized by others at times. However, all of us to a greater or lesser extent are affected by this "other guys" syndrome. It simply is not easy for people to accept responsibility for their acts and the consequences of their acts.

A problem situation is owned when it is spelled out in terms of the client's behavior—what he or she does or does not do—and not just his or her experiences. Let's consider a few examples.

NOT OWNED: I live in a racist society. It even rubs off on me.

OWNED: I choose to live in a neighborhood that excludes minority groups, especially Blacks. And I begin to see that this is only one way in which I express my prejudices. I don't like to see myself as racist, but my actions speak louder than my words.

NOT OWNED: My friends don't seem to care for me, really. They keep me on the margin of their social life.

OWNED: I'm biting and cynical when I'm with my friends. I think sometimes they just say "ugh" quietly and wish I weren't there. I alienate them. I don't listen well to others. I can hardly blame people for not inviting me to their parties and on vacations.

NOT OWNED: My husband is a drunk and I can't do much to change him, though I try. He has ruined the home, and our children suffer a great deal. He should get out of the house and out of our lives.

OWNED: I haven't learned how to cope with my husband's excessive drinking. I know that I've done things that merit having a drunk for a husband. I've always nagged, even before he started drinking. Once the children were born, I showed them much more interest than I showed him. I've put the entire blame for our misery on his drinking, but I should share the blame.

The owned statements are put in terms of behaviors: what the client does or does not do. The statements above, of course, are too good to be true. They indicate a level of self-challenge that is not characteristic of clients. Clients capable of taking that kind of responsibility would not need our help in the first place. Clients need to be helped gradually to complement their exploration of experiences with an exploration of behaviors. Support, empathy, and probing on your part will help them to do so.

One of the reasons that marriage counseling is so difficult is that spouses have a tendency to focus almost exclusively on their experiences—that is, the unacceptable behavior of the other. However, when two human beings find themselves in conflict, it is rare for one of them to be blameless. Helping each to identify what he or she does to contribute to the problem situation is not easy. At one time, when working with married couples in trouble, I made an explicit rule that neither was allowed to talk about the unacceptable behavior of the other. This tended to reduce both spouses to silence.

When we feel we are being dealt with unfairly, the child buried deep (or perhaps not so deep) within us wants to go into a corner and cry. However, even in situations in which clients *are* victims—victims of others, victims of social settings, victims of the organizations and institutions of society, victims of acts of God—they need to be listened to and understood but then helped to mobilize their resources to cope with what they cannot change. In order to help such clients, you need to find out what they are doing or not doing to cope, and help them engage in the kind of "secondary control" discussed in Chapter One. In general, you have to help clients translate experience language into behavior language. "When mother comes for visits, she disrupts our household" needs to be translated into "We do not manage mother's visits well; we allow her to disrupt our household." The first statement does not point to action; the second does.

It is not uncommon for clients to state problems so that they seem unsolvable. This justifies a "poor-me" attitude and a failure to act. It may also elicit the pity and the sympathy of the counselor.

UNSOLVABLE PROBLEM: In sum, my life is miserable now because of my past. My parents were indifferent to me and at times even unjustly hostile. If they had only been more loving, I wouldn't be in this present mess. I am the unhappy product of an unhappy environment.

Of course, clients will not use this rather stilted language, but the message is still the same. The point is that the client's past cannot be changed. Therefore, since she defines her problem in terms of the past, her problem cannot be solved. "You certainly had it rough in the past and are still suffering from the consequences now" might be the kind of response that such a statement is designed to elicit. The client needs to move beyond such a point of view.

SOLVABLE PROBLEM: Over the years I've been blaming my parents for my misery. I still spend a great deal of time feeling sorry for myself. As a result, I sit around and do nothing—I don't make friends, I don't involve myself in the community, I don't take constructive steps to get a better job.

Again, the language is stilted, but the point is that this message is quite different from that of the previous client. The problem, stated in this way, can be managed; the client can stop blaming her parents since she cannot change them, she can increase her self-esteem and therefore stop feeling sorry for herself, and she can develop the interpersonal skills and courage she needs to enter more effectively into relationships with others.

Clients state problems in unsolvable ways when they say "I can't" instead of "I don't."

UNSOLVABLE: I can't get her out of my mind. And I can't start thinking of going out with other women.
SOLVABLE: I don't tell her what I feel. And then I expect her to know anyway.

Saying "I can't" instead of "I don't" may seem to be just a language problem, but often language suggests an underlying attitude. Clients need to own their problems and to state them as solvable. Effective helpers invite them to do so.

CLIENT: I can't get her out of my mind. And I can't start thinking of going out with other women.
HELPER A: It's devastating. It's almost too much to cope with.
CLIENT: I just can't cope with it (he begins crying).

HELPER B: The misery of losing her just won't go away. . . . Tell me a little bit about how this "I can't" feels for you.
CLIENT: Well, I wake up every morning and that's the first thing I think about. And I lie awake at night in agony thinking about it, too. And I. . . .

The first helper responds with empathy alone and the client sinks deeper into his misery. The second helper is empathic, but then gently gets at the "I can't." The client begins to describe experiences, behaviors, and feelings that can be appreciated but that he can also be invited to challenge.

Not only problems but also opportunities need to be owned by clients.

Challenges come from opportunities as well as from danger signals. Opportunities usually do not knock very loudly, and missing a golden opportunity can be just as unfortunate as missing a red-alert warning [Wheeler & Janis, 1980, p. 18].

A social worker who had been out of work for over six months once told me that he had heard the city was hiring social workers for a new "help-the-neighborhoods-help-themselves" program. When I asked him what his response had been, he said that it was probably only a rumor. I saw him in the morning. I did everything but explode. However, by early afternoon he had discovered that the rumor was fact and had set up an interview for the next day.

■ Principles Underlying Effective Challenging

Now that you have at least an initial understanding of the kind of challenging that can help clients develop new perspectives and move on toward problem-managing action, it will be helpful to pause a moment and review the conditions under which challenging is most likely to have a beneficial impact. Challenging well is not a skill that comes automatically; it needs to be learned and practiced (McKee, Moore, & Presbury, 1982; Tamminen & Smaby, 1981). The following principles apply to all forms of challenging. They include both cautions and hints on how to challenge well.

Keep the goal of challenging in mind. Challenge must be integrated into the entire helping process. Keep in mind that the goal is to help clients develop the kinds of alternative perspectives and frames of reference they need to clarify problem situations and to get on with the other steps of the helping process.

Allow for self-challenge. Give clients ample opportunity to challenge themselves. Do not immediately blame the client for lack of progress. You can provide clients with problems and structures that help them engage in self-challenge.

COUNSELOR: People often have blind spots in their relationships with others, especially in close relationships. I wonder whether you are beginning to see any blind spots in your relationship with your son.

Or the same client might be asked to list three things he thinks he does right and three things that need to be reconsidered in his relationship with his son (see Bernstein & Lecomte, 1979; Greenberg & Kahn, 1979; and Greenberg & Higgens, 1980, for ways of helping clients engage in self-challenge).

Earn the right to challenge. Berenson and Mitchell (1974) suggest that some helpers don't have the right to challenge others since they do not fulfill certain essential conditions. Here are some of the factors in earning that right:

• *Quality of relationship.* Challenge only if you have spent time and effort building a relationship with your client. If your rapport is poor or you have allowed your relationship with the client to stagnate, deal with the relationship. The skill of immediacy, to be discussed later, will help you do so.

• *Understanding the client.* Effective challenge is built on understanding and flows from it. Only when you see the world through the client's eyes can you begin to see what he or she is failing to see. Furthermore, if clients feel that you do not understand them, they will probably not listen to your challenges anyway.

• *Being open to challenge.* Don't challenge unless you yourself are open to being challenged. If you are defensive in the counseling relationship, do not expect your clients to set aside their defensiveness. It is unrealistic to expect to address the vulnerabilities of others without at the same time letting yourself be reasonably vulnerable.

• *Living fully.* Berenson and Mitchell claim that only people who are striving to live fully according to their value system have the right to challenge others, for only such persons are potential sources of human nurturing for others. In other words, don't challenge unless you also challenge yourself to develop physically, intellectually, socially, and emotionally.

In other words, ask yourself, "What is there about me that will make clients willing to be challenged by me?"

Be careful about the way you challenge clients.   The same challenging message can be delivered in such a way as to invite the cooperation or arouse the resistance of the client (Wachtel, 1980). Deliver challenges *tentatively,* as *hunches* that are open to discussion (see Strohmer & Newman, 1983), rather than as accusations. Challenging is not an opportunity to browbeat clients or put them in their place. In the following example a teacher is talking to a counselor about problems he's having with fellow faculty and members of the administration.

COUNSELOR A: You don't really swallow your anger, as you claim to. From what you say, it comes dribbling out unproductively all the time.

COUNSELOR B: From what you say, it sounds like the anger you swallow at faculty meetings might not always stay down. I wonder whether others might say that it leaks out at times—perhaps in cynical remarks, in some aloofness, and occasionally in uncooperative behavior. Or am I reading too much into the picture you've painted?

Counselor A's challenge is simply an accusation. The way B qualifies her statement allows the client to explore it without feeling he is arguing with her. Effective challenging is not meant to pin clients down; it leaves them room to move. On the other hand, challenges that are delivered with too many qualifications either verbally or through the helper's tone of voice sound apologetic and can be easily dismissed by clients.

You can go overboard with tentativeness. I once worked in a career-development center. As I listened to one of the clients, it soon became evident that one of the reasons he was getting nowhere was that he engaged in so much self-pity. When I shared this observation with him, I overqualified it. It came out something like this:

"Has it ever, at least in some small way, struck you that one possible reason for not getting ahead, at least as much as you would like, could be that at times you tend to engage in a bit of self pity?"

I'm sure it wasn't that bad, but I still remember his response. He paused, looked at me for a moment, surprise on his face, and said

"A *bit* of self-pity? . . . I *wallow* in self-pity!"

We moved on to explore what he might do to decrease his self-pity, but I knew I had been overly tentative.

Since challenges are often useful hunches that helpers share with clients or that clients share with themselves, there is an interpretive aspect to them. But if you are listening carefully to your clients, your interpretations will be based on cues you receive from your clients: you will not be pulling them out of thin air. Each hunch, of course, will have a different degree of probability and you can expect clients to react strongly if you share hunches with low degrees of probability as if they were facts.

Challenges should be offered caringly. All that has been said about respect applies to challenging. It includes being sensitive to the client's *present* ability to hear and respond to a challenge. If a client is disorganized and confused at the moment, it does little good to add to his or her disorganization by further challenging.

Build on successes. High-level helpers do not urge clients to place too many demands on themselves all at once. Rather, they help clients place reasonable demands on themselves and in the process help them appreciate and celebrate their successes. In the following example, the client is a boy in a detention center.

COUNSELOR A: You're still not standing up for your own rights the way you need to. The other guys are still pushing you around.

COUNSELOR B: I notice two things. In the group meetings you speak up. You say what you want to say. And I get the feeling that you feel good about that. But you still seem to let a couple of the guys push you around a bit. How do you see it?

Counselor A does not reinforce the client for his accomplishment; counselor B does.

Be specific. Your challenges will hit the mark if they are specific. Clients don't know what to do with vague challenges. They may feel they should do *something*, but since they don't know what, they are confused. In the following example, Ted, a member of an alcoholic rehabilitation group, is talking to the counselor outside the group session.

COUNSELOR A: You're too passive, Ted. You have to speak up for what you want.

The concept of "passive" is too general, and the solution offered is too vague to help.

COUNSELOR B: Ted, in group discussions you tend to stay quiet, even when decisions are being made that are going to affect you. For instance, last week the members of the group decided to have a speaker at the next meeting. You didn't say anything, but you didn't show up for the meeting. When people asked you about it, you got angry and said that you didn't want to listen to a speaker. Then the others got angry at you for not going along with the group decision.

Counselor B, instead of labeling Ted as passive, describes an instance of his passive behavior and the consequences it had for him and others.

Challenge strengths rather than weaknesses. Berenson and Mitchell (1974) discovered that successful helpers tend to challenge clients' strengths rather than their weaknesses. Confrontation of strengths means pointing out to clients the assets and resources they have but fail to use. In the following example the helper is talking to a woman in a rape crisis center.

COUNSELOR: Ann, in the group sessions you provide a lot of support for the other women. You have an amazing ability to spot a person in trouble and provide an encouraging word. Yet when you get down on yourself, you don't accept what you provide so freely to others. You are not nearly as kind to yourself as you are to others.

The helper places a demand on Ann to use her resources on her own behalf.

On the other hand, weakness confrontation, as the term implies, dwells on the deficits of the person being confronted. In the following example the helper is talking to a woman living on welfare who has been accused of child neglect.

COUNSELOR: You nagged at your husband and kept a sloppy house until he left. And now it's the kid's turn. You seem to think only of yourself. Life is a rat race and you're its principal victim.

Yelling at clients and putting them down are not creative interventions. Sometimes when the relationship between client and helper is strong and there is a history of respect, strong words like these might do some good. But ordinarily they are dead ends. Ineffective helpers do not know how to help clients mobilize their resources, and so in their frustration they resort to punishment.

Speaking realistically, most challenges have something negative about them. Even when you confront the strengths of others, you are doing so because they are *not* using them effectively. However, the unintentionally punitive effects of challenge are mitigated greatly by emphasizing strengths and potential.

Challenge clients to clarify values.   Challenge clients to clarify their values and to make reasonable choices based on them. Be wary of using challenging to force clients to accept your values.

CLIENT (a 21-year-old woman who is a junior in college): I have done practically no experimenting with sex. I'm not sure whether it's because I think that it's wrong or if I'm just plain scared.

COUNSELOR A: A certain amount of exploration is certainly normal. Maybe it would be good to give you some basic information on contraception. That may help allay your fears a bit.

COUNSELOR B: Are you saying that maybe it's time to find out which it is?

Counselor A edges toward making some choices for the client, while Counselor B challenges her gently to find out what she really wants. Effective helpers have a clear sense of their own values, but have no need to force them on others. "What values am I implicitly pushing here?" is a question that counselors can profitably ask themselves throughout the helping process.

Clients can be helped to explore the consequences of the values they endorse, but this is not the same as attacking their values.

COUNSELOR A: Bill, it seems obvious that you invest too much of yourself in work. Work doesn't really enhance your life any more; it imprisons you. You don't own your work; it owns you.

BILL: It's my life and it's what I like to do. Do I have to be like everyone else?

Work is a legitimate value and, if the counselor attacks it directly, he can expect the client to react defensively. A more effective tactic is to challenge Bill to probe his own values on the subject of work, see how he translates them into behavior, and work out the relationship of his work values to the other values in his life. Value *conflicts* rather than values themselves are the proper object of challenge.

■ Reluctance to Challenge: The "MUM Effect"

Initially some counselor trainees are quite reluctant to place demands on others or (preferably) help others place demands on themselves. They become victims of what has been called the "MUM effect," the tendency to withhold bad news from others even when it is in others' interest to hear that news (Rosen & Tesser, 1970, 1971; Tesser & Rosen, 1972; Tesser, Rosen, & Batchelor, 1972; Tesser, Rosen, & Tesser, 1971). In ancient times the person who bore bad news to the king was sometimes killed. This obviously led to a certain reluctance on the part of messengers to bring such news. Bad news—and, by extension, the kind of "bad news" involved in any kind of challenging—arouses negative feelings in the *challenger,* no matter what he or she thinks the reaction on the part of the receiver might be. If you are comfortable with the supportive dimensions of the helping process but uncomfortable with helping as a social-influence process, you are in danger of falling victim to the MUM effect and of becoming less effective than you might otherwise be.

Reluctance to challenge is not a bad starting position. In my estimation, it is far preferable to being too eager to challenge. However, as we have seen, all helping, even the most client-centered (Rogers, 1951), involves social influence. It is important for you to understand your reluctance (or eagerness) to challenge—that is, to challenge yourself on the issue of challenging and on the notion of helping as a social-influence process. When trainees examine how they feel about challenging others, these are some of the things they say:

> "I am just not used to challenging others. My interpersonal style has had a lot of the live-and-let-live in it. I have *misgivings about intruding into other people's lives.*"
>
> "If I challenge others, *I open myself to being challenged.* I may be hurt or I may find out things about myself that I would rather not know."
>
> "I might find out that I *like* challenging others: that the floodgates will open and my negative feelings about others will flow out. I have some fears that deep down I am a very angry person."
>
> "I am afraid that I will *hurt* others, damage them in some way or other. I have been hurt and I have seen others hurt by heavy-handed confrontations."
>
> "I am afraid that I will delve too deeply into others and find that they have problems that *I cannot help them handle.* The helping process will get out of hand."
>
> "If I challenge others, they will no longer *like me.* I want my clients to like me."

These reactions may not be yours. The point is that it is useful to examine where you stand in terms of the helping process, helping values, and personal feelings with respect to challenging others.

In summary, clients often can benefit from and therefore want not polite talk but *straight talk* from helpers. At times it is painful, but they can take it from helpers motivated by respect and genuineness. The ideal, of course, is to help them engage in straight talk with themselves.

The Summary Box that follows on page 208 suggests some topics for evaluating yourself as a challenger.

■ The Response of the Client Who Is Challenged

Even when challenge is a response to a client's plea to be helped to live more effectively, it can precipitate some degree of disorganization in the client. Different writers refer to this experience by different terms: *crisis, disorganization, a sense of inadequacy, disequilibrium,* and *beneficial uncertainty* (Beier, 1984). However, counseling-precipitated crises *can* be beneficial for the client. Whether they are or not depends to a great extent on the skill of the helper.

As we have seen, social-influence theory suggests that people who feel inadequate are often open to being influenced to a greater degree than people who are managing their lives well. Challenge, since it usually does induce some sense of inadequacy in clients, can render them more open to influence. However, some clients can resist being influenced and respond defensively even to responsible challenge. One way of looking at the manner in which clients resist challenge is from the point of view of cognitive-dissonance theory (Festinger, 1957). Challenge, as we have seen, can induce dissonance (discomfort, crisis, disequilibrium). Since dissonance is an uncomfortable state, the client will try to get out of it. According to dissonance theory, there are five typical ways in which people experiencing dissonance attempt to rid themselves of this discomfort.

1. Discredit challengers. The challenger is confronted and discredited. Some attempt is made to point out that he or she is not better than anyone else.

CLIENT (who has been discussing her marital problems and has been challenged by the helper): It's easy for you to sit there and suggest that I be more responsible in my marriage. You've never had to experience the misery in which we live. You've never experienced his brutality. You probably have one of those nice middle-class marriages.

Counterattack is a common strategy for coping with challenge. Counselors who elicit this kind of response from their clients may be merely the victims of their clients' attempts to reduce dissonance. However, it is best not to jump to that conclusion immediately. The client might be airing a legitimate gripe. It may be that the counselor has been inaccurate or heavy-handed in his or her challenge.

2. Persuade challengers to change their views. In this approach challengers are reasoned with; they are urged to see what they have said as misinterpretation and to revise their views. In the following example the client pursues this strategy by using rationalization.

CLIENT: I'm not so sure that my anger at home isn't called for. I think that it's a way in which I'm asserting my own identity. If I were to lie down and let others do what they want, I would become a doormat at home. I think you see me as a fairly reasonable person. I don't get angry here with you, because there is no reason to.

Sometimes a client like this will lead an unwary counselor into an argument about the issue in question. A client who frequently uses rationalization is difficult to deal with, but arguing with him or her is not the answer.

3. Devalue the issue.   This is another form of rationalization. For instance, if the client is being challenged about her sarcasm, she points out that she is rarely sarcastic, that "poking fun at others" is a minor part of her life and not worth spending time on. The fact that clients sometimes run from topics that are too painful emphasizes the necessity of an accurate understanding of the client's feelings, experiences, and behavior. The client has a right to devalue a topic if it really isn't important, so the counselor has to be sensitive enough to discover which issues are important and which are not.

4. Seek support elsewhere for the views being challenged.   Some clients leave one counselor and go to another because they feel they aren't being understood. They try to find helpers who will agree with them. This is an extreme way of seeking support of one's own views elsewhere. But a client can remain with a counselor and still offer evidence that others contest the helper's point of view.

CLIENT: I asked my wife about my sarcasm. She said she doesn't mind it at all. And she said she thinks that my friends see it as humor and as part of my style.

This is an indirect way of telling the counselor she is wrong. The counselor might well be wrong, but if the client's sarcasm is really dysfunctional in his interpersonal life, the counselor should find some way of pressing the issue. If the counseling takes place in a group, it is much more difficult for clients to use this approach to reducing dissonance.

JUAN: Does anyone else here see me as biting and sarcastic?
SUSAN: I think you do get sarcastic from time to time. The reason I've said nothing about it so far is that you haven't been sarcastic with me. And I'm a bit afraid of you.

Since Juan can get direct feedback on his behavior from the group, it is harder for him to play games.

5. Agree with the challenger.   The client may agree with the counselor. However, the purpose of challenging is not to get clients to agree with their helpers. It is rather to help them reexamine their behavior in order to develop the kinds of perspectives they need to clarify the problem situation and establish goals. Therefore, when clients agree with their challengers, that, too, may be a game.

CLIENT: I think you're right. I'm much too blunt and forward when I speak; I should try to think what impact I'm going to have before I open my mouth.

This response may be mere capitulation rather than self-exploration. Clients can agree with the challenges of helpers in order to get them off their back. If such confessions do not lead to goal-setting behavior, however, it may be just one more way of handling dissonance rather than being a move toward constructive behavior change.

A More Productive Response to Challenge

If clients are challenged reasonably, ideally they are influenced to accept the invitation to reexamine their experiences, behaviors, and feelings. Consider this example in which one member of a counseling group challenges the behavior of another.

GROUP MEMBER A: When I talk to you, you always respond to me very nicely, but you keep putting your interpretation on what I say. What you say sounds so different from what I think I've said.

CLIENT: You mean it sounds like I'm trying to put my words into your mouth so that I can say, "See, we're really saying the same thing!"

This client does what few people spontaneously do when they are challenged: he first checks to see whether he has an accurate understanding of what the other person is saying. However atypical this response might be in everyday life, it is still one that counselors can help their clients to develop. This is the first step in helping clients learn how to challenge themselves.

■ Evaluation Checklist for Step I-C: Challenging

How well are you doing the following as you try to help this client?

GENERAL

- Becoming comfortable with the social-influence dimension of the helping role
- Incorporating challenge into my counseling style without becoming a confrontation specialist
- Using challenge wherever it is needed in the helping process
- Developing enough assertiveness to overcome the "MUM effect."

THE GOALS OF CHALLENGING

- Challenging clients to participate fully in the helping process
- Helping clients become aware of their blind spots in thinking and acting and helping them develop new perspectives
- Helping clients understand more fully the current impact of their experiences, behaviors, and feelings
- Inviting clients to explore the short- and long-term consequences of their behavior
- Challenging clients to own their problems and unused potential
- Giving clients feedback on their successes and failures in the helping process
- Helping clients move beyond discussion to action.

THE STYLE OF CHALLENGING

- Earning the right to challenge by
  - developing an effective working alliance with the client
  - working at seeing his or her point of view
  - being open to challenge yourself
  - living fully yourself
- Inviting clients to challenge themselves
- Being tactful and tentative in challenging without being insipid or apologetic
- Challenging clients' strengths rather than their weaknesses
- Not asking clients to do too much too quickly
- Inviting clients to clarify and act on their own values, not yours.

Eight

The Skills of Challenging

■

Helpers use a variety of challenging skills to help clients understand themselves, others, and the world more fully and act more constructively. As we have already seen, challenging is not limited to Step I-C. The purpose of this chapter is to discuss and illustrate the skills of challenging. They are (1) information sharing, (2) advanced empathy, (3) confrontation, (4) helper self-disclosure, and (5) immediacy.

■ New Perspectives Through Information Sharing

Sometimes clients are not able to explore their problems fully and proceed to action because they lack information of one kind or another. In such cases, helpers can provide the needed information or help clients get it from some other source. Berenson and Mitchell (1974) call this "didactic" confrontation, while Selby and Calhoun (1980) call it "psychodidactics."

> Conveying information about the psychological and social changes accompanying a particular problem situation (e.g., divorce) may be a highly effective addition to any therapeutic strategy. This psychodidactic component has been neglected as an explicit part of treatment in spite of evidence indicating the therapeutic value of information about the client's problem situation [Selby & Calhoun, p. 236].

This skill includes both giving information and correcting misinformation. Since the acquisition of information is an important step in the problem-solving process, a training-as-treatment approach might include teaching clients the life skill of information acquisition (Hudson & Danish, 1980).

This skill or strategy is included under challenging skills because it helps clients develop new perspectives on their problems. In some cases the information can prove to be confirming and supportive. For instance, a parent who feels responsible following the sudden death of a newborn baby may gain relief from an understanding of the features of the "sudden infant-death syndrome" (Selby & Calhoun, p. 239). The client in this case obtains a new perspective that helps him or her handle self-blame.

The new perspectives clients get from information can be both supportive and challenging. Consider the following example.

■

Troy was a college student of somewhat modest intellectual means. He made it through school because he worked very hard. In his senior

210

year he learned that a number of his friends were going on to graduate school. He, too, applied to a number of graduate programs in psychology. He came to see a counselor in the student services center after being rejected by all the schools to which he applied. In the interview it soon became clear to the counselor that Troy thought that many, perhaps even the majority of college students went on to graduate school. After all, most of his closest friends had been accepted in one graduate school or another. The counselor shared with him the statistics of what could be called the educational "pyramid"—the decreasing percentage of students attending school at higher levels. Troy did not realize that the fact that he was finishing college made him part of an elite group. Nor was he completely aware of the extremely competitive nature of the graduate programs in psychology to which he had applied. He found much of this a relief, but then found himself suddenly faced with what to do after finishing school. Up to that point he had not thought of what he might do after college. He felt disconcerted by the sudden need to face the world of work.

In this case Troy is both relieved and challenged by what he learns. The very offer of information can challenge clients to examine issues they may have been avoiding. Giving information is especially useful when ignorance either is one of the principal causes of a problem situation or is making an existing problem worse.

In some medical settings doctors team up with counselors to give clients messages that are hard to hear and to provide them with information needed to make difficult decisions. For instance, Lester, a 54-year-old accountant, has a series of diagnostic tests for a heart condition. The doctor and counselor sit down and talk with him about the findings. Bypass surgery is called for, but there is no absolute assurance that surgery will take care of all of Lester's heart problems. The counselor helps him cope with the news, process the information, and come to a decision. When information is challenging, or even shocking, the helper needs to be tactful and know how to help the client handle the disequilibrium that comes with the news.

Remember these cautions with respect to giving information. Do not overwhelm the client with information. Make sure that it is clear and relevant to the client's problem situation. Do not confuse information giving with advice giving—the latter is seldom useful. Finally, be supportive: help the client process the information.

The relationship between the transmission of personally relevant information and decision making by the client merits some consideration. A therapist might feel reluctant to use a psychodidactic strategy when the client faces a major life decision. Most therapists are careful not to take responsibility for such choices, and clients may be encouraged to postpone decisions until after therapy is completed. Presumably at that time the person will be in a better position to weigh all alternatives. If, however, a significant decision is undertaken, it is important for the therapist to provide whatever relevant information he or she might have concerning the kinds of obstacles and resources associated with each alternative. If a couple is trying to decide whether to stay together or to separate, information concerning the pitfalls involved in each alternative may significantly clarify the decision [Selby & Calhoun, 1980, p. 239].

At times of major decision making, information giving is not to be used by helpers as a subtle (or not so subtle) way of pushing their own values. For instance, helpers should not immediately give clients with unwanted pregnancies information about abortion clinics. Indeed, if abortion is contrary to the helper's values, then he or she may want to let the client looking for abortion counseling know that he or she cannot help her in that area.

■ Advanced Empathy

In the following example the client, a soldier doing a five-year hitch in the army, has been talking about his failure to be promoted. As he talks, it becomes fairly evident that part of the problem is that he is so quiet and unassuming that it is easy for his supervisors to ignore him. He is the kind of person who keeps to himself and keeps everything inside.

CLIENT: I don't know what's going on. I keep getting passed over when promotion time comes along. I think I work as hard as anyone else and I work efficiently, but all of my efforts seem to go down the drain. I'm not as flashy as some others, but I'm just as substantial.

COUNSELOR A: You feel it's quite unfair to do the kind of work that merits a promotion and still not get it.

COUNSELOR B: It's depressing to put in as much effort as those who get promoted and still get passed by. . . . The "not as flashy" bit—what in your style might make it easy for others not to notice you, even when you're doing a good job?

Counselor A tries to understand the client from the client's frame of reference. He deals with the client's feelings and the experience underlying those feelings. Counselor B, however, goes a bit further. From the context, from past interchanges, from the client's manner and tone of voice, she picks up a theme that the client states in passing in the phrase "not as flashy"—that is, that the client is so unassuming that his best efforts go unnoticed. Counselor B uses a combination of basic and advanced empathy to help the client develop a new perspective, but one that is based on the data of the self-exploration process. Advanced empathy, then, goes beyond the expressed to the partially expressed and the implied. Greenberg and Kahn (1979) use the words "stimulation" and "discovery" to describe the process and effect of advanced empathy.

> A view of the mind proposed by James (1892) provides a theoretical framework for understanding the function of stimulation in promoting discovery. In James's view, directing effort to take hold of some marginal impression in the mind, bringing this new information into the center of awareness, and attending fully will precipitate choice, decision, and action. By shifting one's attention and fully attending to some vague feeling, memory, sensory experience, or fleeting thought, people can expand their awareness of possibilities [pp. 139–140].

If, in the example above, the helper is accurate and if her timing is good, this kind of communication helps the client develop a new and useful perspective. Let's take a look at the client's response to each counselor.

CLIENT (in response to Counselor A): I suppose there's nothing I can do but wait it out. (A long silence ensues.)

CLIENT (in response to Counselor B): You mean I'm so quiet I could get lost in the shuffle? Or maybe it's the guys that make more noise—the "squeaky wheels," my dad used to call them—they're the ones that get noticed.

In response to Counselor A, this client merely retreats further into himself. However, in his response to Counselor B he begins to see that his unassuming, nonassertive style may contribute to the problem situation. Once he becomes aware of the self-limiting dimensions of his social style, he might be in a position to do something to better manage the problem situation.

Basic empathy gets at relevant *surface* (not to be confused with *superficial*) feelings and meanings, while advanced accurate empathy gets at feelings and meanings that are buried, hidden, or beyond the immediate reach of the client.

Step I-C continues the process of "piecing together" begun with the use of summaries in Step I-B. Helping clients piece things together can help them see the bigger picture. Advanced empathy is one of the tools in this process. Even when helpers see the world from the point of view of their clients, they often see it more clearly, more widely, more deeply, and more cogently. They not only understand the client's perspective but also see the *implications* of that perspective for effective or ineffective living. The communication of advanced accurate empathy is the helper's way of sharing his or her understanding of those implications with the client. As such it is a bridging response. It helps clients move to more goal-related perspectives.

Advanced empathy can be communicated in a number of different ways. Let's consider some of them.

EXPRESSING WHAT IS ONLY IMPLIED

The most basic form of advanced empathy is to give expression to what the client only implies. In Step I-C, once rapport has been established and the client is exploring his or her experiences, behaviors, and feelings, the helper can begin to point out what the client implies but does not say directly. In the following example the client has been discussing ways of getting back in touch with his wife after a recent divorce, but when he speaks about doing so, he expresses very little enthusiasm.

CLIENT: I could wait to hear from her. But I suppose there's nothing wrong with calling her up and asking her how she's getting along.
COUNSELOR A: As far as you can see, it's okay to take the initiative to find out if everything is well with her.
CLIENT (somewhat drearily): Yeah, I suppose I could.

COUNSELOR B: You've been talking about getting in touch with her but, unless I'm mistaken, I don't hear a great deal of enthusiasm in your voice.
CLIENT: To be honest, I don't really want to talk to her. But I feel guilty: guilty about the divorce, guilty about seeing her out on her own. I'm taking care of her all over again. And that's one of the reasons we got divorced. I mean my constant taking care of her when she was more interested in independence.

Counselor A's response might have been fine at an earlier stage of the helping process, but it misses the mark here and the client grinds to a halt. In Step I-C the counselor needs to help the client dig deeper. Counselor B bases her response not only on the client's immediately preceding remark but also on the entire context of the self-exploration process. Her response hits the mark and the client moves forward. As with basic empathy, the sign of the effective use of advanced accurate empathy is the way in which the client responds. There is no such thing as a good advanced-empathic response in itself. The question is, does it help the client clarify the issue more fully, so that he or she begins to see the need to act differently?

In the following example, the client, a battered woman, is not coming to grips with her problem situation because she is attempting to sweep some important feelings about herself under the rug. She is talking about her husband.

CLIENT: You know . . . usually he's all right. It's only when I do the kinds of things that get under his skin. . . . It's when I mess up. . . . That's the only thing I see. . . . But then he's so violent.
COUNSELOR: Karen, when you talk, you sound so down on yourself all the time. Sometimes you talk almost as if you *deserved* what you get. . . . I'm wondering how much do *you* like yourself.
CLIENT: I . . . I never thought of anything like that before. . . . I've always been a bit down on myself, I guess.

The counselor has been listening to the client's messages, both verbal and nonverbal, and develops a hunch that, if true, is a critical aspect of the problem situation.

Advanced accurate empathy is part of the social-influence process; it places demands on clients to take a deeper look at themselves. The genuineness, respect, understanding, and rapport of the previous steps have created a power base. Helpers now use that power to influence clients to see their problems in a more objective frame of reference. Such demands are still based on an empathic understanding of the client and are made with genuine care and respect, but they are demands nevertheless. Nonassertive helpers can find it difficult to make such demands on their clients.

IDENTIFYING THEMES

Advanced empathy also includes helping clients identify and explore behavioral and emotional themes in problem situations. Themes are self-defeating *patterns* of behavior and emotion. For instance, without stating it explicitly, the following client shows through what she reveals about her feelings, experiences, and behaviors and by the way she acts in the helping sessions that she is a fairly dependent person (a behavioral theme in the client's life).

COUNSELOR: You have not said this in so many words, but it seems that you find it easy at times to let other people make decisions for you. But once they do, you're dissatisfied.

This is something the client has half-said in a number of ways. It is empathic because it *is* the client's point of view, stated in indirect ways. Here are some half-stated themes.

Poor self-image.   Clients such as Karen, above, may hint that they do not think well of themselves. This may run the gamut from occasional dissatisfaction with self to self-hatred.

COUNSELOR: As I listen, this thought is beginning to strike me. In growing up you've seemed to learn one lesson well, and that is, "I am not a fully worthwhile human being." You seem to say this to yourself at work, in your relationships with your friends, and even when you're alone with yourself.
CLIENT: No one's "fully worthwhile" . . . but no, you're right, I can get pretty down on myself.

The client begins to react defensively, then catches herself and lets the truth of what is being said (what she has been saying to herself) sink in.

Dominance.   A client may intimate that she takes a parental role toward her husband.

COUNSELOR: I'd like to pull a few things together. If I understand correctly, you take care of the household finances. You are usually the one who accepts or rejects social invitations. And now you've asked your husband to move because of the location of your new job. You see all of this as a way of making life better or easier for him. Could there be any other theme there?

CLIENT: When you say it like that, it sounds like I'm running his life.

COUNSELOR: What if the roles were reversed?

CLIENT: Hmmm. . . . Well, I'd . . . hmm . . . (laughs) my voice is giving me away.

In each of these cases, the counselor goes beyond what the client has said explicitly. The thematic material might refer to feelings (such as themes of hurt, depression, or anxiety), to behavior (such as themes of controlling others, avoiding intimacy, blaming others, or overwork), to experiences (such as themes of being a victim, being seduced, being feared, or failing), or to combinations of these. Once you recognize a self-defeating theme or pattern, your task is to communicate your perception to the client in a way that enables the client to see it too. This task often demands a high degree of assertiveness, empathy, and tact.

Be careful of overly abstract themes borrowed from schools of therapy. While you might hear clients half-saying things that square with theory, they might not recognize themselves in the way you paraphrase them.

CONNECTING ISLANDS

This metaphor suggests another approach to advanced empathy. The helper attempts to build "bridges" between the "islands" (Ivey, 1971; Ivey & Authier, 1978) of feelings, experiences, and behaviors revealed by the client in the self-exploration stage. For instance, the following client talks about being progressively more anxious and tired in recent weeks. Later he talks about getting ready for his marriage in a few months and about deadlines for turning in papers for current courses. Still later, he talks about his need to succeed, to compete, and to meet the expectatons of his parents and grandparents.

COUNSELOR: John, it could be that your growing fatigue and anxiety have relatively simple explanations. One, you are really working very hard. Two, competing as hard as you do and striving for excellence have to take their physical and emotional toll. And three, the emotional drain involved in getting ready for a marriage can be enormous. Maybe it would be more useful to look at these factors before digging around for deeper causes.

John had been talking about these three "islands" as if they were unrelated to one another.

Advanced empathy means helping the client fill in the missing links in the data produced in the self-exploration process. For instance, if the client presents two separate "islands" of behavior—(1) his general dissatisfaction with his marriage and his disagreements with his wife about sex, training the children, and arranging household finances and (2) his drinking more and more—the missing link, one only hinted at, might be that he is using drinking as a way of punishing his wife.

COUNSELOR: I wonder what the relationship is between your drinking and your disagreements with your wife, Bill. At least at first glance, it seems like a fairly good way of punishing her. Especially since you present your drinking to the family as a separate problem, medical in nature.

The client has presented these two problems as separate. The counselor, in listening to the client, has a hunch that they are not separate. She suggests the concept of punishment as a possible bridge between the two.

Of course, counselors need to be accurate in the connections or relationships they propose. Counselors who work from a controlling rather than from a collaborative model of social influence might well be able to force clients to accept interpretations of their behavior that do not help.

HELPING CLIENTS DRAW CONCLUSIONS FROM PREMISES

Still another way of conceptualizing advanced empathy is to help clients draw their own conclusions from premises. Very often, in the data produced in the self-exploration process, there are certain implied premises from which conclusions can be drawn.

CLIENT: I really don't think I can take my boss' abuse any longer. I don't think she really knows what she's doing. She thinks she's doing me a favor by pointing out what I do wrong all the time. I like the work and I'd like to stay, but, well, I just don't know.

COUNSELOR A: What makes this really frustrating is that your boss might not even realize what she's doing to you.

COUNSELOR B: The alternatives, then, are limited. One is to stay on the job and just take it. But you feel this has become too painful. Another is to talk with your boss directly about this whole destructive relationship. A third is to start thinking about changing jobs, even though you like the work there. We really haven't talked about the second possibility.

Counselor A's basic empathy might help the client probe more deeply into her feelings, but the assumption here is that she has already done that. It is a question of moving forward. Counselor B combs through what has been said in their interaction up to this point and draws some conclusions from the premises laid down by the client. Perhaps the client is avoiding the subject of a direct confrontation with her boss. At some level she might realize that she, too, has some responsibility with regard to this unproductive relationship.

In certain cases, the counselor may draw a tongue-in-cheek conclusion from clients' premises in order to show them that the arguments they are constructing are leading nowhere. Beier (1984) calls this response an "asocial" response, since it is not the kind of response expected by the client. For instance, suppose that a married man has been describing his wife's faults at great length. After a while, the counselor responds:

COUNSELOR: It was a mistake to marry such a woman, and maybe it's time to let her go.

This is not at all what the client has in mind, but since it *is* a logical conclusion to the case the client has been constructing against his wife, it pulls the client up short. He realizes that perhaps he has gone too far, that he is making things sound worse than they really are.

CLIENT: Well, I don't think things are that bad. She does have her good points.

Beier claims that such asocial responses make the client stop and think. They provide what he calls "beneficial uncertainty" for the client. Asocial responses, obviously, can be overused, can be too facetious, and—in the hands of the inept counselor—can actually sound sarcastic. The counselor who is uncomfortable with this kind of communication can get the same result by using a social rather than asocial response. For instance, the counselor in the last example might have said the following:

COUNSELOR: I'm not sure whether you are trying to say that your wife has no redeeming qualities?
CLIENT: Oh! Well, I didn't mean to be so hard on her.

Some clients, in a relationship that is not working out, have to make the other person the scapegoat in order to reduce their own culpability, at least initially. In this example the counselor realizes that the client is engaging in hyperbole and helps the client understand what he is doing.

FROM THE LESS TO THE MORE

The function of advanced empathy is to help clients move from the less to the more. If clients are not clear about some issue or if they speak guardedly, the helper needs to speak directly, clearly, and openly. For instance a client might ramble, touching on sexual issues lightly as he moves along. The counselor helps him face those issues more squarely.

COUNSELOR: George, you have alluded to sexual concerns a few times in passing. My guess is that sex is a pretty touchy issue for you to deal with. But it also seems like a pretty important one.

Through advanced accurate empathy, what is said confusedly by the client is stated clearly by the helper; what is said half-heartedly is stated cogently; what is said vaguely is stated concretely; and what the client presents at a superficial level is re-presented by the helper at a deeper level.

The categories described here are neither exhaustive nor meant to be completely distinct. What they have in common is that they are all different kinds of hunches that, when shared with clients, can help them see a problem situation more clearly.

■ Confronting the Client

Confrontation is a word that inspires fear in many people, for it conjures up images of themselves or others devastated by irresponsible personal attack. They may even see confrontation as a vicious attack, although the attacker often says that it is for their "own good." When confrontation *is* actually an attack, it serves the purpose of helping the confronter get a load off his or her chest rather than helping the other person live more effectively. While some think that even "attack therapy" might be growth-inducing if it takes place in the context of a supportive community (Maslow, 1967), that is not what is meant by confrontation in this chapter. There is such a thing as responsible and caring confrontation. The purpose of this section is to help you understand the nature and techniques of confrontation as one form of challenging and integrate them into your overall counseling style. It is very important to keep in mind that confrontation, too, needs to be related to developing new perspectives and to moving on to goal setting, program development, and action.

At its simplest, confrontation is an invitation to examine some form of behavior that seems to be either self-defeating, harmful to others, or both, and to change the behavior if it is found to be so. Recall Alicia, the not-unattractive woman who experiences herself as unattractive. She is now a member of a counseling group.

GROUP COUNSELOR: You say that you're unattractive, and yet I know that you get asked out a lot. I don't find you unattractive myself. And, if I'm not mistaken, I see people here react to you in ways that say that they like you. I can't put all of this together with your being unattractive.

ALICIA: Okay. What you say is true, and it helps me clarify what I mean. First of all, I'm no raving beauty, and when others find me attractive, I think that means that they find me intellectually interesting, a caring person, and things like that. At times I wish I were more physically attractive, though I feel ashamed when I say things like that. The fact is that much of the time I *feel* unattractive. And sometimes I feel most unattractive at the very moments when people are telling me directly or indirectly that they find me attractive.

GROUP MEMBER: So you've gotten into the habit of telling yourself in various ways that you're unattractive. I wonder where that came from.

ALICIA: Yeah. It's a lousy habit. If I look at my early home life and my experiences in grammar school and high school, I could probably give you the long, sad story of how it happened. But the past is the past.

Since the counselor's experience of Alicia is so different from her experience of herself, he invites her to explore the difference in the group. Her self-exploration clarifies the issue greatly. Now that she wants to stop feeling unattractive, she may not know how. The counselor and group members can help her discover how.

Confrontation focuses on the discrepancies, distortions, evasions, games, tricks, excuse making, and smoke screens in which clients involve themselves, but that keep them mired in their problem situations. All of us have ways of defending ourselves from ourselves, others, and the world. But our defenses are two-edged swords. For instance, daydreaming may help me cope with the dreariness of my everyday life, but it may also keep me from doing something to better myself. Blaming others for my misfortunes helps me to save face, but it disrupts interpersonal relationships and prevents me from developing a healthy sense of self-responsibility. The purpose of confrontation is not to strip clients of their defenses. Rather, the purpose of confrontation is to invite clients to challenge the defenses that keep them from managing problem situations and developing opportunities. There is a fair degree of overlap among the categories discussed below.

CHALLENGING DISCREPANCIES

Confrontation can zero in on discrepancies between what clients think or feel and what they say, between what they say and what they do, between their views of themselves and the views others have of them, between what they are and what they wish to be, between their expressed values and their actual behavior. These discrepancies can refer to their behavior in the counseling sessions or outside. For instance, a helper might challenge the following discrepancies that take place outside the counseling sessions:

- Tom sees himself as witty, while his friends see him as biting.
- Minerva says that physical fitness is important, but she overeats and underexercises.
- George says he loves his wife and family, but he is seeing another woman and stays away from home a lot.
- Penny says she hates her work, but does nothing to look for a new job.
- Leo says he wants to be more assertive, but does not concretely spell out what "being assertive" means for him.
- Clarissa, unemployed for several months, wants a job, but doesn't want to participate in a retraining program.

COUNSELOR: I thought the retraining program would be just the kind of thing you've been looking for.
CLARISSA: Well . . . I don't know if it's the kind of thing I'd like to do. . . . The work would be so different from my last job. . . . And it's a long program.

COUNSELOR: So you feel the fit isn't good.

CLARISSA: Yeah.

COUNSELOR (smiling): What's going on, Clarissa?

CLARISSA: What do you mean?

COUNSELOR (pleasantly): Where's the old fire to get a job? I'm not even sure you believe what you're saying about the retraining program.

CLARISSA: I guess I've gotten lazy. . . . I don't like being out of work, but I've gotten used to it.

The counselor suspects that Clarissa is slipping into what might be called the "culture of unemployment" (see Galbraith, 1979) and challenges her to take a look at what she's doing.

A counselor might challenge the following kinds of discrepancies that take place inside the counseling sessions:

- Mary is obviously confused and hurt, but says she feels fine.
- Bernard says "yes" with his words, but his body language says "no."
- Evita says she wants help, but refuses to disclose herself enough to properly clarify the problem situation.

COUNSELOR: Evita, when we arranged this meeting you talked vaguely about "serious family problems," but it seems that neither you nor I think that what we've talked about so far is that serious. I'm not sure whether there's more and, if there is, what might be keeping you from talking about it.

EVITA: There's a lot more, but I'm embarrassed to talk about it.

The counselor is properly tentative in pointing out this discrepancy and the client moves forward. The client needs support and help to overcome her embarrassment.

CHALLENGING DISTORTIONS

Some clients cannot face the world as it is, and therefore distort it in various ways. For instance,

- Arnie is afraid of his supervisor and therefore sees her as aloof, whereas in reality she is a caring person.
- Edna sees her counselor in some kind of divine role and therefore makes unwarranted demands on him.
- Nancy perceives her stubbornness as commitment.
- Eric, a young gay male who has been beaten up a couple of times by people he's met in gay bars, sees himself as a sexual victim. He blames his problems on an older brother who seduced him during his early years in high school.

COUNSELOR: Eric, every time we begin to talk about your sexual behavior, you bring your brother up.

ERIC: That's where it all began!

COUNSELOR: Your brother's not around any more. . . . Tell me what Eric wants. But tell me straight.

ERIC: I want people to leave me alone.

COUNSELOR: I don't believe it because I don't think you believe it. . . . Be straight with yourself.

ERIC: I want some one person to care about me. But that's deep down inside me. . . . What I seem to want up front is to punish people and make them punish me.

The counselor bluntly but caringly invites Eric to let go of the past and to let himself think more clearly about the present.

CHALLENGING SELF-DEFEATING INTERNAL EXPERIENCES AND BEHAVIOR

As you talk to clients and help them explore their problems, it will soon become clear to you that many clients have ways of thinking that keep them locked into their problem situations. Ellis (1962, 1971, 1973, 1974, 1977a, 1977b; Ellis & Harper, 1975; Bard, 1980; Smith, 1982, 1983) in his "rational-emotive" therapy and Meichenbaum (1974, 1977; Meichenbaum & Genest, 1980) in his "cognitive-behavior modification" both point out that the inner or covert experiences and behavior that sustain self-defeating patterns of overt behavior have to be challenged. They have both developed methodologies for helping clients come to grips with what can be termed self-limiting or self-defeating internal dialogue, or "self-talk."

CLIENT: I've decided not to apply for that job.

COUNSELOR: How come?

CLIENT: Well, it's not exactly what I want.

COUNSELOR: That's quite a change from last week. It sounded then as if it was just what you wanted.

CLIENT: Well, I've thought it over. (Pauses)

COUNSELOR: I've got a hunch based on what we've learned about your style: I think you've been saying something like this to yourself. "I like the job, but I don't think I'm good enough for it. If I try it, I might fall flat on my face and that would be *awful*. So I'll stick to what I've got, even though I don't like it very much." Any truth in any of that?

CLIENT: Maybe more than I want to admit.

Challenging clients' self-limiting ways of thinking can be one of the most powerful methods for behavioral change at your disposal. And, just as negative cognitive states stand in the way of problem solving, so positive cognitive states can contribute greatly to managing problems and developing opportunities (see Fordyce, 1977, 1983).

Some of the common mind-sets that Ellis believes get in the way of effective living are as follows:

• *Being liked and loved.* I *must* always be loved and approved of by the significant people in my life.

- *Being competent.* I *must* always, in all situations, demonstrate competence and I must be talented and competent in some one important area of life.
- *Having my way.* I *must* have my way and my plans must always work out.
- *Being hurt.* People who do anything wrong and especially those who harm me are evil and should be blamed and punished.
- *Being in danger.* If anything or any situation is dangerous in any way, I must be anxious and upset about it.
- *Being problemless.* Things should not go wrong in life and, if by chance they do, there should be quick and easy solutions.
- *Being a victim.* Other people and outside forces are responsible for any misery I experience.
- *Avoiding.* It is easier to avoid facing life's difficulties than to develop self-discipline; making demands of myself should not be necessary.
- *Tyranny of the past.* What I did and especially what happened to me in the past determine how I act and feel today.
- *Passivity.* I can be happy by avoiding, by being passive, by being un-committed, and by just enjoying myself.
- *Catastrophizing.* If any of the above principles are violated in my life, it is terrible, awful, and catastrophic. And, as everyone knows, catastrophes are out of our control.

Daly and Burton (1983), in reviewing the literature on irrational beliefs, found that such beliefs are correlated to a variety of psychological problems including depression, social anxiety, coronary-prone behavior, and lack of assertion. In their own research they found four specific irrational beliefs correlated with low self-esteem and its consequences: demand for approval, overly high self-expectations, anxious overconcern, and problem avoidance. Both research and clinical experience demonstrate vividly that clients can be infected to varying degrees with what Alcoholics Anonymous groups have called "stinkin' thinkin'."

Mike, a man in his mid-thirties, has recently gone through a divorce and lost a well-paying job. He can easily get another job, but not one as plush as the one he has lost. To make things worse, he has just been told that he needs an operation for hemorrhoids. He has been "catastrophizing" over his divorce and the loss of his job and now he feels that he is being completely done in by this new problem. The counselor has spent some time helping him explore the problem situation and communicating support through empathy.

CLIENT: How much can someone stand? The thought of an operation is just beyond me.
COUNSELOR A: You feel you've been on the ropes, and now one more body blow. . . . It's almost too much.

CLIENT: Not "almost." It *is* too much. I've never been like this before. I find my hand shaking at times. I'm not sleeping well.

COUNSELOR B: Mike, you keep saying to yourself that all of this shouldn't be happening to you. When you look at what's happened, what part of it can you change?
CLIENT: Nothing! . . . That's just it. I can't do anything about it.
COUNSELOR B: Right, you can't change it, but maybe you can manage it . . . and get yourself some peace of mind.
CLIENT: What do you mean?
COUNSELOR B: By going over and over what's happened, you keep pushing your nose in it.
CLIENT: And it stinks.
COUNSELOR B: Let's switch roles. You're the counselor and I'm you. I've just gone over the whole story two or three times. I'm at my wit's end. What do you say to me?
CLIENT: I . . . well, I . . .

Counselor A is merely empathic. What she says might well reinforce the client's complaining without helping him move on. Counselor B is also empathic, but he confronts the client's self-defeating thinking. The technique he uses, role reversal, provides the client with some "beneficial uncertainty" and can help him get off the merry-go-round he's on.

These theories of Ellis and Meichenbaum are too important to be given summary treatment here. I find them most useful. However, Ellis is not without his critics (see Ellis, 1982; Eschenroeder, 1982; Patterson, 1986; Rorer, 1983; Smith, 1982, 1983; and Smith, Houston & Zurawski, 1984). I myself object to the way in which Ellis seems to push his own set of values with clients.

CHALLENGING GAMES, TRICKS, AND SMOKE SCREENS

If clients are comfortable with their delusions and profit by them, they will obviously try to keep them. If they are rewarded for playing games, inside the counseling sessions or outside, they will continue a game approach to life (Berne, 1964; Harris, 1969; James & Jongeward, 1971). For instance, Clarence plays "Yes, but . . ."; that is, he presents himself as in need of help and then proceeds to show his helper how ineffective the help he is getting is. Dora makes herself appear helpless and needy when she is with her friends, but when they come to her aid, she gets angry with them for treating her like a child. Kevin seduces others in one way or another and then becomes indignant when they accept his implied invitations. The number of games people can play in order to avoid the work of facing life's tasks squarely is endless. Clients who are fearful of changing will attempt to lay down smoke screens in order to hide from the helper the ways in which they fail to face up to life. Such clients can use communication in order not to communicate (Beier, 1984).

One function of Step I-C is to set up an atmosphere that discourages clients from attempting to play games with you. If clients try, skilled helpers do not get hooked into their games. For instance, since effective helpers don't start out by giving advice, they prevent clients from playing the "Yes, but . . ." game. If a client attempts to lay down diversionary smoke screens during the helping interview, the counselor challenges the behavior. Beier (1984) suggests that some clients play one kind of game or another in an attempt to restrict the helper's response. The helper thus "engaged" is easy to sidetrack.

The following client has just begun to explore a sensitive area: how he manipulates an older brother into coming to his aid financially. He takes financial risks because he knows he can talk his brother into bailing him out.

CLIENT: I really like what you've been doing in these sessions. It feels good to be with such a strong person.
COUNSELOR A (in an angry voice): See, that's exactly what I've been getting at. Now you're manipulating me and not even trying to be subtle!
COUNSELOR B: Thanks. I think that it's important that we respect each other here. And perhaps that's the issue with your brother—respect.

Counselor A gets angry and lets himself be sidetracked, while Counselor B uses the client's game to refocus on the issue at hand.

Helpers can also challenge the games that clients play outside the counseling sessions. In the following example, Sophie, a 55-year-old woman, has been exploring her relationships with her married children. She has her own game. She "confides" in one of them some kind of negative information about herself—for instance, that she can't seem to manage things at the house as well as she used to—and then counts on that one to tell the others. The payoff is that she remains the center of attention much of the time without seeming to do much to demand it. Lately, however, her children seem to be on to her game. She tries to see their behavior as "indifference." She is talking to her pastor about her "loneliness." The pastor has spent a good deal of time exploring the problem situation with her.

PASTOR: I'd like to make a bet with you.
SOPHIE (a bit surprised): About what?
PASTOR: If I've listened carefully to what you've been saying, you've gotten a lot of attention from the kids by playing one off against the other. Nothing evil, mind you, just a bit clever. Maybe just a bit too clever. My bet is that you could relate to them straight and get all the human contact you need. And I think my bet is safe because I see you as a resourceful woman.
SOPHIE (cautiously): Tell me more about this bet.

The helper calls her game. But he challenges her strengths rather than her weaknesses. Casting his challenge in the form of a "bet" adds tentativeness, too. By exploring the "bet" together, they can come up with a goal that will have something to do with restructuring her relationship with her children. Dreikurs (1967) suggests that clients use their symptoms to cover up their real intentions. He sees this as a game that needs challenging. "As Adler pointed out, one of the most effective therapeutic means [of challenging clients' games] is spitting in the patient's soup. He can continue what he's doing, but it no longer tastes so good" (p. 230).

CHALLENGING EXCUSES

Snyder, Higgins, and Stucky (1983; see also Snyder, 1984) examine excuse-making behavior in depth. Excuse making, of course, is universal, part of the fabric of everyday life. As they note, it has its uses in interpersonal transactions. For instance, it helps people save face both with themselves and others. On the other hand, excuse making, together with avoidance behavior, is probably one of the central mechanisms in life contributing to the "psychopathology of the average" (Maslow, 1968) mentioned in Chapter One. And it should be no surprise that Snyder and his colleagues found that excuse making can contribute to severe problems in living (see his Chapter Eight, "Excuses Gone Awry").

Wheeler and Janis (1980) point out categories of excuses that need to be challenged:

Complacency. "It won't happen to me." Clients fail to realize the seriousness of a situation.

> Many middle-aged men and women who have high blood pressure know that they should get more exercise, stop smoking, and eat less fat in order to avoid heart disease. But they do not take the warnings seriously and continue unchanged in their unhealthy way of life [pp. 22–23].

Rationalization. Clients cling to unwarranted assumptions or distort information. "It can't happen to me," or "It's really not that bad." Rationalizations enable clients to avoid what they don't want to do. A member of a counselor-training group, when confronted about her lack of participation, once told me that she was learning in the group by observing and that she was putting what she had learned to work in settings outside the group. Our ability to rationalize seems to know no bounds.

Procrastination. "Nothing needs to be done now." Often enough clients seek the help of counselors only after procrastination has led to some crisis. A husband and wife notice all sorts of cues that their marriage is in trouble, but ignore them ("We'll have to do something about that one of these days"). In the helping process itself clients, often with the complicity of their helpers, explore problems endlessly and put off setting goals, developing strategies, and acting.

Passing the buck.   "I'm not the one who needs to act." Clients pass the buck both outside and inside the counseling sessions.

> In the early days of the Watergate coverup conspiracy . . . a number of high-level aides . . . assumed that their acts of perjury or obstruction of justice were not illegal and were fully justified because they were responding to requests that came from the White House. Most of them were surprised when they learned that they were personally culpable and would be sent to jail [Wheeler & Janis, p. 29].

A surprising number of clients will come to you with the expectation that you are going to do something to fix them. Not only do you have to enter a contract with them right from the start, but you also have to continually challenge them to live up to its provisions.

Giving Feedback

Confrontation involves giving the client feedback on his or her behavior. The following steps (see Remer, 1984; Watson & Remer, 1984; Wallen, 1973) help ensure that feedback will be given in such a way that the receiver is most likely to use it. Since the ideal is self-challenge, the client should be as involved as possible in each of the steps of this process.

1. *Avoid labeling.* Derogatory labels put clients down and make them resistant to accepting and acting on feedback. Words such as *dumb, selfish, arrogant, manipulator, crazy, lazy,* and the like should be avoided. Telling a client "That's a very selfish thing to do," is accusatory, and ordinarily accusations do little to help clients move to problem-managing action. Telling a client that she is a manipulator is not only accusatory, it is not specific; that is, it does not identify the patterns of behavior involved in the manipulation.
2. *Describe the situation and the relevant behaviors.* Instead of labeling the client, describe the context and the self-limiting behaviors in question as specifically and as accurately as possible. For instance, instead of telling a member of a counseling group that he is selfish, describe his behavior. "You interrupt others when they are speaking, not to help them but to bring up your own agendas. You seldom respond to others with empathy. If the topic at hand does not interest you, you become distracted, withdraw, and remain silent. You come late for the meetings." Even when describing his behavior, do not dump everything on him at once. Giving feedback is not the same as building up a case at a trial.

3. *Describe the impact or consequence of the behavior.* Point out how relevant parties are affected by the behavior in terms of both emotions and behavior. Relevant parties can include the client himself or herself, the helper, and others outside the helping relationship. For instance, a member of the counseling group may say, "When you interrupt me repeatedly in order to bring up your own points, I get angry, I feel put down or ignored, and I want to get back at you." In the following example the client is a resident in a home for unmarried women who are expecting children. She is not getting along with the other residents and has been told she might have to leave.

HELPER: What do you think you do that bothers people so much?
CLIENT: I don't bathe as much as they do. I like loud music, so I play a radio loud. When I can't sleep, I move around the dormitory and make noise.
HELPER: How do people react to that?
CLIENT: At first no one said anything. But now people get mad and yell. Some won't talk to me. One girl began crying the other day when I was playing music loud. And of course it has made the supervisor angry enough to tell me that I'm going to be kicked out.

Obviously, many clients will not be as self-challenging as the one in the example. But the ideal stays the same: help clients do as much of the challenging as possible.

4. *Help clients identify what they need to do to manage the problem.* For instance, the woman in the example above can be helped to identify what she needs to start doing and stop doing in order to live peaceably with others in the home.

Giving clients feedback is a way of influencing them to change their behavior to more productive patterns.

■ Helper Self-Sharing

A fourth way of challenging your clients is to share with them something about yourself (Chelune, 1975; Cozby, 1973; McCarthy, 1982; VandeCreek & Angstadt, 1985). Like other forms of challenging, helper self-disclosure is not an end in itself. In one sense you cannot help but disclose yourself.

> The counselor communicates his or her characteristics to the client in every look, movement, emotional response, and sound, as well as with every word. Clients actively construe the personal characteristics, meanings, and causes behind the counselor's behaviors in order to evaluate the personal significance of the counselor's remarks [Strong & Claiborn, 1982, p. 173].

This is indirect disclosure. Direct helper self-disclosure has two principal functions: modeling and the development of new perspectives and new directions for action.

First of all, it can be a form of *modeling*, a way of both showing clients how to disclose themselves and encouraging them to do so (Thase & Page, 1977). Both Jourard (1968, 1971a, 1971b) and Mowrer (1973a, 1973b; Mowrer & Vattano, 1976) were pioneers in urging helper self-disclosure. Self-help groups (Gartner & Riessman, 1977, 1984; Hurvitz, 1970) such as Alcoholics Anonymous use modeling extensively as a way of showing new members what to talk about and of encouraging new members to talk freely about themselves and their problems. Doster and Nesbitt (1979) summarize their findings by noting that "overall . . . the research weighs in favor of the conclusion that therapist modeling of self-disclosure can be an effective method of denoting . . . for clients what is to take place behaviorally in psychotherapy . . ." (p. 204). It is most useful with clients who don't know what to do or who are reluctant to talk about themselves in an intimate or personal way. It can be useful any time clients get "stuck" and are having difficulty revealing themselves.

Second, counselor self-disclosure can help clients develop the kinds of new perspectives that are needed for goal setting and help them see the need for action. If your experience can help clients develop useful alternate frames of reference, sharing yourself seems to be a question of common sense.

■

Ben is a counselor in a drug rehabilitation program. He himself was an addict for a number of years, but "kicked the habit" with the help of the agency where he is now a counselor. It is clear to all addicts in the program that the counselors there have been addicts themselves and are not only rehabilitated but intensely interested in helping others both rid themselves of drugs and develop a lifestyle that helps them stay drug-free. Ben freely shares his experience of being a drug user and his rather agonizing journey to freedom whenever he thinks it can help a client.

■

Ex-alcoholics and ex-addicts can make excellent helpers in programs like this. Sharing their experience is central to their style of counseling and is accepted by their clients. New perspectives are thereby developed and new possibilities for action discovered.

On the other hand, Weigel and his associates (1972) found evidence suggesting that helper self-disclosure can frighten clients or make them see helpers as less well adjusted. In view of this and other difficulties, it seems that helper self-disclosure should follow certain guidelines.

HELPER SELF-DISCLOSURE AS PART OF THE CONTRACT

Derlega, Lovell, and Chaikin (1976) found that helper self-disclosure can easily be misunderstood by naive or uninformed clients and prove counterproductive. However, it can be very useful if, as in the case of the drug counselors just mentioned, it is clear to the clients from the start that "high self-disclosure by the therapist is part of the professional role and is appropriate for effective treatment" (Doster & Nesbitt, 1979, p. 204). In short, if you don't want your disclosures to surprise your clients, prepare them in advance when discussing the "contract."

APPROPRIATE SELF-DISCLOSURE

Sharing yourself is appropriate (Egan, 1976) if it helps clients achieve the treatment goals outlined in this helping process: if it helps them talk about themselves, if it helps them talk about problem situations more concretely, if it helps them develop new perspectives and frames of reference, if it helps them set realistic goals for themselves, and if it moves them to act. Helper self-disclosure that is exhibitionistic or engaged in for effect is obviously inappropriate. Here are some principles to ensure that self-sharing is appropriate.

Keep it selective and focused. Helper self-disclosure is appropriate if it keeps clients on target and does not distract them from investigating their own problem situations.

> COUNSELOR (talking to a graduate student in psychology): Listening to you takes me right back to my own days in graduate school. I don't think I was ever busier in my life. I also believe the most depressing moments of my life took place then. On any number of occasions I wanted to throw in the towel. For instance, I remember once toward the end of my third year, when . . . .

It may be that selective bits of this counselor's experience in graduate school would have been useful in helping the student get a better conceptual and emotional grasp of the problems, but he has wandered off into the kind of reminiscing that meets his needs rather than the client's.

Don't burden the client. Helper self-disclosure is appropriate if it does not add another burden to an already overburdened client. One counselor thought he would make a client who was sharing some sexual problems more comfortable by sharing some of his own experiences. After all, he saw his sexual development as not too different from the client's. However, the client reacted by saying, "Hey, don't tell me your problems. I'm having a hard enough time dealing with my own. I don't want to carry yours around, too!"

This novice counselor shared too much of himself too soon. He was caught up in his own willingness to disclose rather than keeping sight of its potential usefulness to the client.

Don't overdo it. Helper disclosure is inappropriate if it is too frequent. This, too, distracts the client and shifts attention to the counselor. Research (Murphy & Strong, 1972) suggests that if helpers disclose themselves too frequently, clients tend to see them as phony and suspect that they have ulterior motives.

Remain flexible. Adapt your disclosures to differences among clients and situations (Chelune, 1977; Neimeyer & Banikiotes, 1981; Neimeyer & Fong, 1983). Always keep the goals of counseling in mind.

In summary, then, even though the research on helper self-disclosure is somewhat ambivalent (DeForest & Stone, 1980; McCarthy, 1979; Nilsson, Strassberg, & Bannon, 1979; Simonson, 1976), most studies find value in it even when clients do not expect or prefer it (VandeCreek & Angstadt, 1985). Therefore, it is a skill that should be part of any helper's repertory. That is, helpers should be *willing* and *able* to disclose themselves, even deeply, in reasonable ways, but should actually do so only if it is clear that it will contribute to the client's progress.

■ Immediacy: Encouraging Direct, Mutual Talk

Some authors (Danish, D'Augelli, & Brock, 1976; McCarthy, 1979; McCarthy & Betz, 1978; Reynolds & Fischer, 1983) make a distinction between self-disclosing and *self-involving* statements by helpers and tend to see the latter as more useful. Self-involving statements refer to the helper's personal reactions to the client during the counseling session. This is *immediacy.* Carl Rogers, when asked for his current thinking on the role of challenging in counseling (Landreth, 1984), made the following remarks:

> I am quite certain even before I stopped carrying individual counseling cases, I was doing more and more of what I would call confrontation. That is, confrontation of the other person with my feelings. . . . For example, I recall a client with whom I began to realize I felt bored every time he came in. I had a hard time staying awake during the hour, and that was not like me at all. Because it was a persisting feeling, I realized I would have to share it with him. I had to confront him with my feeling and that really caused a conflict in his role as a client. . . . So with a good deal of difficulty and some embarrassment, I said to him, "I don't understand it myself, but when you start talking on and on about your problems in what seems to me a flat tone of voice, I find myself getting very bored." This was quite a jolt to him and he

looked very unhappy. Then he began to talk about the way he talked and gradually he came to understand one of the reasons for the way he presented himself verbally. He said, "You know, I think the reason I talk in such an uninteresting way is because I don't think I have ever expected anyone to really hear me." . . . We got along much better after that because I could remind him that I heard the same flatness in his voice I used to hear [p. 323].

Rogers' talking about what was happening between himself and his client facilitated the helping process. Such cases can be challenging for both client and helper.

It has been suggested that many if not most clients who seek help have trouble with interpersonal relationships. This is either their central concern or part of a wider problem situation. Some of the difficulties clients have in their day-to-day relationships are also reflected in their relationships with their helpers. For instance, if they are compliant outside, they are often compliant in the helping process. If they become aggressive and angry with authority figures outside, they often do the same with helpers. Therefore, the client's interpersonal style can be examined, at least in part, by examining his or her relationship with the helper. If counseling takes place in a group, the opportunity is even greater. The skill or "package" of skills that enables either counselors or clients to initiate an exploration of their relationships has been called *immediacy* (Carkhuff, 1969a, 1969b; Carkhuff & Anthony, 1979), *direct, mutual communication* (Higgins, Ivey, & Uhlemann, 1979; Ivey, 1971; Ivey & Authier, 1978), and *you-me* talk (Egan, 1976, 1977). It is one's ability to explore with another what is happening in their relationship. There are two types: relationship immediacy and here-and-now immediacy.

RELATIONSHIP IMMEDIACY

Relationship immediacy refers to your ability to discuss with a client where you stand in your *overall* relationship to him or her. The focus is not on present interaction but on the way the relationship has developed. In the following example the helper, a 44-year-old woman working in a community mental health agency, is talking to a 36-year-old man she has been seeing once every other week for about two months.

COUNSELOR: We seem to have developed a good relationship here. I feel we respect each other. I have been able to make demands on you and you have made demands on me—there has been a great deal of give-and-take in our relationship. You've gotten angry with me and I've gotten impatient with you at times, but we've worked it out. I'm wondering what our relationship has that is missing in your relationship with your supervisor.

CLIENT: Well, for one thing, you listen to me, and I don't think she does. On the other hand, I listen pretty carefully to you, but I don't think I listen to her at all and she probably knows it.

The counselor is reviewing her good relationship with the client to help him develop some new perspectives on a difficult relationship outside.

Here is another example. Lee, a 38-year-old trainer in a counselor training program, is talking to 25-year-old Carlos, one of the trainees.

TRAINER: Carlos, I'm a bit bothered about some of the things that are going on between you and me. When you talk to me, I get the feeling that you are being very careful. You talk slowly—you seem to be choosing your words, sometimes to the point that what you are saying sounds almost prepared. You have never challenged me on anything in the group. When you talk most intimately about yourself, you seem to avoid looking at me. I find myself giving you less feedback than I give others. I've even found myself putting off talking to you about all this. Perhaps some of this is my own imagining, but I want to check it out with you.

CARLOS: I've been putting it off, too. I'm embarrassed about some of the things I think I have to say.

Carlos goes on to engage Lee in a dialogue about their relationship and how it is affecting his pursuit of the training goals in the group. Again, it is not just some immediate incident that is being discussed, but rather the overall *patterning* of their relationship.

HERE-AND-NOW IMMEDIACY

Here-and-now immediacy refers to the helper's ability to discuss with clients what is happening between them in the here and now of any given transaction. The entire relationship is not being considered, only this specific interaction. In the following example the helper, a 43-year-old woman, is a counselor in an alcoholic rehabilitation program. Agnes, a 49-year-old woman, has stopped drinking and is now taking a look at her current interpersonal lifestyle. Agnes seems to have withdrawn quite a bit, and the interaction has bogged down.

COUNSELOR: I'd like to stop a moment and take a look at what's happening right now between you and me.

AGNES: I'm not sure what you mean.

COUNSELOR: Well, our conversation today started out quite lively and now it seems rather subdued. I've noticed that the muscles in my shoulders have become tense and that I feel a little flushed. I sometimes tense up that way when I feel I might have said something wrong.

AGNES: What could that have been?

COUNSELOR: Agnes, is it just me or do you, too, feel that things are a bit strained between us right now?

AGNES: Well, a little.

COUNSELOR: We were discussing how you can control your friends with your emotions. This gets you what you want, but the price you pay can be too high. For instance, you describe some of your friends as becoming more and more wary of you. Now all of a sudden you've gone a bit quiet and I've been asking myself what I might have done wrong. To be truthful, I'm feeling a bit controlled, too. I'm obviously giving my perspective; I'd like to hear yours.

The counselor does two things. First, she deals with the impasse in the session by examining what is happening in the here and now of the relationship. Second, she begins to explore the possibility that what the client is doing here and now is an example of her self-defeating approach to interpersonal relationships in her day-to-day life. She is tentative in what she says and invites the client to present her perspective.

Immediacy: A Complex Skill

People often fail to be immediate with one another in their interactions. For instance, a husband feels slighted by something his wife says. He says nothing and swallows his feelings. But he becomes a little bit distant from her for the next couple of days, a bit quieter. She notices this, wonders what is happening, but says nothing. Soon little things in their relationship that would ordinarily be ignored become irritating. Things become more and more tense, but still they do not engage in "direct, mutual talk" about what is happening. The whole thing ends in a game of "uproar" (see Berne, 1964)—that is, a huge argument over something quite small. Once they've vented their emotions, they feel both relieved because they've done so but guilty because they've done so in a somewhat childish way.

Immediacy is a difficult, demanding skill. One reason people such as the couple in the example do not engage more readily and more opportunely in direct, mutual talk is that they have never learned to do so. Like other human-relations skills, immediacy or you-me talk has three components: awareness, communication ability, and assertiveness.

THE AWARENESS COMPONENT

If you are going to talk to a client about what is happening between the two of you—either in your overall relationship or in the here and now of *this* interaction—you have to *know* what is happening. You have to be able to read cues both in yourself and in the other. For instance, if you do not read the cues that indicate that the client feels hurt, or if you do not notice the tenseness in your own body, you cannot be immediate. Effective helpers, while not being overly self-conscious about relating to clients, still *monitor* what is happening in those relationships. Turock (1980) sees the focus of immediacy—at least in part—as the unspoken messages of the client, especially those that relate to what is happening in counseling sessions. I would add to those the unspoken messages of the helper. Often in supervision I find that the unspoken messages of both clients and helpers are precisely what needed to be stated and dealt with.

Kagan (1984) has formulated a very useful process called "interpersonal process recall." Helpers are systematically trained to "listen to" themselves as they interact with their clients. After a counseling session, a supervisor helps the trainee counselor reflect on the internal self-talk that took place during the session. Special attention is given to what the counselor said to himself or herself but did not share with the client. After practice counseling sessions, both counselor and client are debriefed. Both have observations that they made to themselves during the session but did not share with the other. The debriefing does at least four things. First, it helps counselors learn the kinds of things that go on in clients' minds. Second, it helps counselors learn how to challenge clients to get more of their significant self-talk into the overt dialogue. Third, it helps counselors become more aware of their own self-talk during sessions instead of afterwards. Fourth, it helps counselors get more of their own significant and relevant self-talk into the overt dialogue with clients.

THE COMMUNICATION COMPONENT

Once you notice something in your relationship with a client that is related to or affecting the helping process, you face the issue of how to communicate your perception. Immediacy is a communication skill formed by a combination of three other skills: empathy, self-disclosure, and challenge.

Empathy.   You must not only perceive what is happening between you and the client, but you must be able to put your perceptions and understandings into words. Very often immediacy calls for *advanced* accurate empathy, because what is happening in the relationship is often not expressed openly and directly.

CLIENT: I'm a bit uncomfortable in these sessions at times.
HELPER: My guess is that some of that discomfort is with me.
CLIENT: That's not a bad guess.

Immediacy, like other forms of challenge, should start with the experience of the client.

Self-disclosure.   Being immediate involves revealing how you think and feel about what is happening in your relationship with the client. You put yourself on the line.

COUNSELOR: I sometimes resent the fact that my job makes me counsel people who would rather not be here. There are days when I tell myself that it's impossible.

CLIENT: Is this one of those days?

Immediacy is not a way of "dealing with" the client. Rather, it is an exercise in mutuality, an expression of the give and take of the helping relationship. The self-disclosure element of immediacy conveys the message, "I want to be open in my relationship to you." Of course, the principles governing helper self-disclosure in general are also applicable here.

Challenge. Immediacy often involves pointing out discrepancies, challenging games, exploring distortions, and the like. Immediacy, however, requires that helpers confront not only the discrepancies they find in their clients but also those they find in themselves. They invite their clients and themselves to discuss whatever might be interfering with a working relationship.

COUNSELOR: Here's what I think has been bogging us down. See if it makes sense to you. I feel that I have let myself gradually adopt the role of "daddy" and that you have gradually let yourself adopt the role of "little girl." I actually find myself talking to you the way I talk to my little girl at home. I think our interactions here lack the kind of robust caring that is found in adult-to-adult relationships. I let myself picture you as fragile and then become overcareful. How do you feel about all this?

CLIENT: It's been very comfortable. But we *are* moving slowly. And I'm not as fragile as I make myself out to be.

Immediacy requires mutuality. It is important to invite clients to explore the relationship. However, if clients do not have the kinds of communication skills required for immediacy, counselors, through empathy and probing, can help them "walk through" an interchange on the relationship.

HELPER: I feel I've been pretty hard on you this session. What do you think?

CLIENT: A bit. Not too bad.

HELPER: I'm not sure what you mean by "a bit."

CLIENT: Well, you seem to be kind of angry a lot. Like you're taking it personally or something.

HELPER: My getting worked up doesn't help much, huh?

CLIENT: Well, I know you care, but you don't have to go overboard.

THE ASSERTIVENESS COMPONENT

Immediacy is not an easy skill for many people, even when they possess the awareness and know-how to engage in it. Basic empathy can be easy because, in a sense, it is giving a gift to the other. The other challenging skills discussed here can be relatively easy because the focus remains on the client. Immediacy is difficult because it is of its nature very self-involving. Helpers who are struggling with intimacy in their own lives can expect to have trouble with this skill.

In the following example, a 17-year-old inmate of a reformatory is talking to the school counselor. He's bright, but failing a subject, and at times is very disruptive. The counselor has seen him three times over a two-month period. He is certainly an involuntary inmate, but is somewhere on the border between voluntary and involuntary as a client.

CLIENT: I don't know why I keep coming here. I keep talking about myself, but nothing happens. I still hate this place, and I can't stand most of the people here.

COUNSELOR: You do talk about yourself, but I'm not sure that I'm helping you talk about the right things. You talk about classes you don't like, teachers you don't like, rules you don't like. But you don't talk a lot about yourself. My hunch is that you still don't trust me very much. At least not enough to talk about yourself instead of just your gripes.

CLIENT: I don't know if it's you. Shrinks turn me off.

COUNSELOR: Well, if I'm still a shrink to you, then something's wrong between you and me. It makes it easy to write me off. If I'm being written off, I'd like to know why. It may be that I just don't like not being liked. Then it's my problem.

CLIENT: Okay. It's not you. (Pause) But why *should* I trust you? The adults in my life haven't been exactly charmers. Why don't you analyze my parents. That'd be a real challenge for any shrink.

They go on to explore how the client's persistent resentment colors almost everything he does and how the only one really being done in by it is himself. An unskilled helper might have continued to encourage the kind of unproductive self-exploration in which the client was engaged, and eventually such a helper might have terminated the relationship on the assumption that the client was not "motivated" to work. This counselor, however, attentive to the cues that the relationship itself is not going right, uses immediacy to help break through the impasse.

Situations Calling for Direct, Mutual Communication

The skill of immediacy can be most useful in the following situations:

- When a session is *directionless* and it seems that no progress is being made: "I feel that we're bogged down right now. Perhaps we could stop a moment and see what we're doing right and what's going wrong."
- When there is *tension* between helper and client: "We seem to be getting on each other's nerves. It might be helpful to stop a moment and clear the air."
- When *trust* seems to be an issue: "I see your hesitancy to talk and I'm not sure whether it's related to me or not. It might still be hard for you to trust me."
- When there is "*social distance*" between helper and client in terms of social class or widely differing interpersonal styles: "There are some

hints here that the fact that I'm Black and you're White is making both of us a bit hesitant."

- When *dependency* seems to be interfering with the helping process. "You don't seem willing to explore an issue until I give you permission to do so. And I seem to have let myself slip into the role of permission giver."
- When *counterdependency* seems to be blocking the helping relationship: "It seems that we're letting this session turn into a struggle between you and me. And, if I'm not mistaken, both of us are bent on winning."
- When *attraction* is sidetracking either helper or client: "I think we've liked each other from the start. Now I'm wondering whether that might be getting in the way of the work we're doing here."

Immediacy is, of course, a means, not an end. The primary goal of the helping process is not to establish and enjoy relationships but to explore and work through problem situations. Immediacy, used effectively, can accomplish two things. First, it can provide new perspectives on the counseling relationship and help client and counselor work more effectively together. Second, what clients learn about themselves in their interactions with helpers can provide new perspectives on how they relate to people outside. The Summary Box at the end of this chapter reviews the skills of challenging. Summarizing, which offers its own kind of challenge, is included.

■ Some Caricatures of Challenging

Gordon (1970), in teaching parents ways of being effective in their relationships with their children, speaks of the "dirty dozen": 12 categories of ineffective parental behaviors. These behaviors are caricatures or perversions of confrontation. They are also ways in which helpers become ineffectually "parental" with their clients. The following is a list of those behaviors. You will notice that some of the categories overlap. You will probably also notice that some of the behaviors might at times be useful, provided that they are not your way of taking over responsibilities that belong to the client.

- *Commanding, ordering, directing:* "Go back to your wife and tell her what we've talked about."
- *Warning, admonishing, threatening:* "If you keep on being dependent, you're going to end up a very lonely woman. I've seen it happen before."
- *Exhorting, moralizing, preaching:* "Try to be more sensitive to her needs. Sensitivity is very important in intimate relationships."

- *Advising, giving suggestions, offering solutions:* "If I were you, I'd quit your teaching job as soon as possible and take one in the business world."
- *Lecturing, giving logical arguments:* "She's not going to give in and neither are you. The conclusion seems to be—end the relationship."
- *Judging, criticizing, disagreeing, blaming:* "If you can admit that getting fired was your own fault, you'll be in a position to start thinking of new jobs."
- *Approving, praising, agreeing with:* "Telling your mother-in-law off was the best thing you could have done. It was your way of regaining your manhood."
- *Name-calling, ridiculing, shaming:* "I can't believe that you'd just drop him without letting him know why. What an awful way to treat someone."
- *Reassuring, consoling, sympathizing:* "Don't let this get you down. He probably didn't know he was hurting you so much."
- *Questioning, interrogating:* "How do you feel right now? What is bothering you the most? What other relationships are going wrong?"
- *Humoring, distracting:* "I bet you can see the humor in all this mess. You're the kind that doesn't let her sense of humor die."

These ordinarily represent failures to respect clients. However, even though clients are not to be badgered and even though tact in challenging clients is often crucial, this does not mean that challenge or invitations to self-challenge cannot be forceful. They can be as forceful as the relationship can tolerate. Some suggest that, once the relationship is established, a certain "impertinence" on the part of the helper is not only allowed but called for (Beier, 1984; Farrelly & Brandsma, 1974). Effective helpers ask impertinent questions, make impertinent observations, and make impertinent demands. They see helping as a caring, but also a robust, activity. However, a caution is in order. I trust "impertinence" in the hands of caring and empathic helpers who have gained the "right" to confront, as outlined in Chapter Seven.

■ Is Challenge Enough?

Some clients are looking for someone to challenge them. Once challenged, they do whatever they have to do to manage their problems. Some are on the brink of challenging themselves and need only a nudge. Others have the resources to manage their lives better, but not the will. They know what they need to do, but are not doing it. The only way you may "be with" such clients is as a gentle or tough challenger. The following conditions must be met: 1. you see clearly that challenge will provide the leverage such clients need in order to move to fruitful action;

2. they see you as empathic, "for" them, in the challenge you offer; and
3. the way you challenge them meets the norms discussed in Chapter
Seven. In no way am I suggesting that you become a specialist in challenging. Rather, sometimes "being with" a client as challenger is meeting
a client at the point of his or her greatest need.

■ A Final Note

As indicated in Chapters One and Two, social influence and challenging
are not limited to Step I-C. Figure 8–1 graphically indicates that challenging or invitations to self-challenge can be part of any stage and any
step. Effective challenge blends in with the rest of the model instead of
standing out, as Block (1981) notes, like a courtroom drama in which
the helper is judge or jury or prosecutor or even apologetic defendant.
Effective challenge, in Block's terms, is not "judgmental, global, stereotyped, lengthy, or complicated," but rather "descriptive, focused, brief,
and simple" (p. 172).

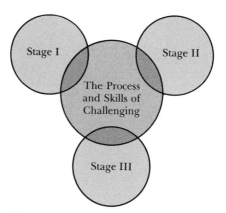

Figure 8–1. Challenge may be useful at any stage or step of the helping
process

■ A Summary of the Communication Skills of Challenging

The following skills are often interrelated in practice. They can be used at any point in the helping process from storytelling to action.

1. *Summarizing:* Summarizing, or inviting clients to summarize, challenges them to see central issues more clearly and to move toward action (from Chapter Six).
2. *Information gathering:* Giving clients needed information or helping them search for it helps them see problem situations in a new light and provides a basis for action.
3. *Advanced empathy:* This skill involves your sharing "hunches" with clients about their experiences, behaviors, and feelings. These hunches can help clients move beyond blind spots and develop needed new perspectives. Some of the forms your hunches can take are:
   a. Helping clients express clearly what they are *implying*.
   b. Identifying *themes* in clients' stories.
   c. Connecting *islands* of experiences, behaviors, feelings.
   d. Helping clients draw *conclusions* from premises.
4. *Confrontation:* This skill takes two forms. First of all, challenging the discrepancies, distortions, smoke screens, and games clients use, knowingly or unknowingly, to keep themselves and others from seeing their problem situations and unused potential. Second, challenging clients to move beyond discussion to action.
5. *Helper self-sharing:* This skill enables you to share your own experience with clients as a way of modeling nondefensive self-disclosure, of helping them move beyond blind spots, and of seeing possibilities for problem-managing action.
6. *Immediacy:* This skill enables you to discuss your relationship with your clients in two ways with a view to improving the working alliance.
   a. *Relationship immediacy:* This refers to your ability to discuss with a client your overall relationship with him or her with a view to managing whatever problems exist and maintaining strengths.
   b. *Here-and-now immediacy:* This refers to your ability to discuss with a client whatever is standing in the way of working together right now.

   Immediacy can involve a whole range of communication skills, including the basic communication skills of attending, listening, and empathy, plus the other challenging skills.

To challenge well, helpers need to be *aware* of situations where it is called for, *competent* in the skills of challenging, and *assertive* enough to use them.

Part Four

Stage II:
Developing Preferred Scenarios

Stage II asks, "What would this problem situation look like if it were being managed successfully?" It has three steps.

Step II-A: Creating new scenarios.   In this step counselors help clients decide what they want to be different in their lives. If the problem situation is Point A, the preferred scenario is Point B.

Step II-B: The critique of possible scenarios.   In this step helpers share with their clients the criteria for evaluating effective goals and help them use those criteria to evaluate possible futures.

Step II-C: Choice and commitment.   In this step counselors help clients choose a preferred scenario or goal or set of goals and commit themselves to working for a better-managed lifestyle.

Stage II emphasizes the need for creativity on the part of helpers and the need to help clients develop their own imaginal resources.

Nine

Stage II:
Creating New Scenarios
and Setting Goals

■

Many clients are clients because they are mired in problem situations from which they see no exit. They don't know where to go, much less how to get there. They lack *direction*. Therefore, one of the most useful ways in which you can be with clients is helping them develop a sense of direction or helping them see new, more constructive directions in which to move. With a sense of direction often comes a sense of hope.

■

I first met Ernesto in the emergency room in a large, urban hospital. He was throwing up blood into a pan. He was a street gang member and this was the third time he had been beaten up in the last year. He had been so severely beaten this time that it was likely that he would suffer permanent physical damage. Ernesto's lifestyle was doing him in, but it was the only one he knew. He was in need of a new way of living, a new scenario, a new way of participating in city life. This time he was hurting enough to consider the possibility of some kind of change.

■

I worked with Ernesto, principally helping him to discover a different purpose in life and a different lifestyle.

FROM POINT A TO POINT B

When clients explore their problem situations in terms of specific experiences, behaviors, and feelings in specific situations, they come to see more clearly *where they are,* Point A. The next step is to help them develop new perspectives on their problem situations so that they can see more clearly *where they want to be,* Point B. For instance, for Delia Point A is the disappointing and dissatisfying job she now has. Since she sees no hope for improvement in her present job, Point B is a new, more satisfying job. The new perspective that she may need in order to actually establish Point B as her goal is that there is no reason why she must persist in a job she does not like. The counselor finds that she is hemming herself in by self-defeating beliefs and attitudes such as "I must always remain loyal to the company for which I work" and "For the sake of stability it is better to stay in a job even though you don't like it." Once the counselor challenges her to examine and move beyond these disabling beliefs, she is able to set the goal of getting a new job. An inadequate examination of Point A, however, will lead to an inadequate conception of Point B.

The discussion of the helping process up till now has focused on the work of helping the client get involved with and "own" both the helping process and the work of problem definition and clarification. But once a problem is clearly defined, it is time to move on. The problem-solving process is organic and cumulative. It is successful if it leads to *problem-handling action*. Listening for the sake of listening, exploring for the sake of exploring, and challenging for the sake of challenging are all useless. The work up to this point is successful if it leads to the kind of problem clarification that contributes to the establishment of realistic, problem-managing goals.

Intentionality in Living

Counseling is a process of helping clients become more *intentional* (Center for Constructive Change, 1984; Ivey, 1983; Wadsworth & Ford, 1983) in their lives. In order to understand what intentionality means, it is helpful to understand the "stuckness" of clients.

> A client comes to an interview *stuck*—having either no alternatives for solving a problem or a limited range of possibilities. The task of the interviewer is to eliminate stuckness and substitute intentionality. *Stuckness* is an inelegant, but highly descriptive, term to describe the opposite of intentionality (see Perls, 1969). Other words that represent the same condition include *immobility, blocks, repetition, compulsion, inability to achieve goals, lack of understanding, limited behavioral repertoire, limited life script, impasse, lack of motivation,* and many other terms. . . . In short, clients often come to the interview because they are stuck for a variety of reasons and seek intentionality [Ivey, 1983, p. 213].

Clients are clients because they are not intentional in their lives or, in some crisis or period of marginality, are not being as intentional as they usually are.

Intentionality implies a number of things, including self-responsibility, a refusal to buckle, a sense of direction, versatility, and the ability to transcend self-interest.

SELF-RESPONSIBILITY

Intentional people know that they are in charge of their own lives.

> Central to intentionality is the ability to recognize that what is happening in our lives is a consequence of how we have gone about our affairs—our habitual approaches to situations and to other people—and we can change these and, thus, change what is happening [Center for Constructive Change, 1984, p. 16].

Intentional people do not waste time and energy blaming others or circumstances for their problem situations. Clients, as we have seen, often have to be challenged to own their problem situations by recasting them in terms of their own behavior rather than in terms of what others and the world are doing to them, and to develop an "I can" spirit.

A REFUSAL TO BUCKLE

In fairness it must be said that many clients experience problem situations due to circumstances beyond their control. The client who has just been told that she has cancer is not to be blamed for not avoiding it. However, a second aspect of intentionality relates to the ability of clients to manage what cannot be changed. If I have a spouse who drinks excessively, I cannot directly change him or her, but I can manage my reaction to my spouse's behavior creatively. I can choose not to give in, not to buckle under unfavorable odds.

A SENSE OF DIRECTION

Intentional people have a sense of direction in their lives. This can be said in a number of ways:

- They have a sense of purpose.
- They live lives that are going somewhere.
- Self-enhancing and other-enhancing patterns of behavior are in place.
- They focus on outcomes and accomplishments.
- They don't mistake aimless action for accomplishments.
- They set long-term and short-term goals and objectives.
- They have a defined rather than an aimless lifestyle.

This sense of purpose and direction is perhaps the central dimension of intentionality. The inevitable crises and problem situations of life are perceived and managed against this background of purpose and direction. Intentional people don't waste time in wishful thinking, but rather "translate abstract wishes and expectations into clearly defined outcomes against which [they] can measure progress" (Center for Constructive Change, 1984, p. 16).

VERSATILITY

The intentional individual is always thinking about and creating options.

> Intentionality is acting with a sense of capability and deciding from a range of alternative actions. The intentional individual has more than one action, thought, or behavior to choose from in responding to changing life situations. The intentional individual can generate alternatives in a given situation and approach a problem from different vantage points, using a variety of skills and personal qualities, adapting styles to suit different cultural groups [Ivey, 1983, p. 3].

Clients become clients because they have few responses to the problems of life or because they become constricted and inflexible in periods of marginality.

MOVING BEYOND SELF-INTEREST

Intentionality includes the ability to appreciate and get involved in the world—the world of other individuals and the world of social settings and systems. Personal goals and objectives are evaluated against the needs and wants of others. Intentional people are not self-referential; they do not "overpersonalize" situations. They are ready to help others and to work for win-win rather than win-lose outcomes. Clients are often people who are either out of community or in community in conflicted ways. They have not developed ways of handling the normal give-and-take of interpersonal relationships. Goals and outcomes are evaluated in terms of their own personal needs rather than the needs of the relationship or community.

Counseling, then, is a process of helping nonintentional people to develop a degree of intentionality, or of helping usually intentional people who have been battered by problems in living to regain a sense of intentionality.

The Centrality of Goal Setting

Goal setting and its relationship to human action is receiving more and more attention in the social sciences (Frese & Sabini, 1985; Locke, Shaw, Saari, & Latham, 1981). Goal setting is the central point of the helping process. On the one hand, everything in Stage I is preparatory. The counseling relationship is established to help the client explore and clarify the problem situation. Focusing helps clients identify points of leverage. The client is challenged in order to develop new perspectives. New perspectives clarify the problem and point out that something needs to be done to manage it. New perspectives also help clients see, at least in some general way, *which* new scenario needs to be substituted. Goal setting completes this process. On the other hand, everything that takes place after goal setting or the development of a preferred scenario— choosing strategies for achieving goals and the actual implementation of action programs—is done to ensure that those goals are actually met.

Sometimes clients want to skip the goal-setting part of the process. Once they see a problem fairly clearly, they want to do something about it immediately.

■

Harry was a sophomore in college who was admitted to one of the state mental hospitals because of an "acute schizophrenic episode" at the university. He was one of the disc jockeys for the university radio station. He came to the notice of college officials one day when he put on a rather bizarre performance that included a lengthy presentation of some grandiose religious ideas. In the hospital it was soon discovered that this pleasant, likable young man was actually a loner. Everyone who knew him at the university thought he had a lot of friends, but in fact he did not. The campus was large and this went unnoticed. Harry was soon released from the hospital, but returned weekly for therapy. The helper discussed with him his lack of contact with women. Once it became clear to him that his meetings with women were perfunctory and almost always took place in groups— he had actually thought he had a rather full social life with women— Harry rushed headlong into a program of dating. This ended in disaster, because he lacked some basic social and communication skills. Furthermore, he had serious doubts about his own worth and therefore found it difficult making a gift of himself to others. With the help of the therapist he returned to the problem clarification and new perspectives part of the helping process, and then established some goals that proved to be more realistic. One of them was to examine his interpersonal style and acquire some communication skills in a safe setting. He accomplished this goal by joining an interpersonal skills group offered by the communication department at the university.

■

Harry's leaping from problem clarification to action without taking time to set some reasonable goals is an example of the nonlinear nature of helping. His lack of success in dating, even though it involved a fair amount of pain, actually helped him see his problem with women more clearly. He then had to backtrack, set some realistic goals, and move more slowly.

The Importance of Imagination in Counseling

A friend of mine is a marriage counselor. He tends not to spend a lot of time in Stage I, at least not in the beginning. His reasoning goes something like this.

■

When a couple comes in, they don't need to spend a lot of time talking about what is going wrong. They *know* what's going wrong because they're living it every day. If I let them tell their stories, they inevitably tell entirely different stories. It's as if they were not even married to each other. They begin to fight in the ways in which they fight at home. I don't find all of this very useful. And so early on I make them focus on the future. I ask them questions like "What would your marriage look like if it were a little bit better—not perfect, but just a little bit better?" If they get stuck, I ask them to think about other couples they know, couples that seem to have decent, if not perfect, marriages. "What's their marriage like? What parts of it would you like to see incorporated into your own marriage?" What I try to do is to help them use their imaginations to create a vision of a marriage that is different from the one they are experiencing. It's not that I never let them talk about the present. Rather I try to help them talk about the present by having them engage in a dialogue between a better future and the unacceptable present. For instance, if one of them says, "I'd like a marriage in which the household tasks were divided up more fairly," then I might let the person explore how they are currently divided up. They then use a better future as a tool to help them clarify a problematic present.

∎

Of course, this is not a quick lesson in how to conduct marriage counseling, but it does give the flavor of one part of his approach.

My friend recognizes the *power* of goals, of direction, of purpose—a power that most if not all clients underestimate and underuse. You can do a great deal for clients if you can help them develop a sense of purpose or direction made specific in clear goals. Clients mired in problem situations do not use the imaginal resources they possess. Stage III can be an exciting one for both client and helper because it involves the stimulation of the unused or underused imaginations or imaginal resources of clients.

> In order to shape [a] preferred future, we need to hold in our minds an image of what it is that we really want. . . . Use of imagination is what propels persons into the future, whether it is by idle dreaming or conscious intention. In ages past, future thinking was generally accepted as the turf of the prophet; more recently, that of the science fiction writer; but now we are beginning to realize that it is within the domain of every thoughtful person [Lindaman & Lippitt, 1979, p 3].

The importance of stimulating the imagination of the client cannot be overestimated.

My hunch is that too many helpers are biased toward Stage I. That is, they spend what I consider an inordinate amount of time helping clients identify, explore, and clarify problem situations; they also spend an inordinate amount of time using a variety of theories to help clients develop insights into themselves and their problems in living. This overemphasis on Stage I is self-defeating. The real challenge of helping is not in the identification and clarification of problem situations, however essential that might be, but in their management. Too many helper training programs begin and end with basic communication skills and the steps of Stage I. A friend of mine in Australia who teaches the model offered in this book once said to me; "If I have two years, I teach the entire model; if I have two months, I teach the entire model; if I have two days, I teach the entire model; if I have two hours, I teach the entire model." The model gives us a picture of the kinds of things people do, however erratically, when they manage problems in living. Helpers who spend most of their time with clients in Stage I may be doing both their clients and themselves a disservice. Their clients are ill served because they are not helped to move to problem-managing action. Helpers are ill served because too much time spent on the problems themselves and even on promoting insights without actually moving on to the management of the problems can lead to burnout.

■ Step II-A: Helping Clients Construct New Scenarios and Set Goals

Problems can make clients feel hemmed in and closed off. Step II-A, indicated in Figure 9–1, helps clients open up the world again. The *goal* of this step is to help clients develop a range of new scenarios or a range of new scenario elements that represent the "solution" or management of a problem situation. A *scenario,* as defined here, is a picture of what the problem situation would look like if it were being managed more effectively. A scenario *element* is one part of the picture. A *goal* is an outcome, an achievement; it is the new scenario *in place.* Clients are helped to envision themselves in the future managing a problem situation or some part of it. They are helped to see themselves engaging in patterns of behavior with outcomes that are more constructive than those of the

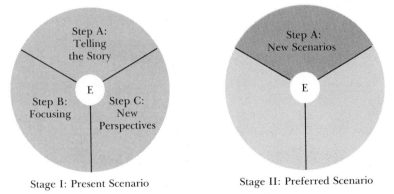

Figure 9–1. Step II-A: New scenario

self-defeating patterns of behavior currently in place. They are helped to imagine themselves accomplishing things that enable them to manage their lives more effectively.

■

Anita is a woman who is experiencing stress because she is simply trying to do too many things: be a wife, be a mother, hold down a part-time job, serve on church committees, and volunteer at a local nursing home. She needs to establish priorities and cut back to a reasonable schedule. One of the associate ministers helps her develop a different picture of the future. Anita, after listing all of the things she really likes to do and feels committed to, puts together different *scenarios* or lifestyle "packages." Then, using the priorities derived from her values, she determines which scenario appeals to her most. Each scenario contains a different mix of activities. Once she has made her choice, she can determine how to go about this change in lifestyle.

■

In this case the client is challenged to use her imagination to develop images of a different, more constructive future.

A new scenario is a simple or complex picture that is drawn up in answer to questions that clients can be helped to ask themselves, such as the following:

- *What would this problem situation look like if it were being managed better?* "I'd be having fewer anxiety attacks. And I'd be spending more time with people rather than by myself."
- *What changes would take place in my present lifestyle?* "I would not be drinking as much. I'd be getting more exercise."
- *What would I be doing differently with the people in my life?* "I would not be letting my mother make my decisions for me. I'd be sharing an apartment with one or two friends."
- *What patterns of behavior would be in place that currently are not?* "I'd be engaging in more of the activities offered here in the nursing home."
- *What patterns of behavior that are currently in place would be eliminated?* "I would not be putting myself down for incontinence I cannot control."
- *What would exist that doesn't exist now?* "I would have my temper under control and would have stopped hitting Jimmy. I would have a better job."
- *What would be happening that is not happening now?* "I would not be experiencing as much chronic pain as I am now. My welfare checks would be arriving on time."
- *What would I have that I don't have now?* "I'd have a place to live that's not rat-infested. I'd have a friend."
- *What decisions would be made and executed?* "I would have taken early retirement. I would be separated from my husband."

· *What accomplishments would be in place that are not now?* "I'd have my degree in practical nursing. I'd have someone to marry."

Although clients are used to looking at problems, because they are mired in them, they are not used to considering solutions.

Some new scenarios are relatively simple to state even though they might not be simple to fulfill. In the following example George has come to the conclusion that drinking is doing him no good. In the beginning of counseling he saw himself as a "social drinker"; he was not ready to see himself as a "problem drinker." However, he is challenged by the helper to explore the effects of drinking in his life. He is now ready to decide what he wants to do about drinking.

■

George, with the help of Evelyn's consultation, realizes that he can set various goals with regard to drinking. For instance, he can stop drinking completely. Or he can decide to stop drinking for a certain period of time, let us say six months. Or he can cut down on his drinking, allowing himself only a certain amount of alcohol in any given day. Or he can choose to restrict his drinking to a certain amount of alcohol on weekends. The goal he chooses is the elimination of drink from his life for a period of at least six months. A six-month "dry" period does not sound as drastic to him as stopping completely. He wants to see what his life will be like without alcohol.

■

The counselor helps George draw up a range of simple scenarios and he chooses the one that suits him best.

A new scenario can also be complex. In this case, clients can be helped to generate a list of possibilities or a list of possible elements in a preferred scenario. For instance Tom, an AIDS victim who found himself abandoned by many of his friends and shunned by society, was helped to come up with the following elements or possibilities. In the new scenario,

· He would have someone such as a minister with whom he could occasionally talk about the "ultimate" issues of life and death.
· He would have found a context for making some kind of sense of his suffering.
· He would have a counselor to whom he could go when things got rocky.
· He would belong to a self-help group of fellow AIDS victims.
· He would have fewer financial worries.
· He would have one or two intimates with whom he could share the ups and downs of daily life.
· He would be engaged in some kind of productive work, whether paid or not.

- He would have a decent place to live.
- He would have access to decent medical attention from medical staff who would not treat him like some kind of New-Age leper.
- He would have access to a community of people who did not fear him.
- He would be managing bouts of anxiety and depression better than at present.
- He would be taking care of unfinished business with relatives.
- He would have made peace with one or two of his closest friends.

Tom is then helped to establish criteria for evaluating each of these elements. Once he has evaluated them and chosen the elements he wants in his preferred scenario, he can be helped to establish priorities among them and determine how he is going to accomplish each. The "package" of elements he chooses constitutes the new and preferred scenario.

When clients are being helped to paint a picture of a better future, the realism of the elements is not an issue. Fantasy can be used to open up the future and engender a sense of hope. In fact, clients should be urged to make the preferred scenario or desired state as concrete and detailed as possible.

> Ideally this "wide-angle" view will be a comprehensive description of the future state. However, the key point is that a *detailed* picture should be produced, be it a "snapshot" or a "movie." . . . When coupled with an assessment of the present state [Stage I], this "picture" of the future condition provides the information necessary for [clients] to develop realistic action plans and time-tables [Stage III] for managing the change [Beckhard & Harris, 1977, p. 20].

Vague scenarios are much less likely to be accomplished because they do not suggest strategies that can be used for their accomplishment. Detailed scenarios can get the client's juices flowing.

Wheeler and Janis (1980) suggest that it is sometimes useful to have clients work through some "gloomy scenarios" (p. 12) such as the dissolution of a marriage, the loss of a job, failing health, and the like. This is not an exercise in pessimism. Working through such scenarios provides useful, often overlooked, information. Also, by putting clients in touch with the "worst case," it helps them mobilize their resources to see to it that the worst case does not happen.

The Advantages of Goal Setting

According to Locke and Latham (1984), helping clients develop new, preferable scenarios and set goals can help them in four ways:

1. Setting goals *focuses* clients' attention and action. New scenarios give clients a vision toward which they can direct their energies. Clients with goals are less likely to engage in aimless behavior.

2. Setting goals *mobilizes* energy and effort. Clients who seem lethargic during the problem-exploration phase come to life when it is a question of spelling out alternate scenarios. Goal setting is not just a cognitive exercise. Clients begin moving toward goals in a variety of ways as soon as they set them.

3. Setting goals *increases persistence.* Clients with goals are not only energized to do something, but they tend to work harder and longer. Clients with clear and realistic goals don't give up as easily as clients with vague goals or no goals at all.

4. Setting goals motivates clients to *search for strategies* to accomplish them. Setting goals, a Stage-II task, leads naturally into a search for means, a Stage-III task.

■ Step II-B: Helping Clients Evaluate Scenarios

Once a range of scenarios or scenario elements has been developed, clients need to evaluate them before they commit themselves to them. Step II-B is added in Figure 9–2. Goals or scenarios need to be "whipped into shape" so that they can drive action. The shaping process means helping clients set goals having the following eight characteristics: stated as accomplishments or outcomes rather than means, clear and specific, measurable or verifiable, realistic, adequate, owned by the client, in keeping with the client's values, and set in a reasonable time frame. These are the *criteria* used to determine whether the new scenario or goal is workable or not. Helping clients criticize or evaluate the scenarios they have developed means helping them apply these seven criteria to their potential choices.

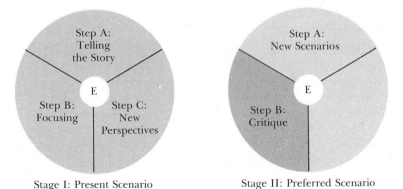

Stage I: Present Scenario   Stage II: Preferred Scenario

Figure 9–2. Step II-B: Critique

1. HELP CLIENTS STATE GOALS IN TERMS OF ACCOMPLISHMENTS RATHER THAN BEHAVIOR

Workable goals are *accomplishments* that help clients manage problem situations. These accomplishments or outcomes constitute the new or preferred scenario: they are not the programs that lead up to the scenario. For instance, if a client says "My goal is to get some training in interpersonal communication skills," she is stating her goal as a program rather than as an accomplishment. However, her goal is achieved only when those skills are *acquired, practiced, and actually used* in interpersonal situations. The processes that lead up to accomplishments are called *programs* and will be considered in the next chapter. The goal of a person who is drinking too much is not to join Alcoholics Anonymous. Joining AA is a program. The person has reached his or her goal when the drinking has stopped.

You can help clients develop this "past-participle" approach (drinking *stopped,* skills *acquired, practiced,* and *used,* the number of marital fights *decreased,* anger habitually *controlled*) to goal setting or scenario development. Stating new scenarios or goals in terms of accomplishments (or at least developing accomplishment-oriented ways of thinking about the future) is not just a question of language. Clients can leap into action (programs) without knowing where they are going (goals, outcomes, accomplishments, preferred scenarios). If a client with AIDS says he thinks he should join a self-help group of fellow AIDS victims, he should be helped to see what he wants to get out of such a group and whether what the group offers will help him manage the problem situations of his life. Programs constitute the *work* clients need to do to manage their lives better, but they need to know the outcomes toward which that work is directed. Knowing where they are going in terms of outcomes helps them work not just hard but smart. Smart workers know precisely what they are trying to accomplish.

2. HELP CLIENTS MAKE SURE THAT THEIR SCENARIOS OR GOALS ARE SPECIFIC ENOUGH TO DRIVE ACTION

Goals stated not only as outcomes but as *specific* outcomes tend to motivate or drive behavior. As mentioned earlier, the work of this step helps clients whip goals or scenarios into shape. Part of the shaping process involves helping them become more and more specific about outcomes. This moving from vagueness to specificity of outcomes can be divided into three steps. If a client states his or her goals in very vague ways, then all three steps might be called for. The steps are (1) a simple declaration of intent, (2) the indication of an aim, and (3) the translation of an aim into a specific outcome.

A declaration of intent.   Some clients, once they see a problem clearly, simultaneously see the need to do something about it. In the following example the client, Jon, has been discussing his relationship to his wife and children. The counselor has been helping him see how some of his behavior is perceived negatively by them. Jon is open to challenge and is a fast learner. He says something like this:

> Boy, this session has been an eye-opener for me. I've really been blind. My wife and kids don't see my investment—rather my overinvestment—in work as something I'm doing for them. I've been fooling myself, telling myself that I'm working hard to get them the good things in life. In fact, I'm spending most of my time at work because I like it. My work is mainly for me. It's time for me to switch some of my priorities.

This statement certainly seems to be well-intentioned. However, it is not yet a goal. It is not a picture of a pattern or behavior he would like to see in place instead of the one that currently is. It is rather *a statement of intent,* an indication on the part of the client that he wants to do something about a problem now that he sees it more clearly.

The following example deals with a 48-year-old woman, Laureen, who has discovered that she has breast cancer and will need a mastectomy. She has had a couple of sessions with a self-help group composed of women who have had to face the same problem. She says to the group:

> As I listen to all of you tell your stories, I've begun to see how passive I've become since I found out the diagnosis. I feel that I'm surrendering myself to doctors and to the whole medical establishment. No wonder I feel so depressed. I'm ordinarily an active woman—I usually take charge of my life. Well, I want to take charge of it again.

Note again, that she does not say *what* she is going to do to handle her passivity, but she is determined to do something. She does not yet outline the pattern of behavior she wants to substitute for the current pattern of passivity. This is a declaration of intent. A good start, but not specific enough to drive action.

An aim. An aim is more than a declaration of intent. It is a declaration of intent that identifies the area in which the client wants to work and that makes some general statement about the area. In the following example, we return to Jon, the client who has been talking about being overinvested in work at the expense of his family life. He says,

> I don't think that I've got so taken up with work deliberately. That is, I don't think I'm running away from family life. But family life is deteriorating because I'm just not around enough. I must spend more time with my wife and kids. No—it's not just a case of "must": I *want* to.

This is more than a declaration of intent because it includes in a general way what Jon wants to do: "spend more time with my wife and kids." It is an aim, but it is not a goal because it still does not say *precisely* what he wants to do, precisely what the new pattern of behavior will look like.

The problem with aims is that their very vagueness makes it too easy to put them off. All of us are familiar with the New Year's-resolution phenomenon. Lots of people indicate in vague ways how they are going to improve during the coming year. "I'm really going to get into shape this year." Few people carry such resolutions out. Vague aims are wishes rather than goals. However, it is useful to help clients move from mere statements of intent to aims. Aims are closer to goals. This is part of the shaping process, developing specific rather than merely general scenarios. The counselor asks Jon such questions as "What will your life with your family look like when you make the change?"

If a problem is defined fairly clearly, aims begin to emerge. For instance Laureen, the woman about to undergo a mastectomy, realizes that she has become passive in various ways. "I used to be careful about my personal appearance, but I notice that I've been letting myself go." One aim, then, might be to reinvest herself in her personal appearance. "I'm going to force myself to take care of how I look." This is not a statement of *precisely what* she wants to do nor is it a statement of *how* she wants to do it, but it is more than a general statement about regaining charge of her life in a specific area.

Goals or specific scenarios.   Goals are clear and specific statements of what a person wants to put in place in order to manage a problem situation or some part of it. For instance Jon says,

> I'm going to consistently spend three out of four weekends a month at home. During the week I'll work no more than two evenings.

Notice how much more specific this is than "I'm going to spend more time with my family." Here Jon talks about a pattern of behavior he wants to establish. He will reach his goal when he is habitually spending the time indicated with his family. Your job is to help the client engage in this shaping process. Notice, however, that this is not the same as setting goals *for* the client.

It helps if clients can *visualize* the accomplishment. "I want to get into physical shape" is not as clear as "Within six months I will be running 3 miles in under 30 minutes at least four times a week." The former is an aim; the latter, a goal. The client can actually see herself or himself engaged in a self-enhancing pattern of behavior. Notice that this goal is also stated as an accomplishment; that is, it is stated in terms of a pattern of exercise that is in place and consistently pursued.

Consider the example of a parent who has identified himself as a child abuser.

AIM: I've got to get my temper under control and not take things out on Tommy.
GOAL: Every time I feel myself getting angry, I'm going to call the "Save the Children" hotline and get some help in talking myself down. I'm going to do

this until I feel I have myself under control. I hate feeling dependent like this, but hurting Tommy is worse.

This parent is talking about a pattern of behavior he wants to put in place. He can visualize himself consistently calling the hotline whenever he experiences cues indicating that he's headed out of control.

In the next example, a marriage has degenerated into constant bickering, especially about finances.

STATEMENT OF INTENT: We want to relate to each other better.

AIM: We want to handle our decisions about finances in a much more constructive way.

GOAL: We try to solve our problems about family finances by fighting and arguing. We'd like to reduce the number of fights we have and increase the number of times we make decisions about money by talking them out. We're going to set up a month-by-month budget. We will have next month's budget ready the next time we see the counselor and will review it and our decision-making process with her.

These two people want to change their style of dealing with finances, which will result in a change in their style of dealing with each other.

3. HELP CLIENTS ESTABLISH OUTCOMES THAT CAN BE MEASURED OR VERIFIED

Clients must be able to tell whether they have achieved their goals or not. Therefore, the criteria for the accomplishment of goals must be clear to them. "I want to have a better relationship with my wife" is an aim, not a goal, because as stated it cannot be verified. Clients have to be helped to ask themselves, "How will I know that I have achieved my goals? How will I know when the new, preferred scenario is in place?"

Clients can't know whether they are making progress if they do not know where they started. If a client wants to reduce the number and severity of his bouts of free-floating anxiety, he needs to know how frequent and how severe the bouts are in the first place. Collection of what behavioral scientists call "baseline data" can be part of the process of problem clarification.

CLIENT: I had been having about four attacks of anxiety a week. Two of them were usually very intense. And usually one of them would last for hours no matter what I'd do. It was driving me crazy. Now I have an attack about once a week or even once every two weeks. It usually doesn't last very long and it's never as intense as it used to be.

In Step II-A this client outlined a future in which his anxiety attacks would be significantly reduced. Since he knew the baseline or starting point, he now realizes how far he has come.

It is not always necessary to count things in order to determine whether a goal has been reached, though sometimes counting is quite helpful. However, goals or outcomes must be able to be verified in some way. For instance, a couple might say something like, "Our relationship is better, not because we've found ways of spending more time together, but because the quality of our time together has improved. By that we mean that we listen better, we talk about more personal concerns, we are more relaxed, and we make more mutual decisions about issues that affect us both, such as finances."

4. HELP CLIENTS SEE WHETHER THEIR SCENARIOS OR GOALS ARE REALISTIC

A goal is realistic if (1) the resources necessary for its achievement are available to the client, (2) external circumstances do not prevent its accomplishment, (3) the goal is under the control of the client, and (4) the cost of accomplishing it is not too high. Let's take a brief look at each of these.

Make sure resources are available.   It does little good to help clients develop clear and verifiable goals if the resources are not available to meet them.

UNREALISTIC: John decides to go to graduate school without having either the financial or academic resources needed to do so.

REALISTIC: John decides to work and to take one graduate course at night in rehabilitation counseling to see whether he is really interested in the field and to determine whether he is capable of the work. His goal is to gather the data he needs to make a good decision.

Clients sabotage their own efforts if they choose goals beyond their reach. Sometimes it is impossible to determine beforehand whether the personal or environmental resources needed are available. If that is the case, it might be best to start first with goals for which resources are certainly available and then move on to those that are more questionable in terms of resources.

Make sure that environmental obstacles can be managed.   A goal is not really a goal if there are environmental obstacles that prevent its achievement—that is, obstacles that cannot be overcome by the use of available resources.

Jessie feels like a second-class citizen at work. He feels that his supervisor gives him most of the dirty work and that in general there is an undercurrent of prejudice against Hispanics in the plant. He wants to quit and get another job, one that would pay the same relatively good wages he is now earning. However, the country is deep into a recession and there are practically no jobs available in the area where he works. For the time being his goal is not workable. He needs another interim goal that helps him cope with his present situation.

■

Sometimes an interim goal can be to find a way around an environmental obstacle. For instance, it may be that there are openings in other departments of the factory in which he works, but not in Jessie's specialty. So Jessie goes to night school and becomes qualified in a trade similar to his own. Once qualified, he gets a job in a different department.

Make sure that the goal is within the control of the client.   Sometimes clients defeat their own purposes by setting goals that are not within their control. For instance, it is common for people to believe that their problems would be solved if only other people would not act the way they do. In most cases, however, we have no direct control over the ways others act.

■

Cybelene wanted a better relationship with her parents. She said the relationship would be better if only they would make fewer demands on her now that she is married and has her own career and home to attend to. It was within her control to let her parents know about some of her needs, but there was relatively little she could do to make them respect those needs. For instance, she wanted her parents to come to her new home for either Thanksgiving or Christmas. Her parents, however, insisted that she and her husband come to their house, since both of those celebrations were "traditional" and therefore best spent "back home." She refused to go home for both and her parents kept telling her how much they were hurt.

■

Clients, however, usually have much more freedom in changing their own behavior. Consider the following example.

■

Tony, a 16-year-old boy, felt that he was the victim of his parents' inability to relate to each other. Each tried to make him a pawn in the struggle, and at times he felt like a ping-pong ball. A counselor helped him see that he could do little to control his parents' behavior, but that he might be able to do a lot to control his reactions to his parents' attempts to use him. For instance, when his parents started to fight, he would simply leave instead of trying to "help." If either tried to enlist him as an ally, he would say that he had no way of knowing who was right. He worked at creating a good social life outside the home. This helped him weather the tension he experienced there.

■

Tony's goal is a new pattern of behavior—that is, a new way of managing his parents' attempts to use him. In Step I-C the necessity of getting clients to own their problems by defining them in terms of their own behavior is stressed. Goals, too, must be defined in terms of outcomes over which the client has control. Clients should know that statements that say either directly or indirectly "My goal is to have him or her do this or that . . ." are unrealistic. However, if a client says "My goal is to engage in a serious attempt to convince my son to stay in school," the goal centers around her behavior, the attempt to influence, not her son's decision.

Help clients set goals that don't cost too much.   Some goals can be reached, but at an exorbitant cost for an inadequate payoff. It may sound overly technical to ask whether any given goal is "cost effective," but the principle remains useful. Skilled counselors help clients budget rather than squander resources.

■

Enid discovered that she had a terminal illness. In talking with several doctors, she found out that she would be able to prolong her life a bit more through a combination of surgery, radiation treatment, and chemotherapy. However, no one suggested that these would lead to any kind of cure. She also found out what each of the forms of treatment and each combination would cost, not so much in terms of money, but in terms of added anxiety and pain. She ultimately decided against all three since none of them and no combination promised much in terms of the quality of life that would be prolonged. Instead, with the help of a doctor she developed a scenario that would ease both her anxiety and her physical pain as much as possible.

■

It goes without saying that another patient might have made a different decision. The words *cost* and *payoff* are relative. Some clients might value an extra month of life no matter what the cost.

Goals should be set neither too high nor too low. If they are set too high, counseling can do more harm than good.

Nothing breeds success like success. Conversely, nothing causes feelings of despair like perpetual failure. A primary purpose of goal setting is to increase the motivation level of the individual. But goal setting can have precisely the opposite effect if it produces a yardstick that constantly makes the individual feel inadequate [Locke & Latham, 1984, p. 39].

The counselor must help clients challenge goals that are set too high.

5. HELP CLIENTS DETERMINE WHETHER THE GOALS THEY ARE SETTING OR THE SCENARIOS THEY ARE DEVELOPING ADEQUATELY ADDRESS THE PROBLEM SITUATION THEY ARE TRYING TO MANAGE

Goals are unrealistic if they are too high, but they are inadequate if they are set too low. To be adequate, the achievement of a goal must be *relevant* to the original problem situation and contribute in some *substantial* way to managing it or some part of it. I knew a man whose "solution" to his marital problems was to go off to some islands in the Indian Ocean and become a beach bum for a few months. His solution, needless to say, was relevant only in the sense that it was a further expression of the problem situation. If a client drinks two fifths of gin a week and one can of beer, her drinking problem will not be effectively handled if she eliminates the can of beer. If the quality of time a man spends at home is no good, merely increasing that time will do little to help him develop a better relationship with his family. If the problem is not clearly defined, it may be impossible to determine whether any given goal is adequate.

Doug was extremely anxious and depressed when he learned that he would have to undergo major surgery for the removal of a brain tumor. There was no way of telling whether it was malignant or benign until after the surgery. A minister talked to him in rather general terms about "the love of God" and suggested that he pray more. Doug became more and more agitated and finally took his own life.

In crisis situations such as this, it might be terribly difficult to help a client identify a goal or scenario that might contribute in some substantial way to handling the emotions experienced. However, suggesting stylized goals or programs that have little meaning for the client might only make things worse. An effective counselor might have been able to identify Doug's desperation and help him develop images of hope and find ways of hanging on until the operation.

6. MAKE SURE THAT THE GOALS SET ARE THE CLIENT'S GOALS

It is essential that the goals chosen be the client's rather than the helper's goals or someone else's. Various kinds of probes can be used to help clients discover what *they* want to do in order to manage some dimension

of a problem situation more effectively. Carl Rogers, in a film of a counseling session (Rogers, Perls, & Ellis, 1965), is asked by a woman what
she should do about her relationship with her daughter. He says, "I think
you've been telling me all along what you want to do." She knew what
she wanted her relationship with her daughter to look like; she was asking
for his *approval*. If he had given it, the goal would, in some way, have
become his instead of hers. At another point he asks, "What is it that
you want me to tell you to do?" This puts the responsibility for goal
setting where it belongs: on the client's shoulders.

■

Cynthia was seeing a lawyer because of her impending divorce. They
had talked about what was to be done with the children, but no decision
had been reached. One day she came in and said that she had decided
on mutual custody; that is, both she and her husband would have
legal custody. She wanted to work out details such as which residence,
hers or her husband's, would be their principal one, and so forth. The
lawyer asked her how she had reached the decision. She said she had
been talking to her husband's parents—she was still on very good
terms with them—and that they had suggested this arrangement. The
lawyer challenged Cynthia to take a closer look at her decision. He
felt he did not want to help her implement a decision that was not
her own.

■

Clients tend to work harder for goals that are their own. Choosing goals
that are not theirs also enables them to blame others when they either
fail to reach the goals or find out that reaching them does little to help
them manage their problem situation.

7. MAKE SURE THAT THE GOALS CHOSEN ARE IN KEEPING WITH THE VALUES OF THE CLIENT

Although helping is, as we have seen, a process of social influence, it
remains ethical only if it respects the values of the client. While helpers
may challenge clients to reexamine their values, they should in no way
inspire them to actions not in keeping with their values. For instance,
the Garzas' son is in a coma in the hospital after an automobile accident.
He needs a life-support system to remain alive. His parents are experiencing great uncertainty, pain, and anxiety. They have been told that
there is very little chance their son will ever come out of the coma, and
that if he does it is very likely that he will be severely handicapped. A
counselor should not urge them to terminate his life-support system if
it goes counter to their values. However, a counselor might well help
them explore and clarify the values involved. For instance, the counselor

might suggest that they talk it over with a clergyman. In doing so, they find out that the termination of the life-support system in this case would not be against the tenets of their religion. Now they are free to explore other values related to their decision.

It is impossible to help clients make good choices without helping them clarify the values and principles on which they are basing those choices. The client with AIDS discussed earlier does not have the time and resources to choose and accomplish all the elements in his scenario. He needs to be helped to review his values and use them to set priorities.

8. HELP CLIENTS DETERMINE A REALISTIC TIME FRAME FOR THE ACCOMPLISHMENT OF GOALS

Goals that are to be accomplished "sometime or other" never seem to be achieved. If Jon says "I'm going to spend three out of every four weekends and three out of every five evenings at home with my family and do so consistently *when business conditions stabilize again*," he violates his goal, because the time frame is not clear. If his business is bad and needs much attention, the deteriorating relationship with his family will have to be managed in some way other than spending more time at home. For instance, another aim might be to increase the quality of the time he does spend there. This, however, is merely an aim and would have to be made much more concrete and specific in order to become a goal.

A goal, to be workable, must meet all of the above requirements. If one is missing, it may prove to be the fatal flaw in a client's movement toward problem-managing action.

Helping Clients Understand the Consequences of Their Choice of Goals

If clients are to make reasonable decisions about goals, they often need help in exploring the consequences of their choice of scenarios or goals. Consider the case of Tom, the man with AIDS described earlier. As we saw, one possible outcome toward which he might work is making peace with one or two of his closest friends who abandoned him when they found out he had AIDS. While he can work for reconciliation, reconciliation itself demands the good will of all parties involved. Since he has not been contacted by his friends, he would have to initiate contact, even though he feels that he is the offended party. His effort might, in the long run, prove futile and he would have to face the pain of rejection once more—perhaps even more intensely. Tom can ask himself how much reconciliation would contribute to the quality of his life now that he knows his life is probably quite limited. It could be that a partial reconciliation would only cause him more anxiety. Tom can ask himself these questions:

- What would life be like if this goal were to be met? What satisfactions would it bring? To what degree would it take care of the concerns I have right now? To what degree would it be an implementation of values I hold dear?
- What would life be like if this goal were not to be reached? Would it mean that my present concerns would not be substantially managed?
- Given the fact that time and resources are limited, are other goals higher in priority?

Tom puts off reconciliation attempts for the time being, because a goal that has higher priority is establishing some kind of community of human resources on which he can depend.

Janice, a woman with an unwanted pregnancy, can be helped to sort out the consequences of different options. She can have an abortion, she can have the child and keep it without getting married, she can marry the father and have and keep the child, or she can have the child and put him or her up for adoption immediately. To assess the consequences adequately, Janice needs to review her own values and become aware of the probable or usual consequences associated with each possibility. For instance, it would help her to know how many women in her situation choose to have and keep the child without getting married and how this works out. In this case, the counselor would need to be informed about the sociology of unwanted pregnancies or know how to help Janice get this information.

An Objection to Goal Setting

Clients can be helped to move from vague statements of intent to setting clear and specific goals. However, some people see the helping process at this point as becoming too "technological." Some suggest that the client's goals be allowed to "emerge" in some more natural way. There are two ways in which such emergence could be productive—that is, contribute to the management of a problem situation or some part of it. First of all, it could mean that once clients are helped, through a combination of probing, empathy, and challenge, to clarify a problem, they begin to see more clearly what they want to do to manage the problem. Second, it could mean that some clients must first act in some way before they find out just what they want to do.

Neither kind of emergence poses a problem. However, if emergence means that clients should wait around until "something comes up" or if it means that clients should try a lot of different programs in the hope that one of them will work, emergence can be a self-defeating process no matter how common or "natural" it might be. Haphazard problem solving is not to be equated with spontaneous living. You will encounter clients who have been trying these kinds of emergence and part of whose problem is that such emergence is not working for them. They are spinning their wheels. Setting specific goals may not be part of a client's ordinary style, but that doesn't make it unnatural or overly technological. In my experience, helping clients set clear and realistic goals has been one of the most useful parts of the helping process. The problem with leaving goal setting to chance is that people may skip goal setting entirely and keep trying one program after another. Failure to set goals can lead to a kind of "tyranny of programs." The client who says "I've tried everything and nothing works" may well be a victim of such tyranny.

In a more direct way, they can be trained to shape their own goals. That is, training clients to set goals that have the characteristics outlined above can be part of a training-as-treatment approach to helping. A client who has goal-setting skills has more freedom; he or she can decide whether to set specific goals or to let them emerge, in the positive sense of the term. The "technology" presented here—both helping clients to set goals and training them in goal-setting skills—can be as human as the person using it.

■ Step II-C: Helping Clients Choose Goals and Commit Themselves to Them

Once clients have put together and critiqued possible courses of action, they need to choose from among them. The choice-and-commitment step of Stage II is added to the helping model in Figure 9–3. This step addresses the distinction between creativity and innovation. Many creative ideas are never translated into action. In counseling and psychotherapy, many insights and creative scenarios go untranslated into action

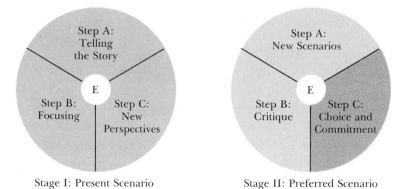

Stage I: Present Scenario   Stage II: Preferred Scenario

Figure 9–3. Step II-C: Choice and commitment

because little attention is paid to commitment and to developing strategies and plans to turn creativity into innovation.

There are a number of ways to help clients choose and commit themselves to new scenarios and goals. Here are a few of them.

CLEAR AND DETAILED SCENARIOS

As suggested earlier, detailed scenarios are more likely to drive behavior than vague ones. The details give the client a feeling for the usefulness of the change.

■

Robert, a computer specialist who had been operated on for testicular cancer, was still suffering from postoperative anxiety and depression a year after the operation. One testicle had been removed, but there was no physical reason that should have interfered with a normal sexual life. His physical recovery had been excellent, and bouts of impotence were seen as psychological in origin. The counselor had Robert imagine a future in which the problems he was experiencing had disappeared. Robert, drawing on his past experience, described in great detail what it was like feeling at peace rather than anxious, and feeling enthusiastic rather than depressed. He pictured himself having normal sexual relations that were as satisfying as any he had had in the past. He pictured himself feeling good about himself and carrying on a positive internal dialogue with himself instead of putting himself down. He developed those detailed images of a better future not only during the counseling sessions but also outside. The positive images gradually drove out the cognitive garbage with which he had become burdened.

■

In this case, images of a better future constituted the centerpiece of the helping process.

OPTIONS

Clients are more likely to commit themselves to goals if they can choose from among options. Therefore, the work done in Step II-A is very important. Counseling at its best results in both freeing and empowering clients.

■

Sandra, a heavy drinker, reviewed the options open to her and chose the option of cutting down on drink rather than eliminating it from her life. While her problems with drink decreased somewhat, she was still a problem drinker. She finally chose to eliminate drink altogether. She said that she felt freer to do so because no one had forced her into such a "radical" decision from the beginning.

Of course Step II-B, evaluating proposed scenarios and goals, is essential, since the options must ultimately be realistic. The counselor might know that alcoholics choosing to restrict rather than eliminate alcoholic intake are courting trouble, but that, as in the case above, it might well be better for a client to make a choice—even thought it is not the "best" one— than to have a choice forced on him or her. Perhaps if Sandra had considered the option of eliminating alcohol entirely for a limited period of time, say two months, she could have experienced the benefits of an alcohol-free life without feeling so constrained.

HURTING

Clients are more likely to commit themselves to goals if they are hurting and see hope in new scenarios. Goals are instruments to help them reduce their emotional pain. People who are hurting, however, are more open to social influence. Therefore, helpers must be careful not to influence clients to adopt their (helpers') goals rather than their own.

Ernesto, the gang member who had been severely beaten three times within a year, was hurting. Since he was wounded both physically and psychologically, he longed for a better future. At first his images of the future included acts of revenge. When challenged to see that it was precisely that kind of behavior that had put him in the hospital, Ernesto began slowly to envision details of a life outside the gang. He needed a great deal of support and challenge to create those images, since practically all of his social rewards had come from membership in a gang.

On the other hand, if a client is hesitant to create new scenarios and set goals, it may be that his or her current lifestyle is not that uncomfortable. Some counselors see challenge (Step I-C) as a way of making clients feel uncomfortable enough to want to change. For instance, a depressed person in a dead-end job who is reluctant to think of other possibilities can be challenged to spell out in detail the consequences of remaining in the job. It could be that the dismal images that surface might make the client hurt enough to want to envision a better future.

SUBSTANTIAL GOALS

In Step II-B you were cautioned to make sure that clients' goals were set neither too high (unrealistic) nor too low (inadequate). A fair amount of research (Locke, Shaw, Saari, & Latham, 1981; Locke & Latham, 1984) suggests that, other things being equal, *harder* goals might be more motivating than easier goals.

> Extensive research . . . has established that, within reasonable limits, the . . . more challenging the goal, the better the resulting performance. . . . [P]eople try harder to attain the hard goal. They exert more effort. . . . In short, people become motivated in proportion to the level of challenge with which they are faced [Locke & Latham, 1984, p. 21].

> Even goals that cannot be fully reached will lead to high effort levels, provided that partial success can be achieved and is rewarded [p. 26].

I once met an AIDS victim who was, in the beginning, full of self-loathing and despair, but who eventually painted a new scenario in which he saw himself not as victim but as helper to other AIDS victims. Till close to the time of his death he worked hard, within the limits of his physical disabilities, seeking out other AIDS victims, getting them to join self-help groups, and generally helping them manage an impossible situation in a humane way. The last two years of his life, though at times very bitter, were among his best. He set his goals high, but they proved to be quite realistic.

MANAGING CURRENT DISINCENTIVES

Clients are more likely to commit themselves to goals if they can be helped to rid themselves of the incentives that are currently holding self-defeating patterns of behavior in place.

■

Joyce, a flight attendant nearing middle age, centered most of her non-flying life around her aging mother who, on Joyce's admission, had been pampered and given her way by her now-deceased husband and her three children all her life. This mother now played the role of the tyrannical old woman who constantly feels neglected and who can never be satisfied—and she played it well. Though Joyce was able to elaborate a number of scenarios in which she lived her own life without abandoning her mother, she found it very difficult to commit herself to any of them. Guilt stood in the way of any change in her relationship to her mother. She even said that being a virtual slave to many of her mother's whims was not as bad as the guilt she experienced when she stood up to her mother or "neglected" her.

The counselor helped Joyce experiment with a few new ways of dealing with her mother. For instance, she went on a two-week trip with a few friends even though her mother objected, saying that it was ill-timed. Although the experiments were successful in that no harm was done to Joyce's mother and Joyce did not experience excessive guilt, counseling did not help her restructure her relationship to her mother in any radical way. The experiments did give her a sense of greater freedom, though. For instance, she felt freer to say no to this or that demand of her mother's. This provided enough slack, it seems, to make life more livable.

In this case, counseling helped the client fashion a life that was "a little bit better," though not as good as the counselor thought it could be. This brings up the issue of what the decision-making literature (Janis, 1983b; Janis & Mann, 1977; Wheeler & Janis, 1980) calls "satisficing."

> [S]ometimes it is more reasonable to choose a satisfactory alternative than to continue searching for the absolute best. The time, energy, and expense of finding the best possible choice may outweigh the improvement in the choice [Wheeler & Janis, 1980, p. 98].

The problem with satisficing, of course, is that the client finds out later on that his or her choice is doing little to make life more acceptable. Joyce's counselor thought that little purpose would be served by continuing to challenge her choice. Her "new" scenario did not differ dramatically from the old, but perhaps it was enough for her. Only time would tell.

HOW DO YOU FEEL ABOUT YOUR CHOICE?

One of the best questions you can ask clients who are tentatively committing themselves to a new scenario is, "How do you feel about your choice?" If, after a reasonable amount of challenge and deliberation, the choice feels right for the client, it is usually a good sign that it's time to make a commitment.

Ernesto, the battered gang member, developed a number of images of a better future. One set turned around his returning to school and developing new relationships. Another set turned around his girlfriend. His relationship with her had always been separate from gang life. Since she didn't want anything to do with gangs, she had a circle of non-gang friends. Ernesto was macho enough to resent a woman's help, however indirect it might be, but was hurting enough to try something new. He even referred to spending time with her friends as "hiding out." When asked how he felt about his choices, he said,

"Why not? Let's face it. When it comes to gang life, I'm a loser. I'd rather be some kind of winner doing something else."

■

Ernesto's statement does not sound like a wholehearted commitment to a new life, but it is a commitment.

INCREASING THE ATTRACTIVENESS OF THE NEW SCENARIO

Clients are more likely to commit themselves to new scenarios if they are helped to see them as attractive. Clients need *incentives* for choice and commitment. They can be helped to compare the new with the old and get a feeling for the advantages of the new, see the possibilities for the general payoff of the new—the "spread effect," and search for incentives for working toward the new.

■

A marriage counselor helped Sheila and Kevin develop a range of elements that could constitute a scenario for a different kind of relationship. Among their top priorities was developing a method for dealing with perceived grievances or "pinches" both quickly—that is, without brooding about them or saving them up—and constructively—that is, without using them to fuel games of "uproar." The counselor, after helping them spell out in detail what such a method would look like, asked them to elaborate, in gory detail, the differences between the new scenario and their present self-defeating method. The contrast was so stark that it heightened their commitment to dealing with small grievances as quickly and sanely as possible.

■

The incentives searched out must, of course, be incentives that motivate this particular client. There are too many individual differences among clients to hope that what is an incentive for one will automatically be an incentive for the next.

HELPING CLIENTS DEVELOP THE RESOURCES CALLED FOR BY THE NEW SCENARIO

It does little good for clients to commit themselves to goals without having the resources needed to achieve them. The principal resources needed are *working knowledge*—that is, information or knowledge that enables clients to *do* something—and *skills*. For instance, a married couple cannot be expected to implement a method for dealing constructively with "pinches" if they do not know what the method is and lack the communication skills called for by the method. Some marriage counselors, working on the assumption that almost every couple that comes for help is having trouble communicating, make training in basic communication skills such as listening, responding with empathy, and using probes at the service of empathy an automatic part of the helping process. One marriage counselor I know works with four couples at a time. He separates men from women for the initial training in communication skills. For further practice he puts man and woman together, but not spouses. Finally, spouses are paired and challenged to use their newly acquired skills to work out their problems. These women and men, once empowered to communicate more effectively, are more likely to commit themselves to new scenarios that call for more constructive forms of communication.

USING CONTRACTS IN HELPING CLIENTS COMMIT THEMSELVES TO THEIR CHOICES

The use of contracts for the helping process itself was discussed in Chapter One. Contracts can also help clients commit themselves to new courses of action (Katz & Torres, 1982). While contracts are promises clients make to themselves to behave in certain ways and to attain certain goals, they are also ways of making new scenarios more focused, more salient. It is not only the expressed or implied promise, but the *explicitness* of the commitment that helps.

■

About a month after one of Dora's two young sons disappeared, she began to grow listless and depressed. She was separated from her husband at the time the boy disappeared. By the time she saw a counselor a few months later, a pattern of depressed behavior was quite pronounced. While her conversations with the counselor helped to ease her feelings of guilt—she stopped engaging in self-blaming rituals—she remained quite listless. She shunned both relatives and friends, kept to herself at work, and even distanced herself emotionally from her other son. She resisted developing images of a better future because the only better future she would allow herself to imagine was one in which her son had returned. Strong confrontation from both the counselor and her sister-in-law, who still visited her from time to time, helped jar her loose from her preoccupation with her own misery. "You're trying to solve one hurt, the loss of Bobby, by hurting Timmy and yourself. I can't imagine in a thousand years that that's what Bobby would want!" her sister-in-law screamed at her one night. Afterwards she and the counselor discussed a "recommitment" to Timmy, to herself, and to their home. Through a series of contracts she began to reintroduce patterns of behavior that had been characteristic of her before the tragedy. For instance, she contracted to opening her life up to relatives and friends once more, to creating a much more positive atmosphere at home, to encouraging Timmy to have his friends over, and so forth. The counselor worked with her in making the patterns of behavior clear, detailed, and realistic.

■

In counseling, contracts are not legal documents but human instruments to be used if they are helpful. They often provide both the structure and the incentives clients need in order to act.

HELPING CLIENTS FIND SUPPORTIVE RELATIONSHIPS

Self-responsibility in no way excludes the use of human resources in managing one's problems in living. In fact, central to self-responsibility is the development of the kind of social system that enables a person to meet social needs. Many clients come to counselors "out of community," with troubled, marginal, or even nonexistent relationships with others. If early on in the counseling process I feel that I am the sole or principal human resource for a client, I view it as part of the problem situation, whether the client describes it as such or not. Then part of the new scenario must be the development of human resources. If the person is "out of community," getting "into community" in a realistic sense of that phrase is an aim.

Some scenarios or goals are unrealistic because their execution assumes, often indirectly, human resources that are not available to clients. To achieve certain goals, clients will need support from people other than the counselor—that is, support in "real" time rather than counseling time.

■

Nick was confronted with his addiction to gambling the hard way. Like other heavy gamblers, he gambled away his liquid assets, gambled away lent money, gambled away money borrowed on nonliquid assets such as his house, and finally gambled away funds he did not have so that he ended up in debt to bookies who began to pressure him for their money. He borrowed money from relatives and friends, used some of it to stave off the bookies and some of it to try to recoup his losses through further bets. The whole situation collapsed when a friend from whom he had borrowed money threatened to tell Nick's wife, his employer, his banks, and his other creditors the whole story unless he immediately sought help.

Under pressure, Nick sought help from Gamblers Anonymous. Part of the program was to put in place a network of people from whom Nick could receive both help and support. For instance, he was put in touch with a couple of people who had gotten in debt as deeply as he had, and they shared with him the ways they had been managing their financial lives. Nick also attended weekly group meetings where he heard horror stories like his own. Meeting people like himself, some of whom were still hurting badly, helped him to begin to de-mythologize for himself the very unreal world of gambling. It struck him that gambling had become his life. For instance, at social gatherings he wasn't really with people; his preoccupation with baseball or basketball scores kept him distracted or on the phone. He made friends and spent time with two GA members who lived near him. They both provided camaraderie and helped him to set financial goals and begin working his way out of his financial mess. In short, GA helped him find a support group, role models, and mentors.

One of Nick's goals was to straighten things out with his family. His wife suspected he was gambling, but had no idea of its extent. What he learned from other GA members helped him a great deal. He met with his wife and teenage children, told them the entire story, and asked for both their forgiveness and their help. There was some resentment and anger to work through, but basically his wife and children became allies instead of adversaries.

■

Each client will have his or her own human resource deficits and needs. They should be diagnosed early on in the helping process, and the development of human resources "out there" should be an aim in almost every counseling case.

HELPING CLIENTS FIND CHALLENGING RELATIONSHIPS

This issue could have been included in the discussion of the development of supportive human relationships, but I believe it is so important as to merit separate consideration. The people in the clients' lives provide, ideally, a judicious mixture of both support and challenge. Or, put in a way that respects clients' self-responsibility, friends can help clients make reasonable demands on themselves. Friendship, like helping, is in part an exercise in social influence. This undermines neither my "unconditional positive regard" for my friend nor my commitment to his or her self-responsibility. Clients, like the rest of us, are afflicted with yes-men and yes-women friends.

■

Neil was extremely afraid of doctors, hospitals, physical tests, inoculations—whatever had anything to do with the medical profession. One evening after some strenuous jogging, he discovered blood in his urine. He wanted to forget about it, believing that it had something to do with the jogging, but he knew that blood in the urine can be symptomatic of many different conditions, some quite serious. His fear of serious illness finally overcame his fear of doctors and he called a doctor he had seen a few times previously. The doctor knew it would be better to talk to Neil face-to-face, so he persuaded him to come into his office the next morning "to talk about it."

The next day he was sensitive to Neil's fears. He said he agreed that what had happened could well be related to the strenuousness of his jogging. But he asked Neil what would set his mind at rest. The outcome Neil wanted, of course, was to know there was nothing seriously wrong. The doctor supported Neil's search for peace of mind, and gently suggested that, despite his fears, he would probably want to do whatever could reasonably give him that peace of mind. He described the kinds of tests called for in such situations. Then he let Neil use him to challenge himself to overcome his fears. "What can I tell you that will help you make a decision, Neil?" Later that morning, Neil checked into the hospital for a kidney test and a cystoscopic examination.

■

As in this example, constructive social pressure in helping situations does not mean a helper's trying to persuade a client to do something not in his or her own interest. Neil uses a friendly, sensitive, and honest doctor to help himself choose and pursue a constructive goal, even though he is fearful of the cost and consequences.

FINDING THE MEANS TO REACH THE NEW SCENARIO

Finally, clients are more likely to commit themselves to goals if they are helped to develop the means needed to achieve those goals. This will be the focus of Step III-A.

In practice, the three steps of Stage II will overlap, just as Stage II itself will overlap with the other two stages. This is illustrated in Figure 9–4. Clients will commit themselves to new scenarios, rework them, act

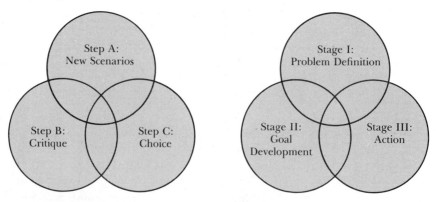

Figure 9–4. Overlap in the steps and stages of the helping process

on them, rework them again, go back and redefine the problem situation, and engage in other permutations of the helping process. In principle there is nothing wrong with this. However, counselors can help clients avoid merely random approaches to working out their problems in living. In other words, some nonlinear approaches to problem management will fit the client and the situation, while others are at best inefficient and at worst strategies for avoidance. One very effective nonlinear approach is outlined in the next section.

■ A Future-Centered Approach to Helping

What has been said about preferred scenarios and goals in this chapter suggests an alternate approach to the steps of the helping model. The focus of this approach is on the future, rather than on a past that cannot be changed or a present that is too problematic. What follows is the approach I currently take in helping people. Obviously I remain flexible and let the needs of clients guide me at any given moment.

1. *The story.* Help clients tell their stories. It is not necessary for the client to reveal all the details of the problem situation at once in the beginning of the helping encounter.

■

Jay, a single man, aged 25, tells a story of drinking and an auto accident in which he was responsible for the death of a friend and his own severe back injuries. He has told the story over and over again to many different people, as if telling it often enough will make what happened disappear.

■

Helping clients retell stories they know only too well is often not useful. At this time a summary of the main points of the story or problem situation may be enough.

2. *Preferred scenario.* Help clients make an initial attempt at formulating the elements of a preferred scenario. This can help them to develop a sense of hope. They identify a better future early in the helping process and that future pervades the rest of the helping process.

■

Jay is helped to spell out a scenario in which he is more responsible for his actions, in which he is not hounded by remorse and guilt, in which he has made peace with his friend's family, in which he is physically rehabilitated within the limits dictated by his injuries, and in which he is coping with whatever cannot be changed about his injuries.

∎

At this point the preferred scenario need not be as detailed as it will be eventually in order to serve the cause of action. The purpose of this quick move to the preferred scenario is to help clients focus on a better future rather than a problematic and unchangeable past.

3. *Return to Stage I.* In light of a preferred scenario, help clients to
- Identify *gaps* between the present scenario and what they want
- Identify points of *leverage*
- Identify and manage *blind spots* and develop new perspectives.

A kind of dialogue takes place between Stage II and Stage I, with the vision of Stage II helping clients complete the work of Stage I.

∎

Jay is helped to explore some of the gaps between the current and the preferred scenario and develop new perspectives. For instance, he comes to see his overpowering remorse and guilt as partially self-inflicted (through his own internal self-dialogue) and as actually standing in the way of managing his life more effectively. When he engages in self-recrimination, he is not in the right frame of mind either to make peace with his friend's family or to get seriously involved in a physical rehabilitation program. Managing the current flood of self-defeating emotions is a point of leverage. One of his blind spots is that he does not see that continual self-chastisement is actually standing in the way of what he wants. He has unwittingly decided that self-chastisement is good and that more is even better.

∎

The current scenario is now seen in the light of the preferred scenario and the clarification of the problem situation is much more upbeat. Points of leverage and blind spots are easier to identify because the client has a better idea where he or she wants to go.

4. *Return to Stage II.* Help clients use what they have learned in their return to Stage I to complete the identification, critiquing, and choice of a new scenario and goals.

∎

Jay sees that he needs to channel the energy that is going into self-recrimination into more useful directions. The part of the preferred scenario that reads "not being hounded by remorse and guilt" needs to be refocused. He now realizes that it should include such things as "refusing to let remorse and guilt dominate and immobilize me," "using remorse and guilt arising from mistakes as stimuli to learn new, more responsible patterns of behavior," and "using this total experience as a way of exploring how I let myself be ruled by my emotions." He uses other Stage I learnings to refashion other parts of his preferred scenario.

■

The exploration of the problem situation is no longer an end in itself. It actually becomes a tool to be used to fashion the preferred scenario.

5. *Transition state.* Help clients formulate strategies and plans to achieve goals and get the new scenario working, and help them to implement their plans.

■

Jay is helped to develop and implement strategies for controlling the flood of emotions that are now victimizing him. He uses his guilt as a stimulus to develop a way of meeting and making peace with his friend's family. He explores with the counselor the ways he has allowed emotions to dominate his behavior, he develops new perspectives, and he begins to find strategies to help him make his emotions allies instead of enemies.

■

This sketchy example illustrates a different, more upbeat sort of movement through the helping process, which might be called a Stage-II-centered approach to helping. It demonstrates that the helping process, at its best, is not a slavish working through the three stages in a linear way. The best helpers let the needs of clients—both what they think they need and what they unknowingly need—guide them through the helping process. The box at the end of this chapter summarizes the main points of this chapter in terms of topics you can use to evaluate your goal—setting goals with clients.

■ Are Scenario Building and Goal Setting Enough?

Some clients need only a clear sense of direction in order to manage their problems more effectively. Others need only the kind of stimulation of imagination that scenario building provides. Therefore, it is possible that the only help you may give a client is help in brainstorming preferred scenarios and setting goals. They already have a clear enough idea of what the problem is and, once they are helped to orient themselves to the future, they can make it on their own. The future orientation provided by Stage II can do much to mobilize clients' resources.

■

One young client, dissatisfied with his life in a poor area of a large city, despaired of ever being able to get out. Getting out didn't seem to be a realistic goal. The counselor said, "Even though you stay physically, are there ways in which you can still 'get out'?" They went on to explore the new ways in which he could live in the old neighborhood.

■

Not everyone can resolve every problem situation. Sometimes *coping* with problem situations is a more realistic goal. Taylor (1983) even suggests a creative use of illusion in coping with personal tragedy. Illusion is not the same as delusion.

> By illusions, I do not mean that the beliefs are necessarily opposite to known facts. Rather, their maintenance requires looking at the known facts in a particular light, because a different slant would yield a less positive picture [p. 1161].

For instance, patients recovering from cancer are often helped by the belief that a positive attitude will keep the cancer from coming back. According to Taylor, clients facing difficult situations can be helped to search for meaning in their lives, gain some sense of mastery over the conditions in their lives, and restore or maintain their self-esteem. Normal people use illusion, myth, metaphor, and belief to cope with some of the harsher realities of life. North American pragmatism gives rise to the delusion that we can solve any problem. Coping creatively with difficult situations is not a second-class solution. To think so is to doom oneself to constant failure as a helper.

Effective helpers, taking cues from what clients say and do, constantly try to identify points of leverage in the helping process. Sometimes merely being with clients is the major point of leverage, but usually that is not enough. The helping model provides nine categories of ways of being with clients. If you are actively with your clients, they will reveal the ways in which you can be with them most constructively.

■ Evaluation Checklist for Stage II

How well am I doing the following as I try to help this client?

STEP II-A: HELPING CLIENTS CREATE NEW SCENARIOS

- Helping the client look beyond his or her problems and failures to a more constructive future
- Helping the client construct alternate scenarios or brainstorm elements that can be grouped into preferred scenarios
- Encouraging clients to be specific about brainstorming scenario elements.

STEP II-B: HELPING CLIENTS CRITIQUE SCENARIOS AND SET SPECIFIC GOALS

This means helping clients set goals that meet the following criteria:

- Stated in terms of outcomes rather than behaviors leading to outcomes
- Specific enough to drive action
- Capable of being measured or verified
- Realistic in terms of client and environmental resources
- Contributing substantially to managing the problem situation
- Chosen by the client rather than by the helper or someone else
- In keeping with the values of the client
- Stated in a realistic time frame.

STEP III-C: HELPING CLIENTS CHOOSE AND COMMIT THEMSELVES TO SPECIFIC GOALS

- Making sure, whenever possible, that the client chooses a preferred scenario from among options
- Making sure that the chosen option is spelled out in sufficient detail
- Helping clients discover incentives for commitment in order to make the new scenario more attractive
- Challenging the client to stretch
- Helping clients identify the resources needed to make the preferred scenario work, including supportive and challenging relationships
- Using contracts as means to enhance commitment.

A PREFERRED-SCENARIO APPROACH TO HELPING

One alternative to a linear approach to helping is a preferred-scenario approach to helping, which follows a sequence something like this:

1. Helping clients tell their stories but not pushing for great detail
2. Helping clients develop a preferred scenario
3. Returning to Stage I in order to identify gaps between the current and preferred scenarios, find points of leverage, and challenge blind spots
4. Finishing the development, critique, and choice of a preferred scenario in light of the newly clarified problem situation
5. Helping clients develop and put into action strategies and plans.

Part Five

Stage III:
Helping Clients Act

■ The Tasks of Stage III

In the next three chapters the steps and tasks of Stage III, moving toward action, are outlined and illustrated. They include the following:

Step III-A: Identifying and assessing action strategies.   Once goals are clear, it is necessary to identify the different routes by which each of them might be reached. One task is to help clients identify a range of strategies or means for making preferred scenarios a reality. A second task is helping clients evaluate the strategies generated and choose those with the greatest potential for success.

Step III-B: Helping clients formulate plans.   Once strategies are chosen, they need to be assembled into a plan. A plan or action program is a step-by-step process leading to goal achievement.

Step III-C: Action—Helping clients implement plans.   Once action plans are formulated, they need to be implemented. There are a number of things counselors can do to help clients implement action programs. For instance it often happens that obstacles arise, and that the client needs guidance, support, and encouragement to stick to the program. These obstacles are discussed and illustrated in Chapter Twelve.

Ten

Stage III: Step III-A
Helping Clients Develop
Strategies for Action

■

Introduction
The development of strategies
     Requirements for creativity
     Helping clients engage in divergent thinking
     Brainstorming as a strategy-development skill
     Using prompts to help clients develop strategies
Training as treatment
Is Step III-A enough?
Evaluation questions for Step III-A

■ Introduction

Some clients, once they have a clear idea of *what* they want to do to manage some problem situation, mobilize their own and whatever environmental resources are necessary to achieve their goals. Other clients, who have a fairly good grasp of the problem situation and know where they want to go, still do not have a clear idea of *how* to get there. They don't know what to do to reach their goals—they still need your help. Consider the following example.

■

Jeff had been in the Army for about ten months. He found himself both overworked and, perhaps not paradoxically, bored. He had a couple of sessions with one of the educational counselors on the base. During the sessions he began to realize that not having a high school diploma was working against him. The counselor mentioned that he could finish high school while in the Army. He then realized that he had heard that during orientation, but hadn't paid any attention. He had joined the Army because he wasn't interested in school and couldn't find a job. He decided to get a high school diploma as soon as possible. He got the authorization needed from his company commander to go to school, found out what courses he needed, and enrolled in time for the next school session. It didn't take him long to finish. Once he received his high school degree he felt better about himself and found that opportunities for more interesting jobs opened up for him in the Army. Achieving his goal of getting a high school degree helped him manage the problem situation.

■

Jeff was one of the fortunate who, with a little help, quickly find out what they need to do to manage a problem situation and then go out and do it.

Jeff's experience is quite different from that of the client in the following example. She needs much more help than he did.

■

As long as she could remember, Grace had been a fearful person. She was especially afraid of being rejected and of being a failure. As a result, she had a rather impoverished social life and had had a series of jobs that were safe but boring. She became so depressed that she made a half-hearted attempt at suicide—probably more a cry of anguish and a cry for help than a serious attempt to get rid of her problems by getting rid of herself.

During her stay in the hospital she had a few therapy sessions with one of the psychiatric staff. The staff member was supportive and helped her handle both the guilt she felt because of the suicide attempt and the depression that had led to the attempt. Just talking to someone about things she usually kept to herself seemed to help. She began to see that her depression was a case of "learned helplessness," and that she had let her choices be dictated by her fears. She also began to realize that she had a number of unused or underused resources. For instance, she was intelligent and, though not good-looking, still attractive in other ways. She had a fairly good sense of humor, though she seldom gave herself the opportunity to use it. She was also sensitive to others and a basically caring person.

After she was discharged from the hospital she returned for a few outpatient sessions. She got to the point of wanting to do something about her general fearfulness and her passivity, especially passivity in her social life. The counselor taught her relaxation and thought-control techniques that helped reduce her anxiety. Once she felt less anxious, she was in a better position to do something about establishing relationships. With the help of the counselor she set a goal of making a few friends and becoming a member of some social group. However, she was at a loss as to how to go about it, since she thought that friendships and a fuller social life were come by "naturally." She soon came to realize that many people had to work at acquiring a more satisfying social life—that for some people there was nothing automatic about it at all.

The counselor helped her identify different kinds of social groups she might join, and helped her to see which of them would best meet her needs without placing too much pressure on her. She finally chose to join an arts-and-crafts group at a local YWCA, which gave her an opportunity to develop some of her talents and to meet people without having to face demands for intimate social contact. It also gave her the chance to look at other more socially oriented programs sponsored by the Y. She began using the relaxation techniques regularly and finally joined the Y program. In the arts group she met a couple of people she liked and who seemed to like her. She began having coffee with them once in a while and then an occasional dinner.

She still needed support and encouragement from the counselor but was gradually becoming less anxious and feeling less isolated. Once in a while Grace would let her anxiety get the better of her. She would skip a Y meeting and then lie to the counselor about having attended. However, as she began to let herself trust the counselor more, she revealed this self-defeating game. The counselor helped her develop coping strategies for those times when anxiety seemed to be highest.

■

Grace's problems were more severe than Jeff's, and she did not have as many immediate resources. Therefore, she needed more time and more attention to develop goals and the programs to achieve those goals.

Helping clients develop strategies to achieve goals can be a most thoughtful, humane, and fruitful way of being with them. This step in the counseling process is another used all too infrequently by helpers. Since it involves helping clients search out viable strategies and tactics for moving from Point A to Point B, it appears to some to be overly "technological." This attitude is especially common among counselors who take a discursive approach to helping that focuses mainly on problems, not solutions. But many clients fail to act in their own behalf simply because they don't know how to do so; I know of many clients who became stuck at the strategy-development stage:

- A client who wanted a new job
- A client who wanted to get away from "bad company" but felt incapable of doing so
- A client who wanted to reduce debilitating anxiety but had simply put up with it for years
- A Black male who wanted to cope better with a prejudiced society
- A victim of a brutal crime who wanted to regain her dignity and equanimity
- A nursing home resident who wanted to stop putting herself down
- A middle-aged man with a back problem who wanted to cope with chronic pain
- A businessman who wanted to get rid of his fear of flying
- An ex-priest who wanted to reorient himself to lay society
- A teenager who wanted to drive away thoughts of suicide
- A wife and mother who wanted to know how to control her sexual promiscuity
- An older man who finally saw that his suspicions were alienating him more and more from others
- A couple who wanted to stop abusing their children.

All these clients had in common some idea of *what* they wanted without knowing *how* to get it. Not to help such people in their search is inhumane. But for many counselors, the preferred way of helping people discover what they can do about problems is to invite them to dig further into the *roots* of their problems. Delving more deeply into the causes of problems can be both extremely seductive and extremely frustrating.

The couple who are abusing their child, however, need immediate help in stopping. Delving into the causes of their unacceptable behavior can complement but not replace practical strategies for controlling themselves. The literature is focusing more and more on methods to help clients develop and use their imaginal resources to identify strategies and tactics that will get them where they want to go (Janis, 1983b).

■ The Development of Strategies

Strategy is the art of identifying and choosing realistic programs for achieving goals or objectives and doing so under adverse (for example, war-time) conditions. The problem situations in which clients are immersed certainly constitute adverse conditions: they often are at war with themselves and the world around them.

Sometimes goals are not achieved because clients rush off and try the first strategy that comes to mind.

■

Tony injured his back and underwent a couple of operations. After the second operation he felt a little better, but then his back began troubling him again. The doctor told him that further operations would not help, so Tony was faced with the problem of handling chronic pain. It soon became clear that his psychological state affected the level of pain he experienced: when he was anxious or depressed the pain always seemed much worse. He was talking to a counselor about all of this when he read about a pain clinic located in a western state. Without consulting anyone he signed up for a six-week program; within ten days he was back, more depressed than ever. He went to the program with extremely high expectations because his needs were so great. The program, a holistic one that helped participants develop a more realistic lifestyle, included seminars on nutrition and the quality of interpersonal life. Group counseling was part of the program, and the groups used a training-as-treatment approach. For instance, participants were trained in behavioral approaches to the management of pain. Tony, however, arrived at the clinic with unrealistic expectations: he expected to find "miracles of modern medicine" that would somehow magically help him. He was extremely disappointed when they talked about reducing and managing rather than eliminating pain. He was not prepared for the kind of program he found.

■

Tony's aim was the elimination of pain, and he refused to acknowledge that it might not be possible. A more realistic aim would have been the reduction and management of pain. He did not spend enough time setting up a realistic goal, and spent no time taking a census of the possibilities available to him.

Taking a census of possible strategies or programs, Step III-A of the helping process illustrated in Figure 10–1, is not an end in itself. The research on problem solving (D'Zurilla and Goldfried, 1971; Heppner, 1978) suggests that the quality and efficacy of a program tends to be higher if it is chosen from among a number of possibilities. For example, Karen, who has come to realize that heavy drinking is ruining her life, sets a goal of stopping drinking. She feels it would not be enough to simply cut down—she has to stop. To her the program seems simple enough: before she drank; now she won't. Because of the novelty of the idea of not drinking, she is successful for a couple of days and then falls off the wagon. This happens a number of times until she finally realizes that she needs some help. Stopping drinking, at least for her, is not as simple as it seemed.

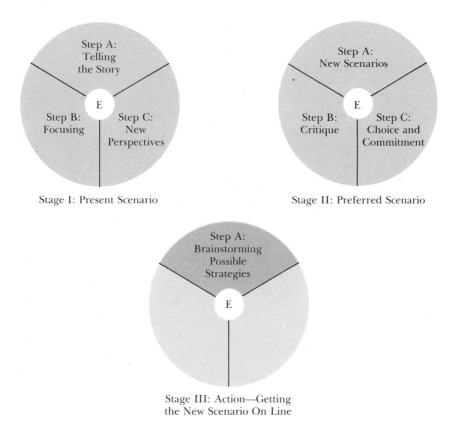

Figure 10–1. Step III-A: Brainstorming possible strategies

A counselor at a city alcohol and drug treatment center helps her explore various techniques that can be used in an alcohol management program. Together they come up with the following possibilities:

- Join Alcoholics Anonymous
- Move someplace declared "dry" by local government
- Take Antabuse, a drug that causes intense nausea when combined with alcohol
- Replace drinking with other rewarding behaviors
- Join a self-help group other than Alcoholics Anonymous
- Get rid of all liquor in the house
- Take the "pledge" not to drink; to make it more binding, take it in front of a minister
- Join a residential hospital detoxification program
- Do not spend time with friends who drink heavily
- Change other social patterns; for instance, find places to socialize other than bars and cocktail lounges
- Try hypnosis to reduce the craving for alcohol
- Use behavior-modification techniques to develop an aversion for alcohol; for instance, pair painful but safe electric shocks with drinking or even thoughts of drinking
- Eliminate self-defeating patterns of self-talk such as "I have to have a drink" or "One drink won't hurt me"
- Become a volunteer to help others stop drinking
- Read books and view films on the dangers of alcohol
- Stay in counseling as a way of getting support and challenge for stopping
- Share the intention to stop drinking with family and a few close friends
- Stop without help from anyone else
- Spend a week with someone who works with alcoholics in the city, going on his rounds with him
- Walk meditatively around Skid Row
- Discuss with family members the impact of the drinking problem on them
- Discover things to eat that might reduce the craving for alcohol
- Develop an interesting hobby or avocation that will call upon personal resources and take up a great deal of attention
- In general, make sure that stopping drinking does not leave a vacuum; take another census on ways to fill the potential void.

While this is not an exhaustive list, it contains many more ideas than Karen would have thought of had she not been stimulated by the counselor to take a census of program possibilities. One of the reasons that clients are clients is that they have never been very creative in looking for solutions to their problems—or at least whatever creativity they do have has not been used. Once goals are established, reaching them is not just a matter of hard work. It also depends on how effective you are in helping clients stimulate their own creativity.

The same techniques are useful to generate strategies for other problems. All of us have looked for a job at one time or another, or have helped others do so. Feingold (1984) has compiled a list of job-hunting strategies. I am sure there are entries on the list that would have helped us in our search.

> All things being equal, the more job-seeking techniques used, the better your chances of locating a truly appropriate position. The following ways can be used. They are not listed in any order of priority.
>
> 1. Newspaper: Place or answer an ad in a periodical.
> 2. Magazine: Place or answer an ad in a periodical.
> 3. Read the *Professional Trade Association Job Finder* (Garrett Park Press, Garrett Park, Maryland 20896).
> 4. Job banks: Use services that list candidates for jobs.
> 5. Job registries: This is another form of job bank.
> 6. Clearinghouse of jobs: Use employment services that list candidates and vacancies.
> 7. Clearinghouse of jobs: Use employment services set up in conjunction with national or regional meetings of professional organizations.
> 8. Cold canvass in person: Call on employers in the hope of finding a vacancy appropriate for your skills, personality, and interests.
> 9. Cold canvass by telephone: Call employers to identify organizations with appropriate vacancies.
> 10. Union hiring hall: Use employment services set up by labor organizations.
> 11. Alumni office contacts: School or college alumni offices may suggest former students in a position to help you.
> 12. Public career counseling services: Use state employment and other public career-oriented services.
> 13. Private career counseling services: The fees charged by these organizations may be more than justified by the job search time saved.
> 14. Employment agencies: These may charge a fee or a percentage commission—but only if you take a job through them.
> 15. Executive search firms: These are "head hunter" organizations retained by employers to identify persons for specialized jobs.
> 16. Volunteer work: Millions have begun their career by first gaining experience as a "foot in the door" through unpaid work.
> 17. Part-time work experience: A part-time job may be easier to obtain than full-time work and may lead to a permanent position.
> 18. Temporary or summer work: These provide experience and an introduction to the employer's organization.
> 19. Make your own job: Freelance work may lead to self-employment or to job with an employer.

20. Join a 40-plus group: Most cities have these job clubs that specialize in older workers.
21. Join a 65-plus group: These organizations provide jobs and other services for senior citizens.
22. Join a job search group: Sharing job hunting experiences can provide new ideas and psychological support.
23. Tell friends and acquaintances: Most studies show that friends and family are the best single source of job leads.
24. Federal job centers: These offices, located in major cities, are a good source of job leads. Look them up in the telephone book under "U.S. Government."
25. Computerized placement services: Many organizations inventory candidates and employers by computers to make job matches.
26. Social agency placement services: Along with social services, many of these groups now provide job counseling and placement assistance.
27. Membership services: Many professional and other organizations maintain employment assistance programs to aid their members.
28. Mail order job campaign: Send out dozens or hundreds of letters to potential employers, hoping to identify suitable openings.
29. School or college placement services: Both current students and alumni generally are eligible for help from these groups.
30. Association placement services: Many professional and other organizations include employment assistance as part of their service programs.
31. Trade placement services: In many occupations, an organized placement program operates.
32. Professional placement services: Use professional career placement specialists, particularly if looking for a high-level job.
33. Hotlines: Use these answering services (many operate 24 hours a day) maintained by community organizations or libraries.
34. Federal civil service offices: Contact employment offices of federal agencies in your area of interest.
35. State merit service offices: Get in touch with appropriate state government agencies.
36. County or city personnel office: File for suitable openings with agencies of local government.
37. Internships: Use a paid or unpaid short-term internship to gain experience and make contact with potential employers.
38. Work-study programs: Use a cooperative work-study program to gain experience and to make contacts in a field of prime interest.
39. Networking: Expand contacts that may help you by working with peers, friends, supervisors, and others.
40. Mentor: Cultivate an older, more experienced person to whom you turn for advice. Such a mentor may take a special interest in your proper placement.
41. Television job and career announcements: Don't overlook ads placed on television for employees.
42. Radio job and career announcements: Many employers, with numerous jobs, use radio to help solicit candidates for them.

43. Bulletin board posting: Check ads placed on career-related bulletin boards.
44. Check the *College Placement Annual,* published by the College Placement Council (P.O. Box 2263, Bethlehem, PA 18001).
45. Check in-house job vacancies: Most progressive employers now post all vacancies for their current employees to examine and, if interested, apply for.
46. DVR job placement services: All state divisions of rehabilitation services offer disabled persons extensive job counseling and placement services.
47. Former employers: Don't hesitate to ask former employers for help.
48. Fellow employees: Persons who work with you might know of suitable vacancies in other offices or organizations.
49. Personnel office counseling: Many times, the personnel office will counsel you about career paths or alternative jobs in your organization.
50. Religious leaders: Often ministers, rabbis, and priests know of potential employers among their members.
51. Library resources: Check Moody's Industrials, the Fortune "500" list, and other library reference books for employment suggestions.
52. Overseas work: Major religious groups and other international agencies may hire for jobs in other countries.
53. Sponsored interviews: If possible, have persons you know set up employment contacts for you.
54. Military services: Enlistment in one of the armed services may provide both an immediate salary and job training in fields of interest [pp. 14–15].

Lists such as this can stimulate a client's imagination and help him or her think of even further possibilities.

The search for strategies is not limited to such pragmatic goals as getting a job. Rook (1985) reviews strategies for helping the lonely and socially isolated. She discusses three general goals: helping lonely people establish satisfying interpersonal ties; helping prevent loneliness from evolving into or contributing to more serious problems such as depression, drug abuse, or suicide; and helping people prevent rather than remedy loneliness. Then in each category she considers individual, group, and environmental strategies. For instance, some strategies to meet the first goal of helping clients establish satisfying interpersonal ties are as follows:

- *An individual approach:* helping them get rid of the cognitive "garbage," the self-defeating things they say to themselves—"I'm no good," "People don't like me," "It won't work," and so forth—that prevent them from appreciating themselves and their resources enough to make contact with others
- *Group approaches:* providing clients with social-skills training or helping them set up or join shyness self-help groups

- *Environmental approaches:* network building or restructuring social settings, such as classrooms, by introducing such things as peer tutoring, teaching, and teacher-feedback sessions

> One project took place in inner-city, single-room occupancy hotels that housed many elderly persons. Physical disability, poverty, and fear of crime prevented most of these inner-city residents from venturing beyond their hotel rooms, and as a result their social contacts were extremely limited. Public health nurses set up stations in the lobbies of these hotels and offered free blood pressure checkups as an initial means of contact. Over the course of several months they were able to identify shared interests among the residents, which provided a basis for linking dyads or larger groupings. After a year of such informal interaction, residents formed their own Senior Activities Club, which came to function as an independent, active support group [Rook, p. 1395].

Note once more how the stimulation of imagination, or creativity, is central to the development of viable strategies. Clients could also be helped to search for individual, group, and environmental strategies to help them pursue the other two social-bonding goals.

Requirements for Creativity

A review of the requirements for creativity (Cole & Sarnoff, 1980; Robertshaw, Mecca, & Rerick, 1978, see pp. 118–120) shows that people in trouble often fail to use the creative resources they have. The creative person is characterized by:

- *Optimism and confidence,* while clients are often depressed and feel powerless
- *Acceptance of ambiguity and uncertainty,* while clients may feel tortured by ambiguity and uncertainty and want to escape from them as quickly as possible
- *A wide range of interests,* while clients may be people with a narrow range of interests or whose normal interests have been severely narrowed by anxiety and pain
- *Flexibility,* while clients may have become quite rigid in their approach to themselves, others, and the social systems of life
- *Tolerance of complexity,* while clients are often confused and looking for simplicity and simple solutions
- *Verbal fluency,* while clients are often unable to articulate their problems
- *Curiosity,* while clients may not have developed a searching approach to life or may have been hurt by being too venturesome
- *Drive and persistence,* while clients may be all too ready to give up
- *Independence,* while clients may be quite dependent or counterdependent

- *Nonconformity or reasonable risk taking,* while clients may have a history of being very conservative, conformist, or of getting into trouble with others and with society precisely because of their particular brand of nonconformity.

A review of some of the principal obstacles to creativity unearths further client-related characteristics. Innovation is hindered by

- *Fear,* and clients are often quite fearful and anxious
- *Fixed habits,* and clients may have self-defeating habits or patterns of behavior that are deeply engrained
- *Dependence on authority,* and clients may come to helpers looking for the "right answers," or be quite counterdependent (the other side of the dependence coin) and block efforts to be helped with "yes, but" and other games
- *Perfectionism,* and clients may come to helpers precisely because they are tortured by this problem and can accept only ideal or perfect solutions.

It is easy to say that imagination and creativity are most useful in Step III-A, but it is another thing to help clients stimulate their own, perhaps dormant creative potential. However, once you know the conditions that favor creativity, you can use responding and challenging skills to help clients awaken whatever creative resources they may have. You can also use training-as-treatment skills to help clients develop creativity-related techniques such as brainstorming.

Helping Clients Engage in Divergent Thinking

I suggest that one of the behavioral mechanisms that holds people in the grip of the "psychopathology of the average" is a failure to develop the ability to think "divergently" (Dirkes, 1978). Let's consider an example. Picture a room with 40 people in it. In the front of the room a woman holds up a red brick. She asks the people to write down how that brick may be used. The odds are that some people in that room will write down only one answer: that it can be used in constructing some kind of building. They take the "one-right-answer" approach to the problem posed. This is called "convergent thinking." In a convergent-thinking approach to problem solving, people look for the "one right answer." Such thinking is not useless. If a person is faced with five electrical wires to handle and is told that only one of them is live but that by tracing the circuits he or she can determine which one it is, the "one right answer" can be extremely important. However, many problem situations in life are too complex to be handled by convergent thinking. Such thinking limits the ways in which people use their own and environmental resources.

Let's return to the example of the brick. Some people in the room might have suggested that it could be used as a paperweight or to construct a bookcase or ground up and used to give paint color and texture—there are all sorts of possibilities. This is divergent thinking. One problem with such thinking is that however useful it might be it is often not rewarded in our culture; sometimes it is even punished. For instance, studies in creativity have shown that students who think divergently can be thorns in the sides of teachers (Guilford, 1962; Holland, 1961). Many teachers feel comfortable only when they ask questions in such a way as to get from students the "one right answer." When students who think divergently give answers different from those expected, even though their responses may be quite useful (perhaps more useful than the expected responses), they may be ignored or even punished. In such cases, the offering of divergent responses, as might be expected, soon disappears. Students learn that divergent thinking is not rewarded—at least not in school—and generalize from their experience to conclude that it is simply not a useful form of behavior. This is especially true when they witness large-scale social dissent and other forms of divergent thinking being ignored or even punished by society.

It is evident that divergent thinking can be extremely useful in problem solving. It is useful in developing new perspectives, in setting workable goals, in finding different ways to achieve those goals, and in searching for needed resources. Helping clients become better divergent thinkers can be a training-as-treatment method with great payoff potential. It is possible to challenge clients to move out of the ruts they have cut for themselves by constant convergent thinking. Einstein is said to have been the amazingly creative scientist he was because he didn't hesitate to ask "impertinent" questions of Nature. Clients, too, can be encouraged to ask "impertinent" questions of themselves and their environment. While a balance between convergent and divergent thinking might be the most useful, it is likely that most clients you meet (and perhaps most helpers you meet) will be overbalanced on the convergent side.

■

Quentin wanted to be a doctor, so he enrolled in the pre-med curriculum in college. He did well, but not well enough to get into medical school. When he received the last notice of refusal, he said to himself, "Well, that's it for me and the world of medicine. Now what will I do?" On graduation, he took a job in his brother-in-law's business; he became a manager and did fairly well financially, but never experienced much career satisfaction. He was glad that his marriage was good and home life rewarding because he obtained little satisfaction from work.

■

Not much divergent thinking went into handling this problem situation. For Quentin, becoming a doctor was the "one right career." He didn't give serious thought to any other career related to the field of medicine, even though there are dozens of interesting and challenging jobs in the allied health sciences.

The case of Miguel, who also wanted to become a doctor but failed to get into medical school, is quite different.

■

Miguel thought to himself, "Medicine still interests me; I'd like to do something in the health field." With the help of a medical career counselor, he reviewed the possibilities. Even though he was in pre-med, he had never realized there were so many careers in the field of medicine. He decided to take whatever courses and practicum experiences he needed to become a nurse. Then, while working in a clinic in the hills of Appalachia, where he found the experience invaluable, he managed to take an M. A. in family-practice nursing by attending a nearby state university part-time. He chose this specialty thinking it would associate him with the delivery of a broad range of services to patients and also enable him to have more responsibility. When he graduated, he entered private practice with a doctor as a nurse practitioner in a small midwestern town. Since the doctor divided his time among three small clinics, Miguel had a great deal of responsibility in the clinic where he practiced. He also taught a course in family-practice nursing at a nearby state school and conducted workshops in holistic approaches to preventive medical self-care. His career satisfaction was very high.

■

A great deal of divergent thinking went into the elaboration of these goals and coming up with the programs to accomplish them.

Brainstorming as a Program-Development Skill

An excellent way of helping clients unearth possible strategies and tactics for meeting goals is *brainstorming* (Maier, 1970; Osborn, 1963). Brainstorming is a technique for generating ideas, possibilities, or alternate courses of action. The brainstormer tries through divergent thinking to identify as many ways of achieving a goal as possible. There are certain rules that help make this technique work (see D'Zurilla & Goldfried, 1971; Osborn, 1963); one must suspend judgment, get rid of normal constraints to thinking, produce as many ideas as possible, use one idea as a takeoff for others, and produce even more ideas by clarifying items on the list.

SUSPEND JUDGMENT

Do not let clients criticize the strategies they are generating and do not criticize them yourself (Bayless, 1967; Davis & Manske, 1966; Parloff & Handlon, 1964). Evidence suggests that this rule is especially effective when the problem situation has been clarified and defined—which would, of course, be the case in a problem-solving approach to helping. In the following example, a man who is in pain after being rejected by the woman he loves is exploring ways of getting her out of his mind.

CLIENT: One possibility is that I could move to a different city, but that would mean that I would have to get a new job.
HELPER: Write it down. We'll take a more critical look at these later.

Having clients suspend judgment is one way of handling the tendency on the part of some to play a "yes, but" game. Don't let yourself say such things as "How would that work?", "Explain what you mean," "I like that idea," "This one is useful," or "I'm not sure about that idea."

"LET YOURSELF GO"

Encourage clients to include even wild possibilities. It is easier to cut suggested strategies down to size than to expand them later on (Maltzman, 1960). The wildest possibilities often have within them at least a kernel of an idea that will work.

HELPER: So you need money for school. Well, what are some wild ways you could go about getting the money you need?
CLIENT: Well, let me think . . . I could rob a bank . . . or print my own money . . . or put an ad in the paper and ask people to send me money.

Clients often need "permission" to let themselves go, even in such a harmless way.

Too often we repress "good" ideas because when they are first stated they sound foolish. The idea is to create an atmosphere where such apparently foolish ideas will not only be accepted but encouraged [*PS News*, #20, 1982, p. 14].

Help clients think of conservative strategies, liberal strategies, radical strategies, and even outrageous strategies.

ENCOURAGE QUANTITY

Help clients develop as many alternatives as possible—it increases the possibility of finding useful strategies. Studies show that some of the best ideas come along later in the brainstorming process (Maier & Hoffman, 1964; Parnes, 1967).

CLIENT: Maybe that's enough. We can start putting it all together.
HELPER: It didn't sound like you were running out of ideas.
CLIENT: I'm not. It's actually fun.
HELPER: Well, let's keep on having fun for a while.

Some claim that the quantity principle is central to strategy development (D'Zurilla & Nezu, 1980).

PIGGYBACK

Without criticizing any of their proposals, help clients both to add on to strategies already generated and to combine different ideas to form new possibilities. In the following example the client is trying to come up with ways of increasing her own self-esteem.

CLIENT: One way I can get a better appreciation of myself is to make a list of my accomplishments every week, even if it means just getting through the ordinary tasks of everyday life.
HELPER: Anything else you might do with that?
CLIENT: (Pause) And I could star the ones that took some kind of special effort on my part and celebrate them with my husband.

Variations and new twists in strategies already identified are actually new ideas.

CLARIFY ITEMS ON LIST

Again without criticizing their proposals, help clients to clarify them. When a proposal is clarified, it can be expanded.

COLLEGE STUDENT (talking about financial support now that he has moved out of the house and his parents have cut off funds): ... And I suppose there might be the possibility of loans.
COUNSELOR: Are there different kinds of loans?
CLIENT: Well, my grandfather talked about taking out a stake in my future, but at the time I didn't need it. (Pause) And then there are the low-interest state loans. I usually never think of them because none of the people I know use

them. I bet I'm eligible. I'm not sure, but the school itself might even have some loans.

Helping clients clarify ideas often leads to new possibilities.

Two basic assumptions of brainstorming are that the suspension of judgment increases productivity and that quantity breeds quality. For our purposes the evidence supporting these assumptions seems to be substantial enough (Brilhart & Jochem, 1964; Meadow, Parnes, & Reese, 1959; Weisskopf-Joelson & Eliseo, 1961; also see D'Zurilla & Goldfried, 1971, and Heppner, 1978, for reviews of that research).

Brainstorming is not the same as free association. Although clients are encouraged to think of even wild possibilities, still those possibilities must in some way be stimulated by and relate to the client's problem situation and the goals that have been established to manage it. Therefore, brainstorming itself is influenced by the way in which the problem situation has been defined and the clarity and concreteness of the goals that have been set. Concreteness is as important in this program-census step as it is in the problem-clarification and goal-setting stages (Crutchfield, 1969; D'Zurilla & Goldfried, 1971; Goldfried & D'Zurilla, 1969; Hackman, 1967; Maier, 1960, 1970).

Using Prompts to Help Clients Identify Strategies

Without taking over responsibility for the census of strategies, you can use certain prompts to stimulate the imagination of your clients. For instance, a client, Jason T., has terminal cancer. He has been in and out of the hospital several times over the past few months and knows that he probably will not live more than a year. He would like the year to be as full as possible, and yet he wants to be realistic. He hates being in the hospital, especially a large hospital where it is so easy to be anonymous, and one of his goals is to die outside it. He would like to die as benignly as possible and be in possession of his faculties as long as possible. How is he to achieve his goal?

You could use the following interrelated and overlapping prompts to help him identify possible strategies.

Persons. What people might help him achieve his goal? Jason has heard of a doctor in Wisconsin who specializes in the treatment of chronic pain by teaching people to use a variety of techniques to manage it. He also says that perhaps his wife and daughter can learn how to give simple injections to help him control the pain. In addition, Jason thinks that talks every once in a while with a friend whose wife died of cancer, a man he respects and trusts, will help him find the courage he needs.

Models. Does the client know people who are presently doing what he or she wants to do? One of Jason's fellow workers died of cancer at home. Jason visited him a couple of times; that's what gave him the idea of dying outside the hospital. He noticed that his friend never allowed himself "poor-me" talk. He refused to see dying as anything but part of living. This touched Jason deeply at the time, and now reflecting on that experience may help him develop realistic attitudes, too.

Places. Are there particular places that might help? Jason immediately thinks of Lourdes, the shrine where believers flock with all sorts of human problems. He doesn't expect miracles, but feels that he might experience life more deeply there. It's a bit wild, but why not a pilgrimage? He still has the time and also enough money to do it.

Things. What things exist that can help the client achieve the goal? Jason has read about the use of combinations of drugs to help stave off pain and the side effects of chemotherapy. He notices that the use of marijuana by terminal cancer patients to help control nausea has just been legalized in his state. He has also heard that certain kinds of electric stimulation can ward off chronic pain for relatively long periods.

Organizations. Are there any organizations that help people with this kind of problem? Jason knows there are mutual-help groups of cancer patients. He has heard of one at the hospital and believes there are others in the community. He learns that there are such things as hospices for those terminally ill with cancer.

Programs. Are there any ready-made programs for people in the client's position? A hospice for the terminally ill has just been established in the city. They have three programs. One helps people who are terminally ill stay out in the community as long as they can. A second makes provision for part-time residents. The third provides a residential program for those who can spend little or no time in the community. The goals of these programs are practically the same as Jason's.

The skills, working knowledge, and inner resources of the client. What resources does the client have himself or herself that can be used to achieve the goal? Jason knows something about the principles of behavior, such as reinforcement, aversive conditioning, and shaping. He has read that these principles can be used in the management of pain (Fordyce, 1976). He also has strong religious convictions that can help him face adversity. These resources suggest possible courses of action.

If a client is having a difficult time coming up with strategies, the helper can "prime the pump" by offering a few suggestions of his or her own. This can be done in such a way that the principal responsibility for the production of possible strategies stays with the client.

■ Training as Treatment

D'Zurilla and Goldfried (1971) suggest a "deficiency" rather than a "pathology" view of client behavior.

> Much of what we view clinically as "abnormal behavior" or "emotional disturbance" may be viewed as *ineffective* behavior and its consequences, in which the individual is unable to resolve certain situational problems in his life and his inadequate attempts to do so are having undesirable effects, such as anxiety, depression, and the creation of additional problems [p. 107].

It often happens that people get into trouble or fail to get out of it because they lack the kinds of *life skills* (Gazda, 1982, 1984) needed to do so and do not know how to mobilize internal and environmental resources to cope with problem situations. If this is the case, training clients in the life skills they need to cope more effectively will be an important part of the helping process. For some clients, one of the most important ways of helping them make their preferred scenarios a reality is to help them acquire the life skills associated with those new scenarios. A constant question throughout the helping process should be, "What kinds of skills does this client need to get where he or she wants to go?" Skills training is another all-too-often-overlooked strategy.

One of the definitions of the word *skill* suggested by *Webster's New Collegiate Dictionary* is "a learned power of doing something competently." Skills are physical, intellectual, and social competencies that are necessary for effective living in the areas of learning, self-management, involvement with others, and participation in groups and other social settings of life. Working knowledge informs and enhances skills, and skills translate working knowledge into effective—that is, accomplishment-producing—patterns of behavior. Whether skills deficit is a cause, a consequence, or a feature of a client's disturbance (Brady, 1984a, 1984b), training in relevant life skills can be an extremely useful part of the helping process.

Anthony (1977, 1979), Carkhuff (1969a, 1969b, 1971b; Carkhuff & Berenson, 1976), Egan and Cowan (1979; Egan, 1984), and Kanfer and Goldstein (1980) suggest that educating clients in the kinds of working knowledge and training them in the kinds of skills they need to work through problems in living—in the words of Carkhuff (1971), "training as treatment"—can be an extremely important part of the helping process. Part of "giving psychology away" (Larson, 1984; Miller, 1969, 1980) is giving clients the working knowledge and skills they need to cope (Guerney, 1982, 1984; Ivey & Galvin, 1982). Let us consider an example.

■

Jerzy and Zelda fall in love. They marry and enjoy a relatively trouble-free "honeymoon" period of about two years or so. Eventually, however, the problems that inevitably arise from living together in such intimacy assert themselves. They find, for instance, that they counted too heavily on positive feelings for each other and that now, in their absence, they cannot "communicate" about finances, sex, and values. Jerzy really has little working knowledge of the developmental demands of a 20-year-old woman; Zelda has little working knowledge of the kinds of cultural blueprints that affect her 26-year-old husband. The relationship begins to deteriorate. Since they have few problem-solving skills, they don't know how to handle their situation. Things get worse until they settle down into living miserably, or separate, or divorce, or perhaps take their problems—for better or worse—to a helper.

■

In the case of this young couple, it seems reasonable to assume that helping will necessarily include both education and training as essential elements of an action plan. As suggested in Chapter One, one of the most important sets of skills that can become part of a training-as-treatment program are basic problem-solving skills. The box at the end of the chapter provides a summary of topics you can use to evaluate your performance as you help clients develop strategies for action.

■ Is Step III-A Enough for Some Clients?

The answer, as usual, is a qualified yes. Some clients know *where* they are headed but are not sure *how* to get there. If the client's need is in the area of "how," the greatest point of leverage may well be helping him or her develop a broad range of strategies from which to choose. Stimulating the imagination of clients, even clients who have a hard time imagining anything about the future, is often one of the best ways of being with them. If clients have a hard time with the future, ask them what has worked for them or others in the past. Use past experience as a way of stimulating their imaginations. Many people think that they are without imagination simply because no one has ever challenged them to use it.

■ Evaluation Checklist for Step III-A

How well am I doing the following as I try to help the client?

THE GENERATION OF STRATEGIES

- Trying to stimulate the imagination of the client at the service of action
- Helping the client to engage in divergent thinking
- Helping the client brainstorm as many ways as possible to get a preferred scenario, or some part of it, on line
- Using probes and prompts to stimulate the client's thinking about strategies.

TRAINING AS TREATMENT

- Helping the client see which skills he or she needs to implement goals
- Training the client in essential skills or helping him or her find out where this training can be obtained.

Eleven

Stage III: Step III–B
Helping Clients Choose Strategies and Formulate Action Plans

■

Some clients, once they are helped to see different program possibilities, move forward on their own—that is, they choose strategies, put together an action plan that fits their needs, and implement it. Others, however, still need help in putting together a viable action program. They need help in completing Step III-B, illustrated in Figure 11–1—help that can take two forms. The first is for the counselor, once possible strategies have been identified, to help the client choose those that provide the best "fit": those are most in keeping with the client's values, resources, and circumstances. Having a large number of possible strategies can be a problem in itself, because individuals then have a hard time picking the best (Johnson, Parrott, & Stratton, 1968). It is useless to have clients brainstorm if they don't know what to do with the possibilities they generate. Another form of help is to assist clients in translating their

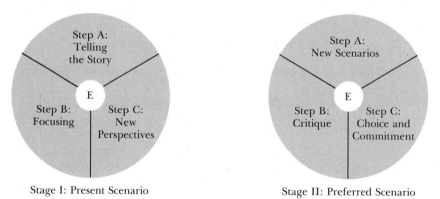

Stage I: Present Scenario   Stage II: Preferred Scenario

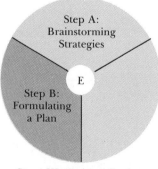

Stage III: Action—Getting
the New Scenario On Line

Figure 11–1. Step II-B: Formulating a plan

preferred strategies in a step-by-step plan. Let us take a look at both of these.

■ Helping Clients Choose Best-Fit Strategies

First we will consider the general criteria for choosing strategies and then take a look at the balance sheet as a method of helping clients choose those best for them.

The Criteria for Choosing Strategies

The criteria for choosing a program do not differ from those for choosing a goal outlined in StepII-B, so they are reviewed only briefly here through a series of examples. Strategies to achieve goals must have certain characteristics.

SPECIFIC

Like goals, strategies need to be specific if they are to motivate the client to action.

When Karen says, "My goal is to stop drinking. In order to achieve this goal, I'm going to lessen the amount of stress in my life. If I feel less stress, I won't be tempted to drink as much," she is violating the specificity criterion. While the principle she suggests may be sound, her application of it is much too vague to be of any use. In contrast, if John's goal is to reduce and manage the pain of a chronic back condition, learning to control his reaction to pain through a biofeedback program is a specific way of moving toward his goal.

Note that being specific is important *throughout* the helping process: in clarifying and defining the problem situation, in setting goals, and now in elaborating strategies.

MEASURABLE OR VERIFIABLE

The relationship between the strategy and the achieving of the goal must be capable of being verified.

■

Susan intends to take some kind of communication course as a way of helping her be more assertive in class, in talking with her parents, and in her relationships with her peers. The course she takes, however, is a "sensitivity-training" program characterized by "planned goal-lessness." She attends the meetings, but does not know exactly what she is learning, if anything. There is no way of telling whether the program is helping her become more assertive. Trish, on the other hand, with the same goal takes a course in interpersonal communication skills. She is given a clear idea of what each skill is and how it can be used. She learns and practices the skills in the training group and is given help in transferring them to other settings. She knows what she is learning and how it contributes to her goal.

■

If the impact of a course of action is not capable of being verified, it is not a viable strategy.

REALISTIC

The course of action must be within the resources of the client, under his or her control, and environmentally possible.

■

Desmond is in a halfway house after leaving a state mental hospital. From time to time he still has bouts of depression that incapacitate him for a few days. He wants to get a job because he thinks it will help him feel better about himself, become more independent, and manage his depression better. He answers want ads in a rather random way and keeps getting turned down after being interviewed. He simply does not yet have the kinds of resources needed to show himself in a favorable light in job interviews—and he is not yet ready for a regular full-time job. The counselor helps him explore some sheltered-workshop possibilities. She helps him find a workshop that is not a dead end but rather a step toward a more usual type of job. Desmond does have the psychological resources to work successfully in a sheltered workshop.

■

There is, of course, a difference between realism and selling a client short. Strategies that make clients "stretch" for a valued goal can be most rewarding.

ADEQUATE

Strategies must contribute in a substantial way to accomplishing the client's goal of putting a new scenario in place. Sometimes goals do not get accomplished because strategies are too insubstantial or irrelevant.

■

Stacy was admitted to a mental hospital because she had been exhibiting bizarre behavior in her neighborhood. She dressed in a slovenly way and went around admonishing the residents of the community for their "sins." She was diagnosed as schizophrenic, simple type. She had been living alone for about five years since the death of her husband. It seemed that she had become more and more alienated from herself and others. In the hospital, medication helped control some of her symptoms: she stopped admonishing others and took reasonable care of herself, but she was still quite withdrawn. She was assigned to "milieu" therapy, a euphemism meaning that she followed the more or less benign routine of the hospital. She remained withdrawn and usually seemed moderately depressed. No therapeutic goals had been set and the nonspecific program to which she was assigned was totally inadequate.

■

Sometimes courses of action are inadequate because the resources needed are not available. In this example, "milieu" therapy indicates that the hospital lacked adequate therapeutic resources.

OWNED BY THE CLIENT

Strategies, like goals, must be owned by the client. Advice giving is the opposite of this: "Why don't you try . . . ". This is a sure way of getting into trouble. However, there is a "prompt-and-fade" technique that can be used with clients who are having a hard time coming up with possible strategies. The counselor can say, "Here are some possibilities. . . . Do any of them make sense to you?" Or, "Here are some of the things that people with this kind of problem situation have tried. . . . How do they sound to you?" The goal is clear: make sure the client is committing to his or her own strategies, not to yours.

IN KEEPING WITH THE VALUES OF THE CLIENT

Strategies, like goals, can either be in keeping with the values of the client or violate them.

■

Glenn was cited for battering his 2-year-old child. Mandatory counseling was part of the suspended sentence he received. He had a violent temper; that is, he got angry easily, did little to control it, and vented it on others, including the child. The counselor discovered that Glenn and his wife were having sexual problems and that sexual frustration had a great deal to do with his anger. The counselor suggested that Glenn lower his frustration (and therefore control his anger) by engaging in sexual relations with other women. Glenn did so, but felt guilty and became depressed.

■

The counselor is in the wrong for suggesting a course of action without consideration of the client's values. He might do so because he thinks that Glenn's having sex with other women, if an evil, is less of an evil than abusing his child, but it is not his decision to make.

SET IN A REASONABLE TIME FRAME

This implies that clients have a clear idea of the course of action and know when they are to do what.

■

Tammy, after consulting with her doctor, undertook a physical fitness program as part of an overall weight-reduction program. Her counselor gave her a book that outlined both a variety of exercises and a running schedule. The book indicated three different programs— slow, medium, and fast—scaled according to age groups. Tammy decided that she needed a taste of success. She chose the slow program for her age group. The book indicated each objective and the time allotted to it, so each day Tammy had a very clear idea of just what to do. She stuck to the schedule and began feeling much better about herself.

■

If a client does not know what the steps of a program are and when each is to be accomplished, it militates against his or her starting at all.

The Balance Sheet as a Method for Helping Clients Choose Strategies

The decision balance sheet is a decision-making aid that counselors can use to help clients choose the kinds of programs that best fit their needs (Janis & Mann, 1977; Wheeler & Janis, 1980). It is a way of helping clients examine the consequences of different courses of action in the light of both values and usefulness. The balance sheet addresses *utility*— "Will this course of action get me where I want to go?"—and *acceptability*— "Can I live with this course of action?" It helps clients consider not just themselves but also significant others and the social settings of their lives. The issues considered in the balance sheet are possible gains, possible losses, and the acceptability or unacceptability of each. The balance sheet form is illustrated in Table 11–1. In this step you are helping clients make the kinds of decisions they can live with.

• *Benefits or gains.* If I follow this course of action, what benefits or gains are in it
  for me?
  for significant others in my life?
  for the social settings of which I am a member?

Table 11–1. The decision balance sheet

If I choose this course of action:		
The Self		
Gains for self:	Acceptable to me because:	Not acceptable to me because:
Losses for self:	Acceptable to me because:	Not acceptable to me because:
Significant Others		
Gains for significant others:	Acceptable to me because:	Not acceptable to me because:
Losses for significant others:	Acceptable to me because:	Not acceptable to me because:
Social Setting		
Gains for social setting:	Acceptable to me because:	Not acceptable to me because:
Losses for social setting:	Acceptable to me because:	Not acceptable to me because:

- *Acceptability of benefits.* In each case, these potential benefits or gains are *acceptable* to me because

    my gains would be . . .

    the gains of significant others would be . . .

    the gains for relevant social settings would be . . .

- *Unacceptability of benefits.* In each case these potential benefits or gains are *unacceptable* to me because

    my gains would be . . .

    the gains for significant others would be . . .

    the gains for relevant social settings would be . . .

- *Losses or costs.* If I choose this program or follow this course of action, what losses or costs can I expect to incur

    for myself?

    for significant others?

    for relevant social settings?

- *Acceptability of losses.* In each case, these potential losses are *acceptable* to me because

    my losses would be . . .

    the losses to significant others would be . . .

    the losses to relevant social settings would be . . .

- *Unacceptability of losses or costs.* In each case these potential losses or costs are *unacceptable* to me because

    my losses or costs would be . . .

    the losses or costs to significant others would be . . .

    the losses or costs to relevant social settings would be . . .

Some examples will clarify the use of the balance sheet. Let's return to Karen, the woman who has admitted she is an alcoholic and whose goal is to stop drinking. One possible strategy is to spend a month as an inpatient at an alcoholic treatment center. This possibility intrigues her. Since choosing this possibility would be a serious decision, the counselor, Joan, helps her use the balance sheet to weigh possible costs and benefits. Joan tells her to mark the spots she feels a need to discuss after filling it out. She returns with the following:

BENEFITS OF CHOOSING THE RESIDENTIAL PROGRAM

For me: It would help me because it would be a dramatic sign that I want to do something to change my life. It's a clean break, as it were. It would also give me time just for myself; I'd get away from all my commitments to family, relatives, friends, and work. I see it as an opportunity to do some planning. I'd have to figure out how I would act as a sober person.

For significant others: I'm thinking mainly of my family here. It would also give them a breather, a month without an alcoholic wife and mother around the house. I'm not saying that to put myself down. I think it would give them time to reassess family life and make some decisions about any changes they'd like to make. I think something dramatic like my going away would give them hope. They've had very little reason to hope for the last five years.

For relevant social settings: I can't think of many benefits for social settings apart from the family. I'd probably be more "with it" in my part-time job, but they've never had any real complaints.

ACCEPTABILITY OF BENEFITS

For me: I feel torn here. But looking at it just from the viewpoint of acceptability, I feel kind enough toward myself to give myself a month's time off. Also, something in me longs for a new start in life.

For significant others: I think that my family would have no problem in letting me take a month off. I'm sure that they'd see it as a positive step from which all of us would benefit.

For relevant social settings: This does not seem to be an issue at work. They like me now. I might be more efficient, and most likely I'd be less moody.

UNACCEPTABILITY OF BENEFITS

For me: Going away for a month seems such a luxury, so self-indulgent. Also, while taking such a dramatic step would give me an opportunity to change my current lifestyle, it would also place demands on me. My fear is that I would do fine while "inside," but that I would come out and fall on my face. I guess I'm saying it would give me another chance at life, but I have misgivings about having another chance. *I need some help here.*

For significant others: The kids are young enough to readjust to a "new"me, but I'm not sure how my husband would take this "benefit." He's more or less worked out a lifestyle that copes with my being drunk a lot. Though I have never left him and he has never left me, still I wonder whether he wants me "back"—sober, I mean. Maybe this belongs under the "cost" part of this exercise. *I need some help here.* I notice that some of my misgivings relate not to a residential program as such but to a return to a lifestyle free of alcohol. Doing this exercise has helped me see that more clearly.

For relevant social settings: As far as I can see there's nothing unacceptable about my being more efficient or more personable at work.

COSTS OF CHOOSING A RESIDENTIAL PROGRAM

For me: Well, there's the money. I don't mean the money just for the program, but I would be losing four weeks' wages. The major cost seems to be the commitment I have to make about a lifestyle change. Also, I guess the residential program won't be all fun. I don't know exactly what they do there, but some of it must be demanding.

For significant others: It's a private program and it's going to cost the family a lot of money. The services I have been providing will be missing for a month. It's also going to disturb their patterns of living, because the probability is that they're going to get some kind of "new" me back and they'll have to learn to live with me all over again.

For relevant social settings: There may be one cost here. If I change my lifestyle, I may want a better job or I may make a decision not to work at all. In that case, they would lose someone they see as a decent employee.

ACCEPTABILITY OF COSTS

For me: I have no problem at all with the money nor with whatever the residential program demands of me physically or psychologically. I'm willing to pay. The demand the program places on me for a new lifestyle? Well, in principle I'm willing to pay what that costs. *I need some help here.*

For significant others: They will have to make financial sacrifices, but I have no reason to think that they would be unwilling. Still, I can't be making decisions for them. I see much more clearly the need to have a counseling session with my husband and children present. I think they're also willing to have a "new" person around the house, even if it means making adjustments and changing their lifestyle a bit. I want to check this out with them, but I think it would be helpful to do so with the counselor present. I think they would be willing to come.

For relevant social settings: If getting better means not working or getting a different job, let it be. I can hardly base my decision on what they will think at work.

UNACCEPTABILITY OF COSTS

For me: While I'm ready to change my lifestyle, I hate to think that I will have to accept some dumb, dull life. I think I've been drinking at least in part to get away from dullness; I've been living in a fantasy world, a play world a lot of the time. A stupid way of doing it perhaps, but it's true. I have to do some life planning of some sort. *I need some help here.*

For significant others: It strikes me that my family might have problems with a sober me if it means that I will strike out in new directions. I wonder if they don't just want the traditional homebody wife and mother. I don't think I could stand that. *I need some help here.*

For relevant social settings: They can get along without me for a month at work—and if necessary they can get along without me completely.

All in all, it seems like the residential program is a good idea. There is something much more "total" about it than an outpatient program. But that's also what scares me.

Karen's use of the balance sheet helps her make an initial program choice, and also enables her to discover issues that she has not yet worked out completely. By using the balance sheet, she returns to the counselor with work to do; she does not come merely wondering what will happen next. This highlights the usefulness of exercises and other forms of structure that help clients take more responsibility for what happens both in the helping sessions and outside.

Program Sampling

Some clients find it easier to choose strategies if they first sample some of the possibilities.

■

Karen, surprised by the number of program possibilities there were to achieve the goal of getting liquor out of her life, decided to sample some of them. She went to an open meeting of an Alcoholics Anonymous group, attended a meeting of a women's consciousness-raising group, visited the hospital with the residential treatment program, joined up for a two-week trial physical fitness program at a YWCA, and had a couple of strategy meetings with her husband and children. While none of this was done frantically, it did occupy her energies and strengthened her resolve to do something about her alcoholism.

■

It goes without saying that some clients could use strategy sampling as a way of putting off action. However, if a course of action is going to require a high cost in terms of time, energy, and/or money, sampling it to see how it fits one's resources, values, and preferences makes sense.

1. *The "wish" strategy.* In the "wish" strategy the client chooses a course of action that *might* (he or she hopes) lead to the attainment of a goal, regardless of risk, cost, or probability. For instance, Jenny wants her ex-husband to increase the amount of support he is paying for the children. She tries to accomplish this by constantly nagging him and trying to make him feel guilty. She does not consider the risk (he might get angry and stop giving her anything), the cost (she spends a lot of time and emotional energy arguing with him), or the probability of success (he does not react favorably to nagging and views it as one reason for the divorce). In the "wish" strategy the client operates blindly, using some preferred course of action without taking into account its usefulness. Clients who "work hard" and "still get nowhere" might well be using the "wish" strategy; they are persevering in using means they prefer but that are of doubtful efficacy.

2. *The "safe" strategy.* In the "safe" strategy the client chooses only safe courses of action—ones with little risk and a high degree of producing

at least limited success. For instance, Liam, a man in his early forties, is very dissatisfied with his job, but afraid of losing the one he has if anyone finds out he is thinking of changing. He chooses only those job possibilities for which interviews are given in the evening, and he excludes possibilities he thinks might be too competitive or too challenging. He simply wants a job different from the one he has. The trouble with this strategy is that it places limitations on the kinds of goals that can be pursued. Goals have to be tailored to safe and probable means. Clients might well end up being safe but also sorry.

3. *The "escape" strategy.* In the "escape" strategy clients choose means likely to help them avoid *the worst possible result;* it minimizes the maximum danger. Let's say that a client has had fits of violence. He commits himself to a mental hospital, for he feels that there he will be protected from his own violence. The greatest danger, in his view, is harming another person. By placing himself in custodial care, he minimized that danger. The obvious problem with such a strategy is that it is an avoidance strategy based on negative reinforcement, and can prevent any learning from taking place.

4. *The "combination" strategy.* In the "combination" strategy clients choose courses of action that, although involving risk, both minimize danger and increase the probability of achieving a goal in the way and to the degree they desire. This "combination" strategy is the most difficult to apply, for it involves the hard work needed to devise a clarification of objectives, a solid knowledge of one's personal values, the ability to rank a variety of action programs according to those values, and the ability to predict results from a given course of action. Sometimes clients have neither the time nor the will for this kind of detailed work. Or it may be that helpers frequently do not have the decision-making skills to help clients do this work.

■ Helping Clients Formulate Plans

Some strategies are quite simple and obviate the need to help clients work out a step-by-step procedure to accomplish their goal. Others are more complicated and require that clients determine what steps must be taken and in what order. Some clients are able to do the kind of sequencing of steps required by a plan on their own, while others still need a counselor's help.

Many clients are not good at formulating specific plans. It takes too much time or concentration, and they are not patient enough. Or we the helpers feel that a plan will hem us in. We want to live as freely as possible, and we bring those feelings with us in our interactions with clients. However, helping clients work out a step-by-step program increases the probability that they will act in their own interest. Carroll and Tosi (1973, pp. 81–82) summarize the reasons why action plans help people attain goals. I have adapted them to the counseling process.

· Formulating action plans helps clients search for more useful ways of reaching goals—that is, even better strategies.

When the Johnson family (wife and children) began to formulate a plan for coping with their reactions to Mr. Johnson's alcoholism, they realized they had not been very inventive in the strategy-census phase. They went back to the drawing board.

· Action plans provide an opportunity to evaluate the realism and adequacy of new scenarios and goals.

When Walter began tracing out a plan to cope with the loss he experienced when a tornado killed his wife and destroyed his home, he realized that his goals were unrealistic. He scaled back his expectations.

· Such plans give clients a good idea of the time required and the psychological costs involved in working toward a goal.

When Lynn was helped to get an overview of the rehabilitation program she was about to undertake after an automobile accident, she saw clearly that the psychological costs were going to be quite high. She talked with the counselor about ways of keeping her spirits up.

· They help clients determine what kind of resources, especially human resources, they will need to attain goals.

When Nancy was helped by a counselor to formulate a plan to pull her life together after the disappearance of her younger son, she came to realize that she couldn't do it alone. She had retreated from friends and even relatives, but now she knew she had to get back into community.

· Formulating plans helps clients uncover unanticipated snags or obstacles to the achievement of goals.

Only when Ernesto, the badly beaten gang member, started putting together a plan for a different kind of lifestyle did he realize what an obstacle his not finishing high school would be. He came to realize that he needed the equivalent of a high school diploma, and now had to figure out how to fit it into the overall scenario.

∎

• Plans identify areas in which the counselor can provide support or challenge.

∎

Peg was a woman with several physical disabilities, who still claimed that she suffered the most from what she did to herself psychologically. In working out a program to increase her self-esteem, it became clear that she was depending too much on the counselor. It was evident that she needed to develop further human resources in her everyday life.

∎

A step-by-step plan enables clients to answer such questions as "What do I need to do today? What do I need to do tomorrow? How will these steps help me get what I want?"

Shaping the Plan: Developing Subgoals and Strategies to Achieve Them

If a problem situation is complex, any given goal chosen by the client may have a number of subgoals. A subgoal is a step toward a larger goal. For instance, if an automobile is to move smoothly down an assembly line, all sorts of subgoals need to be met first. It does little good to have the chassis moving down the line if the other parts are not available for assembling. "Fenders *manufactured, shipped,* and *in place* for assembly" would be an important subgoal or objective. Without that subgoal, further goals would be impossible.

The simpler the programs the better, provided that they help clients achieve their goals. However, simplicity is not an end in itself. The question is not whether any given program is complicated or not but whether it is well *shaped* or organized. If complicated programs are broken down into subgoals and their accompanying strategies, they are as capable of being achieved, if the time frame is realistic, as are simpler ones. In schematic form, program shaping looks like this:

Subprogram 1 leads to subgoal 1.
Subprogram 2 leads to subgoal 2.
Subprogram n (the last in the sequence) leads to the achievement of the major goal.

Your job is to help clients identify subgoals—that is, *major steps* on the way to the achievement of an important goal—and organize those subgoals into a *sequence* leading to the major goal. This is a *plan.*

Wanda is a client who has set a number of goals in order to manage a complex problem situation. One of them is finding a job. The program leading to this goal can be divided into a number of steps. Another way of putting this is that each step leads to the accomplishment of a *subgoal.* The following subgoals are part of Wanda's job-finding program.

Subgoal 1: kind of job wanted *determined,* resume *written*
Subgoal 2: job possibilities *canvassed*
Subgoal 3: best job prospects *identified*
Subgoal 4: job interviews *arranged*
Subgoal 5: job interviews *completed*
Subgoal 6: job *chosen*
Major goal in total program:
job *started*

If all of this is accomplished, Wanda achieves one of the major goals in her overall program: satisfactory employment.

For each of these subgoals a program is established. For instance, the program for the subgoal "job possibilities *canvassed*" might include such things as reading the help-wanted section of the local papers, contacting friends or acquaintances who might be able to offer jobs or provide leads, reading the bulletin boards at school, visiting employment agencies, and talking with someone in the job placement office at school. Remember that clients often tend to overlook program possibilities and that one of your tasks, even in the elaboration of subprograms, is to help them break out of overly narrow patterns of thinking. As usual, both support and challenge are still needed to help clients move beyond their own narrow perspectives.

WANDA: I'm beginning to panic. I've been reading the help-wanted sections of the local paper and a couple of the papers in nearby towns, but I haven't seen anything that seems right for me.

COUNSELOR: Newspapers are only one source of job possibilities. Let's see if we can come up with other ways of finding out what kind of work is available. For instance, most people don't know that more jobs are obtained through word of mouth than through newspaper ads. It's called *networking.*

WANDA: Well, I could call some places where I would like to work. I could ask some of my friends who are already working to keep their eyes open.

And she goes on to explore further possibilities.

Hints for Effective Elaboration of Plans

There are a number of things you can do to help clients put together reasonable plans for action.

QUALITY OF SUBGOALS

Each major step in a plan has some kind of subgoal; a goal that, if accomplished, will lead to the achievement of the major goal of the plan. And of course there will be strategies to achieve each subgoal. The number of subgoals and strategies to achieve them will differ according to the complexity of each problem situation. First of all, a subgoal must fulfill the same requirements as a goal; that is, it must be

- Stated as a clear, specific, behaviorial *accomplishment;* "job possibilities thoroughly canvassed" is a goal that is stated as a clear accomplishment.
- *Adequate*—that is, clearly related both to the next subgoal and to the major goal toward which it is directed. If Wanda does a good job of canvassing job possibilities, she is ready to pick out the best prospects (the next subgoal in the program) and is moving toward her major goal of getting a job.
- Within the *control* of the client and something the client rather than someone else is to do; in the example, Wanda takes responsibility for canvassing job possibilities.
- *Realistic*—that is, within the resources and capabilities of the client and in keeping with the environmental (social-system) constraints within which the client is operating. Wanda needs some encouragement from the counselor, but she has the resources needed to search out job possibilities.
- *Compatible* with the other subgoals of the program and with the values of the client. Job possibilities must be discovered before Wanda can decide which ones look most promising; she holds no values that would keep her from finding out what the job market has to offer.
- Capable of being *verified;* it will be quite evident both to Wanda and to the counselor whether or not she has done a reasonably adequate job of canvassing possibilities.
- Assigned a reasonable *time frame* for completion; Wanda gives herself two weeks for this task and gets it done within that time.

Let us consider the example of a young man trying to cope with an impoverished social life.

■

One of Leroy's problems is that he is "out of community"; he has no close friend and no group with which he interacts regularly. It becomes clear that many of his other problems are related to having such an impoverished social life. Therefore, one major goal of this total program is "getting into community"—participating in groups and establishing friendships. Although Leroy is somewhat fearful of making contact with others, he is lonely enough to want to do something about his social life. Through discussions with the counselor, he comes up with the following subgoals that would contribute to becoming a member of some kind of social group:

group possibilities *identified* within two weeks
best possibilities *explored*
social group *chosen*
social group *joined*

Leroy has never thought of taking such direct action to improve his social life, and at first is put off by it. He has been "waiting for something to happen." But—predictably—nothing has happened. It now is clear to him that he has to make it happen. He evaluates each of his subgoals. For instance, in looking carefully at the subgoal "group possibilities identified" he finds that it is

- Stated as an accomplishment: he can picture himself with a list of possibilities in front of him.
- Clearly related to the next subgoal "group *chosen*"—for it is better to choose from a number of possibilities—and it is related to the ultimate goal of actually participating in a social group.
- Within his control: though he might need some suggestions from both the counselor and others, he can come up with a list of possibilities.
- Realistic, for he has the minimal skills needed to come up with a list.
- Compatible, for it doesn't interfere with any other goal or go against any value he holds.
- Capable of being verified: he either has a list of possibilities or he does not.
- Adequate: it is fairly easy to see whether the list is too short or if it gives evidence of poorly thought-out possibilities.
- Assigned a time frame: he judges two weeks to be an adequate amount of time.

■

It is clear that it is not necessary to apply each of these criteria explicitly to each subgoal. The methodology is not a thing in itself; it is a means to accomplish goals.

THE STRATEGIES LEADING TO SUBGOALS

Each strategy leading to the attainment of a subgoal should have the characteristics of strategies discussed earlier in this chapter—that is, each should be

- *Clear*: the client should know exactly what to do.

- *Clearly related to the next step:* the progression of steps should be clear to the client.
- *Clearly related to the subgoal:* the client should see the steps as a more or less direct line toward the subgoal.
- *Not too large:* the "size" of a step should be in proportion to both the client's actual resources and circumstances and the client's feelings about any given step—what does he or she see as too large? This issue is dealt with more fully below.
- *Not too small:* although some helpers suggest that there is no such thing as a step that is too small, some clients feel they are being treated like children if asked to do too little.
- *Reasonably scheduled:* there should be a realistic time frame for each step.

SIZE OF STEPS

It is not enough that subgoals be identified and subprograms established. In setting up both programs and subprograms there is one cardinal rule: *no step should be too large.* Watson and Tharp (1985) suggest that helpers too often mistakenly attribute lack of will power to their clients. The problem, they say, is not lack of will power but rather poorly shaped programs, plans that ask clients to do too much at one time. If any given step in a program seems too formidable for a client, he or she might balk or become disorganized. Any step that seems too large can be broken up into one or more smaller steps.

■

Jason T., the terminal cancer patient met in Chapter Ten, felt a lot of the emotions that can sweep through people facing death: confusion, denial, rage, fear, isolation, hurt, and depression. One day he talked with a minister from his church who was making his weekly rounds in the hospital. After talking briefly with Jason, the minister suggested that he find someone with whom, or some forum in which, he could talk about his illness, his feelings, his values, and what he would like to do in the time he had left. This sounded good to Jason, but when the minister—who was somewhat rushed because he had a lot of patients to see—left, Jason had no idea what to do. Finding such a forum was too big a step for him, because he was still struggling with his emotions. His brief conversation with the minister had done little to lessen his turmoil, so after he left Jason felt even more depressed than usual.

The next day a counselor from the pastoral ministry staff of the hospital stopped by. She provided support by helping him express his feelings. After he ventilated and explored his feelings about dying, they addressed the idea of a forum in which he could continue to talk in this fashion. She helped Jason become an *agent* rather than just a patient. He now wanted to do something about his illness other than merely endure it. "What do terminal cancer patients do for support?" he asked himself, and with the help of the counselor began to identify some of the possibilities. There were more possibilities than he suspected: for instance, living-at-home programs, hospital-based mutual-help groups, one-to-one counseling, family counseling, group programs supported by various church agencies, and hospice-based programs. Exploring some of the possibilities included attending a couple of sessions of the hospital-based mutual-help group and a visit to a hospice, where he ultimately decided to spend the rest of his time.

■

The simple steps here were ventilating feelings, identifying the need for support, brainstorming possibilities, sampling a few forums of support, and choosing one. None proved too large.

Helping Clients Develop Contingency Plans

One important reason for helping clients choose a program from among alternatives is the possibility that the chosen program or part of it, might not work. Since this is always possible, it is wise to help clients determine back-up or contingency programs. We have already seen the need for contingency plans in Stage II.

■

Jason made plans to become a resident of the hospice he had visited. He thought this would be the best way both for him and for his family to handle his dying. However, although he had visited the hospice and liked what he had seen, he could not be absolutely sure that it would work out. Therefore, with the help of the counselor he settled on two other possibilities as back-up plans. One was living at home with some outreach services from the hospice. A second was spending his last days in a smaller hospital in a nearby town. The latter plan would not be as convenient for his family, but he would feel more comfortable there, since he hated large hospitals. Jason came to these decisions after being helped to weigh the pro's and con's by means of the balance-sheet approach.

■

Contingency plans are needed especially when clients choose a high–risk program to achieve a critical goal. Having back–up plans also helps clients develop more responsibility. If they see that a plan is not working, they have to decide whether to try the contingency plan. Back–up plans need not be complicated. A counselor might merely ask, "If that doesn't work, then what will you do?"

Some Problems Associated with Developing Plans

There are a number of problems associated with the development of plans to reach subgoals and goals: resisting the work involved, getting lost in details, trying to accomplish too much or too little, post-decision depression, and the inevitable quirks of the entire decision-making process.

Resisting the work of developing programs.   Some clients and some helpers resist the work involved in setting up effective programs because it seems too complicated. Clients come to counseling feeling disorganized and do not want that feeling intensified. Since you as the helper are aware of the logic involved in program development, you can use that logic to guide clients who are too disorganized or too resistant to use it directly themselves. The point is that some systematic process should serve as a framework or guideline for elaborating plans. Clients who work more intuitively may see detailed planning as overly rational. Although intuition can be a valuable resource, doing all the planning work intuitively, especially in the case of complicated problem situations, is expecting too much of intuition. Put more positively, intuitions that are guided by the logic of the planning process are likely to be more useful than raw intuition.

Getting lost in the details.   A common mistake made by novices who use planning and program-development "technology" to help others is to become too detailed. If you keep using it in your own life to help yourself elaborate programs to achieve your own goals, it will become second nature to you. You can quickly learn the skill of breaking problems and goals into smaller parts, and "chaining" together the steps needed to accomplish both subgoals and major goals. Experience will teach you neither to overload clients and run the risk of discouraging them nor to cause them to "loaf" through the helping process and run the risk of giving it up because it appears ineffectual. Learning and using planning and program-development skills is like learning any other skill. At first it feels awkward, but with practice the entire process becomes much easier.

A balance between too much and too little.   Janis and Mann (1977; see Wheeler & Janis, 1980) suggest that many people make poor decisions because they take a "minimal" approach to decision making; that is, they tend to make decisions that fulfill minimum requirements. Let us say that a woman decides she wants a job that pays $225 per week and that is within walking distance of her apartment. She accepts the first job that meets these minimum requirements and becomes secretary to the manager of a nearby laundry firm. It is not long before she becomes dissatisfied with the job and begins to realize that there were really other requirements she had not considered. For instance, she likes companionship at work but now works alone all day. For her, a minimal approach has proved very inefficient (though it may have seemed efficient at the time), for it has left her dissatisfied, and she now faces the prospect of searching for a new, more fulfilling job.

On the other hand, taking an "optimal" approach to decision making can be just as self-defeating. Optimizing means that a person continues looking for and evaluating options until she or he is completely satisfied that the decision being made is absolutely the "best" one. The problems with this approach to decision making are evident. For instance, optimizing can be a way of never making a decision because any given course of action might not be the "best" one. It is also an expensive approach to decision making in terms of the cost of counseling.

There is a continuum between minimal and optimal approaches. One of your tasks as a counselor is to help clients find the best "point" on this continuum for the decisions they must make. The "best point" depends on such variables as time available, the seriousness of the problem, the needs, wants, and resources of the client, and environmental constraints. However, it should be noted that people with problems usually fail to give *enough* consideration to decision-making processes: when clients face problems, they often drift toward the minimal end of the continuum.

Postdecision depression. Sometimes people get depressed after making a relatively important decision like buying a house or car or choosing a course of action to face up to some problem situation (see Janis & Mann, 1977). They keep asking themselves whether they could have made a better one. They feel sad that their resources are now committed. In a sense, they have given up some of their freedom and are in mourning for it. The best way to help clients manage such depression is to get them started in implementing the courses of action they have chosen.

The quirks of the decision-making process. The helping model described in these pages involves a great deal of decision making. Counselors help clients decide which issues to focus on, which scenarios to pursue, and which strategies to use. The rationality of the process is stressed. In real life, however, the decision-making process is never as straightforward and rational as it is in books.

[D]ecisions are influenced by many factors: by long-established habits, by deeply held beliefs and values, by assessments of risks and the prospects for personal or social gain, and by knowledge, which has the potential to affect all of the others. . . .

[I]n defining a problem, people dislike thinking about unpleasant eventualities, have difficulty in assigning . . . values to alternative courses of action, have a tendency toward premature closure, overlook or undervalue long-range consequences and are unduly influenced by the first formulation of the problem. In evaluating the consequences of alternatives, they attach extra weight to those risks that can be known with certainty. They are more subject to manipulation . . . when their own values are poorly thought through. . . . A major problem . . . for individuals is knowing when to search for additional information relevant to decisions [Goslin, 1985, pp. 7–9].

Many clients make decisions based on impulse, bias, and taste rather than on the analysis of information and values. Even when counselors help them use the logic of decision making outlined here, success is only partial. Indeed, helpers themselves do not escape this "shadow side" of the problem-solving and decision-making process. The box at the end of this chapter summarizes the topics you can use to evaluate your performance as you help clients to choose best fit strategies and to formulate action plans.

■ Is Step III-B Enough for Some Clients?

Yes, if this is what they need. Some clients are filled with great ideas for getting things done, but they never seem to do anything. They lack the discipline to evaluate their ideas, choose the best, and then cast them into a step-by-step plan. This kind of work seems too tedious for them, even though it is precisely what they need. Therefore, the first and only way you may be with this kind of client is as a planner or rather as a consultant to their planning. Questions such as: What are you going to do today? Tomorrow? The next day? may sound very simple, but it is surprising how much leverage they can provide.

■ Evaluation Checklist for Step III-B

How well am I doing the following as I try to help this client?

CHOOSING ACTION STRATEGIES

- Helping clients choose strategies that best fit their capabilities, personal and environmental resources, and environmental constraints
- Making sure that the chosen strategies are specific, verifiable, realistic, substantially related to the desired outcome, owned by the client, in keeping with the client's values, and set in a reasonable time frame
- Helping the client use the balance sheet as a way of choosing strategies, outlining principal benefits and costs for self, others, and relevant social settings
- Helping clients balance risk-taking behavior and probability of success.

HELPING CLIENTS TURN STRATEGIES CHOSEN INTO AN ACTION PLAN

- Helping clients overcome their resistance to planning
- Helping clients see the wisdom of formulating a plan instead of leaving action to chance
- Helping clients shape the plan in terms of goals and subgoals, while avoiding getting lost in details
- Determining the sequence of steps to be taken and the time frame for each
- Helping clients manage postdecisional depression
- Being careful to challenge clients when they plan to do too much too soon
- Helping clients develop contingency plans.

Twelve

Stage III: Step III-C
Action—Helping Clients
Implement Programs

■

Skills needed to help clients implement action programs
    Understanding inertia and entropy
    Force-field analysis: Forewarned is forearmed
    The use of "check" or "think" steps
    Training clients to be assertive in implementing programs
    Helping clients use self-contracts
    Helping clients get feedback
    Making use of the principles of behavior
Is Step III-C enough?
Evaluation questions for Step III-C
Cautions concerning Stage III

Some clients, once they have a clear idea of just what to do to handle a problem situation, go ahead and do it. They need little or nothing in terms of further support and challenge from a helper. They either find the resources they need within themselves or they get further support and challenge from the significant others in the social settings of their lives. Other clients, however, still need a greater or lesser degree of support and challenge from a helper at the implementation stage of the problem-solving process. For one reason or another they still feel uncertain about taking action. For instance, they still don't trust their own resources or they see the program as too demanding. Many clients fall somewhere between these two extremes. For instance, although a client may be able to handle most of the implementation process on her own, she may find that one part of the action program seems so difficult that she needs help with it.

■

Luisa, an unmarried woman in her early fifties, was living in a halfway house after a five-year stay in a mental hospital located in a rural area of the state. At the halfway house she had been trained in various social skills to help her cope with her new urban environment. The aim of the program was to help her develop greater independence, with the view of ultimately leaving the halfway house and living on her own. One of the programs involved helping her and other residents learn how to use the transportation system of the city. As part of the program she had already ridden both buses and subways to various locations in the city—for instance, the social security office, the state welfare office, and the park along the lake front—but the staff members had up to this point accompanied residents on those journeys. Luisa was now about to "solo," and she was frightened. The counselor helped her talk through her fears and encouraged her to take the short and simple trip that was the next part of the program. Luisa wanted to become more independent, but she had learned dependence in the hospital and was finding it hard to overcome.

■

Luisa needed help at the implementation stage. The training programs gave her some of the skills she needed to become more independent, but she still needed further support and challenge.

■ Skills Needed to Help Clients Implement Action Programs

Up to this point in the helping process *strategy* has been emphasized—that is, the overall action program or plan for achieving goals and objectives. In the implementation phase the focus is switched from strategy to *tactics* and *logistics*. Figure 12–1 adds the final step, Step III-C, to the helping model. Tactics is the art of being able to adapt a general plan to the immediate situation. This includes being able to change the plan on the spot in order to handle unforeseen complications. Logistics is the art of being able to provide the *resources* needed for the implementation of any given plan.

■

During the summer Rebecca wanted to take an evening course in statistics so that her first semester of the following school year would be lighter. Having more time would enable her to act in one of the

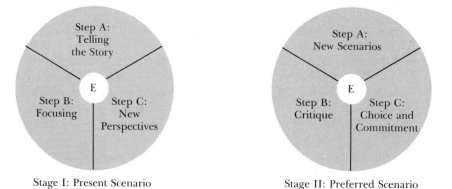

Stage I: Present Scenario   Stage II: Preferred Scenario

Stage III: Action—Getting
the New Scenario On Line

Figure 12–1. Step III-C: Action

school plays, a high priority for her. Her goal and program were adequate, but she didn't have the money to pay for the course when it was needed. At this university prepayment for summer courses was the rule. Rebecca had counted on paying for the course from her summer earnings, but that meant that she would not have the money until later. However, she did some quick shopping around and found that the same course was being offered by a community college not too far from where she had intended to go. Her tuition there was minimal since she was a resident of the area the college served. She switched schools.

■

In this example, Rebecca keeps to her overall plan (strategy). However, she adapts the plan to an unforeseen circumstance (tactics) by locating another resource (logistics).

All of us have experienced the common problems in trying to implement programs. We make plans and they seem realistic to us. We start into the initial steps of a program with a good deal of enthusiasm. However, we soon run into tedium, obstacles, and complications. What seemed so easy in the planning stage now seems quite difficult. We become discouraged, flounder, recover, flounder again, and finally give up, offering ourselves rationalizations as to why we did not want to accomplish those goals anyway.

■

Tina launched herself on a long-needed diet. She found that the novelty of the program carried her along for the first two weeks. However, during the third week the program lost its novelty, her ultimate goal seemed as distant as ever, and she kept reminding herself of how hungry she was. She became discouraged and depressed. During the middle of the fourth week, she quit the program. She talked about her probably incurable "glandular imbalance" and the stupid way our culture views "heavier" people.

■

Tina did not know the principles of effective implementation, nor did she have the skills to put them into practice.

The following strategies will enable you to help clients stick to programs. However, this does not mean that all strategies are to be applied to every action program of every client. Overburdening clients with too much "technology" is obviously self-defeating. Helpers who have the following strategies in their repertory of helping methods can use them when they judge that they will be useful. These strategies are understanding inertia and entropy, applying force-field analysis, using "check" steps, training clients to be assertive in implementing programs, making use of the principles of behavior, helping clients use self-contracts, and helping clients get feedback on performance.

Understanding Inertia and Entropy

Stage III of the helping process is sometimes called the "transition state" (Beckhard, 1977, 1985). It deals actively with the transition from the current, unacceptable state or scenario (Stage I) to the preferred scenario (Stage II). As Ferguson (1980) notes, clients often feel at risk during this state—it's the "trapeze" feeling. During the action or transition phase, clients are asked (or rather ask themselves) to let go of one trapeze bar—familiar but dysfunctional patterns of behavior—and grab ahold of a new trapeze bar—new and more productive patterns of behavior. For some, the time spent between the two bars is so terrifying that they need help in letting go of the first one. All action programs are subject to *inertia* (Egan, 1985), the tendency either to keep on doing the same old things or not to start new things. Put in its simplest form, action programs tend not to get off the ground.

Action plans are also subject to *entropy,* the tendency of things to fall apart over time. Put in its simplest form, if action programs do get off the ground, they tend to fall apart. Schramski and his associates (1984) review the factors that contribute to and inhibit the persistence of therapeutic change. For instance, clients whose socioeconomic status is low may well be at greater risk of deterioration once therapy is formally terminated. Clients are at risk if the environment does not support the action programs and lifestyle changes worked out in the helping sessions. Helpers need to become aware of factors that might contribute to entropy as clients work to change their lives.

None of this means that clients who get stuck or who "backslide" are exhibiting ill will. Rather, inertia and entropy are part of the human condition. If we don't monitor them, they get us—all of us. With respect to inertia, I often say to clients, "The action program you've come up with seems to be a sound one. The main reason that sound action programs don't work, however, is that they are never tried. Don't be surprised if you feel reluctant to act or are tempted to put off the first steps. That's quite natural. Ask yourself what you can do to get past that initial barrier." With respect to entropy, I might say, "Even sound action programs tend to fall apart over time, so don't be surprised when your initial enthusiasm seems to wane. That's only natural. Rather, ask yourself what you need to do to keep yourself at the task." Stein (1980) suggests that action programs need to be buttressed by "ratchets": strategies and tactics designed to keep programs in place, keep them from falling apart. Force-field analysis helps clients identify the ways in which entropy might sabotage their programs.

Force-Field Analysis: Forewarned is Forearmed

Force-field analysis (Lewin, 1969; Spier, 1973), despite its rather sophisticated name, is, conceptually at least, relatively simple and can be a useful tool in helping clients cope with obstacles and develop resources during the implementation of an action program.

> A force-field is the social-psychological field that immediately surrounds a decision or action. It includes the forces that compel or restrain against alternative actions as they are perceived by an individual. . . . An examination or analysis of an [client's] force field, especially one that focuses on the resources available and the obstacles to action, is frequently useful for four reasons: (a) by focusing on the [client's] perceptions of environmental influences, the nature of these perceptions becomes open to scrutiny, revision, . . . and test; (b) a complete account of obstacles and resources decreases the likelihood that pitfalls or potentials will be overlooked in the [execution of an action program]; (c) using knowledge of the influences in the [client's] environment helps to capitalize on opportunities . . . that go beyond the resources under a [client's] direct control; and (d) alternative strategies . . . to implement an [action plan] can be created and assessed in the context of the force field [Gottfredson, 1984, p. 1105].

Once clients see what their goals are and draw up plans to achieve them, they can be helped to discover what forces will keep them from implementing their programs (restraining forces) and what forces will help them implement those programs (facilitating forces). The first step, then, is the *identification* of both restraining and facilitating forces.

RESTRAINING FORCES

Restraining forces are the obstacles that might be encountered during the implementation process, while facilitating forces are the resources at hand for moving toward a goal. This process is illustrated in Figure 12–2. The identification of possible obstacles to the implementation of a program helps make clients forewarned.

■

Raul and Maria live in a large midwestern city. They have been married for about five years and have not been able to have children.

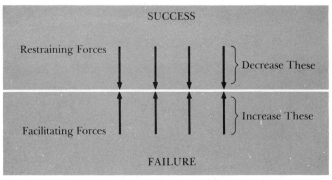

Figure 12–2. Force-field analysis

They finally decide that they would like to adopt a child, so they consult a counselor familiar with the adoption process. The counselor helps them work out a plan of action that includes examining their motivations and lifestyle, contacting an agency, and preparing themselves for an interview. After the plan has been worked out, Raul and Maria, with the help of the counselor, identify two restraining forces: the negative feelings that often arise on the part of prospective parents when they are being scrutinized by an adoption agency, and the feelings of helplessness and frustration caused by the length of time and uncertainty involved in the process.

■

The assumption here is that if clients are aware of some of the "wrinkles" that can accompany a course of action, they will be less disoriented when they encounter them. This part of the force-field analysis process is, at its best, a straight-forward census of probable pitfalls rather than a self-defeating search for every possible thing that could go wrong.

Once a restraining force is identified, ways of coping with it can be discussed. Sometimes simply being aware of a pitfall is enough to help clients mobilize their resources to handle it. At other times a more explicit coping strategy is needed. For instance, the counselor arranged a couple of role-playing sessions with Raul and Maria in which she played the role of the examiner at the adoption agency and took a "hard line" in her questioning. These rehearsals helped them stay calm during the actual interviews. The counselor also helped them locate a mutual-help group of parents working their way through the adoption process. The members of the group shared their hopes and frustrations and provided support for one another. In a word, Raul and Maria were trained to cope with the restraining forces they might encounter on the road toward their goal.

Restraining forces can come from within the clients themselves, from others, and from the social systems of their lives. Sometimes programs go awry because people fail to take into consideration the latter.

■

Horace had counted heavily on getting a loan to see him through his third year of college, but he put off applying for it. When he finally applied, it was a few months after national elections and a predicted push to control the federal budget deficits arrived on schedule. He had failed to consider what might happen to a federally funded loan program under such circumstances. By the time he applied for the loan, not only were there no funds available but he was told that it might be a year or more before new applications would be taken. He had to leave school and get a job.

■

Both clients and counselors can easily overlook environmental realities unless they are trained to assess them.

FACILITATING FORCES

In a more positive vein, force-field analysis can help clients identify important *resources* to be used in implementing programs. These are the facilitating forces. Facilitating forces can be persons, places, or things.

■

Shirley was going to stop smoking as part of a physical fitness program. She listed her mother as a facilitating force because she, too, had decided to quit. Shirley knew that their friendly vying with each other and the mutual encouragement that they got from talking to each other would provide much of the challenge and support they would need.

Les had let his social life get the better of his academic life, though he knew that his coming semester exams would be crucial. If he did not do well, he would be forced to leave school. He listed the smaller study rooms in the library among the facilitating forces in his study program. He found it easier to study when everyone around him was also studying. In the dorm he could always find someone to talk to and in the library's large study hall there were too many temptations to get together with friends. The people who went to the smaller rooms usually meant business.

Nora found it extremely depressing to go to her weekly dialysis sessions. She knew that without them she would die but wondered whether it was worth living if she had to depend on a machine. The counselor helped her see that she was making life more difficult for herself by thinking such discouraging thoughts. He helped her learn to concentrate on thoughts that would broaden her vision of the world instead of narrowing it down to herself, her pain and discomfort, and the machine. She was a religious person and found in the Bible a rich source of positive thinking. The day before she visited the clinic she began to prepare herself psychologically by reading from the Bible. Then, as she traveled to the clinic and underwent treatment, she meditated on what she had read.

■

In this last case the client substituted positive thinking, a facilitating force, for "stinkin' thinkin'," a restraining force.

SYSTEMATIC STEPS IN THE USE OF FORCE-FIELD ANALYSIS

The following steps may be followed in helping clients use force-field analysis.

1. Help clients list all the restraining forces that might keep them from participating in the program. Brainstorming is used in this step.

■

Deryl was about to join a fraternity as a way of helping himself develop a fuller social life. He identified the restraining forces that he thought might stand in the way of a successful fraternity experience, but made no attempt to rank them in order of importance. Deryl's list included the following:

- "I'm afraid to meet new people. I feel shy and inadequate, and I end up by running away or making myself as unobtrusive as possible."
- "I feel that I'm physically unattractive. I fear that I alienate people just by my looks."
- "I keep thinking of my past social failures—the friends I have alienated—and I fear that the same thing is going to happen in the fraternity."
- "I don't have anything interesting to say to others. My conversation is dull."

- "I'm awkward in my manner of presenting myself to others. For instance, because of my shyness and self-consciousness, I end up not listening to what people are saying. Then I can't respond to them and I feel stupid."
- "When I'm with people, in my anxiety I talk too much about myself. So others see me as self-centered and boring."
- "I want others to love me, but few even like me. My needs for attention are great and I'm looking for too much."

Deryl continues to list any further restraining forces, in whatever order they come tumbling from his mind. When he has finished, he sets his list aside and proceeds to the next step.

■

This process can be self-defeating if it merely depresses a client and makes him or her think that the action plan will not work.

2. Help clients list all the facilitating forces at work helping them participate in a program.   This step addresses resources. It forces clients to look at what they have going for themselves.

■

Deryl asks himself, "What do I have going for me?" He lists everything he can think of that might help him become a good member of the fraternity. His list includes the following:

- "I am a caring person. I care about others and would like to be helpful when I can."
- "I'm an intelligent human being. I'm smart enough to know what's called for in social situations, even though I'm awkward in responding."
- "Tom and Bill are members of the fraternity and they seem to see me as an ordinary guy."
- "I'm pretty lonely right now, so my motivation to do something about it is high."
- "I have a number of skills. I'm a good carpenter. I know how to manage finances. I've got something to contribute to the fraternity."

And Deryl continues to list any other facilitating forces that come to mind.

■

The client can treat the construction of these lists as a homework assignment and finish filling them out with the help of the counselor. Once the lists are reasonably complete, the client is ready for the next step.

3. Have clients underline the forces in each list (facilitating and re-straining) that seem most critical with respect to carrying out the action plan.   This helps simplify the process. Clients cannot deal with every facilitating and every restraining force. Some are more important than others.

■

Deryl now asks himself, "Which restraining forces are most critical as I join the fraternity? Which facilitating forces can help me the most?" As he reads the list of restraining forces, he notices a most important theme: he keeps telling himself in a variety of ways that he is not the kind of person that other people will like. He does himself in even before he meets others. In reading over the facilitating forces list, he is struck by the fact that two of the members of the fraternity relate to him as they would anyone else. That is, he begins to see that others are not saying to themselves or to one another all the negative things he's saying to himself.

■

Not every facilitating or restraining force need be uncovered and man-aged. Counselors can help clients deal with those that are seen to have the most leverage for the least cost. Good counselors help clients place their resources where the payoff will be greatest.

4. Help clients identify ways of reducing significant restraining forces and of strengthening significant facilitating forces.   Simple techniques are preferred.

■

Deryl, with the help of the counselor, hits on a simple way of decreas-ing restraining forces and increasing facilitating forces at the same time. Whenever he finds himself saying self-defeating things to himself about his ability to relate to others, he says to himself internally, "Stop!" Then he immediately says something to himself about a positive qual-ity he has that contributes to his ability to relate. In a word, he wants to stop *apologizing* for himself, whether those apologies are directed to himself or others. For instance, when he catches himself saying to himself, "You're not very physically attractive," he says, "Stop!" He then says something like, "Listen, you're not ugly or repulsive and even what you look like physically is perceived in terms of your human qualities, like your ability to care for others. The *total package* is at-tractive to others."

■

This technique helps Deryl get rid of a lot of the "static" or "noise" that has long surrounded his relationship to others. Note that force-field analysis need not be restricted to the action stage of the problem-management process. It can also be used in Step III-B, choosing new scenarios, and in Step III-A, choosing strategies.

The Use of "Check" or "Think" Steps

A practical concept that helps clients bridge the planning and implementation of programs is what Carkhuff and Anthony (1979) and Anthony, Pierce, and Cohen (1979) call "check" or "think" steps.

> Check steps are actually "question steps." That is, they indicate to clients what they should be asking themselves during the implementation stage. Check steps are used to guide clients' . . . performance. There are three types of check steps: "before" check steps; "during" check steps; and "after" check steps. As the names suggest, "before" check steps indicate what clients should think about before performing a certain behavior; "during" check steps indicate what clients should think about while performing the step; "after" check steps indicate what clients should think about after performing the step [Anthony, Pierce, & Cohen, 1979, p. 53].

These authors suggest that the last step before implementation of a course of action is to draw up a list of practical check steps.

The following example follows up on Luisa, the person who went to a halfway house after five years in a mental hospital.

■

Luisa has spent almost a year in the halfway house. She has gotten a decent part-time job and is now considering moving out of the halfway house as the next step toward becoming more independent. She does not yet feel ready to live on her own, and would like to live with a family or a friend for a while. The staff of the halfway house acts as an intermediary between its residents and families or individuals who are open to having residents live with them for a while. Luisa has a couple of friends and knows one family she might ask.

With the help of the counselor she decides to talk with a couple of families and a couple of single people. However, it is made clear to both parties that these chats are exploratory. No final decision is being made by either party on the basis of this one talk. This makes Luisa feel less pressured, but she still wants to put her best foot forward in these meetings. The counselor helps her deal with her misgivings by the use of check steps.

"BEFORE" CHECK STEPS:

- Is it clear in my mind what I want to say about myself?
- Am I going to these meetings with an open mind, without already feeling rejected?

"DURING" CHECK STEPS:

- Am I trying to be myself instead of some person I think these people would like me to be?
- Am I listening to these people, trying to understand their point of view?
- Am I ready to see some negative signs without getting down on myself or thinking ill of these people?
- What do I do if people seem to be putting me down or making a "case" of me—what do I do with my feelings?

"AFTER" CHECK STEPS:

- Am I avoiding letting myself get depressed because everything did not go perfectly?
- Is there anything I'd like to add to what I said to them?
- Do I have any further questions of the people I talked to?

Obviously check steps should be added to the program if they will be helpful. Cluttering up the program-development process with unneeded check steps can make clients overly self-conscious, however. A force-field analysis of the facilitating and restraining factors in the implementation of a program can help pinpoint the need for check steps.

Training Clients to Be Assertive in Implementing Programs

The implementation phase, by definition, places demands on clients to be assertive. If change is to take place, they must cease being "patients" and become "agents" in their own behalf. Lange and Jakubowski (1976) suggest a number of basic causes for a lack of assertiveness on the part of clients.

Clients may not know what they want. If clients' preferences, desires, and feelings are unclear, they will either not act or act aimlessly. This highlights the need for both clear preferred scenarios and clear courses of action to bring them into effect.

Clients may hold irrational beliefs that stand in the way of assertive behavior. Often clients are not even aware of the beliefs that keep them from implementing programs or that slow them down. They include such sentiments as the following:

"My rights are not important, at least not as important as others'."
"I am a fragile person. If I act, I will hurt myself."
"Others are fragile. If I act, I will hurt them."

"I am not entitled to express my own opinions either verbally or through action."

"If I act assertively, I will lose the affection and approval of others."

"If I act assertively, others will see me as "out of role" and consider me stupid or foolish."

"If I act I might fail, and failure is always disgraceful."

If it is clear to you that a client is plagued by irrational beliefs that are thwarting action, "cognitive restructuring" procedures may be useful both before and during the implementation of a program (see Bard, 1980; Ellis & Harper, 1975; Goldfried & Goldfried, 1980; Lange & Jakubowski, 1976; Meichenbaum & Genest, 1980).

Clients may lack skills and practice in assertiveness.   There is always some kind of "leap" to take between planning and action. For some clients this "leap" seems too great, especially if they have a history of nonassertiveness. Techniques such as rehearsal and roleplaying (see Lange & Jakubowski, 1976, Chapters 6 and 7) can help clients bridge the gap. Counselors who take a training-as-treatment approach to helping first make sure that clients have the skills they need to be assertive and then help clients make assertiveness demands on themselves throughout the helping process. In this case moving from planning to action is less of a leap for clients than it is in approaches to helping in which clients take a much more passive role.

Clients may stumble over their feelings and emotions.   Clients often feel overwhelmed by their feelings and emotions. When action stimulates emotions they are not used to handling well, they retreat. Feelings interfere with their ability to act assertively. According to Lange and Jakubowski, this can be seen as a skills deficit. "People may lack strategies for coping with their own excessive anxiety, anger, and guilt—feelings which interfere with their ability to act assertively" (p. 275). Clients may fail to implement programs because they have not developed strategies to cope with normal, but action-inhibiting, feelings.

■

Luisa, the middle-aged woman trying to make her way back into society, begins her meetings with people who might take her into their homes temporarily. In a meeting with a single person slightly older than herself, she feels as if she's being treated like a child. She gets angry but manages to keep it to herself. She sees no use in sabotaging the program just because of this woman's overprotectiveness.

■

Because Luisa had formulated the "during" check step—"What do I do if people seem to be putting me down during the meeting?"—she knew how to handle her anger. Instead of indulging in self-defeating angry remarks, she kept telling herself she was glad she found out what this person was like before it was too late.

Clients can tend to see themselves as the victims of their emotions. They develop an irrational belief—one that all of us fall prey to at one time or another—that "I can't control my feelings." They say "I can't" instead of "I don't." Failure to take responsibility for one's feelings and emotions is ultimately self-defeating (see Passons, 1975, pp. 186–192).

> First, he [that is, the person who does not see himself or herself as responsible for and in some way able to control his or her feelings] is "at the mercy" of his feelings rather than being the creator or master of them. As such, an unpleasant degree of powerlessness and, in some cases, hopelessness is experienced. Second, the person will be unable to dismiss or substitute an alternative feeling for one which is inappropriate or destructive for him. These both involve choices which the person is not aware of having. Third, the person will not know how he brought about his pleasant feelings and thereby does not have ready access to them [Passons, p. 186].

Some clients are so used to assuming that their problems are caused by others that they resist the idea of being responsible for their own feelings. Passons outlines some exercises that can help clients gain some degree of control over their emotional lives. These exercises can be used as preparation for program implementation.

While it is true that feelings and emotions arise spontaneously, it is also true that people can exercise control over the stimuli that elicit emotions and over the intensity of feelings and emotions once they do arise. For many clients this is a novel idea, and their first reaction might be one of skepticism. But research and practice has shown that they can learn simple "environmental-planning" (Thoresen & Mahoney, 1974) or "stimulus-control" (Goldiamond, 1965) methods to decrease the intensity of the emotion-arousing event. For instance, one client found that whenever she talked to her ex-husband alone, she would let her anger get the better of her. However, when she talked to him with at least one other person present, she was more relaxed during their discussions. On the occasions when she would be alone with him she found that "thought-stopping" methods (Cautela & Wisocki, 1977; Hackman & McLean, 1975; Rimm & Masters, 1974) helped quite a bit. That is, internally she would yell "Stop!" to herself when she began to dwell on the aspects of his behavior that were stimulating her anger. In this case, she could not control the stimuli, but she could control the amount of attention she paid to them.

Clients may lack the ability to discriminate between assertiveness and compliance and between assertiveness and aggression. As was pointed out earlier, clients often have difficulty seeing themselves as others see them. That is one of the reasons why the "new perspectives" step in the helping process is so important. But even when clients come to see that what they consider assertive in their behavior is actually a form of compliance, or that what they see as assertive is actually a form of aggression, they find it difficult to translate those insights into behavior. If that is the case, it is important for them to attempt to translate their insights into action *during the counseling sessions themselves,* so that they are prepared to make accurate discriminations during the implementation phase.

Helping clients become more assertive is another way of saying helping them take reasonable risks. Clients are usually not big risk-takers. If they are to take reasonable risks, they sometimes need a structure to help them do so.

Helping Clients Use Self-Contracts

As we have seen, a contract, whether implicit or explicit, gives direction to the helping process. Contracts are also useful in specific ways at the implementation stage. Clients can keep themselves on track in implementing action programs by setting up contracts with themselves that specify precisely what they are to do and indicate rewards for success and sanctions for failures (see Baucom, 1982; Cormier & Cormier, 1979, pp. 506–512; Rudestam, 1980, pp. 122–127). Many clients find it rewarding to make contracts with themselves and keep them. They see it as a reflection of their personal integrity. Such contracts are especially helpful for more difficult aspects of action programs; they help focus clients' energies. If a self-contract directly or indirectly involves things that others must do, those others need to be aware of and agree to its stipulations. Cormier and Cormier (1979, pp. 507, 509) outline the basic features of a contract:

- The contract terms should be negotiated, not proclaimed, by all involved parties (client, counselor, significant others).
- The contract terms should be clear to all involved parties. The behavior to be achieved and an acceptable criterion level should be specified.
- The contract should include a balance of rewards and sanctions appropriate to the desired behavior.
- Oral and written commitment to the contract should be obtained.
- The client (and any other person involved) should carry out the contractual procedures systematically and regularly.
- The contract should include a recording system (a progress log) that specifies the desired behavior, the amount (frequency or duration) of the behavior, and the rewards and sanctions administered. If possible, the recording system should be verified by one other person.
- The contract should be reviewed at a later time and revised if necessary.

• The counselor should provide reinforcement to the client as the client implements the contractual procedures.

These provisions apply to both the helping contract and self-contracts. Our focus now, however, is the latter.

■

Eunice and Edgar are involved in a deteriorating marriage. The assessment stage indicates that the problems are multiple. One aim agreed to by both of them is that the present chaos in the home needs to be reduced. For instance, Eunice does very little housework (neither does Edgar) and Edgar comes and goes as he pleases, missing meals (however poorly prepared) without notice. They seem to be deeply committed to punishing each other by this chaotic behavior. An initial contract to which both agree includes Eunice's keeping the house clean and orderly for a week and Edgar's sticking to a schedule that allows him to take care of work commitments but still leaves him time at home. Actually both are committing themselves to self-contracts, because each agrees to carry out his or her program despite what the other does.

■

In this case the contract proves most useful in introducing a degree of order into their home life. Neither counselor nor clients assume that fulfilling these contracts will solve all the problems of the relationship, but they are trying to create the kind of *climate* that will enable them to begin to work together to sort out issues critical to their marriage. Here is another example.

■

A boy in the seventh grade was causing a great deal of disburbance by his outbreaks in class. The usual kinds of punishment did not seem to work. The teacher talked it over with the school counselor, who called a meeting of all the stakeholders—the boy, his parents, the teacher, and the principal—and suggested this simple contract. When the boy disrupted the class, one and only one thing would happen: he would go home. Once the teacher identified his behavior as disruptive, he was to go to the principal's office and check out without receiving any kind of lecture. He was then to go immediately home and check in with whichever parent was there, again without receiving further punishment. The next day he was to return to school. All agreed to the contract, though both principal and parents said they would find it difficult not to add to the punishment.

During the first month the boy spent a fair number of days or partial days at home. In the second month, however, he missed only two partial days, the third month only one. He really wanted to be in school with his classmates. That's where the action was. And so he paid the price of self-control in order to get what he wanted. The contract proved an effective tool for behavioral change.

■

Counselors can use Cormier and Cormier's self-contract checklist to draw up and implement these agreements. When a contract is drawn up, the time when it is to be reviewed should be stipulated.

Helping Clients Find Social Support

Clients often find counseling goals both attractive and threatening. Since adherence to stressful decisions is painful, both social support and challenge (Janis, 1983a) can help them move to action, persevere in action programs, and maintain gains. We have already discussed how necessary it is to help isolated clients develop social resources. These resources are critical when clients are acting on their own. Protracted contact with the helper is usually not feasible and yet support is essential.

> Despite the enormous research literature on social influences . . . we still know relatively little about when, how, and why social support is effective in helping people change their actions. . . . In a recent review of pertinent research, Judith Rodin (in press) concludes that social support can buffer the individual from potentially unfavorable effects of all sorts of crises and environmental changes by facilitating coping and adaptation. She cites numerous empirical studies indicating that men and women who have social support from significant others . . . tend to manifest higher morale, to have fewer somatic illnesses, and to live longer than those who do not [p. 144].

Such support is not an admission of defeat or an abdication of the principles of self-responsibility advocated in Chapter One. Rather it is an exercise in common sense. Support groups and self-help groups (Gottlieb & Schroter, 1978; Pancoast, Parker, & Froland, 1983; Pearson, 1982, 1983) seem to be especially needed in socially fragmented and high-tech societies (Naisbitt, 1982). Effective helpers are aware of such resources in the community and are prepared to develop them if they do not exist.

Helping Clients Get Feedback on Performance

Gilbert (1978), in his book on human competence, claims that "improved information has more potential than anything else I can think of for creating more competence in the day-to-day management of performance" (p. 175). If clients are to be successful in implementing programs, they need adequate information about how well they are performing. The purpose of feedback is not to pass judgment on the performance of clients but rather to provide guidance and support. Feedback can be

- *Confirmatory*, when it lets clients know when they are on course—that is, moving successfully through the steps of an action program toward a goal
- *Corrective*, when it provides clients who have strayed with information they need in order to get back on course
- *Motivating*, when it points out the *consequences* of both adequate and inadequate program implementation.

According to Gilbert, good feedback does not eliminate client responsibility. He urges those who give feedback to "supply as much backup information as needed to help people troubleshoot *their own* performance" (p. 179, emphasis added). Furthermore, when people give corrective feedback, it should be *concrete*: it should "relate various aspects of poor performance to specific remedial actions" (p. 179).

SCENARIO 1

CLIENT: I can't seem to control myself. I want to stay on the diet, but sometimes almost without knowing what I'm doing I find myself eating. I followed it only a few times earlier in the week.

COUNSELOR A: You don't seem to be motivated enough to stop overeating. I think the diet plan we worked out together is a good one.

CLIENT: I think it's a good one, too. I seem to be lying to myself when I say that I want to lose weight.

SCENARIO 2

CLIENT: I can't seem to control myself. I want to stay on the diet, but sometimes almost without knowing what I'm doing I find myself eating.

COUNSELOR B: Tell me as concretely as possible what happened.

CLIENT: (describes what she did and didn't do the previous week with respect to dieting)

COUNSELOR B: Tell me what you think went wrong.

CLIENT: Well, I just blew it. I bought too much food, for one thing. And the wrong kinds of things.

COUNSELOR B: The times you followed your diet were early in the week, when your enthusiasm was still high. It seems that you have shown yourself you can do it when the incentives are there. As for the rest of the week, I see two problems. First of all, you forgot to set up immediate rewards for keeping to your diet schedule and perhaps mild punishments for not doing so. Second, you are probably right in thinking that you can do something about stimulus control. You couldn't have eaten what you did if it hadn't been in the refrigerator! But that seems fairly clear to you now.

Counselor A's "feedback" is vague and at least mildly judgmental. Counselor B offers some confirmatory and some corrective feedback without a judgmental tone.

Don't wait for perfect performance before giving encouraging or confirmatory feedback. Counselor B, in her last response, follows Krumboltz and Thoresen's (1976) suggestion to use Homme's "sandwiching" technique for feedback. The first "slice of bread" is some kind of encouragement or reinforcement for what was done right. The "filling" is a description of what was done wrong or a suggestion for improving performance. Finally, the second "slice of bread" is some kind of reinforcement.

According to McKeachie (1976, p. 824), feedback will be helpful if three conditions are met:

1. *Client motivation.* The person receiving the feedback should be motivated to improve. But as Gilbert (1978) and Watson and Tharp (1985) suggest, lack of motivation on the part of the client should not immediately be suspected if the implementation process is running into difficulty. Motivation has two aspects: the internal "motives" or values of the client and the incentives that bring those motives to life. If motivation seems to be a problem, look first at issues related to incentives, reinforcement, punishment, avoidance, extinction, and shaping before coming to the conclusion that the client is not motivated.

2. *Moderate dosages.* Feedback should provide an adequate but not excessive dose of information. Again, shaping is important here. If a client needs a lot of feedback, give it to her or him in doses that can be handled—information overload is a punishment rather than an incentive. In counselor training groups I consistently see a tendency in novice trainees to give one another feedback that is both vague and long-winded.

3. *Suggestions.* Good feedback helps clients identify and implement alternative approaches to implementing a program. This does not necessarily mean that it is the helper who always comes up with alternatives. Effective helpers leave as much responsibility for change as possible up to the client. In feedback sessions clients need not be given alternatives, but rather can be helped to uncover them.

SOURCES OF FEEDBACK

There are at least three sources of feedback available to clients: clients themselves, counselors, and significant others in their day-to-day environments.

Clients themselves.   We live in a society in which people think feedback necessarily comes from others. If people have a clear idea of what they want to accomplish, then they themselves should be the first source of feedback (Egan, 1985). The same is true in counseling. Effective helping is an enabling process. It teaches clients how to monitor their own behavior as they implement programs. Seeing themselves become more and more responsible for their own behavior can be extremely rewarding for clients and helpers alike. Clients can be trained to give themselves all three kinds of feedback: confirmatory, corrective, and motivating. However, if they are to do so, they must first be working toward clear and concrete goals and have a clear grasp of the step-by-step action programs leading to those goals. If strategies and goals are general and vague, feedback from whatever source will necessarily be general and vague. Also, as we have seen before, clients can learn to make the "right" comments to themselves instead of self-defeating ones. Sentences such as "You're on track" or "You really did that well" can be an important source of reinforcement.

The counselor. It goes without saying that counselors are also important sources of all three kinds of feedback, but the counselor's feedback should *complement* the feedback clients give themselves. Counselors who fail to give feedback often lack the skills reviewed earlier: basic empathy, information giving, advanced empathy, confrontation, and immediacy. Sometimes counselors, falling prey to the MUM effect described in Chapter Seven, fail to give direct, unequivocal feedback because they are afraid of clients' reactions. And yet clients usually find feedback—even corrective feedback—rewarding rather than punishing because, if given well, it is so useful in helping them achieve their goals.

Others. Ideally clients have one or more persons in their everyday lives on whom they can count for supportive and challenging feedback. It was suggested earlier that a common aim of the counseling process is to help clients get "into community." Getting into community includes developing complementary feedback resources.

■

Lamar had developed a drinking problem. He was not an alcoholic, but when he drank he became a different person. Ordinarily he was quite personable and thoughtful, but when he drank heavily he became harsh, loud, sarcastic, and manipulative. It became embarrassing to go to social events with him. Finally, his wife and a couple of his friends talked to him about the problem. They told him that although ordinarily he was a person of great interpersonal power (first "slice of bread"), when he began drinking heavily he lost his charm. They went on to describe his annoying behavior and how they felt about being with him at such times (the "filling"). They finished by telling him that when he drank moderately, he was great fun to be with and that everyone had a better time because of his pleasant, rather than biting, wit (second "slice of bread"). At his request they agreed to give him preventive feedback in drinking situations. For instance, in a social situation when he had been drinking moderately but had had enough, his wife or a friend would say something like, "It's fun being with you right now." This served to cue him that he was nearing his limit. He gradually learned to make that discrimination himself. All this was done without making Lamar an "identified patient" within his group of friends.

Direct, unequivocal feedback in day-to-day living is not common. Counselors can help clients develop such resources, however.

Making Use of the Principles of Behavior

Counselors can help clients make the principles of behavior such as reinforcement, punishment, extinction, avoidance, shaping, and the like work for rather than against them as they implement action programs.

INCENTIVES AND REWARDS

Clients are more likely to embark on any given step of a program if there are clear and meaningful incentives. Distant goals may not appear to be rewarding, so it is often necessary to help clients identify both the intrinsic and the extrinsic reinforcements or rewards for each step of any given course of action. Perhaps one of the best things a helper can do is to join a client in celebrating the successful completion of a step, or even in savoring the learnings that can come even from unsuccessful or only partially successful attempts to implement a program.

Randall is seeing a counselor associated with the county probation office. He has been given a suspended sentence for petty larceny and possession of drugs. One of his goals is to get a job, and the strategy leading to that goal includes identifying job possibilities, ranking them according to desirability, and checking them out one by one either through telephone calls or face-to-face interviews. He goes to his first interview with a relatively high degree of enthusiasm, but comes back somewhat dejected because they didn't think he was qualified for the job. He discusses his principal learning with his counselor: that finding a job is a full-time job in itself. Since he is going to be repeating the interview process a number of times, he asks himself, "What incentives will help me sustain my search?" At this point, the reward of actually getting a job is too distant. He and the counselor explore the possibilities. Some intrinsic reward may come from knowing that he has

352 PART FIVE HELPING CLIENTS ACT

put in a good day's work searching for a job. There will also be the support and encouragement he receives from the counselor for sticking to a task that can be discouraging. They also discuss the possibility of his participation in a weekly mutual-support group of people like himself looking for employment. Randall also thinks it important to reward himself for putting in a good day's search, or even after each job interview in which he feels he has done a reasonable job of presenting himself as an applicant. He thinks of such things as watching television, going to movies, spending time with friends, eating favorite foods, reading magazines, having a few beers, and other simple activities that might serve as extrinsic rewards. He then sets about choosing the incentives he thinks will work best and makes them contingent on successfully completing substeps in his job-search program.

■

This example may not be realistic in that it assumes a great deal of cooperation on the part of a kind of client not known for being cooperative. The example is used only to illustrate that incentives and rewards are important in the implementation of programs. Reluctant and resistant clients too, it should be remembered, are moved by incentives and work for rewards. If they do not cooperate, they obviously find not cooperating more rewarding (or less punishing) than cooperating. The search for incentives is a constant theme in the helping process, especially with reluctant and resistant clients.

Ideally, once self-enhancing behaviors are learned and developed, they become self-sustaining; that is, they generate their own positive consequences so that there is no longer any need for programmed reinforcement. If Susan, who is fearful of dating, embarks on a realistic course of action to develop relationships with men, the rewards found in relating well to men will hopefully sustain that behavior. There are, of course, certain disagreeable tasks in life that may always demand programmed reinforcement. The person who must submit to dialysis if she is to stay alive may have to engage in an ongoing search for reinforcers.

■ **Principle**

Don't immediately blame clients who do not participate in programs. It may be that they do not see strong enough short-term or even long-term incentives for doing so. Do work at helping clients find the kinds of intrinsic and extrinsic incentives that will help them stick to programs.

PUNISHMENT OR SANCTIONS

The use of punishment is ordinarily a relatively poor way of changing behavior. There are, of course, exceptions to this.

> Many of us have been brought up in the school of "sin and suffer." Consequently, self-punishment in the wake of symptomatic behavior may seem like a just reward and, paradoxically, *increase* the future likelihood of the behavior [Rudestam, 1980, p. 128].

In this case, the grief and frustration associated with searching for a job would actually increase the likelihood that the client would continue his or her search. However, it is best not to count heavily on the "sin and suffer" school of thought in clients, even when they seem to be good students of that school.

■

Moira was avoiding a complete physical checkup even though certain physical symptoms were persisting. She planned on taking a weekend trip to see a very good friend. She contracted with herself to put off the trip until she had had the checkup.

■

Moira terminated her procrastinating behavior by withholding a reward.

Rudestam suggests a caution in the use of self-punishment. "Be sure that the penalty you pay for undesirable behavior is something you can afford to lose" (p. 130).

■

Beatrice was both gregarious and a heavy eater. She decided that whenever she even opened the door of the refrigerator after supper, she would call a friend and cancel some upcoming social event. She soon discovered that she was punishing not just herself but others too. Also, on the days that this self-punishment technique made people disappear from her life, she was more tempted than ever to eat. She soon discovered that this form of self-punishment was something she could ill afford.

■

Self punishment is not a goal, but an aid in getting action programs in place.

It is not sufficient to punish negative behavior. You also need to encourage alternative, more desirable behaviors by reinforcing them.

■

Constance, an elderly widow, would put off her flexibility exercises when her arthritis flared up even a bit, so she contracted with herself not to turn on music until she had done them. When she did her exercises even with pain in her joints, she rewarded herself with a brief long-distance call to a close friend who had moved to a neighboring state. It was a luxury, but one she could still afford.

■

Punishment works best when it is not used in isolation—it leaves a bad taste in the mouth. It is far more effective when coupled with incentives and rewards.

■ **Principle**

Although punishment is usually a poor way of changing behavior, in some cases clients can be helped to stick to programs by a reasonable use of self-punishment. However, since punishment is related to decreasing and eliminating unconstructive behavior, make sure that clients couple this approach with rewards for carrying out the steps of a program.

AVOIDANCE

Avoidance mechanisms are potent restraining forces in the implementation of programs. Avoidance will take place if the rewards for *not* doing something are stronger than the rewards for doing it. In your dealings with clients at the implementation stage, it can be a mistake to confuse avoidance with ill will. All of us have a tendency to put off the difficult or distasteful, and we break out of that pattern only under certain conditions. If clients are not implementing some step of a program, if they are putting it off, or if they are implementing it in only a desultory way, use the following checklist:

· What punishing consequences would result from implementing any given step of a program and what can be done to minimize them?
· What rewards are there for *not* implementing a step and how can they be neutralized?
· Is there a reasonable but firm time line for completing the step?
· Are there rewards for completing the step, and are they clear to the client and suited to his or her needs and wants?

■ **Principle**

Never underestimate the power of incentives and rewards for *not* doing things. If clients are avoiding participating in action programs, help them increase the rewarding consequences and decrease the punishing consequences of participating.

EXTINCTION

If any given step is seen by the client as neither rewarding *nor* punishing, the client's behavior is likely to *extinguish*—that is, grind to a halt. In such cases clients will often express ignorance of why they have stopped implementing a program.

COUNSELOR: Tell me how your diet has been going.
CLIENT: Well, I think I've sort of fallen off the wagon.
COUNSELOR: You found it too difficult.
CLIENT: No, it was reasonable. I wasn't starving myself. In fact, when I was busy, I didn't even notice I was on it.
COUNSELOR: Then it's not clear why you let it go.
CLIENT: I don't know. It wasn't really a decision. I just trailed off.

This client felt neither any punishing effects from dropping the diet *nor* any particular reward for sticking to it. Dieting behavior extinguished. Simple extinction is a common form of entropy.

■ **Principle**

Help clients specify incentives for sticking to action programs. In the absence of specific incentives and rewards, action programs may grind to a halt.

SHAPING

Shaping can mean the rewarding of gradual movements toward a desired goal or scenario. For instance, a patient in a mental hospital is rewarded for getting up in the morning even though she merely lounges around and remains ungroomed. This is at least a step toward a more acceptable lifestyle. Shaping can also refer to the proper sequencing of behaviors toward a goal together with seeing to it that there are incentives for carrying out each step (Bandura & Schunk, 1981). Consider the following interchanges.

COUNSELOR A: Perhaps we could review how your diet is going.
CLIENT (sheepishly): Well, as you know, I had been eating over 3000 calories a day and it seemed reasonable to drop down to 1500 for a few weeks. But to be honest, this past week I've averaged about 1900 a day.
COUNSELOR A: You probably feel bad about violating the contract you made with yourself. Let's review the contract once more and find out what's going wrong.

COUNSELOR B: What do you think would be best to focus on today?
CLIENT (sheepishly): I think I should talk about my diet. I had contracted to move from over 3000 down to 1500 calories a day. And I haven't done it. I've only managed to drop to around 1900 a day.

COUNSELOR B: You sound a bit down on yourself.

CLIENT: Well, I think I should be. I did fail.

COUNSELOR B: You talk as if you failed totally.

CLIENT: Well, I did *something*, but not everything I wanted to do.

COUNSELOR B: Well, you *didn't* do everything but you also *did* do something. It's possible to celebrate what you did and use it as a springboard for what you want to do.

Counselor B chooses to reinforce an approximation to a goal rather than dwell on a contractual failure. The difference between Counselor A and Counselor B is not that the latter is soft while the former is hard-nosed. The important thing is the actual implementation of programs that achieve goals. In this example, shaping in the sense of rewarding an approximation to a goal seems to make more sense than the rigid fulfillment of a contract.

■ Principle

Help clients who are having difficulty involving themselves in programs move through small steps toward their goals. Help them emphasize what they are doing right.

The steps leading to a remote goal are sometimes called *proximal* goals. Research shows that "self-motivation is best summoned and sustained by adopting attainable subgoals that lead to large future ones" (Bandura, 1982, p. 134).

Not all the suggestions in this chapter will be used with all clients or with any single client. Each one has to be viewed in terms of both his or her needs and his or her capabilities. Therefore, the process needs to be adapted to the resources of the person, while helping him or her stretch a bit.

As indicated earlier, Stage III will in practice overlap the other two stages. "Skipping around" will not be unusual but, since you as helper know the territory, you can act as guide. You will be able to help clients see the difference between random behavior and creative violations of the model's linearity. Therefore, like the steps of previous stages, the steps of Stage III will also in practice overlap one another, as illustrated in Figure 12–3. For instance, clients may act on their own hunches before spending time developing a range of action strategies from which to choose. Or they may make step-by-step plans and then ignore the order of the steps—sometimes creatively, sometimes not. The main problem, of course, would be no action at all. The box that follows summarizes the main points of Step III-C to help you evaluate your performance as you help clients implement action programs.

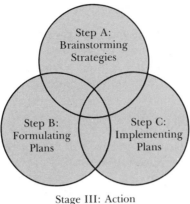

Stage III: Action

Figure 12–3. Overlap in the steps of Stage III

■ Is Step III-C Enough for Some Clients?— A Final Look at Evaluation

It is not uncommon to have clients who are already acting on their own behalf but need help to stay on target. With a little guidance, support, and challenge from a helper, they do quite well. However, some clients at this stage may have to backtrack. They may be having trouble because:

• they have failed to identify the problem clearly and accurately;
• they are working on the wrong problem;
• they are still being lead astray by their blind spots;
• they have no clear idea of what they really want;
• they have set unrealistic goals;
• they are not committed to the goals they have set;
• the strategies they have chosen to use are ineffective;
• they have no real plan and are going off in all directions at once.

The helping process, whether carried out by clients themselves or in conjunction with helpers, is cumulative. Mistakes made at an early stage of the process come back to haunt clients at the time of action. Whenever a client comes to you, you need to discover what step he or she has reached in the problem-management process and what foundation has been laid for it. If the client is not prepared to do the work of any given step, return to a step that will provide leverage. The ultimate evaluation question is always: "Is the client managing his or her life better through his or her interactions with you?"

■ Cautions Concerning Stage III

Balking at the mechanistic flavor of systematic behavioral-change programs. A friend of mine, after reading a short book dealing with a comprehensive problem-solving methodology even more extensive and complicated than the one outlined here, exclaimed, "Who would go through all that?" There is a problem inherent in any comprehensive problem-solving methodology: it can be overly analytic, and unskilled helpers and clients can both get lost in detail. They can be used by the methodology instead of using it. The caution mentioned a number of times already bears repeating here: this methodology is not an end in itself; it should be expanded or abridged or laid aside according to the needs of the client. The process should only be as detailed as is necessary to stimulate effective action. Weick (1969, 1979) counsels against overplanning.

> The point is simply that planning can insulate members from the very environment which they are trying to cope with. Planning in the absence of action is basically unconstrained; the only actions available for reflective attention are the planning acts themselves. The members can learn more and more about how to plan and how they are planning, but they can lose sight of what they were originally planning for [1969, p. 103].

Counseling can involve too much talk and too little action. While it is true that a client's being with a helper in an emotionally reeducative way and learning to revalue himself or herself can be a constructive action program in itself, most clients need more than that. There is a life "out there" that needs to be managed more effectively. Planning means putting order and reason into experience. Problem solving that is not based on the relevant experience of the client is doomed from the outset. Nor is problem solving an all-at-once process, because action produces reaction. When clients act differently toward their environment during the execution of an action program, the environment reacts, often enough, in unexpected ways. When the client's environment reacts, it is essential to modify previously planned action programs. Stage III demands a productive dialogue between planning and action.

The client who chooses not to change. There is a kind of inertia and passivity in the makeup of many people that makes change difficult and distressing for them. Therefore, some clients who seem to do well in Stages I and II of the counseling program end up by saying, in effect if not directly, something like this:

CLIENT: Even though I've explored my problems and understand why things are going wrong—that is, I understand myself and my behavior better and I realize the behavioral demands I should be making on myself—right now I don't want to pay the price called for by action. The price of more effective living is too high for me.

There are at least two kinds of client dropouts. Some are being helped by unskilled counselors and realize they are going nowhere. Others, with high-level counselors, may consider the price of change too high. The question of human motivation seems almost as enigmatic now as it has ever been. So often we seem to choose our own misery. Worse, we choose to stew in it rather than endure the relatively short-lived pain of behavioral change.

Never getting to Stage III.   Some low-level counselors stay in the safe waters of Stage I, exploring the client's problems in a rather circular way and hoping that the exploratory phase will suffice. Such helpers are ineffective even in what they think they are doing well, for counseling is about change and not problem exploration. High-level helpers are themselves doers, change agents in their own lives, and therefore at home with action programs. Some counselors are unable to help in the action phase of the counseling process because they themselves are basically passive people—nondoers. Therefore, in this respect they are not living more effectively than their clients and cannot be expected to help.

Starting with Stage III.   Some counselors move to action-oriented advice giving almost immediately. They fail to see that, in most cases, action for the sake of action is rootless. Stages I and II ordinarily provide the roots for action. Moving too quickly into action programs satisfies the needs of the helper rather than those of the client, violating one of the primary principles of counseling: helping is for the client. There is no problem in starting with Stage III if the groundwork has already been laid by the client himself or herself, or if there is an ongoing dialogue among all the stages.

■ Evaluation Checklist for Step III-C

How well am I doing the following as I try to help this client?

- Understanding how widespread both inertia and entropy are and how they are affecting this client
- Using force-field analysis to help clients discover and manage obstacles to action
- Using force-field analysis to help clients discover resources that enable them to act
- Helping clients use before, during, and after "think" steps as they implement programs
- Encouraging clients to develop the kind of assertiveness called for by their action programs
- Helping clients draw up and live up to realistic contracts with themselves
- Providing feedback for clients on the results of their action programs and encouraging them to seek out other sources of feedback.

THE USE OF THE PRINCIPLES OF BEHAVIOR

- Helping clients identify the kinds of incentives that move them toward action
- Making sure that clients use self-punishment sparingly and intelligently as a stimulus for action; helping them manage the punitive side-effects of the programs in which they are involved
- Making clients aware of the incentives and rewards that exist for avoiding action; helping them find incentives to counteract avoidance
- Helping clients shape their action programs, so that they do not try to do too much too soon, on the one hand, or too little, on the other.

Epilog

■

This book outlines a model of helping that is rational, linear, and systematic. "What good is that," you well may ask, "in a world that is often irrational, nonlinear, and chaotic?" One answer is that rational models help clients bring much needed discipline and order into their chaotic lives. And so, effective helpers do not apologize for using such models.

Helpers who understand and use the helping model found in this book, together with the skills and techniques that make it work, can be said to be "doing a smart thing." But it is not enough to be smart: Helpers must move from smart to wise. Effective helpers understand the limitations not only of helping models but also of helpers, the helping professions, clients, and the environments that affect the entire helping process. One dimension of wisdom is the ability to understand and manage these limitations, which constitute what I call the *arational* dimensions, or the "shadow side," of life. Helping models are flawed; helpers are sometimes selfish, lazy, and even predatory. Helpers are not immune to burnout. Clients are sometimes selfish, lazy, and predatory, even in the helping relationship; they are the joy and the curse of the helping professions.

Indeed, if the world were completely rational, the pool of clients would soon dry up, since many clients cause their own problems. However, there is no danger of this since, as Cross and Guyer (1980) note, people knowingly choose paths that lead to trouble. They go on to suggest that the popular view that people lacking foresight deserve what they get in life

> is itself based on the optimistic premise that human behavior is (or should be) determined by a goal-oriented intellectual process of evaluating alternative destinations and then following the path to the best one, rather than on the simpler and more direct procedure of permitting immediate rewards and punishments to dictate direction [p. 41].

Life is not a straight road; it is often more like a maze. It is not vanilla but fudge ripple with opposites such as good and evil, the comic and the tragic, cowardice and heroism inextricably intermingled.

The philosopher who said, "Know thyself," understood that it is too easy to be deceived about oneself. Part of the wisdom of Jesus can be attributed to the fact that "He knew what was in men and women." Both of these—knowing both yourself and others in caring, reflective, unvarnished ways—will help you develop the wisdom that enables you to move beyond the technology of helping, the helping alliance, and even the "real relationship" to the kind of authenticity celebrated by Rogers in *A Way of Being*. The ability to befriend the "shadow side" of yourself and your clients, without becoming its victim, is not the fruit of raw experience, but experience wrestled with, reflected on, and learned from, not mere reflection but meditation with yourself, your colleagues, your intimates, your demons, and your deities.

Bibliography

■

Adkins, W. R. (1984). Life skills education: A video-based counseling/learning delivery system. In D. Larson (Ed.), *Teaching psychological skills: Models for giving psychology away*. Monterey, Calif.: Brooks/Cole.

Alpert, J. L., & Rosenfield, S. (1981). Consultation and the introduction of social problem-solving groups in schools. *Personnel and Guidance Journal, 60*, 37–41.

American Psychiatric Association Commission on Psychotherapies (1982). *Psychotherapy research: Methodological and efficacy issues*. Washington, D. C.: American Psychiatric Association.

Anderson, C. M., & Stewart, S. (1983). *Mastering resistance: A practical guide to family therapy*. New York: Guilford Press.

Anthony, W. A. (1977). Psychological rehabilitation: A concept in need of a model. *American Psychologist, 32*, 658–662.

Anthony, W. A. (1979). *The principles of psychiatric rehabilitation*. Amherst, Mass.: Human Resource Development Press.

Anthony, W. A., Pierce, R. M., & Cohen, M. R. (1979). *The skills of rehabilitation programming*. Amherst, Mass.: Carkhuff Institute of Human Technology.

Argyris, C. (1982). *Reasoning, learning, and action*. San Francisco: Jossey-Bass.

Ashinger, P. (1985). Using social networks in counseling. *Journal of Counseling and Development, 63*, 519–521.

Bandura, A. (1977a). Self-efficacy: Toward a unifying theory of behavioral change. *Psychological Review, 84*, 191–215.

Bandura, A. (1977b). *Social learning theory*. Englewood Cliffs, N. J.: Prentice-Hall.

Bandura, A. (1980). Gauging the relationship between self-efficacy judgment and action. *Cognitive Therapy and Research, 4*, 263–268.

Bandura, A. (1982). Self-efficacy mechanism in human agency. *American Psychologist, 37*, 122–147.

Bandura, A., & Schunk, D. A. (1981). Cultivating competence, self-efficacy, and intrinsic interest through proximal self-motivation. *Journal of Personality and Social Psychology, 41*, 386–398.

Bard, J. A. (1980). *Rational-emotive therapy in practice*. Champaign, Ill.: Research Press.

Barrett-Lennard, G. T. (1981). The empathy cycle: Refinement of a nuclear concept. *Journal of Counseling Psychology, 28,* 91–100.

Baucom, D. H. (1982). A comparison of behavioral contracting and problem-solving/communications training in behavioral marital therapy. *Behavior Therapy, 13,* 162–174.

Bayless, O. L. (1967). An alternative pattern for problem-solving discussion. *Journal of Communication, 17,* 188–197.

Beck, J. T., & Strong, S. R. (1982). Stimulating therapeutic change with interpretations: A comparison of positive and negative connotation. *Journal of Counseling Psychology, 29,* 551–559.

Beckhard, R. (1985). *Managing change in organizations: Participant's workbook.* Reading, Mass.: Addison-Wesley.

Beckhard, R., & Harris, R. T. (1977). *Organizational transitions: Managing complex change.* Reading, Mass.: Addison-Wesley.

Beier, E. G., & Young, D. M. (1984). *The silent language of psychotherapy: Social reinforcement of unconscious processes (2nd ed.).* New York: Aldine.

Benjamin, A. (1981). *The helping interview (3rd ed.).* Boston: Houghton Mifflin.

Bennett, M. I., & Bennett, M. B. (1984). The uses of hopelessness. *American Journal of Psychiatry, 141,* 559–562.

Berensen, B. G., & Mitchell, K. M. (1974). *Confrontation: For better or worse.* Amherst, Mass.: Human Resource Development Press.

Berger, D. M. (1984). On the way to empathic understanding. *American Journal of Psychotherapy, 38,* 111–120.

Berger, P. L., & Neuhaus, R. J. (1977). *To empower people: The role of mediating structures in public policy.* Washington, D. C.: American Enterprise Institute for Public Policy Research.

Bergin, A. E. (1971). The evaluation of therapeutic outcomes. In A. E. Bergin & S. L. Garfield (Eds.), *Handbook of psychotherapy and behavior change.* New York: Wiley.

Bergin, A. E. (1980). Negative effects revisited: A reply. *Professional Psychology, 11,* 93–100.

Bergin, A. E., & Lambert, M. J. (1978). The evaluation of therapeutic outcomes. In S. L. Garfield & A. E. Bergin (Eds.), *Handbook of psychotherapy and behavior change: An empirical analysis (2nd ed.).* New York: Wiley.

Berne, E. (1964) *Games people play.* New York: Grove Press.

Bernstein, B. L., & LeComte, C. (1979). Self-critique technique training in a competency-based practicum. *Counselor Education and Supervision, 19,* 69–76.

Black, D. R., & Scherba, D. S. (1983). Contracting to problem solve versus contracting to practice behavioral weight loss skills. *Behavior Therapy, 14,* 100–109.

Block, P. (1981). *Flawless consulting: A guide to getting your expertise used.* Austin, Texas: Learning Concepts.

Bobbe, R. A., & Schaffer, R. H. (1968). *Mastering change: Breakthrough projects and beyond.* AMA Management Bulletin, No. 120. New York: American Management Association.

Brabeck, M. M., & Welfel, E. R. (1985). Counseling theory: Understanding the trend toward eclecticism from a developmental perspective. *Journal of Counseling and Development, 63,* 343–348.

Brady, J. P. (1984a). Social skills training for psychiatric patients, I: Concepts, methods, and clinical results. *American Journal of Psychiatry, 141,* 333–340.

Brady, J. P. (1984b). Social skills training for psychiatric patients, II: Clinical outcome studies. *American Journal of Psychiatry, 141,* 491–498.

Brammer, L. (1973). *The helping relationship: Process and skills.* Englewood Cliffs, N. J.: Prentice-Hall.

Brammer, L., & Shostrom, E. (1977). *Therapeutic psychology: Fundamentals of actualization counseling and psychotherapy (3rd ed.).* Englewood Cliffs, N. J.: Prentice-Hall.

Bransford, J. D., & Stein, B. S. (1984). *The ideal problem solver: A guide for improving thinking, learning, and creativity.* New York: Freeman.

Braswell, M., & Seay, T. (1984). *Approaches to counseling and psychotherapy.* Prospect Heights, Ill.: Waverly.

Brickman, P., Rabinowitz, V. C., Karuza, Jr., J., Coates, D., Cohn, E., & Kidder, L. (1982). Models of helping and coping. *American Psychologist, 37,* 368–384.

Brilhart, J. K., & Jochem, L. M. (1964). Effects of different patterns on outcome of problem-solving discussion. *Journal of Applied Psychology, 45,* 175–179.

Bronfenbrenner, U. (1977). Toward an experimental ecology of human development. *American Psychologist, 32,* 513–531.

Brown, S. (1983). Coping skills training: Attitude toward mental illness, depression, and quality of life 1 year later. *Journal of Counseling Psychology, 30,* 117–120.

Buber, M. (1970. Originally published 1937). *I and thou.* New York: Scribner's.

Burke, J. P., Haworth, C. E., & Brantley, J. C. (1980). Scientific problem solver model: A resolution for professional controversies in school psychology. *Professional Psychology, 11,* 823–832.

Caplan, N., & Nelson, S. D. (1973). The nature and consequences of psychological research on social problems. *American Psychologist, 28,* 199–211.

Carkhuff, R. R. (1969a). *Helping and human relations.* Vol. I: *Selection and training.* New York: Holt, Rinehart, & Winston.

Carkhuff, R. R. (1969b). *Helping and human relations.* Vol. II: *Practice and research.* New York: Holt, Rinehart, & Winston.

Carkhuff, R. R. (1971a). *The development of human resources.* New York: Holt, Rinehart, & Winston.

Carkhuff, R. R. (1971b). Training as a preferred mode of treatment. *Journal of Counseling Psychology, 18,* 123–131.

Carkhuff, R. R. (1985). *The exemplary organization.* Amherst, Mass.: Human Resource Development Press.

Carkhuff, R. R., & Anthony, W. A. (1979). *The skills of helping: An introduction to counseling.* Amherst, Mass.: Human Resource Development Press.

Carkhuff, R. R., & Berensen, B. G. (1976). *Teaching as treatment.* Amherst, Mass.: Human Resource Development Press.

Cautela, J. R., & Wisocki, P. A. (1977). The thought stopping procedure: Description, application, and learning theory interpretations. *Psychological Record, 27,* 255–264.

Cavanaugh, M. E. (1982). *The counseling experience.* Monterey, Calif.: Brooks/Cole.

Center for Constructive Change (1984). How intentional is your life? *Journal for Constructive Change, 6* (1), 16–17. (The entire issue deals with intentionality.)

Chamberlain, P., Patterson, G., Kavanagh, K., & Forgatch, M. (1984). Observations of client resistance. *Behavior Therapy, 15,* 144–155.

Chelune, G. (1975). *Self-disclosure: An elaboration of its basic dimensions. Psychological Reports, 36,* 79–85.

Chelune, G. (1977). Disclosure flexibility and social-situational perceptions. *Journal of Consulting and Clinical Psychology, 45,* 1139–1143.

Chelune, G. J. (Ed.) (1979). *Self-disclosure: Origins, patterns, and implications of openness in interpersonal relationships.* San Francisco: Jossey-Bass.

Claiborn, C. D. (1979). Counselor verbal intervention, nonverbal behavior, and social power. *Journal of Counseling Psychology, 26,* 378–383.

Claiborn, C. D. (1982). Interpretation and change in counseling. *Journal of Counseling Psychology, 29,* 439–453.

Clark, K. B. (1980). Empathy: A neglected topic in psychological research. *American Psychologist, 35,* 187–190.

Clifford, J. S. (1983). Self-efficacy counseling and the maintenance of sobriety. *Personnel and Guidance Journal, 62,* 111–114.

Cole, H. P., & Sarnoff, D. (1980). Creativity and counseling. *Personnel and Guidance Journal, 59,* 140–146.

Combs, A. (1965). *The professional education of teachers.* Boston: Allyn & Bacon.

Combs, A. (1982). *A personal approach to teaching: Beliefs that make a difference.* Boston: Allyn & Bacon.

Conyne, R. K., & Clack, R. J. (1981). *Environmental assessment and design.* New York: Praeger.

Cooper, T. D., & Lewis, J. A. (1983). The crisis of relativism: Helping counselors cope with diversity. *Counselor Education and Supervision, 22,* 290–295.

Corey, G. (1986). *Theory and practice of counseling and psychotherapy.* Monterey, Calif.: Brooks/Cole.

Cormier, W. H., & Cormier, L. S. (1979). *Interviewing strategies for helpers: A guide to assessment, treatment, and evaluation.* Monterey, Calif.: Brooks/Cole.

Cormier, W. H., & Cormier, L. S. (1985). *Interviewing strategies for helpers: Fundamental skills and cognitive behavioral interventions (2nd ed.).* Monterey, Calif.: Brooks/Cole.

Corrigan, J. D., Dell, D. M., Lewis, K. N., & Schmidt, L. D. (1980). Counseling as a social influence process: A review. *Journal of Counseling Psychology Monograph, 27,* 395–431.

Corsini, R. (1984). *Current psychotherapies (3rd ed.).* Itasca, Ill.: Peacock.

Cowen, E. L. (1982). Help is where you find it. *American Psychologist, 37,* 385–395.

Coyne, J. C., & Widiger, T. A. (1978). Toward a participatory model of psychotherapy. *Professional Psychology, 9,* 700–710.

Cozby, P. C. (1973). Self-disclosure: A literature review. *Psychological Bulletin, 79,* 73–91.

Cross, J. G., & Guyer, M. J. (1980). *Social traps.* Ann Arbor, Mich.: University of Michigan Press.

Crutchfield, R. S. (1969). Nurturing the cognitive skills of productive thinking. In *Life skills in school and society*. Washington, D. C.: Association for Supervision and Curriculum Development.

Cummings, N. A. (1979). Turning bread into stones: Our modern antimiracle. *American Psychologist, 34,* 1119–1129.

Daly, M. J., & Burton, R. L. (1983). Self-esteem and irrational beliefs: An exploratory investigation with implications for counseling. *Journal of Counseling Psychology, 30,* 361–366.

Danish, S. J., D'Augelli, A. R., & Brock, G. W. (1976). An evaluation of helping skills training: Effects on helpers' verbal responses. *Journal of Counseling Psychology, 23,* 259–266.

Davis, G. A., & Manske, M. E., (1966). An instructional method of increasing originality. *Psychonomic Science, 6,* 73–74.

Deffenbacher, J. L. (1985). A cognitive-behavioral response and a modest proposal. *Counseling Psychologist, 13,* 261–269.

Deforest, C., & Stone, G. L. (1980). Effects of sex and intimacy on self-disclosure. *Journal of Counseling Psychology, 27,* 93–96.

Derlega, V. J., & Grzelak, J. (1979). Appropriateness of self-disclosure. In G. J. Chelune (Ed.), *Self-disclosure: Origins, patterns, and implications of openness in interpersonal relationships*. San Francisco: Jossey-Bass.

Derlega, V. J., Lovell, R., & Chaikin, A. L. (1976). Effects of therapist self-disclosure and its perceived appropriateness on client self-disclosure. *Journal of Consulting and Clinical Psychology, 44,* 866.

Deutsch, M. (1954). Field theory in social psychology. In G. Lindzey (Ed.), *The handbook of social psychology*. Vol. I. Cambridge, Mass.: Addison-Wesley.

Dimond, R. E., Havens, R. A., & Jones, A. C. (1978). A conceptual framework for the practice of prescriptive eclecticism in psychotherapy. *American Psychologist, 33,* 239–248.

Dirkes, M. A. (1978). The role of divergent production in the learning process. *American Psychologist, 33,* 815–820.

Dixon, D. N., Heppner, P. P., Petersen, C. H., Ronning, R. R. (1979). Problem-solving workshop training. *Journal of Counseling Psychology, 26,* 133–139.

Dorn, F. J. (1984). *Counseling as applied social psychology: An introduction to the social influence model*. Springfield, Ill.: Charles C Thomas.

Doster, J. A., & Nesbitt, J. G. (1979). Psychotherapy and self-disclosure. In G. J. Chelune (Ed.), *Self-disclosure: Origins, patterns, and implications of openness in interpersonal relationships*. San Francisco: Jossey-Bass.

Dreikurs, R. (1967). Goals in psychotherapy. In A. Maher (Ed.), *The goals of psychotherapy*. New York: Appleton-Century-Crofts.

Dumont, M. P. (1984). The nonspecificity of mental illness. *American Journal of Orthopsychiatry, 54,* 326–334.

Dyer, W. W., & Vriend, J. (1975). *Counseling techniques that work: Applications to individual and group counseling*. Washington, D. C.: APGA Press.

D'Zurilla, T. J., & Goldfried, M. R. (1971). Problem solving and behavior modification. *Journal of Abnormal Psychology, 78,* 107–126.

D'Zurilla, T. J., & Nezu, A. (1980). A study of the generation-of-alternatives process in social problem solving. *Cognitive Therapy and Research, 4,* 67–72.

Edelwich, J. (1980). *Burn-out: Stages of disillusionment in the helping professions.* New York: Human Sciences Press.

Egan, G. (1970). *Encounter: Group processes for interpersonal growth.* Monterey, Calif.: Brooks/Cole.

Egan, G. (1976). *Interpersonal living: A skills-contract approach to human-relations training in groups.* Monterey, Calif.: Brooks/Cole.

Egan, G. (1977). *You and me: The skills of communicating and relating to others.* Monterey, Calif.: Brooks/Cole.

Egan, G. (1984). People in systems: A comprehensive model for psychosocial education and training. In D. Larson (Ed.), *Teaching psychological skills: Models for giving psychology away.* Monterey, Calif.: Brooks/Cole.

Egan, G. (1985). *Change agent skills in helping and human-service settings.* Monterey, Calif.: Brooks/Cole.

Egan, G. (1986). *Exercises in helping skills (3rd ed.)* Monterey, Calif.: Brooks/Cole.

Egan, G., & Cowan, M. A. (1979). *People in systems: A model for development in the human-service professions and education.* Monterey, Calif.: Brooks/Cole.

Egan, G., & Cowan, M. A. (1980). *Moving into adulthood: Themes and variations in self-directed development for effective living.* Monterey, Calif.: Brooks/Cole.

Ekman, P. (1982). *Emotion in the human face (2nd ed.).* New York: Cambridge University Press.

Ekman, P., & Friesen, W. V. (1969). The repertoire of nonverbal behavior: Categories, origins, usage, and coding. *Semiotica, 1,* 49–98.

Ellis, A. (1962). *Reason and emotion in psychotherapy.* New York: Lyle Stuart.

Ellis, A. (1971). *Growth through reason.* Palo Alto, Calif.: Science and Behavior Books.

Ellis, A. (1973). *Humanistic psychotherapy: The rational-emotive approach.* New York: Julian Press (also New York: McGraw-Hill Paperbacks, 1974).

Ellis, A. (1974). *Disputing irrational beliefs (DIBS).* New York: Institute for Rational Living.

Ellis, A. (1977a). The basic clinical theory of rational-emotive therapy. In A. Ellis & R. Grieger (Eds.), *Handbook of rational-emotive therapy.* New York: Springer.

Ellis A. (1977b). Rational-emotive therapy: Research data that support the clinical and personality hypotheses of RET and other modes of cognitive-behavior therapy. *Counseling Psychologist, 7* (1), 2–42.

Ellis, A. (1979). *New developments in rational-emotive therapy.* Monterey, Calif.: Brooks/Cole.

Ellis, A. (1982). A reappraisal of rational-emotive therapy's theoretical foundations and therapeutic methods: A reply to Eschenroeder. *Cognitive Therapy and Research, 6,* 393–398.

Ellis, A. (1984). Must most psychotherapists remain as incompetent as they are now? In J. Hariman (Ed.), *Does psychotherapy really help people?* Springfield, Ill.: Charles C Thomas.

Ellis, A. (1985). *Overcoming resistance: Rational-emotive therapy with difficult clients.* New York: Springer.

Ellis, A., & Harper, R. A. (1975). *A new guide to rational living.* Englewood Cliffs, N. J.: Prentice-Hall.

Erikson, E. H. (1964). *Insight and responsibility.* New York: Norton.

Eschenroeder, C. (1982). How rational is rational-emotive therapy? A critical appraisal of its theoretical foundations and therapeutic methods. *Cognitive Therapy and Research, 6,* 381–392.

Evans, H. M. (1984). Increasing patient involvement with therapy goals. *Journal of Clinical Psychology, 40,* 728–733.

Eysenck, H. J. (1984). The battle over psychotherapeutic effectiveness. In J. Hariman (Ed.), *Does psychotherapy really help people?* Springfield, Ill.: Charles C Thomas.

Farrelly, F., & Brandsma, J. (1974). *Provocative therapy.* Cupertino, Calif.: Meta Publications.

Feingold, S. N. (1984). Emerging careers: Occupations for post-industrial society. *The Futurist, 18,* (1), 9–16.

Felton, B. J., & Revenson, T. A. (1984). Coping with chronic illness: A study of illness controllability and the influence of coping strategies on psychological adjustment. *Journal of Consulting and Clinical Psychology, 52,* 343–353.

Ferguson, M. (1980). *The aquarian conspiracy: Personal and social transformation in the 1980's.* Los Angeles: J. P. Tarcher.

Festinger, S. (1957). *A theory of cognitive dissonance.* New York: Harper & Row.

Fine, M. J. (1985). Intervention from a systems-ecological perspective. *Professional Psychology, 16,* 262–270.

Fordyce, M. W. (1977). Development of a program to increase personal happiness. *Journal of Counseling Psychology, 24,* 511–521.

Fordyce, M. W. (1983). A program to increase happiness: Further studies. *Journal of Counseling Psychology, 30,* 483–498.

Fordyce, W. E. (1976). *Behavioral methods for control of chronic pain and illness.* St. Louis: Mosby.

Frances, A., Clarkin, J., & Perry, S. (1984). *Differential therapeutics in psychiatry.* New York: Brunner/Mazel.

Frank, J. D. (1973). *Persuasion and healing (2nd ed.).* Baltimore: Johns Hopkins University Press.

Freire, P. (1970). *Pedagogy of the oppressed.* New York: Seabury.

Frese, M., & Sabini, J. (Eds.) (1985). *Goal directed behavior: The concept of action in psychology.* Hillsdale, N. J.: Lawrence Erlbaum Associates.

Fretz, B. R., Corn, R., Tuemmler, J. M., & Bellet, W. (1979). Counselor nonverbal behaviors and client evaluations. *Journal of Counseling Psychology,* 304–311.

Frey, D. H., & Raming, H. E. (1979). A taxonomy of counseling goals and methods. *Personnel and Guidance Journal, 58,* 26–33.

Galbraith, J. K. (1979). *The nature of mass poverty.* Cambridge, Mass.: Harvard University Press.

Gallo, P. S., Jr. (1978). Meta-analysis—A mixed meta-phor? *American Psychologist, 33,* 515–517.

Gambrill, E. (1984). Social skills training. In D. Larson (Ed.), *Teaching psychological skills: Models for giving psychology away.* Monterey, Calif.: Brooks/Cole.

Garfield, S. L., & Kurtz, R. (1974). A survey of clinical psychologists: Characteristics, activities, and orientations. *The Clinical Psychologist, 28,* 7–10.

Garfield, S. L., & Kurtz, R. (1977). A study of eclectic views. *Journal of Consulting and Clinical Psychology, 45,* 78–83.

Gartner, A., & Riessman, F. (1977). *Self-help in the human services.* San Francisco: Jossey-Bass.

Gartner, A., & Riessman, F. (Eds.) (1984). *The self-help revolution.* New York: Human Sciences Press.

Gazda, G. M. (1973). *Human relations development: A manual for educators.* Boston: Allyn & Bacon.

Gazda, G. M. (1982). Life skills training. In E. K. & P. D. Kurtz (Eds.), *Interpersonal helping skills: A guide to training methods, programs, and resources.* San Francisco: Jossey-Bass.

Gazda, G. M. (1984). Multiple impact training: A life skills approach. In D. Larson (Ed.), *Teaching psychological skills: Models for giving psychology away.* Monterey, Calif.: Brooks/Cole.

Gelatt, H. B., Varenhorst, B., & Carey, R. (1972). *Deciding: A leader's guide.* Princeton, N. J.: College Entrance Examination Board.

Gelso, C. J., & Carter, J. A. (1985). The relationship in counseling and psychotherapy: Components, consequences, and theoretical antecedents. *Counseling Psychologist, 13,* 155–243.

Genther, R. W., & Moughan, J. (1977). Introverts' and extroverts' responses to nonverbal attending behavior. *Journal of Counseling Psychology, 24,* 144–146.

Gibb, J. R. (1968). The counselor as a role-free person. In C. A. Parker (Ed.), *Counseling theories and counselor education.* Boston: Houghton Mifflin.

Gibb, J. R. (1978). *Trust: A new view of personal and organizational development.* Los Angeles: The Guild of Tutors Press.

Gilbert, T. F. (1978). *Human competence: Engineering worthy performance.* New York: McGraw-Hill.

Gladstein, G. (1974). Nonverbal communication and counseling/psychotherapy. *Counseling Psychologist, 4,* 34–57.

Gladstein, G. A. (1983). Understanding empathy: Integrating counseling, developmental, and social psychology perspectives. *Journal of Counseling Psychology, 30,* 467–482.

Gladstein, G. A., & Feldstein, J. C. (1983). Using film to increase counselor empathic experiences. *Counselor Education and Supervision, 23,* 125–131.

Goldenberg, I., & Goldenberg, H. (1980). *Family therapy: An overview.* Monterey, Calif.: Brooks/Cole.

Goldfried, M. R. (Ed.) (1982). *Converging themes in psychotherapy: Trends in psychodynamic, humanistic, and behavioral practice.* New York: Springer.

Goldfried, M. R., & Davidson, G. C. (1976). *Clinical behavior therapy.* New York: Holt, Rinehart & Winston.

Goldfried, M. R., & D'Zurilla, T. J. (1969). A behavioral-analytic model for assessing competence. In C. D. Spielberger (Ed.), *Current topics in clinical and community psychology.* Vol. I. New York: Academic Press.

Goldfried, M. R., & Goldfried, A. P. (1980). Cognitive change methods. In F. H. Kanfer & A. P. Goldstein (Eds.), *Helping people change: A textbook of methods (2nd ed.).* New York: Pergamon.

Goldfried, M., & Robins, C. (1982). On the facilitation of self-efficacy. *Cognitive Therapy and Research, 6,* 361–379.

Goldiamond, I. (1965). Self-control procedures in personal behavior problems. *Psychological Reports, 17,* 851–868.

Goldstein, A. P. (1980). Relationship-enhancement methods. In F. H. Kanfer & A. P. Goldstein (Eds.), *Helping people change: A textbook of methods (2nd ed.).* New York: Pergamon.

Goldstein, A. P., Gershaw, N. J., & Sprafkin, R. P. (1984). Structured learning therapy: Background, procedures, and evaluation. In D. Larson (Ed.), *Teaching psychological skills: Models for giving psychology away.* Monterey, Calif.: Brooks/Cole.

Goldstein, A. P., Heller, K., & Sechrest, L. B. (1966). *Psychotherapy and the psychology of behavior change.* New York: Wiley.

Goodyear, R. K., & Bradley, F. O. (1980). The helping process as contractual. *Personnel and Guidance Journal, 58,* 512–515.

Gordon, T. (1970). *Parent effectiveness training.* New York: Wyden.

Goslin, D. A. (1985). Decision making and the social fabric. *Society, 22* (2), 7–11.

Gottfredson, G. D. (1984). A theory-ridden approach to program evaluation. *American Psychologist, 39,* 1101–1112.

Gottlieb, B. H. (1983). Social support as a focus for integrative research in psychology. *American Psychologist, 38,* 278–287.

Gottlieb, B. H., & Schroter, C. (1978). Collaboration and resource exchange between professionals and natural support systems. *Professional Psychology, 9,* 614–622.

Greenburg, L. S., & Higgins, H. M. (1980). Effects of two-chair dialogue and focusing on conflict resolution. *Journal of Counseling Psychology, 27,* 221–224.

Greenberg, L S., & Kahn, S. E. (1979). The stimulation phase in counseling. *Counselor Education and Supervision, 19,* 137–145.

Greenson, R. R. (1967). *The technique and practice of psychoanalysis.* Vol. 1. New York: International Universities Press.

Grieger, R., & Boyd, J. (1980). *Rational-emotive therapy: A skills-based approach.* New York: Van Nostrand Reinhold.

Guerney, B., Jr. (1982). Relationship enhancement. In E. K. Marshall & P. D. Kurtz (Eds.), *Interpersonal helping skills.* San Francisco: Jossey-Bass.

Guerney, B., Jr. (1984). Relationship enhancement therapy and training. In D. Larson (Ed.), *Teaching psychological skills: Models for giving psychology away.* Monterey, Calif.: Brooks/Cole.

Guilford, J. P. (1962). Factors that aid and hinder creativity. *Teachers College Record, 63,* 380–392.

Haase, R. F., and Tepper, D. (1972). Nonverbal components of empathic communication. *Journal of Counseling Psychology, 19,* 417–424.

Hackman, A., & McLean, C. (1975). A comparison of flooding and thought-stopping in the treatment of obsessional neurosis. *Behavior Theory and Research, 13,* 263–269.

Hackman, J. R. (1967). The nature of the task as a determiner of job behavior. Paper presented at the meeting of the American Psychological Association, Washington, D. C.

Hackney, H. (1978). The evolution of empathy. *Personnel and Guidance Journal, 57,* 35–38.

Hackney, H., & Cormier, L. S. (1979). *Counseling strategies and objectives (2nd ed.).* Englewood Cliffs, N. J.: Prentice-Hall.

Hall, E. (1982). Schooling children in a nasty climate: Jerome Bruner interviewed by Elizabeth Hall. *Psychology Today, 16* (1), 57–63.

Hall, E. T. (1977). *Beyond culture.* Garden City, N. J.: Anchor Press.

Halleck, S. L. (1982). The concept of responsibility in psychotherapy. *American Journal of Psychotherapy, 36,* 292–303.

Ham, M. D. (1980). The effects of the relationship between client behavior and counselors' predicted empathic ability upon counselors' in-session empathic performance: An analogue study (Doctoral dissertation, University of Rochester). *Dissertation Abstracts International,* 1981, *41,* 2939A (University Microfilms No. 8025044).

Hare-Mustin, R. T., Marecek, J., Kaplan, A. G., & Liss-Levinson, N. (1979). Rights of clients, responsibilities of therapists. *American Psychologist, 34,* 3–16.

Hariman, J. (Ed.) (1983). *The therapeutic efficacy of the major psychotherapeutic techniques.* Springfield, Ill.: Charles C Thomas.

Hariman, J. (Ed.) (1984). *Does psychotherapy really help people?* Springfield, Ill.: Charles C Thomas.

Harre, R. (1980). *Social being.* Totowa, N. J.: Adams, Littlefield.

Harris, T. (1969). *I'm OK—You're OK: A practical guide to transactional analysis.* New York: Harper & Row.

Hatcher, C., Brooks, B., & Associates (1978). *Innovations in counseling psychology.* San Francisco: Jossey-Bass.

Heath, D. H. (1980a). The maturing person. In G. Walsh & D. Shapiro (Eds.), *Beyond health and normality.* New York: Van Nostrand Reinhold.

Heath, D. H. (1980b). Wanted: A comprehensive model of health development. *Personnel and Guidance Journal, 58,* 391–399.

Held, B. S. (1984). Toward a strategic eclecticism: A proposal. *Psychotherapy, 21,* 232–241.

Heppner, P. P. (1978). A review of the problem-solving literature and its relationship to the counseling process. *Journal of Counseling Psychology, 25,* 366–375.

Heppner, P. P., Baumgardner, A. H., & Jackson, J. (in press). Problem-solving styles, depression, and attribution styles: Are they related? *Cognitive Therapy and Research.*

Heppner, P. P., Hibel, J., Neal, G. W., Weinstein, C. L., & Rabinowitz, F. E. (1982). Personal problem solving: A descriptive study of individual differences. *Journal of Counseling Psychology, 29,* 580–590.

Heppner, P. P., Neal, G. W., & Larson, L M. (1984). Problem-solving training as prevention with college students. *Personnel and Guidance Journal, 62,* 514–519.

Heppner, P. P., & Petersen, C. H. (1982). The development and implications of a personal problem-solving inventory. *Journal of Counseling Psychology, 29,* 66–75.

Heppner, P. P., & Reeder, B. L. (in press). The effect of problem-solving training with residence hall staff: Do you think you need it? *Journal of College Student Personnel.*

Heppner, P. P., Reeder, B. L., & Larson, L. M. (1983). Cognitive variables associated with personal problem-solving appraisal: Implications for counseling. *Journal of Counseling Psychology, 30,* 537–545.

Higgins, W., Ivey, A., & Uhlemann, M. (1970). Media therapy: A programmed approach to teaching behavioral skills. *Journal of Counseling Psychology, 17,* 20–26.

Highlen, P. S., & Hill, C. E. (1984). Factors affecting client change in individual counseling: Current status and theoretical speculations. In S. D. Brown & R. W. Lent (Eds.), *The handbook of counseling psychology.* New York: Wiley.

Hills, M. D. (1984). Improving the learning of parents' communication skills by providing for the discovery of personal meaning (Doctoral dissertation, University of Victoria, Victoria, British Columbia, Canada).

Hiltonsmith, R. W., & Miller, H. R. (1983). What happened to the setting in person-setting assessment? *Professional Psychology, 14,* 419–434.

Hogan, R. (1969). Development of an empathy scale. *Journal of Consulting and Clinical Psychology, 33,* 307–316.

Holland, J. L. (1961). Creative and academic performance among talented adolescents. *Journal of Educational Psychology, 52,* 136–147.

Howell, W. S. (1982). *The empathic communicator.* Belmont, Calif.: Wadsworth.

Hudson, J., & Danish, S. J. (1980). The acquisition of information: An important life skill. *Personnel and Guidance Journal, 59,* 164–167.

Hulse, D., & Jennings, M. L. (1984). Toward comprehensive case conceptualizations in counseling. *Professional Psychology, 15,* 251–259.

Hurvitz, N. (1970). Peer self-help psychotherapy groups and their implication for psychotherapy. *Psychotherapy: Theory, Research, and Practice, 7,* 41–49.

Hurvitz, N. (1974). Similarities and differences between conventional psychotherapy and peer self-help psychotherapy groups. In P. S. Roman & H. M. Trice (Eds.), *The sociology of psychotherapy.* New York: Aronson.

Hussian, R. A., & Scott, L. P. (1981). Social reinforcement and problem-solving training in the treatment of depressed elderly patients. *Cognitive Therapy and Research, 5,* 57–69.

Hutchins, D. E. (1979). Systematic counseling: The T-F-A model for counselor intervention. *Personnel and Guidance Journal, 57,* 529–531.

Hutchins, D. E. (1982). Ranking major counseling strategies with the TFA/matrix system. *Personnel and Guidance Journal, 60,* 427–431.

Hutchins, D. E. (1984). Improving the counseling relationship. *Personnel and Guidance Journal, 62,* 572–575.

Huxley, A. (1963). *The doors of perception.* New York: Harper & Row (Originally published by Colophon, 1954).

Ivey, A. E. (1971). *Microcounseling: Innovations in interviewing training.* Springfield, Ill.: Charles C Thomas.

Ivey, A. E. (1980). *Counseling and psychotherapy: Skills, theories, and practice.* Englewood Cliffs, N.J.: Prentice-Hall.

Ivey, A. E. (1983). Intentional interviewing and counseling. Monterey, Calif.: Brooks/Cole.

Ivey, A. E., & Authier, J. (1978). *Microcounseling (2nd ed.).* Springfield, Ill.: Charles C Thomas.

Ivey, A. E., & Galvin, M. (1982). *Skills training: A model for treatment.* In E. K. Marshall & P. D. Kurtz (Eds.), *Interpersonal helping skills.* San Francisco: Jossey-Bass.

Ivey, A., & Gluckstern, N. (1984). *Basic influencing skills (2nd ed.).* Amherst, Mass.: Microtraining Associates.

Ivey, A. E., & Matthews, W. J. (1984). A meta-model for structuring the clinical interview. *Journal of Counseling and Development, 63,* 237–243.

Jacobson, N. S. (1977). Problem solving and contingency contracting in the treatment of marital discord. *Journal of Consulting and Clinical Psychology, 45,* 92–100.

James, M., & Jongeward, D. (1971). *Born to win: Transactional analysis with Gestalt experiments.* Reading, Mass.: Addison-Wesley.

James, W. (1892). *Psychology: Briefer Course.* New York: Holt.

Janis, I. L. (1983a). The role of social support in adherence to stressful decisions. *American Psychologist, 38,* 143–160.

Janis, I. L. (1983b). *Short-term counseling: Guidelines based on recent research.* New Haven, Conn.: Yale University Press.

Janis, I. L., & Mann, L. (1977). *Decision making: A psychological analysis of conflict, choice, and commitment.* New York: The Free Press.

Janosik, E. H. (Ed.) (1984). *Crisis counseling: A contemporary approach.* Belmont, Calif.: Wadsworth.

Johnson, D. M., Parrott, G. R., & Stratton, R. P. (1968). Production and judgment of solutions to five problems. *Journal of Educational Psychology, 59* (No. 6, Pt. 2).

Jones, G. B. (1976). Evaluation of problem-solving competence. In J. D. Krumboltz & C. E. Thoresen (Eds.), *Counseling methods.* New York: Holt, Rinehart & Winston.

Jourard, S. M. (1968). *Disclosing man to himself.* New York: Van Nostrand Reinhold.

Jourard, S. M. (1971a). *Self-disclosure: An experimental analysis of the transparent self.* London: Wiley-Interscience.

Jourard, S. M. (1971b). *The transparent self* (Rev. ed.). New York: Van Nostrand Reinhold.

Journal of Abnormal Psychology (1978). Learned helplessness as a model of depression. Special Issue, Vol. *87,* No. 1, February.

Jurjevich, R-R. M. (Ed.) (1973). *Direct psychotherapy: Twenty-eight American originals.* Vols. I, II. Coral Gables, Fla.: University of Miami Press.

Kagan, N. (1973). Can technology help us toward reliability in influencing human interaction? *Educational Technology, 13,* 44–51.

Kagan, N. I. (1981). Influencing human interaction—Eighteen years with IPR. In A. K. Hess (Ed.), *Psychotherapy supervision: Theory, research, and practice.* New York: Wiley.

Kagan, N. I. (1984). Interpersonal process recall: Basic methods and recent research. In D. Larson (Ed.)., *Teaching psychological skills: Models for giving psychology away.* Monterey, Calif.: Brooks/Cole.

Kagan, N. I., with McQuellon, R. (1981). IPR: A structured method for applying videotape technology in psychotherapy. In R. Corsini (Ed.), *Handbook of innovative psychotherapies.* New York: Wiley.

Kanfer, F. H. (1980). Self-management methods. In F. H. Kanfer & A. P. Goldstein (Eds.), *Helping people change: A textbook of methods (2nd ed.).* New York: Pergamon.

Kanfer, F. H., & Goldstein, A. P. (Eds.) (1980). *Helping people change: A textbook of methods (2nd ed.).* New York: Pergamon.

Kanter, R. M. (1983). *Change masters: Innovation for productivity in the American corporation.* New York: Simon & Schuster.

Katz, J. H., & Torres, C. (1982). Couples contracting workshops: A proactive counseling strategy. *Personnel and Guidance Journal, 60,* 567–570.

Kerr, B. A., Olson, D. H., Claiborn, C. D., Bauers-Gruenler, S. J., & Paolo, A. M. (1983). Overcoming opposition and resistance: Differential functions of expertness and attractiveness in career counseling. *Journal of Counseling Psychology, 30,* 323–331.

Kimble, G. A. (1984). Psychology's two cultures. *American Psychologist. 39,* 833–839.

Kirschenbaum, H., & Glaser, B. (1978). *Developing support groups: A manual for facilitators and participants.* San Diego: University Associates.

Knapp, M. L. (1978). *Nonverbal communication in human interaction (2nd ed.).* New York: Holt, Rinehart & Winston.

Krumboltz, J. D., & Thoresen, C. E. (Eds.) (1976). *Counseling methods.* New York: Holt, Rinehart, & Winston.

LaCrosse, M. B. (1975). Nonverbal behavior and perceived counselor attractiveness and persuasiveness. *Journal of Counseling Psychology, 22,* 563–566.

LaForge, R. (1977). Interpersonal check list (ICL). In J. E. Jones & J. W. Pfeiffer (Eds.), *The 1977 annual handbook for group facilitators.* San Diego: University Associates Press.

Lambert, M. J., Bergin, A. E., & Collins, J. L. (1977). Therapist-induced deterioration in psychotherapy. In A. S. Gurman & A. M. Razin (Eds.), *Effective psychotherapy: A handbook of research.* New York: Pergamon.

Landreth, G. L. (1984). Encountering Carl Rogers: His views on facilitating groups. *Personnel and Guidance Journal, 62,* 323–326.

Lange, A. J., & Jakubowski, P. (1976). *Responsible assertive behavior: Cognitive/behavioral procedures for trainers.* Champaign, Ill.: Research Press.

Larrabee, M. J. (1982). Working with reluctant clients through affirmation techniques. *Personnel and Guidance Journal, 61,* 105–109.

Larson, D. (Ed.) (1984). *Teaching psychological skills: Models for giving psychology away.* Monterey, Calif.: Brooks/Cole.

Laungani, P. (1984). Do psychotherapists meet clients' perceived needs? In J. Hariman (Ed.), *Does psychotherapy really help people?* Springfield, Ill.: Charles C Thomas.

Lauver, P. J., Holliman, M. A., & Kazama, S. W. (1982). Counseling as battleground: Client as enemy. *Personnel and Guidance Journal, 61,* 99–101.

Lazarus, A. A. (1976). *Multimodal behavior therapy.* New York: Springer.

Lazarus, A. A. (1981). *The practice of multimodal therapy.* New York: McGraw-Hill.

Lebow, J. (1982). Consumer satisfaction with mental health treatment. *Psychological Bulletin, 91,* 244–259.

Lee, C. (1983). Self-efficacy and behaviour as predictors of subsequent behaviour in an Assertiveness Training Programme. *Behaviour Research and Therapy, 21,* 225–232.

Leichenbaum, D. (1980). The assessment of interpersonal problem-solving skills. In P. C. Kendall & S. D. Hollon (Eds.), *Cognitive-behavioral interventions: Assessment methods.* New York: Academic Press.

Levinson, D. J., with Darrow, C. N., Klein, E. B., Levinson, M. H., & McKee, B. (1978). *The seasons of a man's life.* New York: Knopf.

Levy, L. H. (1968). Fact and choice in counseling and counselor education: A cognitive viewpoint. In C. A. Parker (Ed.), *Counseling theories and counselor education.* Boston: Houghton Mifflin.

Lewin, K. (1969). Quasi-stationary social equilibria and the problem of permanent change. In W. G. Bennis, K. D. Benne, & R. Chin (Eds.), *The planning of change.* New York: Holt, Rinehart & Winston.

Lichtenstein, E. (1980). *Psychotherapy: Approaches and applications.* Monterey, Calif.: Brooks/Cole.

Lieberman, M. A., Yalom, I. D., & Miles, M. B. (1973). *Encounter groups: First facts.* New York: Basic Books.

Lindaman, E. B., & Lippitt, R. O. (1979). *Choosing the future you prefer: A goal setting guide.* Washington, D. C.: Development Publications.

Livneh, H. (1984). Psychiatric rehabilitation: A dialogue with Bill Anthony. *Journal of Counseling and Development, 63,* 86–90.

Locke, E. A., & Latham, G. P. (1984). *Goal setting: A motivational technique that works.* Englewood Cliffs, N. J.: Prentice-Hall.

Locke, E. A., Shaw, K. N., Saari, L. M., & Latham, G. P. (1981). Goal setting and task performance: 1969–1980. *Psychological Bulletin, 90,* 125–152.

Lynd, H. M. (1958). *On shame and the search for identity.* New York: Science Editions.

Mahon, B. R., & Altmann, H. A. (1977). Skill training: Cautions and recommendations. *Counselor Education and Supervision, 17,* 42–50.

Mahoney, M. J. (1977). Reflections on the cognitive-learning trend in psychotherapy. *American Psychologist, 32,* 5–13.

Mahoney, M. J., & Arnkoff, D. B. (1978). Cognitive and self-control therapies. In S. L. Garfield & A. E. Bergin (Eds.), *Handbook of psychotherapy and behavior change (2nd ed.).* New York: Wiley.

Maier, N. R. F. (1960). Screening solutions to upgrade quality: A new approach to problem solving under conditions of uncertainty. *Journal of Psychology, 49,* 217–231.

Maier, N. R. F. (1970). *Problem solving and creativity in individuals and groups.* Monterey, Calif.: Brooks/Cole.

Maier, N. R. F., & Hoffman, L. R. (1964). Financial incentives and group decision in motivating change. *Journal of Social Psychology, 64,* 369–378.

Mallory, L. (1984). *Leading self-help groups: A guide for training facilitators.* New York: Family Service America.

Maltzman, I. (1960). On the training of originality. *Psychological Review, 67,* 229–242.

Mansfield, R. S., & Busse, T. V. (1977). Meta-analysis of research: A rejoinder to Glass. *Educational Researcher, 6,* 3.

Manthei, R. J., & Matthews, D. A. (1982). Helping the reluctant client engage in counselling. *British Journal of Guidance and Counselling, 10,* 44–50.

Marshall, E. K., & Kurtz, P. D. (Eds.) (1982). *Interpersonal helping skills: A guide to training methods, programs, and resources.* San Francisco: Jossey-Bass.

Maslow, A. H. (1967). Synanon and Eupsychia. *Journal of Humanistic Psychology, 7,* 28–35.

Maslow, A. H. (1968). *Toward a psychology of being (2nd ed.).* New York: Van Nostrand Reinhold.

Maslow, A. H. (1971). *The farther reaches of human nature.* New York: Viking.

Mayeroff, M. (1971). *On caring.* New York: Perennial Library (Harper & Row).

Mays, D. T., & Franks, C. M. (1980). Getting worse: Psychotherapy or no treatment—The jury should still be out. *Professional Psychology, 11,* 78–92.

Mays, D. T., & Franks, C. M. (1985). *Negative outcome in psychotherapy and what to do about it.* New York: Springer.

McCarthy, P. R. (1979a). Differential effects of self-disclosing versus self-involving counselor statements across counselor-client gender pairings. *Journal of Counseling Psychology, 26,* 538–541.

McCarthy, P. R. (1979b). Differential effects of self-disclosing versus self-giving counselor statements across counselor-client gender pairings. *Journal of Counseling Psychology, 26,* 538–541.

McCarthy, P. R. (1982). Differential effects of counselor self-referent responses and counselor status. *Journal of Counseling Psychology, 29,* 125–131.

McCarthy, P. R., & Betz, N. E. (1978). Differential effects of self-disclosing versus self-involving counselor statements. *Journal of Counseling Psychology, 25,* 251–256.

McFall, R. M. (1976). Behavioral training: A skill-acquisition approach to clinical problems. In J. T. Spence & R. C. Carson (Eds.), *Behavioral approaches to therapy.* Morristown, N. Y.: General Learning Press.

McKeachie, W. J. (1976). Psychology in America's bicentennial year. *American Psychologist, 31,* 819–833.

McKee, J. E., Moore, H. B., & Presbury, J. H. (1982). A model for teaching counselor trainees how to make challenging responses. *Counselor Education and Supervision, 22,* 149–153.

Meadow, A., Parnes, S. J., & Reese, H. (1959). Influence of instructions and problem sequence on a creative problem-solving test. *Journal of Applied Psychology, 43,* 413–416.

Mehrabian, A. (1971). *Silent messages.* Belmont, Calif.: Wadsworth.

Mehrabian, A., & Epstein, N. (1972). A measure of emotional empathy. *Journal of Personality, 40,* 525–543.

Mehrabian, A., & Reed, H. (1969). Factors influencing judgments of psychopathology. *Psychological Reports, 24,* 323–330.

Meichenbaum, D. H. (1974). *Cognitive behavior modification.* Morristown, N. J.: General Learning Press.

Meichenbaum, D. (1977). *Cognitive-behavior modification: An integrative approach.* New York: Plenum.

Meichenbuam, D., & Genest, M. (1980). Cognitive behavioral modification: An integration of cognitive and behavioral methods. In F. H. Kanfer & A. P. Goldstein (Eds.), *Helping people change: A textbook of methods (2nd ed.).* New York: Pergamon.

Miller, G. A. (1969). Psychology as a means of promoting human welfare. *American Psychologist, 24,* 1063–1075.

Miller, G. A. (1980). Giving away psychology in the 80's: George A. Miller interviewed by Elizabeth Hall, *Psychology Today, 13* (8), 38–50, 97–98.

Miller, G. A., Galanter, E., & Pribram, K. H. (1960). *Plans and the structure of behavior.* New York: Holt, Rinehart & Winston.

Miller, L. M. (1984). *American spirit: Visions of a new corporate culture.* New York: William Morrow.

Mowrer, O. H. (1968a). Loss and recovery of community: A guide to the theory and practice of integrity therapy. In G. M. Gazda (Ed.), *Innovations in group psychotherapy.* Springfield, Ill.: Charles C Thomas.

Mowrer, O. H. (1968b). New evidence concerning the nature of psychopathology. *University of Buffalo Studies, 4,* 113–193.

Mowrer, O. H. (1973a). Integrity groups today. In R-R. M. Jurjevich (Ed.), *Direct psychotherapy: Twenty-eight American originals.* Vol. 2. Coral Gables, Florida: University of Miami Press.

Mowrer, O. H. (1973b). My philosophy of psychotherapy. *Journal of Contemporary Psychotherapy, 6* (1), 35–42.

Mowrer, O. H., & Vattano, A. J. (1976). Integrity groups: A context for growth in honesty, responsibility, and involvement. *Journal of Applied Behavioral Science, 12,* 419–431.

Murphy, K. C., & Strong, S. R. (1972). Some effects of similarity self-disclosure. *Journal of Counseling Psychology, 19,* 121–124.

Naisbitt, J. (1982). *Megatrends: Ten new directions for transforming our lives.* New York: Warner Books.

Neimeyer, G. J., & Banikiotes, P. G. (1981). Self-disclosure flexibility, empathy, and perceptions of adjustment and attraction. *Journal of Counseling Psychology, 28,* 272–275.

Neimeyer, G. J., & Fong, M. L. (1983). Self-disclosure flexibility and counselor effectiveness. *Journal of Counseling Psychology, 30,* 258–261.

Newman, B. M., & Newman, P. R. (1984). *Development through life: A psycho-social approach* (3rd ed.). Homewood, Ill.: Dorsey.

Nezu, A., & D'Zurilla, T. J. (1981). Effects of problem definition and formulation on decision making in the social problem-solving process. *Behavior Therapy, 12,* 100–106.

Nicholson, R. A., & Berman, J. S. (1983). Is follow-up necessary in evaluating psychotherapy? *Psychological Bulletin, 93,* 261–278.

Nilsson, D. E., Strassberg, D. S., & Bannon, J. (1979). Perceptions of counselor self-disclosure: An analogue study. *Journal of Counseling Psychology, 26,* 399–404.

Norcross, J. C., & Wogan, M. (1983). American psychotherapists of diverse persuasions: Characteristics, theories, practices, and clients. *Professional Psychology: Research and Practice, 14,* 529–539.

Oblas, A. S. (1978). Rampant passivity. *Personnel and Guidance Journal, 56,* 550–553.

Osborn, A. F. (1963). *Applied imagination: Principles and procedures of creative problem solving (3rd ed.).* New York: Scribner's.

Pancoast, D. L., Parker, P., & Froland, C. (Eds.) (1983). *Rediscovering self-help: Its role in social care.* Vol. 6. Social Service Delivery System. Beverly Hills, Calif.: Sage.

Paradise, L. V., & Wilder, D. H. (1979). The relationship between client reluctance and counseling effectiveness. *Counselor Education and Supervision, 19,* 35–41.

Parloff, M. B., & Handlon, J. H. (1964). The influence of criticalness on creative problem-solving in dyads. *Psychiatry, 27,* 17–27.

Parnes, S. J. (1967). *Creative behavior guidebook.* New York: Scribner's.

Passons, W. R. (1975). *Gestalt approaches in counseling.* New York: Holt, Rinehart & Winston.

Patterson, C. H. (1985). *The therapeutic relationship: Foundations for an eclectic psychotherapy.* Monterey, Calif.: Brooks/Cole.

Patterson, C. H. (1986). *Theories of counseling and psychotherapy (4th ed.).* New York: Harper & Row.

Pearson, R. E. (1982). Support: Exploration of a basic dimension of informal help and counseling. *Personnel and Guidance Journal, 61,* 83–87.

Pearson, R. E. (1983). Support groups: A conceptualization. *Personnel and Guidance Journal, 61,* 361–364.

Perlman, H. H. (1979). *Relationship: The heart of helping people.* Chicago: University of Chicago Press.

Perls, F. (1969). *Gestalt therapy verbatim.* Moab, Utah: Real People Press.

Phillips. S. D., Pazienza, N. J., & Ferrin, H. H. (1984). Decision-making styles and problem-solving appraisal. *Journal of Counseling Psychology, 31,* 497–502.

Piaget, J. (1954). *Construction of reality in the child.* New York: Basic Books.

Plum, A. (1981). Communication as skill: A critique and alternative proposal. *Journal of Humanistic Psychology, 21,* 3–19.

Presby, S. (1978). Overly broad categories obscure important differences between therapies. *American Psychologist, 33,* 514–515.

Prochaska, J. O., & Norcross, J. C. (1982). The future of psychotherapy: A Delphi poll. *Professional Psychology, 13,* 620–627.

PS News: A Sharing of Ideas About Problem Solving, #20. (1982).

Puryear, D. A. (1979). *Helping people in crisis: A practical, family-oriented approach to effective crisis intervention.* San Francisco: Jossey-Bass.

Rappaport, J. (1981). In praise of paradox: A social policy of empowerment over prevention. *American Journal of Community Psychology, 9,* 1–26.

Raths, L., Harmin, M., & Simon, S. B. (1960). *Values and teaching.* Columbus, Ohio: Charles E. Merrill.

Redl, F. (1966). *When we deal with children.* New York: Free Press.

Remer, P., & O'Neill, C. (1980). Clients as change agents: What color should my parachute be? *Personnel and Guidance Journal, 58,* 425–429.

Remer, R. (1984). The effects of interpersonal confrontation on males. *AMHCA Journal, 6,* 56–70.

Reynolds, C. L., & Fischer, C. H. (1983). Personal versus professional evaluations of self-disclosing and self-involving counselors. *Journal of Counseling Psychology, 30,* 451–454.

Richardson, B. K. (1984). Empirically derived typologies—A missing link to the evaluation of the rehabilitation counseling process. *Journal of Counseling Psychology, 31,* 132–138.

Ridley, C. R. (1984). Clinical treatment of the nondisclosing black client. *American Psychologist, 39,* 1234–1244.

Rimland, B. (1979). Death knell for psychotherapy? *American Psychologist, 34,* 192.

Rimm, D. C., & Masters, J. C. (1974). *Behavior therapy.* New York: Academic Press.

Riordan, R. J., Matheny, K. B., & Harris, C. W. (1978). Helping counselors minimize reluctance. *Counselor Education and Supervision, 18,* 6–13.

Robertshaw, J. E., Mecca, S. J., & Rerick, M. N. (1978). *Problem-solving: A systems approach.* New York: Petrocelli Books.

Robin, A. L. (1981). A controlled evaluation of problem-solving communication training with parent-adolescent conflict. *Behavior Therapy, 12,* 593–609.

Rogers, C. R. (1951). *Client-centered therapy.* Boston: Houghton Mifflin.

Rogers, C. R. (1957). The necessary and sufficient conditions of therapeutic personality change. *Journal of Consulting Psychology, 21,* 95–103.

Rogers, C. R. (1961). *On becoming a person.* Boston: Houghton Mifflin.

Rogers, C. R. (Ed.) (1967). *The therapeutic relationship and its impact.* Madison, Wis.: University of Wisconsin Press.

Rogers, C. R. (1975). Empathy: An unappreciated way of being. *Counseling Psychologist, 21,* 95–103.

Rogers, C. R. (1980). *A way of being.* Boston: Houghton Mifflin.

Rogers, C. R., Perls, F., & Ellis, A. (1965). Three approaches to psychotherapy I: A film distributed by Psychological Films, Inc. Orange, Calif.

Rogers, C. R., Shostrom, E., & Lazarus, A. (1977). Three approaches to psychotherapy II. A film distributed by Psychological Films, Inc., Orange, Calif.

Rogers, C. R., & Truax, C. B. (1967). The therapeutic conditions antecedent to change: A theoretical view. In C. R. Rogers (Ed.), *The therapeutic relationship and its impact.* Madison, Wis.: The University of Wisconsin Press.

Rook, K. S. (1985). Promoting social bonding: Strategies for helping the lonely and socially isolated. *American Psychologist, 39,* 1389–1407.

Rorer, L G. (1983). "Deep" RET: A reformulation of some psychodynamic explanations of procrastination. *Cognitive Therapy and Research, 7,* 1–10.

Rosen, S., & Tesser, A. (1970). On the reluctance to communicate undesirable information: The MUM effect. *Sociometry, 33,* 253–263.

Rosen, S., & Tesser, A. (1971). Fear of negative evaluation and the reluctance to transmit bad news. *Proceedings of the 79th Annual Convention of the American Psychological Association, 6,* 301–302.

Rosenthal, R. (1983). Assessing the statistical and social importance of the effects of psychotherapy. *Journal of Consulting and Clinical Psychology, 51,* 4–13.

Rosenthal, T. L., Hung, J. H., & Kelley, J. E. (1977). Therapist social influence: Sternly strike while the iron is hot. *Behavior Research and Therapy, 15,* 253–259.

Rothbaum, F. M., Weisz, J. R., & Snyder, S. S. (1982). Changing the world and changing self: A two-process model of perceived control. *Journal of Personality and Social Psychology, 42,* 5–37.

Rotter, J. B. (1971). Generalized expectancies for interpersonal trust. *American Psychologist, 26,* 443–452.

Rubenstein, E. A., & Parloff, M. B. (Eds.) (1959). *Research in psychotherapy.* Washington, D. C.: American Psychological Association.

Rudestam, K. E. (1980). *Methods of self-change: An ABC primer.* Monterey, Calif.: Brooks/Cole.

Ryan, W. (1971). *Blaming the victim.* New York: Pantheon.

Rychlak, J. F. (1985). Eclecticism in psychological theorizing: Good and bad. *Journal of Counseling and Development, 63,* 351–353.

Schiff, J. L. (1975). Cathexis reader. *Transactional analysis treatment of psychosis.* New York: Harper & Row.

Schramski, T. G., Beutler, L. E., Lauver, P. J., Arizmendi, T. A., & Shanfield, S. B. (1984). Factors that contribute to posttherapy persistence of therapeutic change. *Journal of Clinical Psychology, 40,* 78–85.

Schwebel, R. S., Schwebel, A. T., & Schwebel, M. (1985). The psychological/mediation intervention model. *Professional Psychology, 16,* 86–97.

Scott, C. (1984). Empathy: Examination of a crucial concept. *Journal of British Association for Counselling,* #49, August, 3–6.

Scott, N. A. (1979). Beyond assertiveness training: A problem-solving approach. *Personnel and Guidance Journal, 57,* 450–452.

Searight, H. R., & Openlander, P. (1984). Systematic therapy: A new brief intervention model. *Personnel and Guidance Journal, 62,* 387–391.

Selby, J. W., & Calhoun, L. G. (1980). Psychodidactics: An undervalued and underdeveloped treatment tool of psychological intervention. *Professional Psychology, 11,* 236–241.

Seligman, M. E. P. (1975). *Helplessness: On depression, development, and death.* San Francisco: Freeman.

Selye, H. (1974). *Stress without distress.* Philadelphia: Lippincott.

Shaffer, H. (1978). Psychological rehabilitation, skills-building, and self-efficacy. *American Psychologist, 33,* 394–396.

Shapiro, S. B. (1968). Some aspects of a theory of interpersonal contracts. *Psychological Reports, 22,* 171–183.

Shure, M. B., & Spivack, G. (1978). *Problem-solving techniques in childrearing.* San Francisco: Jossey-Bass.

Simonson, N. R. (1976). The impact of therapist disclosure in patient disclosure. *Journal of Counseling Psychology, 23,* 3–6.

Smaby, M., & Tamminen, A. W. (1979). Can we help belligerent counselees? *Personnel and Guidance Journal, 57,* 506–512.

Smith, M. L., Glass, G. V., & Miller, T. I. (1980). *The benefits of psychotherapy.* Baltimore: Johns Hopkins University Press.

Smith, T. W. (1982). Irrational beliefs in the cause and treatment of emotional distress. A critical review of the rational-emotive model. *Clinical Psychology Review, 2,* 505–522.

Smith, T. W. (1983). Change in irrational beliefs and the outcome of rational-emotive psychotherapy. *Journal of Consulting and Clinical Psychology, 51,* 156–157.

Smith, T. W., Houston, B. K., & Zurawski, R. M. (1984). Irrational beliefs and the arousal of emotional distress. *Journal of Counseling Psychology, 31,* 190–201.

Smith-Hanen, S. (1977). Effects of nonverbal behaviors on judged levels of counselor empathy and warmth. *Journal of Counseling Psychology, 24,* 87–91.

Snow, C. P. (1964). *The two cultures and a second look.* London: Cambridge University Press.

Snyder, C. R. (1984). Excuses, excuses. *Psychology Today, 18,* 50–55.

Snyder, C. R., Higgins, R. L., & Stucky, R. J. (1983). *Excuses: Masquerades in search of grace.* New York: Wiley.

Spier, M. S. (1973). Kurt Lewin's "force-field analysis." In J. W. Pfeiffer & J. E. Jones (Eds.), *The 1973 annual handbook for group facilitators.* San Diego: University Associates.

Spinks, S., & Birchler, G. (1982). Behavioral-systems marital therapy: Dealing with resistance. *Family Process, 21,* 169–185.

Spivack, G., Platt, J. J., & Shure, M. B. (1976). *The problem-solving approach to adjustment: A guide to research and intervention.* San Francisco: Jossey-Bass.

Spivack, G., & Shure, M. B. (1974). *Social adjustment of young children: A cognitive approach to solving real-life problems.* San Francisco: Jossey-Bass.

Spivack, J. D. (1984). Animals at the crossroads: A perspective on credentialing in the mental health field. *Counseling Psychologist: 12,* 175–182.

Staats, A. W. (1981). Paradigmatic behaviorism, unified theory, unified theory construction methods, and the Zeitgeist of separatism. *American Psychologist, 36,* 239–256.

Stadler, H. A., & Rynearson, D. (1981). Understanding clients and their environments: A simulation. *Counselor Education and Supervision, 21,* 153–162.

Standal, S. (1954). The need for positive regard: A contribution to client-centered theory (Unpublished doctoral dissertation, University of Chicago).

Stein, B. A. (1980). Quality of work life in context: What every practitioner should know (Unpublished manuscript). Cambridge, Mass.: Goodmeasure.

Stensrud, R., & Stensrud, K. (1981). Counseling may be hazardous to your health: How we teach people to feel powerless. *Personnel and Guidance Journal, 59,* 300–304.

Stone, G. L., & Morden, C. J. (1976). Effect of distance on verbal productivity. *Journal of Counseling Psychology, 23,* 486–488.

Stream, H. S. (1985). *Resolving resistances in psychotherapy.* New York: Wiley.

Strohmer, D. C., & Newman, L. J. (1983). Counselor hypothesis-testing strategies. *Journal of Counseling Psychology, 30,* 557–565.

Strong, S. R. (1968). Counseling: An interpersonal influence process. *Journal of Counseling Psychology, 15,* 215–224.

Strong, S. R., & Claiborn, C. D. (1982). *Change through interaction: Social psychological processes of counseling and psychotherapy.* New York: Wiley.

Strupp, H. H., Hadley, S. W., & Gomes-Schwartz, B. (1977). *Psychotherapy for better or worse: The problem of negative effects.* New York: Jason Aronson.

Sue, D. W., & Sue, D. (1977). Barriers to effective cross-cultural counseling. *Journal of Counseling Psychology, 24,* 420–429.

Swan, G. E. (1979). On the structure of eclecticism: Cluster analysis of eclectic behavior therapists. *Professional Psychology, 10,* 732–739.

Talland, G. A., & Clark, D. H. (1954). Evaluation of topics in therapy group discussion. *Journal of Clinical Psychology, 10,* 131–137.

Tamminen, A. W., & Smaby, M. H. (1981). Helping counselors learn to confront. *Personnel and Guidance Journal, 60,* 41–45.

Taylor, S. E. (1983). Adjustment to threatening events: A theory of cognitive adaptation. *American Psychologist, 38,* 1161–1173.

Tennov, D. (1975). *Psychotherapy: The hazardous cure.* New York: Abelard-Schuman.

Tepper, D., & Haase, R. (1978). Verbal and nonverbal communication and facilitative conditions. *Journal of Counseling Psychology, 25,* 35–44.

Tesser, A., & Rosen, S. (1972). Similarity of objective fate as a determinant of the reluctance to transmit unpleasant information: The MUM effect. *Journal of Personality and Social Psychology, 23,* 46–53.

Tesser, A., Rosen, S., & Batchelor, T. (1972). On the reluctance to communicate bad news (the MUM effect): A role play extension. *Journal of Personality, 40,* 88–103.

Tesser, A., Rosen, S., & Tesser, M. (1971). On the reluctance to communicate undesirable messages (the MUM effect): A field study. *Psychological Reports, 29,* 651–654.

Thase, M., & Page, R. A. (1977). Modeling of self-disclosure in laboratory and nonlaboratory interview settings. *Journal of Counseling Psychology, 24,* 35–40.

Thoreson, C. E., & Mahoney, M. J. (1974). *Behavioral self-control.* New York: Holt, Rinehart, & Winston.

Thorne, F. C. (1973a). An eclectic evaluation of psychotherapeutic methods. In R-R. M. Jurjevich (Ed.), *Direct psychotherapy: Twenty-eight American originals.* Vol. II. Coral Gables, Fla.: University of Miami Press.

Thorne, F. C. (1973b). Eclectic psychotherapy. In R. Corsini (Ed.), *Current Psychotherapies.* Itasca, Ill.: Peacock.

Truax, C. B., & Carkhuff, R. R. (1965). Client and therapist transparency in the psychotherapeutic encounter. *Journal of Counseling Psychology, 12,* 3–9.

Tryon, W. W. (1976). A system of behavioral diagnosis. *Professional Psychology, 7,* 495–506.

Turock, A. (1980). Immediacy in counseling: Recognizing clients' unspoken messages. *Personnel and Guidance Journal, 59,* 168–172.

Tyler, F. B., Pargament, K. I., & Gatz, M. (1983). The resource collaborator role: A model for interactions involving psychologists. *American Psychologist, 38,* 388–398.

Urbain, E. S., & Kendall, P. C. (1980). Review of social-cognitive problem-solving interventions with children. *Psychological Bulletin, 88,* 109–143.

VandeCreek, L., & Angstadt, L. (1985). Client preferences and anticipations about counselor self-disclosure. *Journal of Counseling Psychology, 32,* 206–214.

Voss, J. (in press). Problem solving and the educational process. LRDC, University of Pittsburg.

Wachtel, P. (Ed.) (1982). *Resistance: Psychodynamic and behavioral approaches.* New York: Plenum.

Wachtel, P. L. (1980). What should we say to our patients? On the wording of therapists' comments. *Psychotherapy: Theory, Research, and Practice, 17,* 183–188.

Wadsworth, M., & Ford, D. H. (1983). Assessment of personal goal hierarchies. *Journal of Counseling Psychology, 30,* 514–526.

Wagman, M. (1979). Systematic dilemma counseling: Theory, method, research. *Psychological Reports, 44,* 55–72.

Wagman, M. (1980a). PLATO DCS: An interactive computer system for personal counseling. *Journal of Counseling Psychology, 27,* 16–30.

Wagman, M. (1980b). Systematic dilemma counseling: Transition from counselor mode to autonomous mode. *Journal of Counseling Psychology, 27,* 171–178.

Wallen, J. L. (1973). Developing effective interpersonal communication. In R. W. Pace, B. D. Peterson, & T. R. Radcliffe (Eds.), *Communicating interpersonally*. Columbus, Ohio: Merrill.

Ward, D. E. (1983). The trend toward eclecticism and the development of comprehensive models to guide counseling and psychotherapy. *Personnel and Guidance Journal, 62,* 154–157.

Wasik, B. H., & Fishbein, J. E. (1982). Problem solving: A model for supervision in professional psychology. *Professional Psychology, 13,* 559–564.

Watson, D. L., & Tharp, R. G. (1985). *Self-directed behavior: Self-modification for personal adjustment (4th ed.)*. Monterey, Calif.: Brooks/Cole.

Watson, J. J., & Remer, R. (1984). The effects of interpersonal confrontation on females. *Personnel and Guidance Journal, 62,* 607–611.

Weick, K. E. (1969). *The social psychology of organizing*. Reading, Mass.: Addison-Wesley.

Weick, K. E. (1979). *The social psychology of organizing (2nd ed.)*. Reading, Mass.: Addison-Wesley.

Weigel, R. G., Dinges, N., Dyer, R., & Straumfjorn, A. A. (1972). Perceived self-disclosure, mental health, and who is liked in group treatment. *Journal of Counseling Psychology, 19,* 47–52.

Weisskopf-Joelson, E., & Eliseo, S. (1961). An experimental study of the effectiveness of brainstorming. *Journal of Applied Psychology, 45,* 45–49.

Weisz, J. R. (1983). Can I control it? The pursuit of veridical answers across the life span. In P. B. Baltes & O. G. Brim (Eds.), *Life span development and behavior*. Vol. 5. New York: Academic Press.

Weisz, J. R., Rothbaum, F. M., & Blackburn, T. C. (1984). Standing out and standing in: The psychology of control in America and Japan. *American Psychologist, 39,* 955–969.

Wheeler, D. D., & Janis, I. L. (1980). *A practical guide for making decisions*. New York: Free Press.

Williams, R. L., & Long, J. D. (1983). *Toward a self-managed life style (3rd ed.)*. Boston: Houghton Mifflin.

Wills, T. A. (1978). Perceptions of clients by professional helpers. *Psychological Bulletin, 85,* 968–1000.

Wollersheim, J. P., McFall, M. E., Hamilton, S. B., Hickey, C. S., & Bordewick, M. C. (1980). Effects of treatment rationale and problem severity on perceptions of psychological problems and counseling approaches. *Journal of Counseling Psychology, 27,* 225–231.

Wright, B. A., & Fletcher, B. L. (1982). Uncovering hidden resources: A challenge to assessment. *Professional Psychology, 13,* 229–235.

Zielinski, J. J. (1978). Maintenance of therapeutic gains: Issues, problems, and implementation. *Professional Psychology, 9,* 353–360.

Zins, J. E. (1984). A scientific problem-solving approach to developing accountability procedures for school psychologists. *Professional Psychology, 15,* 56–66.

Author Index

Subject Index

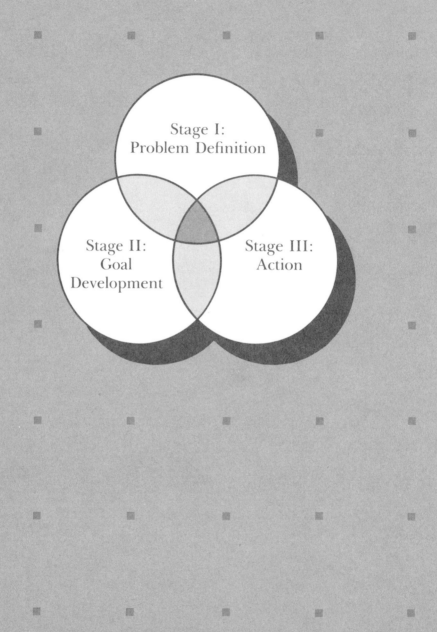